How to Make Sure Your Money Lasts in Retirement

J A M E S   B R A S S

ISBN: 145641996X
ISBN-13: 9781456419967

Chapter 1

It has begun! My generation of baby boomers has started to enter retirement. Over the next 15-20 years, approximately 80 million of this much-talked about group will be flooding the retirement "market". The experts have been telling us for years how this will impact our country. From finances to medical care, from job opportunities to the commercials we see on television, big changes are coming. Much has been written about the strain this will put on such government programs as Social Security and Medicare.

Effect of ERISA

A law passed back in 1974 is also impacting the baby boomer generation. Called ERISA, it stands for Employee Retirement Income Security Act. This act made 401k and similar retirement plans possible. The net effect of this law was to, in many cases; shift the burden of the cost of an employee's retirement plan from the employer to the employee. It allowed for the change from a Defined Benefit plan to a Defined Contribution plan.

Defined Benefit Plan

A defined benefit plan promises a specific monthly benefit at retirement usually based on your years of service. It used to be that you would work for a company for 30, 35, or even 40 years. At your retirement you would get a specified amount of dollars per month based on your years of service. The company's pension plan covered the cost of your retirement and you just collected your monthly check. Some plans also had built-in COLAs or Cost of Living Adjustments. You basically knew what you would receive each month and could figure your retirement lifestyle accordingly. In other words, your retirement income was "defined" ahead of time and the employee didn't need to do much financial planning, at least as far as his or her pension was concerned.

This defined benefit lasted for the rest of your life regardless of how long you lived.

Defined Contribution Plan

Unlike a defined benefit plan, a defined contribution plan does not promise a specific amount of benefit at retirement. Instead the employee or the employer (or often both) "contribute" to the employee's account. Generally, employees can "contribute" whatever they want up to a set limit. Oftentimes the employer will match the employee's contribution with a certain percentage of whatever the employee contributes. This percentage match is often 50% or 100% of the first set percentage the employee contributes. The Department of Labor, on their website, states the following about the ultimate value to the employee of the defined contribution plan:

"The employee will ultimately receive the balance in their account, which is based on contributions plus or minus investment gains or losses. The value of the account will fluctuate due to the changes in the value of the investments. Examples of defined contribution plans include 401(k) plans, 403(b) plans, employee stock ownership plans, and profit-sharing plans".

Notice that, unlike the set monthly amount of the Defined Benefit plan, the Defined Contribution plan has no set monthly amount. Instead, when you retire, your account will have so much money in it. At that point you have several options. One option is to annuitize it. Under this option, you basically buy an annuity from, for example, a life insurance company. The insurance company then guarantees you monthly payments for a set amount for a set period of time which could include, for the rest of your life.

Another option would be to take full control of your retirement plan(s) yourself. This book cannot tell you which option is the best for you. You need to consult your tax person, lawyer or accountant for all your options. What this book will do is help you answer some very important questions if you decide to self-annuitize. In other words, if you would like to take this lump sum and take full control of it yourself. This book will help you answer questions like:

1. *How long will my money last if I take out $X a month?*
2. *What percentage of my nest egg can I safely withdraw annually if I expect to earn X% on my money?*
3. *If I take out $X each month, will my nest egg be growing or shrinking after 10 years? After 15 years? After 20 Years?*
4. *How will I know when I am taking out too much?*
5. *How will inflation affect my nest egg?*

Using the information in this book, you will be able to obtain answers to specific customized questions that will most likely fit your situation. For example:

Age: 62
Nest Egg Value: $500,000
Expected Return on Investment 6%

1. *How long will my money last if I withdraw 4% ($20,000/year)?*
2. *How much will I have left at age 82 if I withdraw $2500 a month?*
3. *If inflation is averaging 4%, can I initially safely withdraw 5% ($25,000/yr)?*
4. *If I think I need to have $3000 a month income, should I work until I'm 65?*
5. *If my Return On Investment is only 5%, can I still withdraw 5% a year?*
6. *If I start out needing $2500 a month, what will I need at age 82, given 3% inflation?*
7. *At what age will my nest egg drop below $500,000; which is what I started with? How much longer will it last, at that point?*
8. *If inflation grows at 4% instead of 3%, how much can I safely withdraw annually? If I withdraw the same amount, how much sooner does my money run out?*

The Insidiousness of Inflation

Webster's New World Dictionary defines insidious as "more dangerous than seems evident". This definition is a perfect characterization of the effects of inflation on your retirement planning. We tend to think in linear terms when it comes to numbers. The problem with inflation is it affects our finances geometrically not linearly. Inflation "compounds" as the years pass. Small initial differences grow into huge differences down the road.

Inflation's Effects Can Be Profound Over Time

The table below shows the "compounding" effect of inflation. The first few years the difference is negligible. But as time passes the effects of a higher inflation rate are enormous. Imagine if you budget $2,000 per month the first year, how much a month would you need to "keep up with inflation" in the successive years. The compounding effect is as shown.

Table 1.1

Inflation Rate	First Year	Second Year	Start Year 6	Start Year 11	Start Year 21	Start Year 31
0%	$ 2,000	$ 2,000	$ 2,000	$ 2,000	$ 2,000	$ 2,000
1%	$ 2,000	$ 2,020	$ 2,102	$ 2,209	$ 2,440	$ 2.696
2%	$ 2,000	$ 2,040	$ 2,208	$ 2,438	$ 2,972	$ 3,623
3%	$ 2,000	$ 2,060	$ 2,319	$ 2,688	$ 3,612	$ 4,855
4%	$ 2,000	$ 2,080	$ 2,433	$ 2,960	$ 4,382	$ 6,487
5%	$ 2,000	$ 2,100	$ 2,553	$ 3,258	$ 5,307	$ 8,644
6%	$ 2,000	$ 2,120	$ 2,676	$ 3,558	$ 6.414	$11,487

After 30 years of just 3% annual inflation, you would "need" $4,855 just to maintain the same buying power you had 30 years earlier. A 60 year-old retiree, who is budgeting $2,000 a month from his or her nest egg, must take into account that at age 90, he or she will need to budget almost $5,000 a month just to "stay even". In fact, just one year later, he or she will need exactly $5,000 a month to keep up with the ravages of just 3% inflation. Imagine if inflation would "heat up" to 6% for any extended period of time!

Obviously your nest egg must be financially strong enough to withstand progressively bigger "hits" each year. If you start out taking out too much initially, your nest egg can be in trouble too soon. At a time your inflated "hits" reach the higher levels 20 or 30 years down the road, your money just can't hold out. To make matters worse, no one knows for sure what the inflation rate will be 10, 20, or 30 years into the future. If you plan on 3% inflation and we hit a stretch of 6% inflation, the effects on your nest egg can be devastating.

The tables that follow in this book will allow you to plan a safe monthly withdrawal amount that will give your nest egg the best likelihood of outlasting you. The last thing anyone wants is to see their nest egg in a tailspin. The tables give you detailed information for almost any financial scenario you can imagine, including the trend line of the growth or decline of your nest egg in the years ahead. The information in these tables can be very valuable in helping you decide the "safe" amount to withdraw so that you don't run into trouble in your later retirement years. Obviously, if you knew how long your retirement years were going to last, you could calculate your withdrawals more precisely. But do you really want to know how long you will need your nest egg? Because you don't know, you need to plan for a possible long retirement. It is possible you could need your nest egg to last 35 or 40 years. Ask any 100 year-old if they thought they were going to live as long as they have?

While you are at it, ask them if they wished they had planned better for retirement.

Inflation: What You Can Do About It

Inflation averaged 4.66% from Jan, 1972 to Jan, 2007; a 35 year time span. At that rate, a beginning withdrawal of $2000 a month in Jan 1972 would have "grown to" $9,410 a month in Jan, 2007, if you wanted to "keep up" with inflation. But there is a way to "fight back". Each year inflation is gradual. You don't necessarily notice its bite in a year's time. Sure you may notice prices are higher, but usually not uncomfortably so. So what would happen if, when the figures came out that the inflation rate was say 5% the past year, you decided to only "inflate" your withdrawals 4%. You probably would hardly notice that you money doesn't seem to go as far. There is no law that says you have to inflate your monthly withdrawals at the reported inflation rate. If the tables show you running out of money too soon, just change the inflated withdrawal amount down a point. This will often "allow" your nest egg to last several more years. In other words, change your Cost of Living Adjustment or COLA to an amount less than the current inflation rate.

Effects of Inflation: Often Overlooked

It seems that too many financial planning books just mention inflation in passing. Yes, they mention inflation but its effects are often not thoroughly explained. These books often mention how the stock market has averaged almost 10% in the past century. Therefore, they state that if your nest egg can just return the "normal" 10% return and you withdraw that 10% a year, you will never "touch" your principal. The percentages may be different from book to book, but they basically show you that if you just withdraw what your investment "earned" that year, your nest egg will last forever. It sounds great, and would actually work, if you could actually stand to do it. But the following table shows the fallacy of not figuring in inflated withdrawals each successive year .I'll use a more realistic return of 8%, but any return would work.

Table 1.2

	Beginning Balance	Annual % Return	Annual Withdraw-al	Inflated Value Needed (4%)
After 1 Year	$250,000	8%	$20,000	$20,800
After 5 Years	$250,000	8%	$20,000	$24,333
After 10 Years	$250,000	8%	$20,000	$29,605
After 20 Years	$250,000	8%	$20,000	$43,822
After 30 Years	$250,000	8%	$20,000	$64,869

Given the above scenario, how long could you "stand" to live on withdrawing just what your investment was making (in this case - $20,000). As you saw your buying power shrinking each year, at what point would you start withdrawing more than what your nest egg was returning. You would need to build in a self-chosen COLA to try to keep up with inflation. At that point, you would start cutting into you nest egg. Once you begin to bite into your principal, the effect is like a snowball rolling down a hill. Each year your nest egg is shrinking while your "needed" withdrawal amount (+COLA) is increasing. As the tables later in this book clearly reveal, you must always keep your withdrawal % LESS then your Rate of Return %.

Prudent Planning: ALWAYS Withdraw Less Than Your Investment Earns

We've all heard the maxim; "Live beneath your means." It simply means to always spend less than you make. Or negatively, never spend more than you make. As we have seen above, when it comes to retirement planning; never withdraw as much as your investment returns. In fact, a general rule of thumb is to always keep your withdrawal rate to AT LEAST 2 % below your investment return rate. And that is figuring a 3% inflation rate! At 4% & 5% inflation rates, you may need to keep your withdrawal rate to 3% below your investment return rate.

Example At 4% Inflation

Table 1.3

Return On Investment	Withdrawal % Rate	Begin Payout $500,000	Begin Payout $750,000	Begin Payout $1,000,000	Nest Egg Lasts
6	3	$1,250	$1,875	$2,500	Over 40 Yrs
6	4	$1,667	$2,500	$3,334	34 Yrs 11 Mths
6	5	$2,083	$3,124	$4,166	25 Yrs 10 Mths
6	6	$2,500	$3,750	$5,000	20 Yrs 7 Mths

Notice how quickly your money would be gone if you simply withdrew at a 6% rate when you were getting a 6% return – less than 21 years! Even if you withdrew 2% less than your projected investment return, or 4%, your money would run out in just under 35 years. Given this scenario, a 62 year-old retiree would start to feel uncomfortable about his nest egg several years BEFORE his nest egg was completely gone at age 97. Would you want to enter your 90's wondering if your nest egg would last? Granted, most retirees won't live 35 years in retirement, but what if you are one of the fortunate ones. Only a 3% withdrawal rate would "guarantee" your nest egg would outlast you (Over 40 years).

One other observation worth noting; the durations of the above nest eggs are the same whether we are talking about $500,000, $750,000 or $1,000,000. This is because we are dealing with percentages. You could plug in any nest egg amount and the above durations would still hold true. In other words, if you started with $358,179, a 4% withdrawal rate would equal $1,194 a month initially. This nest egg would last; you guessed it, 34 years and 11 months.

Planning For The Unknowns

Life is a continuum of unknowns. Some affect us financially:

- We don't know how long we will live, so we don't know how long our nest egg needs to last
- We don't know what inflation will be in the future
- We don't know what our investment return will be

Given that we don't know the above answers, it would seem prudent to plan for a possible worst financial case scenario. If we plug in possible values that might materialize in our future that would most adversely affect our nest egg, we can then run the numbers to see what withdrawal amount would 'allow' our nest egg to still survive. Our number one objective must always be:

OUR NEST EGG MUST OUTLAST US!

Since our nest egg MUST last longer than us, we should pick a withdrawal amount that will withstand the following possible scenarios:

- Duration: Our nest egg must last until we are at least 100 years old or so
- COLA: Our nest egg must allow for a reasonable COLA raise
- Investment Return: Our nest egg must be able to sustain returns of as little as 3%

The tables in this book that follow will show you how much you can safely withdraw to give your nest egg the best chance of surviving the above scenarios. A wide range of scenarios are presented so you can best plan on your initial withdrawal amount. Obviously if you are 80 years old and have already been retired a few years, your nest egg need not last as long as a newly retired 60 year-old.

Duration of Nest Egg Table

Age	60	65	70	75	80	85	90	95
Duration	40 Years	35 Years	30 Years	25 Years	20 Years	15 Years	10 Years	5 Years

Depending on your current age, the tables will reveal the "best" withdrawal amount that will "allow" your nest egg the best change of lasting until you are at least 100. If you are 70 years old you could choose the withdrawal table that shows a duration of at least 30 years. Here is a sample of how your age might affect your withdrawal amount.

Current Nest Egg: $500,000
COLA Projection: 4%

Investment Return Projection: 5%

Table 1.4

Age	60	65	70	75	80	85
Withdraw	3%	3.42%	3.90%	4.56%	5.58%	7.26%
Monthly	$1250	$1425	$1625	$1900	$2325	$3025
Duration	Over 40yr	35 Yrs	30 Yrs	25 Yrs	20 Yrs	15 Yrs

Importance of Yearly Reexamination

Each year it is important that you reexamine your withdrawal amount. The tables make this easy to do. Since inflation and investment return rates are constantly changing from year to year, it would be wise to 'recalculate' your withdrawal amount annually. If at any time during your retirement you are withdrawing too much too fast, your nest egg could be in 'trouble' too soon. It would be better to make minor adjustments to your withdrawal amounts on an annual basis instead of drastic cuts if you wait for longer periods to reexamine and find out you have been withdrawing way too much for the current financial conditions at the time.

Plan Conservatively

In good times, it will be tempting to withdraw at higher amounts. For example, In a year where your investment returns are running at 5% or higher it will be tempting to use the 5% tables and use those withdrawal rates. Those tables will "allow" you to withdraw at a higher amount and still have your nest egg last. The problem is the tables are calculating at a 5% return for up to 40 years – every year. This scenario is not realistic if you stick with conservative investments. In 2009, you were hard pressed to find a 'safe' investment yielding more than 3%.

Therefore the best approach is to use the tables with lower % returns and higher inflation rates. You will end up withdrawing less according to the tables. The net result is most often an increasing nest egg. In high yield years when there is low inflation you may be pleasantly surprised at the end of the year how much your nest egg as grown. With a growing nest egg, your next year's withdrawal amount can actually be higher because it is based on your balance for the current year. Since your balance is higher, your payout will be higher, using the same withdrawal percentage. (For example: 4% of 700,000 is greater than 4% of 600,000).

Aim For Balanced Withdrawals Year End & Year Out

As we have said, your number one goal is to have a plan in place to make sure your nest egg outlasts you. But a close second is to come up with a withdrawal amount that is level and slopes up slowly at or near the rate of inflation as the years go by. The last scenario you want is to start with one amount but have to slash it in half 5 years into retirement because you're running out of money too quickly. So you need to fight the temptation to increase your withdrawal amount in the years when your investment returns are high and the inflation rates are low. You must always think long term and plan accordingly.

The Numbers Don't Lie

To best illustrate the validity of the above paragraph, let's look at the following scenario:

John Doe, Age 62
Nest Egg $600,000
Current Return: 6%, 2% Inflation

Withdrawal Rate	3% ROI	4% ROI	5% ROI	6% ROI
5%	22 Yrs & 6 Mths	25 Yrs & 8 Mths	30 Yrs & 5 Mths	38 Yrs & 11Mths

Because the inflation rate is low at 2%, John figures he can withdraw 5% a year and his money will last him until age 101 (62 + 38Yrs&11Mths). Therefore he figures he can withdraw $2,500 a month ($600,000 x 5%=30,000 yr/12 months). Gradually over the next three years the financial environment changes. The next thing John knows the inflation rate has creeped up to 4% but he can only find "safe" investments that pay 4%.The tables show a disturbing truth.

Table 1.5

Withdrawal Rate	3% ROI	4% ROI	5% ROI	6% ROI
3%	29 Yrs & 5 Mths	33 Yrs & 11Mths	Over 40 Years	Over 40 Years
4%	22 Yrs & 10Mths	25 Yrs & 6 Mths	29 Yrs & 3 Mths	34 Yrs & 11Mths
5%	18 Yrs & 8 Mths	20 Yrs & 5 Mths	22 Yrs & 8 Mths	25 Yrs & 10Mths

At 4% inflation(if he uses a 4% COLA) the tables show if he continues withdrawing 5%, he is out of money in 20 years & 5 months. Now age 65, he'll run of money at age 85! Alarmed he realizes he'll need to cut back to a 3% withdrawal rate if he wants his money to last to near age 100. Instead of over $2,600 a month (after 3 years with a 2% COLA raise), John will have to cut back to just $1,500 a month if he wants a 4 % COLA to keep up with inflation.

After looking at the tables, he decides his best and least drastic approach is to cut back to a 4% withdrawal rate with 2% COLAs. The following table shows his nest egg lasting over 34 years. This means cutting back to around $2,000 a month. His choice was basically: $1500 a month with a 4% COLA or $2000 a month with a 2% COLA. He figured the second choice was the least painful of the two. Remember, he was used to almost $2,600 a month.

2% COLA

Table 1.6

Withdrawal Rate	3% ROI	4% ROI	5% ROI	6% ROI
2%	Over 40 Years	Over 40 Years	Over 40 Years	Over 40 Years
3%	Over 40 Years	Over 40 Years	Over 40 Years	Over 40 Years
4%	28 Yrs & 11Mths	34 Yrs & 9 Mths	Over 40 Years	Over 40 Years
5%	22 Yrs & 6 Mths	25 Yrs & 8 Mths	30 Yrs & 5 Mths	38 Yrs & 11Mths

Some Things To Remember

This chapter has revealed a lot of ramifications to the choices you make concerning your retirement withdrawals or monthly payouts. As you can see, there are many things to consider. But several crucial goals must ALWAYS be kept in the forefront of your thinking:

- Your Nest Egg Must Outlast You!
- Aim For Balanced Withdrawals Year End & Year Out
- Check These Tables Yearly

In the next chapter, we will present a hypothetical case that will help you see how this whole process can work. It will show you several scenarios which may develop in your retirement planning and how to deal with them.

CHAPTER 2

What Happens If I Start Withdrawing...?

Meet Sam Makeitlast. Sam is our imaginary retiree that allows us to vary our scenarios, some of which may seem almost ridiculous but since he is fictitious, no one gets hurt. Unfortunately some of Sam's choices are all too real in some retirees' lives. Here are some of Sam's numbers:

- Age: 62 about to retire, current monthly income of about $3800
- Married: wife Mary, age 61
- Social Security monthly payment: $1435 at current age
- Retirement savings: $527,000 combined with Mary's
- Mary, who will soon retire at age 62, has a monthly income of about $2200.
- Mary's Social Security at age 62 will be $1065
- Current Monthly Savings: $1000, living comfortably
- House Payment: none

Sam and Mary have always considered themselves to be good savers and are quite proud that they have been able to accumulate a sum of about $527,000. They have not really sacrificed too much to be able to save this sum. They always have taken nice vacations, driven somewhat newer vehicles and eaten out regularly. They have just been consistent savers because they realized they would be funding their own retirement using their companies' retirement plans and their IRAs. Given this sum, they are looking forward to a comfortable retirement.

Overview of the Makeitlasts financial situation:

- Current monthly income: about $6000

- SS Income in retirement: $2500
- Desired retirement income before taxes: $5000 (83% of preretirement income)

Sam's Plan

- Buy a new car to be able to travel; cost around $25,000
- Invest remainder, around $500,000
- Desired monthly income from investments: $2500
- Projected needed investment return: 6%
- The Math: $500,000 x 6% = $30,000 / 12 months = $2,500 a month

With the above as a framework, we will create several different possible scenarios of how Sam's plan might work out. Financial planners like to talk about asset allocation and risk tolerance. In other words, how much risk are you willing to live with in order to receive the greatest return. Over long periods of time (decades), it is true that stocks outperform bonds. But it is also true that stocks tend to be more volatile in their price fluctuations. Experts therefore debate what is the best ratio of stocks and bonds in your portfolio. My purpose is not to enter that debate but to show some possible outcomes of what Sam might choose.

Scenario 1 – 100% stocks

In this scenario, Sam decides he wants to go with stocks 100%.

Table 2.1

Possible Outcome #1 – if his returns match the S&P 500 from 1999-2008

Balance	$ 500,000			
Monthly Payout	$ 2,500			
Year	Return	Monthly Payout	Prepayout	PostPayout
1	21.04	$ 2,500	$ 605,200	$ 575,200
2	-9.11	$ 2,500	$ 522,799	$ 492,799
3	-11.89	$ 2,500	$ 434,205	$ 404,205
4	-22.10	$ 2,500	$ 314,876	$ 284,876
5	28.68	$ 2,500	$ 366,578	$ 336,578
6	10.88	$ 2,500	$ 373,198	$ 343,198

7	4.91	$ 2,500	$ 360,049	$ 330,049
8	15.79	$ 2,500	$ 382,164	$ 352,164
9	5.49	$ 2,500	$ 371,498	$ 341,498
10	-37.00	$ 2,500	$ 215,144	$ 185,144

After ten years, Sam's money would be almost 2/3 gone. Obviously, Sam would not have been very pleased with this result, just as many investors during that time period were very disappointed with their returns. If the above scenario would happen, in the 11th year, Sam would need to increase his return from 6% (of 500,000) to over 16.2% (of $185,144) in order to continue withdrawing $2500 a month. If he earned much less of a return, say 10%, and continued withdrawing $30,000 a year he would soon be out of money.

Table 2.2

Trying To Recover From A Down Decade Takes Huge Returns

Year	Return	Monthly Payout	Prepayout	PostPayout
11	16.20	$ 2,500	$ 215,145	$ 185,145
12	10.00	$ 2,500	$ 203,659	$ 173,659
13	10.00	$ 2,500	$ 191,025	$ 161,025
14	10.00	$ 2,500	$ 177,128	$ 147,128
------	------	-----	-----	-----
21	10.00	$ 2,500	$ 32,095	$ 2,095

On the other hand, if the stock market performs like the 1990's, Sam would end up being very happy! Let us see how those numbers might look.

Table 2.3

Possible Outcome #2 – if his returns match the S&P 500 from 1990-1999

Balance	$ 500,000			
Monthly Payout	$ 2,500			
Year	Return	Monthly Payout	Prepayout	PostPayout
1	-3.11	$ 2,500	$ 484,450	$ 454,450
2	30.47	$ 2,500	$ 592,921	$ 562,921
3	7.62	$ 2,500	$ 605,815	$ 575,815
4	10.08	$ 2,500	$ 633,858	$ 603,858
5	1.32	$ 2,500	$ 611,829	$ 581,829

6	37.58	$ 2,500	$ 800,480	$ 770,480
7	22.96	$ 2,500	$ 947,382	$ 917,382
8	33.36	$ 2,500	$ 1,223,421	$ 1,193,421
9	28.58	$ 2,500	$ 1,534,500	$ 1,504,500
10	21.04	$ 2,500	$ 1,821,047	$ 1,791,047

What a difference a decade can make! The problem is no one knows what the next decade may bring. Stocks averaged 9.5% over the last century. This would easily allow Sam to make his goal of a 6% return if stocks continued that average. Unfortunately an initial down year like 2008 (-37%) would set his nest egg in such a hole, that he would be hard-pressed to recover without reducing his monthly withdrawal amount.

Downs and Ups

There is an unfortunate truth about a negative return on an investment. In order to recover from any loss a person will need to have a greater percentage gain than his previous percentage loss. You would think a 37% gain after a loss of 37% would bring a person back to where they were before the loss. The numbers show otherwise.

Table 2.4

Year	Return	Monthly Payout	Prepayout	PostPayout
1	-37.00	$ -	$ 315,000	$ 315,000
2	37.00	$ -	$ 431,550	$ 431,550

The larger the loss, the larger the gain needed to return to where you started:

Table 2.5

100% Gain Needed After A 50% Loss

Year	Return	Monthly Payout	Prepayout	PostPayout
1	-50	$ -	$ 250,000	$ 250,000
2	100	$ -	$ 500,000	$ 500,000

Notice it takes a 100% gain to make up a 50% loss and that is with NO withdrawals! If you take into account the withdrawals, the picture is even bleaker. That is because the 100% is based on the lower balance after the withdrawals ($220,000). After two years, he is down $90,000, though he only withdrew $60,000. (See Table 1.5 below)

Table 2.6

Effect Of Withdrawals After 50% Loss

Year	Return	Monthly Payout	Prepayout	PostPayout
1	-50	$ 2,500	$ 250,000	$ 220,000
2	100	$ 2,500	$ 440,000	$ 410,000

The above table shows why negative returns are so damaging to your portfolio balance once you begin making withdrawals from it. The above example also reveals the danger of just relying on "average" returns. In the above example the two-year average would be 25%. Who wouldn't love a two year return that averaged 25% per year.

Table 2.7

Year	Return	Monthly Payout	Prepayout	PostPayout
1	25	$ 2,500	$ 625,000	$ 595,000
2	25	$ 2,500	$ 743,750	$ 713,750

Both examples averaged 25% gain per year. But what a difference in results!

Again the above information just shows the pain any significant downturn can cause, especially once you are making withdrawals from your balance. In 2008, the reality of a large negative return was brought home to a lot of people as they saw the S&P 500 portion of their portfolio drop by 37%. Retirees that were making withdrawals from their portfolios during the year were especially hard hit. They were in effect, "selling low". Once the money is withdrawn it is no longer there to grow when the returns turn positive again.

The difference between a saver, one who is still working and contributing to his retirement nest egg, and a withdrawer, a retiree living off his nest egg; is quite stark in a down decade. The saver can usually recover from a down decade. The retiree who is withdrawing from his nest egg all during the down years is hard-pressed to come back.

Saving Versus Withdrawing During 2000-2007

Compare the year-end balances of a saver saving $1,000 per month and a retiree withdrawing $2,500 a month (like Sam) during the years of 2000-2007 starting with $500,000.

Table 2.8

Year	Return	Withdrawing $2,500/ month	Adding $1,000/month
2000	-9.11	$ 424,450	$ 466,450
2001	-11.89	$ 343,983	$ 422,989
2002	-22.1	$ 237,963	$ 341,509
2003	28.68	$ 276,210	$ 451,453
2004	10.88	$ 276,262	$ 512,571
2005	4.91	$ 259,827	$ 549,738
2006	15.79	$ 270,853	$ 648,542
2007	5.49	$ 255,723	$ 696,147

Despite having the down years of 2000-2002, the saver was able to rally nicely in the positive years of 2003-2007. He started with $500,000 and by the end of 2007 had increased his nest egg to $696,147 which meant a gain of $196,147 of which $96,000(1,000x96 months) was made up of his own contributions.

The retiree, on the other hand was down by almost HALF. In fact, if you will notice, by the end of 2002, he was down by more than half. It was the only the nice positive returns of 2003-2007 that allowed him to keep from losing even more ground. Unfortunately 2008 came with its negative return of 37%, and he would have ended 2008 with only $131,105 left. Remember he was withdrawing $2,500 a month which is $30,000 a year. In just 9 short years his money is almost ¾ gone. Unless the stock market would sky rocket for multiple years, there is no way the retiree could continue to withdraw $2,500 a month for long.

Scenario 2 – Conservative blend of investments

Most people tend to become more conservative with their investments once they enter retirement. They figure they can't afford to risk a period like 2000-2008. Let's pretend that Sam agrees and picks a blend of stocks, bonds, and certificates of deposit(CD's).

Possible Outcome #1: if his return yields 6% - which is Sam's goal

Table 2.9

Year	Return	Monthly Payout	Prepayout	PostPayout
1	6	$ 2,500	$ 530,000	$ 500,000
2	6	$ 2,500	$ 530,000	$ 500,000
3	6	$ 2,500	$ 530,000	$ 500,000
4	6	$ 2,500	$ 530,000	$ 500,000
5	6	$ 2,500	$ 530,000	$ 500,000

In an ideal world, Sam's plan would work beautifully. But to earn 6% consistently year after year in mostly conservative investments is unrealistic. In 2009, you were hard-pressed to earn much more than 2% on your CD's. But let's say that Sam could lock in an investment that would pay 6% year after year. Is Sam's plan then bulletproof? At first glance; yes, BUT... Sam has forgotten one small detail that will actually be a big headache in his future. Sam has forgotten about INFLATION!. What will that $2,500 buy in 10 years, 15 years, 20 years???

Table 2.10

Effect of 3% Inflation on Sam's Plan

Year	Return	Monthly Payout	Prepayout	PostPayout
1	6.00	$ 2,500	$ 530,000	$ 500,000
2	6.00	$ 2,575	$ 530,000	$ 499,100
3	6.00	$ 2,652	$ 529,046	$ 497,219
4	6.00	$ 2,732	$ 527,052	$ 494,270
5	6.00	$ 2,814	$ 523,927	$ 490,161

If Sam increases his withdrawal by 3% to keep up with inflation each year, will his plan still work? After 5 years he will only be down $10,000. It looks like his plan can easily keep up with 3% inflation. Even after 10 years it looks like he will be okay.

Table 2.11

Year	Return	Monthly Payout	Prepayout	PostPayout
6	6.00	$ 2,898	$ 519,571	$ 484,793
7	6.00	$ 2,985	$ 513,880	$ 478,059
8	6.00	$ 3,075	$ 506,742	$ 469,846
9	6.00	$ 3,167	$ 498,037	$ 460,034
10	6.00	$ 3,262	$ 487,636	$ 448,493

After 10 years he is down about 10% from his original $500,000. If he wouldn't have inflated his monthly payment for those 10 years he would still have $500,000 but his $2,500 monthly payout wouldn't be keeping up with the inflated value of that $2,500 which would then be $3262. That would be like a 23% paycut in the first 10 years. Sam doesn't think he would like to give up his 3% COLA so if he keeps it up, what would happen in the next ten years:

Table 2.12

Year	Return	Monthly Payout	Prepayout	PostPayout
11	6.00	$ 3,360	$ 475,402	$ 435,085
12	6.00	$ 3,461	$ 461,190	$ 419,663
13	6.00	$ 3,564	$ 444,842	$ 402,070
14	6.00	$ 3,671	$ 426,194	$ 382,138
15	6.00	$ 3,781	$ 405,066	$ 359,688
16	6.00	$ 3,895	$ 381,270	$ 334,531
17	6.00	$ 4,012	$ 354,602	$ 306,461
18	6.00	$ 4,132	$ 324,849	$ 275,263
19	6.00	$ 4,256	$ 291,779	$ 240,706
20	6.00	$ 4,384	$ 255,149	$ 202,543

Shocking, isn't it!

Twenty years into retirement, at age 82, Sam would be down 60% just keeping up with 3% inflation. And it quickly gets even worse.... Sam and Mary would be broke in just a little over 24 years! Maybe neither one will live to be 86, but what if one or both do?

Table 2.13

Year	Return	Monthly Payout	Prepayout	PostPayout
21	6.00	$ 4,515	$ 214,696	$ 160,513
22	6.00	$ 4,651	$ 170,144	$ 114,335
23	6.00	$ 4,790	$ 121,195	$ 63,712
24	6.00	$ 4,934	$ 67,534	$ 8,327
25	6.00	$ 5,082	$ 8,826	$ -

What happened? Can this be possible?

After 10 years everything looked so manageable. Sam was only down about 10% at age 72. But by age 82 (year 20), he was down to $202,000 and was withdrawing over $50,000 a year ($4,384*12) just to keep up with an inflation rate of 3%. What would Sam be thinking at age 82?

- Am I going to run out of money?
- What could I have done different?
- Should I try the stock market to increase my returns?
- Should I have stuck with $2,500 a month and not done the COLAs?

Inflation, which seems so innocent at first, would wreak havoc on Sam's plan. In just 25 years, he would need $5,082 a month just to keep up with 3% inflation. But he would have no money left! The effects of inflation over the long term must be accounted for or some really tough decisions may come. Sam and Mary may not live long enough for inflation to be a major headache, but what if they make to their eighties? Or what if inflation hits 4%...?

Possible Outcome #2: 5% return with 4% inflation

Table 2.14

Year	Return	Monthly Payout	Prepayout	PostPayout
1	5.00	$ 2,500	$ 525,000	$ 495,000
2	5.00	$ 2,600	$ 519,750	$ 488,550
3	5.00	$ 2,704	$ 512,978	$ 480,530
4	5.00	$ 2,812	$ 504,556	$ 470,810
5	5.00	$ 2,925	$ 494,351	$ 459,255
6	5.00	$ 3,042	$ 482,218	$ 445,718
7	5.00	$ 3,163	$ 468,004	$ 430,044
8	5.00	$ 3,290	$ 451,546	$ 412,069

9	5.00	$ 3,421	$ 432,672	$ 391,615
10	5.00	$ 3,558	$ 411,196	$ 368,496
11	5.00	$ 3,701	$ 386,921	$ 342,514
12	5.00	$ 3,849	$ 359,639	$ 313,456
13	5.00	$ 4,003	$ 329,129	$ 281,098
14	5.00	$ 4,163	$ 295,153	$ 245,200
15	5.00	$ 4,329	$ 257,460	$ 205,510
16	5.00	$ 4,502	$ 215,786	$ 161,757
17	5.00	$ 4,682	$ 169,845	$ 113,656
18	5.00	$ 4,870	$ 119,338	$ 60,901
19	5.00	$ 5,065	$ 63,947	$ 3,172
20	5.00	$ 5,267	$ 3,331	$ -

What Happened To The Dream Retirement?

The above table reveals an even more troubling possibility; out of money in less than 20 years. If Sam could only average a 5% return and inflation kicked up to 4%, his money situation would begin to be uncomfortable even in his mid to late seventies (years 13-17). This may seem like a worse-case scenario and it may never happen. But an inflation rate of 4% is quite feasible, especially given the increased rate of government borrowing of late. Remember that the inflation rate averaged 4.66% from 1972 to 2007. If higher inflation rates return, you need to be plan accordingly.

So What Could Sam Do?

One possible option:

- Start out withdrawing $2,000 a month instead or $2,500
- Keep COLA to 1% less than inflation – 3% COLA in a 4% inflation environment

Table 2.15

Year	Return	3% COLA	4% Inflation	Prepayout	PostPayout
1	5.00	$ 2,000	$2,000	$ 525,000	$ 501,000
2	5.00	$ 2,060	$2,080	$ 526,050	$ 501,330
3	5.00	$ 2,122	$2,163	$ 526,397	$ 500,935
4	5.00	$ 2,185	$2,250	$ 525,982	$ 499,756
5	5.00	$ 2,251	$2,340	$ 524,744	$ 497,732

6	5.00	$ 2,319	$2,433	$ 522,618	$ 494,796
7	5.00	$ 2,388	$2,531	$ 519,536	$ 490,878
8	5.00	$ 2,460	$2,632	$ 515,422	$ 485,905
9	5.00	$ 2,534	$2,737	$ 510,201	$ 479,798
10	5.00	$ 2,610	$2,847	$ 503,788	$ 472,473
11	5.00	$ 2,688	$2,960	$ 496,097	$ 463,843
12	5.00	$ 2,768	$3,079	$ 487,035	$ 453,814
13	5.00	$ 2,852	$3,202	$ 476,504	$ 442,286
14	5.00	$ 2,937	$3,330	$ 464,400	$ 429,156
15	5.00	$ 3,025	$3,463	$ 450,613	$ 414,311
16	5.00	$ 3,116	$3,602	$ 435,027	$ 397,636
17	5.00	$ 3,209	$3,746	$ 417,517	$ 379,004
18	5.00	$ 3,306	$3,896	$ 397,955	$ 358,286
19	5.00	$ 3,405	$4,052	$ 376,201	$ 335,342
20	5.00	$ 3,507	$4,214	$ 352,109	$ 310,025

After 20 years, Sam would still have over $310,000 left. At 82, he would still be comfortable. Each year he would feel somewhat pinched with inflation, but it would work.

What Sam and Mary Really Need

Obviously, there are many scenarios that could happen in Sam and Mary's future. In order to properly and safely plan their retirement, what they really need is an easy way to compare almost limitless possible scenarios. To intelligently plan their withdrawal strategy, they need easy to use information for the wide-ranging variables of what might happen in the future, especially with inflation. As we have seen in this chapter, inflation is insidious. It starts out so gradual and is therefore so easy to overlook in one's planning. If there was just an easy way to compare varying inflation rates at varying withdrawal rates, their planning could be so much easier. That is exactly the information the tables in this book provide.

Retirement Planning Made Easy

The tables are so easy to use. Once you pick your general scenario, the appropriate table for that scenario will give you all the information you need to make comparative judgments ON ONE PAGE! There is no need to jump all over the tables to find the comparisons you need. The tables are set up so that you can make all your comparisons of varying withdrawal rates and varying inflation rates in one table. You will know how long your money will last and what your withdrawal amounts will inflate to. Again – ALL ON ONE PAGE!

In the next chapter we will show you how easy the tables are to use and explain everything about them. We will continue to use Sam and Mary for our example. Be prepared to be amazed at how eye-opening and helpful the tables can be.

A Word About COLAs

Because retirement can last 20, 30 or even more years, a retiree must take into account the effect inflation will have on his retirement planning. As we have seen, the COLA or Cost of Living Adjustment, can help ease the pain of persistent inflation. Each year you can increase your withdrawal amount by a certain percentage. There are at least two benefits to giving yourself a COLA. First, it will help you keep up with inflation. But secondly, it will give you a psychological boost. Each year you can look forward to a "raise".

Back in chapter one and earlier in this chapter, we dealt with the possible devastating effects of inflation. The COLA is a way to mitigate the effects of inflation. COLAs must be managed carefully, however, or they can deplete your nest egg rapidly. In an high inflation environment, it is tempting to give yourself a "high" COLA to keep up. To do so, as we have seen, can quickly run you out of money. It is best to use the tables to find the highest COLA you can give yourself and still have your money last as long as you think it must.

I have read many financial planning books that often have a section on how to make your money last in retirement. They often recommend setting up a spreadsheet to look at various scenarios. Or they give various websites to visit. Many sites are somewhat confusing to use or only allow one set of criteria per calculation. Then you have to go back and forth changing the variables to come up with the new answer, which by then you may have forgotten the previous answer. The tables in this book are set up to show the main variables and their results ON ONE PAGE. This makes it very easy to compare your options.

CHAPTER 3

How To Use The Tables

In this chapter, we will continue to use Sam & Mary Makeitlast for our sample couple. You will remember that Sam figured he would have about $500,000 in investments after buying his new car. He calculated that if he could average a 6% return on that $500,000 that would yield him $30,000 a year or $2,500 a month. As we saw in chapter 2, this plan sounds good on paper. The tables will show the plan has some serious flaws. Fortunate for Sam, he picks up this book of tables and begins to follow the numbers and Sam soon develops a more enlightened plan.

First Things First

The first objective in retirement is to set up an emergency fund. You need to set up a fund to cover potential needs. You may need a new roof, new furnace, etc. The unexpected costs of life can arise at anytime. It is best to have a fund set aside so that you will not touch your portfolio that you are using to plan your withdrawals. The tables are set up in increments of $25,000 ($50,000 for amounts over $750,000) with this in mind. For example, although Sam has $500,000 in retirement funds, he will not use the $500,000 balance tables but rather the $475,000 tables allowing the remaining $25,000 to fund his emergency fund. Whether he actually sets that $25,000 in a separate fund or just leaves it separate in his calculations is up to him.

Find You Current Balance

The tables are set to run from $200,000 up to $750,000 in increments of $25,000. A second set of tables run from $750,000 to $1.5 million in increments of $50,000. In Sam's case he locates the tables with a beginning balance of $475,000. There are four tables that have a beginning balance of $475,000. They vary from 3% to 6% Return On Investment. Because Sam expects to average a 6% return he finds the following table:

$475,000 Balance					6% Return On Investment			

No COLA

Monthly Amount	15 Yr Inflated	30 Yr Inflated	Money Lasts	5 Years	10 Years	15 Years	20 Years	30 Years
$1,250	$1,250	$1,250	Over 40 Yrs	$548,564	$647,010	$778,753	$955,054	$1.507 Mil
$1,500	$1,500	$1,500	Over 40 Yrs	$531,146	$606,282	$706,831	$841,387	$1.262 Mil
$1,750	$1,750	$1,750	Over 40 Yrs	$513,726	$565,552	$634,905	$727,715	$1.018 Mil
$2,000	$2,000	$2,000	Over 40 Yrs	$496,308	$524,823	$562,982	$614,048	$773,837
$2,250	$2,250	$2,250	Over 40 Yrs	$478,889	$484,094	$491,060	$500,383	$529,554
$2,500	$2,500	$2,500	Over 40 Yrs	$461,471	$443,366	$419,138	$386,715	$285,264
$2,750	$2,750	$2,750	31 Y & 4 M	$444,052	$402,637	$347,214	$273,046	$40,970

The table actually has 4 smaller minitables laid out using progressively higher COLAs.

The top minitable of the four is labeled No COLA. This one shows how long your money will last if you never pay yourself a COLA. It consists of nine columns which are here explained.

Monthly Amount – this is the monthly amount you will begin to withdraw at retirement

15 Yr Inflated – this is the amount your beginning amount will grow to in 15 years given the COLA percentage. Obviously with No COLA it would stay the same.

30Yr Inflated – this is the amount your beginning amount will grow to in 30 years given the COLA percentage. Again with no COLA it is still the same.

Money Lasts – This column shows how long your beginning balance (in this case $475,000) will last for each of the monthly amounts.(in this case from $1,250 to $2,750).

THE "Money Lasts" COLUMN IS THE MOST IMPORTANT ONE IN THE TABLES

5 Yrs thru 30 Yrs – These remaining 5 columns show the remaining balances, in dollars, for each of the subsequent time spans. For example, looking at the table above, if you begin withdrawing $2,500 a month, after 5 yrs you would have $461,471 left. If the column equals zero, YOU ARE OUT OF MONEY!

Obviously if you never give yourself a COLA, you can have a higher monthly withdrawal and still have your money last. In Sam's case, if he never gave himself a COLA, his $475,000 would last over 40 years if he withdrew $2,500 a month. If there was no inflation, Sam would be just fine. But if inflation comes in at just a modest 2% a year and Sam pays himself a 2% COLA to keep up with that inflation rate, everything changes.

2% COLA

Monthly Amount	15 Yr Inflated	30 Yr Inflated	Money Lasts	5 Years	10 Years	15 Years	20 Years	30 Years
$1,250	$1,650	$2,220	Over 40 Yrs	$545,219	$629,775	$732,529	$858,557	$1.209 Mil
$1,500	$1,979	$2,664	Over 40 Yrs	$527,131	$585,598	$651,366	$725,603	$905,563
$1,750	$2,309	$3,108	Over 40 Yrs	$509,045	$541,424	$570,205	$592,659	$601,862
$2,000	$2,639	$3,552	38 Y & 1 M	$490,955	$497,245	$489,034	$459,687	$298,081
$2,250	$2,969	$3,996	29 Y & 11 M	$472,866	$453,067	$407,868	$326,724	$0
$2,500	$3,299	$4,440	24 Y & 10 M	$454,780	$408,900	$326,719	$193,791	$0
$2,750	$3,629	$4,884	21 Y & 4 M	$436,693	$364,726	$245,550	$60,821	$0

This 2% minitable shows the results of the monthly amounts growing by 2% a year. In just 15 years, Sam would be withdrawing $3,299 just to keep up with a 2% inflation rate (see 15 Yr Inflated amount). If he had enough money he would be withdrawing $4,440 a month after 30 years. BUT his money wouldn't last that long. Notice he runs out of money in just 24 years and 10 months! By age 87 he would be broke. Not knowing how long he and Mary will live, he is not comfortable with the results of a 2% COLA on the $2,500 monthly amount. He would like their money to last at least 35 years which would get them to age 97. Sam is beginning to see that he will need to decrease his expectations concerning his monthly withdrawal amount. As he looks down the tables at the 3% and 4% COLAS, he realizes that he may have to cut back to even below $2,000 per month.

3% COLA

Monthly Amount	15 Yr Inflated	30 Yr Inflated	Money Lasts	5 Years	10 Years	15 Years	20 Years	30 Years
$1,250	$1,891	$2,946	Over 40 Yrs	$543,497	$620,484	$706,493	$801,863	$1.020 Mil
$1,500	$2,269	$3,535	Over 40 Yrs	$525,065	$574,449	$620,108	$657,535	$678,651
$1,750	$2,647	$4,124	37 Y & 6 M	$506,634	$528,423	$533,759	$513,285	$337,250
$2,000	$3,025	$4,713	29 Y & 11 M	$488,199	$482,371	$447,344	$368,906	$0
$2,250	$3,403	$5,302	24 Y & 11 M	$469,771	$436,353	$361,002	$224,652	$0
$2,500	$3,782	$5,891	21 Y & 7 M	$451,337	$390,314	$274,618	$80,337	$0
$2,750	$4,160	$6,481	18 Y & 11 M	$432,904	$344,277	$188,232	$0	$0

4% COLA

Monthly Amount	15 Yr Inflated	30 Yr Inflated	Money Lasts	5 Years	10 Years	15 Years	20 Years	30 Years
$1,250	$2,165	$3,899	Over 40 Yrs	$541,742	$610,710	$678,246	$738,501	$796,768
$1,500	$2,598	$4,678	37 Y & 9 M	$522,957	$562,719	$586,227	$581,537	$410,520
$1,750	$3,031	$5,458	30 Y & 5 M	$504,175	$514,725	$494,185	$424,528	$24,194
$2,000	$3,463	$6,237	25 Y & 6 M	$485,395	$466,754	$402,200	$267,626	$0
$2,250	$3,896	$7,017	21 Y & 11 M	$466,611	$418,761	$310,168	$110,633	$0
$2,500	$4,329	$7,796	19 Y & 4 M	$447,827	$370,768	$218,143	$0	$0
$2,750	$4,762	$8,576	17 Y & 3 M	$429,043	$322,778	$126,108	$0	$0

Considering Sam's Options

After examining the minitables above, Sam believes he has about 3 options if he wants his money to last at least 35 years. They are:

1. Begin with $2,000 a month payout with a 2% COLA – his money will last over 38 years
2. Begin with $1,750 a month payout with a 3% COLA – his money will last 37.5 years
3. Begin with $1,500 a month payout with a 4% COLA – His money will last 37.75 years

After 15 Years

Given those three options, Sam then considers where he would be in 15 years. Using the minitables above, Sam comes up with the following:

	Beginning Monthly	COLA	15 Year Inflated	15 Year Balance
Option 1	$2,000	2%	$2,639	$489,034
Option 2	$1,750	3%	$2,647	$533,759
Option 3	$1,500	4%	$2,598	$586,227

Sam notices that after 15 years all 3 inflated amounts will be almost the same, around $2,600 a month. So Sam has a decision to make. Should he start out with less (Option 3), $1,500 a month, and end up with a 15 year balance almost $100,000 more then with Option 1. Sam doesn't think he wants to cut back to $1,500 and decides he wants to run some figures using Option 1. Starting at $2,000 a month is more palatable for his retirement plans. Even though he will only give himself a 2% COLA per year, he will still end up with the same amount per month after 15 years as the other options. Plus he will still have MORE money than he started with - $489,034. Not as much as the other options but an easier ride getting to that 15 year mark since he starts with more ($2,000).

Good Planning Pays

If Sam's hypothetical 15 year plan works out, he would go back to the tables at age 77, and run the new numbers at $475,000 because he would put the difference (489,034 - $475,000 = $14,034) back in his emergency fund. Here's how the new plan works out:

$475,000 Balance   6% Return On Investment

3% COLA

Monthly Amount	15 Yr Inflated	30 Yr Inflated	Money Lasts	5 Years	10 Years	15 Years	20 Years	30 Years
$1,250	$1,891	$2,946	Over 40 Yrs	$543,497	$620,484	$706,493	$801,863	$1.020 Mil
$1,500	$2,269	$3,535	Over 40 Yrs	$525,065	$574,449	$620,108	$657,535	$678,651
$1,750	$2,647	$4,124	37 Y & 6 M	$506,634	$528,423	$533,759	$513,285	$337,250
$2,000	$3,025	$4,713	29 Y & 11 M	$488,199	$482,371	$447,344	$368,906	$0
$2,250	$3,403	$5,302	24 Y & 11 M	$469,771	$436,353	$361,002	$224,652	$0
$2,500	$3,782	$5,891	21 Y & 7 M	$451,337	$390,314	$274,618	$80,337	$0
$2,750	$4,160	$6,481	18 Y & 11 M	$432,904	$344,277	$188,232	$0	$0

4% COLA

Monthly Amount	15 Yr Inflated	30 Yr Inflated	Money Lasts	5 Years	10 Years	15 Years	20 Years	30 Years
$1,250	$2,165	$3,899	Over 40 Yrs	$541,742	$610,710	$678,246	$738,501	$796,768
$1,500	$2,598	$4,678	37 Y & 9 M	$522,957	$562,719	$586,227	$581,537	$410,520
$1,750	$3,031	$5,458	30 Y & 5 M	$504,175	$514,725	$494,185	$424,528	$24,194
$2,000	$3,463	$6,237	25 Y & 6 M	$485,395	$466,754	$402,200	$267,626	$0
$2,250	$3,896	$7,017	21 Y & 11 M	$466,611	$418,761	$310,168	$110,633	$0
$2,500	$4,329	$7,796	19 Y & 4 M	$447,827	$370,768	$218,143	$0	$0
$2,750	$4,762	$8,576	17 Y & 3 M	$429,043	$322,778	$126,108	$0	$0

Notice at this stage, Sam doesn't even need to look at the lower COLA minitables because he is 77 and only needs his money to last 20 years or so. Sam, who was planning on around $2,600 a month in the 15th year of the previous options could actually jump to $2,750 a month at age 78 and with a 3% COLA would have his money last almost 19 more years. Because he was willing to take a little bit less in the earlier years of his retirement, he will be able to keep up his monthly withdrawals with healthy 3 or 4% COLAs even in his later years. So his plan looks like the following:

Years	Beginning Monthly	Annual COLA	Inflated Monthly	Ending Balance
1 Thru 15	$2,000	2 %	$2,639 after 15	$489,034
16 Thru 30	$2,750	3 %	$4,160 after 30	$188,232

Even though Sam's plan looks like it will work and keep his monthly payouts reasonably uniform allowing for some inflation, so many variables can change in such a short time. Therefore it is recommended that he reevaluates his plan YEARLY. Each year, like Sam, you would do well to run the new numbers with your new beginning of the year balance.

What If My Return Is Really High During The Year?

Sam ran his numbers with a 6% Return On Investment or ROI. What if your ROI comes in really high one year, how can you still use the tables? After all, they only show a high of 6% ROI? This is done as a safeguard. Remember these tables are to be used as an estimate to determine what you can safely withdraw and still have your nest egg last. If you have a really good investment year and your ROI is say 33%, you wouldn't run your numbers at that rate. That would be unrealistic. But even running them at a 6% ROI will increase your monthly payout for the next year because your beginning balance is now 33% higher. Here are the new numbers:

$625,000 Balance							**6% Return On Investment**	

2% COLA

Monthly Amount	15 Yr Inflated	30 Yr Inflated	Money Lasts	5 Years	10 Years	15 Years	20 Years	30 Years
$2,000	$2,639	$3,552	Over 40 Yrs	$691,689	$765,873	$848,519	$940,759	$1.160 Mil
$2,250	$2,969	$3,996	Over 40 Yrs	$673,602	$721,697	$767,356	$807,800	$855,857
$2,500	$3,299	$4,440	Over 40 Yrs	$655,514	$677,526	$686,201	$674,860	$552,148
$2,750	$3,629	$4,884	34 Y & 7 M	$637,427	$633,352	$605,032	$541,889	$248,359

$3,000	$3,958	$5,327	29 Y & 2 M	$619,341	$589,179	$523,873	$408,946	$0
$3,250	$4,288	$5,772	25 Y & 4 M	$601,248	$544,990	$442,683	$275,940	$0
$3,500	$4,618	$6,215	22 Y & 5 M	$583,163	$500,825	$361,541	$143,019	$0

3% COLA

Monthly Amount	15 Yr Inflated	30 Yr Inflated	Money Lasts	5 Years	10 Years	15 Years	20 Years	30 Years
$2,000	$3,025	$4,713	Over 40 Yrs	$688,933	$751,000	$806,830	$849,978	$857,010
$2,250	$3,403	$5,302	39 Y & 1 M	$670,504	$704,980	$720,484	$705,720	$515,548
$2,500	$3,782	$5,891	32 Y & 7 M	$652,070	$658,941	$634,102	$561,408	$173,997
$2,750	$4,160	$6,481	27 Y & 11 M	$633,639	$612,905	$547,718	$417,080	$0
$3,000	$4,538	$7,070	24 Y & 7 M	$615,208	$566,871	$461,349	$272,790	$0
$3,250	$4,916	$7,659	21 Y & 11 M	$596,776	$520,846	$374,990	$128,513	$0
$3,500	$5,294	$8,248	19 Y & 10 M	$578,341	$474,796	$288,583	$0	$0

Because you are using a higher balance notice that you could raise your monthly payout from $2,000 (using Sam's plan which used $475,000) to $2,750 (using your new balance of $625,000 which is $475,000 + a 33% return rounded down to the nearest $25,000) if you would use the 2% COLA minitable. Notice your money would last almost 35 years which if you are Sam's age would be about right.

A General Plan

Now you are beginning to understand how to use these tables. If any variables such as inflation or your ROI are abnormally high, low or even negative, you just roll with the punches and stay with the norms in your future calculations. If inflation would hit 10 % one year, just run your numbers with the 4% COLA minitable. It would be painful for that year, but remember you control how much your monthly payout will be. Keep to the tables' guidelines and plan ahead wisely. Don't let abnormal years upset your planning. Stay with the norms. Plan on between 3% to 6% ROI and 2% to 4% COLAs. Over the years the numbers will even out.

Make It Easy

As we have said the tables contain a lot of information. They can seem to be overwhelming at first, especially if you are not a "numbers" person. But if you use three simple steps, the tables will focus you like a laser beam to the best monthly payout so that your money will outlast you. Here are the three steps:

First Step Take you current age and subtract it from 97. This is your *Money Lasts Age.*

Second Step: Pick a realistic ROI between 3% to 6% inclusive. This is your PLANNED ROI

Third Step: Pick a COLA (2% to 4%) you can feel comfortable with for your retirement years.

That's it! The rest is simple!

1. At the beginning of each year, figure out the value of your nest egg. Example $637,250
2. Round down to the nearest $25,000 (or the nearest $50,000 if your nest egg is above $750,000) and put the remainder in your emergency fund.
3. Find that amount in the tables with your corresponding PLANNED ROI from step 2 above. Our example:. $625,000 with a ROI of 6% see above table
4. Look at the COLA minitable you picked in step 3 above. For example: 3% COLA
5. Look in the Money Lasts column. Find the number that is at least as much as your *Money Lasts Age* from Step 1 above: For example a 70 year-old would pick out 27Y 11M
6. Follow that row across to the amount in the Monthly Payout column. That is your beginning monthly payout. In our example ,his beginning payout = $2,750

Sam Reevaluates His Plan

As Sam and Mary talk about their retirement planning, Mary, who is more financially conservative, asks a simple question. "What if our investments only average 4% ROI?" Mary reminds Sam that their CD's were only paying about 2% in 2009. Sam, who is generally very optimistic, looks again at chapter two and what happened to the stock market and decides that he will probably be finding more conservative investments for their retirement years. Sam agrees to run the tables at a 4% ROI at least until the economy looks more robust and "safe".

Sam's Revised Plan

First Step Sam subtracts 62 from 97 = 35
Second Step: Sam picks 4% instead of 6% for his ROI
Third Step: Sam picks a 2% COLA since inflation is currently really low.

Sam uses the table as follows:

1. Nest Egg: $500,000
2. Amount to invest: $475,000 after setting aside $25,000 for his emergency fund
3. Look up the table:

$475,000 Balance	4% Return On Investment

4. Use the 2% COLA minitable

2% COLA

Monthly Amount	15 Yr Inflated	30 Yr Inflated	Money Lasts	5 Years	10 Years	15 Years	20 Years	30 Years
$1,000	$1,320	$1,776	Over 40 Yrs	$509,014	$543,224	$576,928	$609,198	$664,167
$1,250	$1,650	$2,220	Over 40 Yrs	$491,793	$503,261	$507,310	$501,304	$445,035
$1,500	$1,979	$2,664	37 Y & 7 M	$474,568	$463,286	$437,683	$393,417	$225,960
$1,750	$2,309	$3,108	30 Y & 3 M	$457,346	$423,316	$368,060	$285,539	$6,901
$2,000	$2,639	$3,552	25 Y & 4 M	$440,121	$383,345	$298,433	$177,643	$0
$2,250	$2,969	$3,996	21 Y & 10 M	$422,897	$343,370	$228,804	$69,747	$0
$2,500	$3,299	$4,440	19 Y & 2 M	$405,675	$303,408	$159,195	$0	$0

5. Look in the Money Lasts column for the first time period greater than 35 years (Step 1)
6. Look across to the Monthly Amount column: $1,500

Sam and Marys' Compromise

As Sam and Mary look at the numbers, they are a little bit discouraged how little they would initially withdraw: $1,500 a month. Sam remembers that before he looked at the tables, he was planning on $2,500 a month. Sam's first temptation is to return to his first ROI projection of 6%. That at least gave them a beginning monthly payout of $2,000. But they both agree that this book has reminded them to be realistic. They must stick with the 4% ROI projection, at least for now. Things will hopefully improve. They also looked at the 3% COLA minitable and saw that they would have to start at $1,250 a month to allow their money to last over 35 years.

$475,000 Balance						4% Return On Investment		

3% COLA

Monthly Amount	15 Yr Inflated	30 Yr Inflated	Money Lasts	5 Years	10 Years	15 Years	20 Years	30 Years
$1,000	$1,513	$2,357	Over 40 Yrs	$507,678	$536,252	$558,047	$569,528	$541,649
$1,250	$1,891	$2,946	38 Y & 6 M	$490,119	$494,534	$483,696	$451,714	$291,923
$1,500	$2,269	$3,535	30 Y & 11 M	$472,563	$452,818	$409,338	$333,886	$42,131
$1,750	$2,647	$4,124	25 Y & 11 M	$455,006	$411,110	$335,010	$216,119	$0
$2,000	$3,025	$4,713	22 Y & 4 M	$437,444	$369,375	$260,622	$98,239	$0
$2,250	$3,403	$5,302	19 Y & 8 M	$419,890	$327,675	$186,301	$0	$0
$2,500	$3,782	$5,891	17 Y & 6 M	$402,331	$285,955	$111,944	$0	$0

After weighing the differences, they decided to stick with the 2% COLA and start with $1,500 a month. According to the 2% COLA minitable, after 5 years they would still have almost $475,000 left, which is what they are starting with. A 3% COLA would be nice but it would mean starting with only $1,250 a month according to the 3% COLA minitable as shown above.

To Be Forewarned

Until Sam picked up this book of tables, he really had no idea how the numbers would work in retirement. He has now learned how insidious inflation can be. It must be carefully planned for, especially if you happen to have a long retirement. He and Mary also learned the importance of using a realistic, sustainable, ROI or return-on-investment. They found it is best to use a lower, more conservative ROI in their planning. If it turns out their investments return a greater ROI, it can only help them in later years. On the other hand, if their actual ROI ends up being less than their planned ROI, they can withdraw too much in their early years and end up having to make drastic withdrawal cuts in their later years.

ALWAYS REMEMBER YOUR #1 GOAL: YOUR NEST EGG MUST OUTLIVE YOU!!!

Required Minimum Distributions

Some retirement investment vehicles, such as regular IRA's, require you to begin withdrawing certain set percentages at older ages beginning at age 70½ (Currently, at least). These are important to know and are legally binding. You should check with your legal/tax advisor to learn the specifics of these RMD's. It is important to realize that they need not affect your use of these tables. A required RMD withdrawal does not mean you have to spend the amount you withdraw. It simply means you must withdraw that amount from your IRA which then becomes taxable as income. It is still yours to do with what you want. You can simply put that money into another savings vehicle. It can remain part of your nest egg (unless you need to use part of it to pay your taxes) in which you continue to use for your retirement planning.

Be Careful With That Million Dollars

Most people dream of becoming a millionaire someday. With careful planning, most people can actually save a million dollars by the time they retire. (But the how-to is for another book). This book is here to show you that a million dollars at retirement does not mean you can live like a king. Take a look at the tables for that amount and I think you might be surprised how little you can "safely" withdraw monthly and still have that million dollars sure to outlast you. A 62 year-old who wants to have his money last until at least age 100 would see the following.

For a planned 4% ROI:

$1,000,000 Balance				4% Return On Investment				

3% COLA

Monthly Amount	15 Yr Inflated	30 Yr Inflated	Money Lasts	5 Years	10 Years	15 Years	20 Years	30 Years
$2,000	$3,025	$4,713	Over 40 Yrs	$1.076 Mil	$1.147 Mil	$1.206 Mil	$1.249 Mil	$1.245 Mil
$2,500	$3,782	$5,891	Over 40 Yrs	$1.041 Mil	$1.063 Mil	$1.057 Mil	$1.013 Mil	$746,053
$3,000	$4,538	$7,070	32 Y & 11 M	$1.006 Mil	$979,650	$908,739	$777,362	$246,543
$3,500	$5,294	$8,248	27 Y & 7 M	$970,841	$896,207	$760,018	$541,710	$0
$4,000	$6,050	$9,426	23 Y & 8 M	$935,726	$812,781	$611,332	$306,109	$0
$4,500	$6,807	$10,605	20 Y & 9 M	$900,609	$729,350	$462,635	$70,487	$0
$5,000	$7,563	$11,783	18 Y & 6 M	$865,494	$645,913	$313,919	$0	$0

A millionaire living on $2500-$3000 a month! It may seem hard to believe but with just a 3% COLA, those are the numbers. Without these tables, one would think a millionaire could "afford" to withdraw $4000-$5000 a month easily. After all he is worth a million dollars! Notice that if he begins withdrawing $5000 a month, an inflation rate of just 3% (if he used the corresponding 3% COLA) could make a millionaire a pauper in less than 20 years!

Financial Rules For Retirement

1. Plan so that your money outlasts you.
2. Don't forget to plan for inflation.
3. Never withdraw more than 4% of your nest egg a year.

  We've all read about these financial rules and many others in financial planning books. We understand their importance. But the big question is always; how do we implement them? This book has even emphasized many of these rules but without the numbers to substantiate these rules, they will just remain good ideas. If this book ended here, without the numbers, you would know why you need to follow the above rules but not how to implement them.

The Tables Work!

  The tables that follow give you the numbers you need to make this all work. If you use the tables correctly, you will end up adhering to the above rules almost automatically. You will have the numbers at your fingertips that will make your plan work. No more guessing. No more complicated website wandering that too often yields only one answer at a time. As you get comfortable with how the tables work, you will actually have fun with all kinds of what-if scenarios.

Some Final Notes

  All the numbers in these tables are believed to be accurate (allowing for round-off differences) but are not guaranteed. Remember these tables will guide you in the right direction but to be most beneficial, you should review your numbers at least yearly. Actual ROI's will constantly change. Inflation varies. The financial world is constantly in a state of flux. Consistent usage of these tables will help guide you through the financial maze which lies in front of all of us.

What About Higher Beginning Balances?

  The tables are given for amounts up to $1.5 million. If you are fortunate enough to have a greater amount in your nest egg, you can still quite easily use the tables. For example, if you have $3 million simply use the the $1.5 million tables and DOUBLE all the dollar amounts. The time your money lasts REMAINS THE SAME. You DO NOT double the time your nest egg lasts. The following tables show the doubling of the dollar amounts as the beginning balances double. The amounts double as you move the $1.5 million table to a

$3 million table. But notice the time frames REMAIN THE SAME, in the "Money Lasts" columns.

$1,500,000 Balance					3% Return On Investment			

3% COLA

Monthly Amount	15 Yr Inflated	30 Yr Inflated	Money Lasts	5 Years	10 Years	15 Years	20 Years	30 Years
$2,750	$4,160	$6,481	Over 40 Yrs	$1.550 M	$1.579 M	$1.577 M	$1.534 M	$1.273 M
$3,500	$5,294	$8,248	36 Y & 3 M	$1.499 M	$1.460 M	$1.370 M	$1.214 M	$627,054
$4,250	$6,429	$10,016	29 Y & 11 M	$1.448 M	$1.340 M	$1.162 M	$893,758	$0
$5,000	$7,563	$11,783	25 Y & 5 M	$1.396 M	$1.221 M	$955,190	$573,384	$0

Simply DOUBLING the above amounts gives you the dollar amounts for $3 million.

$3,000,000 Balance					3% Return On Investment			

3% COLA

Monthly Amount	15 Yr Inflated	30 Yr Inflated	Money Lasts	5 Years	10 Years	15 Years	20 Years	30 Years
$5,500	$8,319	$12,961	Over 40 Yrs	$3.101 M	$3.158 M	$3.154 M	$3.069 M	$2.546 M
$7,000	$10,588	$16,496	36 Y & 3 M	$2.998 M	$2.919 M	$2.739 M	$2.428 M	$1.254 M
$8,500	$12,857	$20,031	29 Y & 11 M	$2.895 M	$2.681 M	$2.325 M	$1.788 M	$0
$10,000	$15,126	$23,566	25 Y & 5 M	$2.792 M	$2.443 M	$1.910 M	$1.147 M	$0

This is true for any amount you may use. If, for example, you start with $5 million, simply take FIVE times the dollar amounts in the $1 million table. Remember that the times REMAIN THE SAME, in the "Money Lasts" columns.

If you would like further information about these tables, or have questions or comments, please contact me at howtomakeitlast@gmail.com.

| $200,000 Balance | | | | 3% Return On Investment | | | | |

No COLA

Monthly Amount	15 Yr Inflated	30 Yr Inflated	Money Lasts	5 Years	10 Years	15 Years	20 Years	30 Years
$600	$600	$600	Over 40 Yrs	$193,056	$185,005	$175,672	$164,852	$137,771
$800	$800	$800	32 Y & 5 M	$180,123	$157,079	$130,365	$99,397	$21,877
$1,000	$1,000	$1,000	22 Y & 11 M	$167,190	$129,154	$85,059	$33,941	$0
$1,200	$1,200	$1,200	17 Y & 11 M	$154,257	$101,228	$39,753	$0	$0
$1,400	$1,400	$1,400	14 Y & 8 M	$141,323	$73,301	$0	$0	$0
$1,600	$1,600	$1,600	12 Y & 6 M	$128,390	$45,375	$0	$0	$0
$1,800	$1,800	$1,800	10 Y & 10 M	$115,456	$17,448	$0	$0	$0

2% COLA

Monthly Amount	15 Yr Inflated	30 Yr Inflated	Money Lasts	5 Years	10 Years	15 Years	20 Years	30 Years
$400	$528	$710	Over 40 Yrs	$204,963	$207,918	$208,257	$205,239	$185,395
$600	$792	$1,066	32 Y & 10 M	$191,520	$177,488	$156,585	$127,232	$35,306
$800	$1,056	$1,421	23 Y & 7 M	$178,073	$147,052	$104,910	$49,235	$0
$1,000	$1,320	$1,776	18 Y & 5 M	$164,628	$116,622	$53,243	$0	$0
$1,200	$1,583	$2,131	15 Y & 1 M	$151,182	$86,189	$1,577	$0	$0
$1,400	$1,848	$2,487	12 Y & 10 M	$137,738	$55,757	$0	$0	$0
$1,600	$2,111	$2,842	11 Y & 2 M	$124,292	$25,326	$0	$0	$0

3% COLA

Monthly Amount	15 Yr Inflated	30 Yr Inflated	Money Lasts	5 Years	10 Years	15 Years	20 Years	30 Years
$400	$605	$942	Over 40 Yrs	$204,439	$205,219	$201,063	$190,381	$141,075
$600	$908	$1,414	28 Y & 3 M	$190,731	$173,438	$145,794	$104,940	$0
$800	$1,210	$1,886	21 Y & 2 M	$177,017	$141,638	$90,494	$19,463	$0
$1,000	$1,513	$2,357	16 Y & 11 M	$163,311	$109,864	$35,246	$0	$0
$1,200	$1,815	$2,828	14 Y & 2 M	$149,603	$78,082	$0	$0	$0
$1,400	$2,118	$3,299	12 Y & 1 M	$135,893	$46,292	$0	$0	$0
$1,600	$2,420	$3,770	10 Y & 7 M	$122,188	$14,518	$0	$0	$0

4% COLA

Monthly Amount	15 Yr Inflated	30 Yr Inflated	Money Lasts	5 Years	10 Years	15 Years	20 Years	30 Years
$200	$346	$624	Over 40 Yrs	$217,876	$235,573	$252,406	$267,435	$286,656
$400	$693	$1,248	35 Y & 7 M	$203,899	$202,354	$193,193	$173,602	$87,726
$600	$1,039	$1,871	25 Y & 1 M	$189,919	$169,148	$134,020	$79,848	$0
$800	$1,385	$2,494	19 Y & 4 M	$175,947	$135,954	$74,864	$0	$0
$1,000	$1,732	$3,119	15 Y & 9 M	$161,968	$102,736	$15,646	$0	$0
$1,200	$2,078	$3,743	13 Y & 4 M	$147,990	$69,524	$0	$0	$0
$1,400	$2,424	$4,366	11 Y & 6 M	$134,011	$36,314	$0	$0	$0

$200,000 Balance	4% Return On Investment

No COLA

Monthly Amount	15 Yr Inflated	30 Yr Inflated	Money Lasts	5 Years	10 Years	15 Years	20 Years	30 Years
$600	$600	$600	Over 40 Yrs	$203,553	$207,876	$213,135	$219,534	$236,793
$800	$800	$800	Over 40 Yrs	$190,294	$178,486	$164,118	$146,639	$99,498
$1,000	$1,000	$1,000	27 Y & 1 M	$177,035	$149,093	$115,100	$73,742	$0
$1,200	$1,200	$1,200	20 Y & 1 M	$163,775	$119,703	$66,082	$842	$0
$1,400	$1,400	$1,400	16 Y & 1 M	$150,517	$90,314	$17,068	$0	$0
$1,600	$1,600	$1,600	13 Y & 5 M	$137,258	$60,922	$0	$0	$0
$1,800	$1,800	$1,800	11 Y & 6 M	$123,999	$31,531	$0	$0	$0

2% COLA

Monthly Amount	15 Yr Inflated	30 Yr Inflated	Money Lasts	5 Years	10 Years	15 Years	20 Years	30 Years
$400	$528	$710	Over 40 Yrs	$215,772	$232,093	$248,787	$265,600	$298,126
$600	$792	$1,066	Over 40 Yrs	$201,993	$200,113	$193,076	$179,266	$122,781
$800	$1,056	$1,421	27 Y & 1 M	$188,213	$168,133	$137,369	$92,949	$0
$1,000	$1,320	$1,776	20 Y & 5 M	$174,436	$136,158	$81,671	$6,642	$0
$1,200	$1,583	$2,131	16 Y & 5 M	$160,656	$104,178	$25,969	$0	$0
$1,400	$1,848	$2,487	13 Y & 9 M	$146,877	$72,200	$0	$0	$0
$1,600	$2,111	$2,842	11 Y & 10 M	$133,098	$40,222	$0	$0	$0

3% COLA

Monthly Amount	15 Yr Inflated	30 Yr Inflated	Money Lasts	5 Years	10 Years	15 Years	20 Years	30 Years
$400	$605	$942	Over 40 Yrs	$215,239	$229,306	$241,236	$249,742	$249,158
$600	$908	$1,414	32 Y & 11 M	$201,194	$195,938	$181,760	$155,485	$49,320
$800	$1,210	$1,886	23 Y & 8 M	$187,143	$162,548	$122,247	$61,183	$0
$1,000	$1,513	$2,357	18 Y & 6 M	$173,098	$129,186	$62,790	$0	$0
$1,200	$1,815	$2,828	15 Y & 2 M	$159,053	$95,813	$3,309	$0	$0
$1,400	$2,118	$3,299	12 Y & 10 M	$145,005	$62,435	$0	$0	$0
$1,600	$2,420	$3,770	11 Y & 2 M	$130,962	$29,071	$0	$0	$0

4% COLA

Monthly Amount	15 Yr Inflated	30 Yr Inflated	Money Lasts	5 Years	10 Years	15 Years	20 Years	30 Years
$200	$346	$624	Over 40 Yrs	$229,010	$261,206	$296,604	$335,078	$419,664
$400	$693	$1,248	Over 40 Yrs	$214,690	$226,351	$232,989	$231,876	$190,495
$600	$1,039	$1,871	28 Y & 4 M	$200,371	$191,516	$169,422	$128,764	$0
$800	$1,385	$2,494	21 Y & 3 M	$186,056	$156,688	$105,867	$25,671	$0
$1,000	$1,732	$3,119	16 Y & 11 M	$171,736	$121,835	$42,249	$0	$0
$1,200	$2,078	$3,743	14 Y & 2 M	$157,416	$86,990	$0	$0	$0
$1,400	$2,424	$4,366	12 Y & 2 M	$143,097	$52,149	$0	$0	$0

| $200,000 Balance | | | | | 5% Return On Investment | | | |

No COLA

Monthly Amount	15 Yr Inflated	30 Yr Inflated	Money Lasts	5 Years	10 Years	15 Years	20 Years	30 Years
$600	$600	$600	Over 40 Yrs	$214,478	$232,956	$256,539	$286,637	$374,077
$800	$800	$800	Over 40 Yrs	$200,883	$202,010	$203,451	$205,289	$210,627
$1,000	$1,000	$1,000	34 Y & 5 M	$187,290	$171,071	$150,370	$123,949	$47,191
$1,200	$1,200	$1,200	23 Y & 3 M	$173,698	$140,129	$97,286	$42,607	$0
$1,400	$1,400	$1,400	17 Y & 10 M	$160,105	$109,188	$44,203	$0	$0
$1,600	$1,600	$1,600	14 Y & 7 M	$146,512	$78,246	$0	$0	$0
$1,800	$1,800	$1,800	12 Y & 4 M	$132,919	$47,305	$0	$0	$0

2% COLA

Monthly Amount	15 Yr Inflated	30 Yr Inflated	Money Lasts	5 Years	10 Years	15 Years	20 Years	30 Years
$400	$528	$710	Over 40 Yrs	$227,015	$258,554	$295,563	$339,216	$452,664
$600	$792	$1,066	Over 40 Yrs	$212,893	$224,939	$235,444	$243,473	$246,725
$800	$1,056	$1,421	32 Y & 6 M	$198,773	$191,325	$175,329	$147,748	$40,872
$1,000	$1,320	$1,776	23 Y & 1 M	$184,652	$157,712	$115,215	$52,024	$0
$1,200	$1,583	$2,131	17 Y & 11 M	$170,532	$124,100	$55,108	$0	$0
$1,400	$1,848	$2,487	14 Y & 10 M	$156,411	$90,487	$0	$0	$0
$1,600	$2,111	$2,842	12 Y & 7 M	$142,290	$56,874	$0	$0	$0

3% COLA

Monthly Amount	15 Yr Inflated	30 Yr Inflated	Money Lasts	5 Years	10 Years	15 Years	20 Years	30 Years
$400	$605	$942	Over 40 Yrs	$226,473	$255,678	$287,639	$322,273	$398,367
$600	$908	$1,414	Over 40 Yrs	$212,083	$220,631	$223,565	$218,064	$165,267
$800	$1,210	$1,886	27 Y & 2 M	$197,686	$185,560	$159,450	$113,800	$0
$1,000	$1,513	$2,357	20 Y & 6 M	$183,297	$150,519	$95,397	$9,639	$0
$1,200	$1,815	$2,828	16 Y & 6 M	$168,905	$115,468	$31,321	$0	$0
$1,400	$2,118	$3,299	13 Y & 9 M	$154,512	$80,411	$0	$0	$0
$1,600	$2,420	$3,770	11 Y & 10 M	$140,123	$45,368	$0	$0	$0

4% COLA

Monthly Amount	15 Yr Inflated	30 Yr Inflated	Money Lasts	5 Years	10 Years	15 Years	20 Years	30 Years
$200	$346	$624	Over 40 Yrs	$240,587	$289,211	$347,404	$416,969	$599,087
$400	$693	$1,248	Over 40 Yrs	$225,917	$252,631	$278,992	$303,220	$333,610
$600	$1,039	$1,871	33 Y & 1 M	$211,248	$216,069	$210,626	$189,564	$68,407
$800	$1,385	$2,494	23 Y & 9 M	$196,582	$179,514	$142,275	$75,934	$0
$1,000	$1,732	$3,119	18 Y & 7 M	$181,914	$142,940	$73,863	$0	$0
$1,200	$2,078	$3,743	15 Y & 3 M	$167,245	$106,369	$5,473	$0	$0
$1,400	$2,424	$4,366	12 Y & 11 M	$152,574	$69,800	$0	$0	$0

$200,000 Balance	6% Return On Investment

No COLA

Monthly Amount	15 Yr Inflated	30 Yr Inflated	Money Lasts	5 Years	10 Years	15 Years	20 Years	30 Years
$800	$800	$800	Over 40 Yrs	$211,905	$227,837	$249,158	$277,689	$366,967
$1,000	$1,000	$1,000	Over 40 Yrs	$197,969	$195,253	$191,617	$186,751	$171,527
$1,200	$1,200	$1,200	28 Y & 5 M	$184,036	$162,672	$134,082	$95,824	$0
$1,400	$1,400	$1,400	20 Y & 4 M	$170,101	$130,089	$76,543	$4,888	$0
$1,600	$1,600	$1,600	15 Y & 11 M	$156,166	$97,507	$19,006	$0	$0
$1,800	$1,800	$1,800	13 Y & 4 M	$142,230	$64,922	$0	$0	$0
$2,000	$2,000	$2,000	11 Y & 5 M	$128,296	$32,340	$0	$0	$0

2% COLA

Monthly Amount	15 Yr Inflated	30 Yr Inflated	Money Lasts	5 Years	10 Years	15 Years	20 Years	30 Years
$600	$792	$1,066	Over 40 Yrs	$224,234	$252,146	$284,506	$322,301	$419,618
$800	$1,056	$1,421	Over 40 Yrs	$209,764	$216,803	$219,569	$215,930	$176,629
$1,000	$1,320	$1,776	27 Y & 2 M	$195,292	$181,458	$154,632	$109,555	$0
$1,200	$1,583	$2,131	20 Y & 2 M	$180,822	$146,117	$89,700	$3,187	$0
$1,400	$1,848	$2,487	16 Y & 2 M	$166,352	$110,776	$24,757	$0	$0
$1,600	$2,111	$2,842	13 Y & 6 M	$151,881	$75,433	$0	$0	$0
$1,800	$2,375	$3,197	11 Y & 7 M	$137,414	$40,105	$0	$0	$0

3% COLA

Monthly Amount	15 Yr Inflated	30 Yr Inflated	Money Lasts	5 Years	10 Years	15 Years	20 Years	30 Years
$600	$908	$1,414	Over 40 Yrs	$223,410	$247,695	$272,023	$295,108	$328,938
$800	$1,210	$1,886	32 Y & 6 M	$208,661	$210,853	$202,891	$179,607	$55,559
$1,000	$1,513	$2,357	23 Y & 2 M	$193,917	$174,037	$133,817	$64,208	$0
$1,200	$1,815	$2,828	18 Y & 1 M	$179,171	$137,209	$64,717	$0	$0
$1,400	$2,118	$3,299	14 Y & 10 M	$164,426	$100,379	$0	$0	$0
$1,600	$2,420	$3,770	12 Y & 7 M	$149,681	$63,558	$0	$0	$0
$1,800	$2,723	$4,242	10 Y & 11 M	$134,938	$26,737	$0	$0	$0

4% COLA

Monthly Amount	15 Yr Inflated	30 Yr Inflated	Money Lasts	5 Years	10 Years	15 Years	20 Years	30 Years
$400	$693	$1,248	Over 40 Yrs	$237,592	$281,379	$332,054	$390,223	$530,538
$600	$1,039	$1,871	Over 40 Yrs	$222,562	$242,989	$258,447	$264,675	$221,639
$800	$1,385	$2,494	27 Y & 3 M	$207,541	$204,616	$184,867	$139,168	$0
$1,000	$1,732	$3,119	20 Y & 7 M	$192,513	$166,216	$111,216	$13,523	$0
$1,200	$2,078	$3,743	16 Y & 6 M	$177,487	$127,824	$37,596	$0	$0
$1,400	$2,424	$4,366	13 Y & 10 M	$162,460	$89,433	$0	$0	$0
$1,600	$2,771	$4,990	11 Y & 11 M	$147,432	$51,041	$0	$0	$0

| $225,000 Balance | | | | | | 3% Return On Investment | | |

No COLA

Monthly Amount	15 Yr Inflated	30 Yr Inflated	Money Lasts	5 Years	10 Years	15 Years	20 Years	30 Years
$600	$600	$600	Over 40 Yrs	$222,037	$218,603	$214,622	$210,008	$198,456
$800	$800	$800	39 Y & 11 M	$209,104	$190,676	$169,313	$144,547	$82,554
$1,000	$1,000	$1,000	27 Y & 4 M	$196,170	$162,749	$124,006	$79,091	$0
$1,200	$1,200	$1,200	20 Y & 11 M	$183,239	$134,827	$78,704	$13,641	$0
$1,400	$1,400	$1,400	17 Y & 1 M	$170,306	$106,900	$33,395	$0	$0
$1,600	$1,600	$1,600	14 Y & 5 M	$157,372	$78,973	$0	$0	$0
$1,800	$1,800	$1,800	12 Y & 6 M	$144,440	$51,047	$0	$0	$0

2% COLA

Monthly Amount	15 Yr Inflated	30 Yr Inflated	Money Lasts	5 Years	10 Years	15 Years	20 Years	30 Years
$400	$528	$710	Over 40 Yrs	$233,947	$241,518	$247,208	$250,393	$246,076
$600	$792	$1,066	37 Y & 9 M	$220,500	$211,085	$195,534	$172,386	$95,989
$800	$1,056	$1,421	26 Y & 11 M	$207,055	$180,652	$143,863	$94,392	$0
$1,000	$1,320	$1,776	20 Y & 11 M	$193,610	$150,219	$92,193	$16,399	$0
$1,200	$1,583	$2,131	17 Y & 2 M	$180,165	$119,788	$40,528	$0	$0
$1,400	$1,848	$2,487	14 Y & 6 M	$166,719	$89,355	$0	$0	$0
$1,600	$2,111	$2,842	12 Y & 7 M	$153,274	$58,922	$0	$0	$0

3% COLA

Monthly Amount	15 Yr Inflated	30 Yr Inflated	Money Lasts	5 Years	10 Years	15 Years	20 Years	30 Years
$400	$605	$942	Over 40 Yrs	$233,420	$238,815	$240,010	$235,531	$201,752
$600	$908	$1,414	31 Y & 9 M	$219,712	$207,034	$184,741	$150,091	$29,482
$800	$1,210	$1,886	23 Y & 10 M	$205,999	$175,235	$129,445	$64,617	$0
$1,000	$1,513	$2,357	19 Y & 1 M	$192,292	$143,460	$74,194	$0	$0
$1,200	$1,815	$2,828	15 Y & 11 M	$178,586	$111,679	$18,927	$0	$0
$1,400	$2,118	$3,299	13 Y & 7 M	$164,875	$79,890	$0	$0	$0
$1,600	$2,420	$3,770	11 Y & 11 M	$151,168	$48,112	$0	$0	$0

4% COLA

Monthly Amount	15 Yr Inflated	30 Yr Inflated	Money Lasts	5 Years	10 Years	15 Years	20 Years	30 Years
$200	$346	$624	Over 40 Yrs	$246,859	$269,172	$291,356	$312,589	$347,340
$400	$693	$1,248	39 Y & 4 M	$232,880	$235,952	$232,144	$218,758	$148,413
$600	$1,039	$1,871	27 Y & 10 M	$218,901	$202,748	$172,972	$125,004	$0
$800	$1,385	$2,494	21 Y & 6 M	$204,928	$169,551	$113,810	$31,266	$0
$1,000	$1,732	$3,119	17 Y & 7 M	$190,950	$136,335	$54,596	$0	$0
$1,200	$2,078	$3,743	14 Y & 10 M	$176,972	$103,122	$0	$0	$0
$1,400	$2,424	$4,366	12 Y & 10 M	$162,994	$69,913	$0	$0	$0

| $225,000 Balance | | | | 4% Return On Investment | | | | |

No COLA

Monthly Amount	15 Yr Inflated	30 Yr Inflated	Money Lasts	5 Years	10 Years	15 Years	20 Years	30 Years
$600	$600	$600	Over 40 Yrs	$233,969	$244,881	$258,157	$274,311	$317,876
$800	$800	$800	Over 40 Yrs	$220,709	$215,490	$209,140	$201,415	$180,580
$1,000	$1,000	$1,000	33 Y & 11 M	$207,451	$186,099	$160,122	$128,517	$43,282
$1,200	$1,200	$1,200	24 Y & 3 M	$194,192	$156,710	$111,106	$55,621	$0
$1,400	$1,400	$1,400	18 Y & 11 M	$180,933	$127,318	$62,088	$0	$0
$1,600	$1,600	$1,600	15 Y & 9 M	$167,673	$97,927	$13,070	$0	$0
$1,800	$1,800	$1,800	13 Y & 5 M	$154,415	$68,537	$0	$0	$0

2% COLA

Monthly Amount	15 Yr Inflated	30 Yr Inflated	Money Lasts	5 Years	10 Years	15 Years	20 Years	30 Years
$400	$528	$710	Over 40 Yrs	$246,189	$269,099	$293,809	$320,377	$379,211
$600	$792	$1,066	Over 40 Yrs	$232,409	$237,119	$238,098	$234,042	$203,864
$800	$1,056	$1,421	31 Y & 9 M	$218,630	$205,140	$182,395	$147,730	$28,602
$1,000	$1,320	$1,776	23 Y & 8 M	$204,852	$173,163	$126,692	$61,416	$0
$1,200	$1,583	$2,131	18 Y & 10 M	$191,072	$141,185	$70,993	$0	$0
$1,400	$1,848	$2,487	15 Y & 9 M	$177,294	$109,207	$15,280	$0	$0
$1,600	$2,111	$2,842	13 Y & 6 M	$163,514	$77,229	$0	$0	$0

3% COLA

Monthly Amount	15 Yr Inflated	30 Yr Inflated	Money Lasts	5 Years	10 Years	15 Years	20 Years	30 Years
$400	$605	$942	Over 40 Yrs	$245,655	$266,313	$286,262	$304,522	$330,249
$600	$908	$1,414	37 Y & 11 M	$231,610	$232,942	$226,781	$210,261	$130,398
$800	$1,210	$1,886	26 Y & 11 M	$217,559	$199,553	$167,269	$115,960	$0
$1,000	$1,513	$2,357	21 Y & 1 M	$203,514	$166,190	$107,811	$21,747	$0
$1,200	$1,815	$2,828	17 Y & 3 M	$189,470	$132,821	$48,335	$0	$0
$1,400	$2,118	$3,299	14 Y & 7 M	$175,422	$99,442	$0	$0	$0
$1,600	$2,420	$3,770	12 Y & 8 M	$161,377	$66,076	$0	$0	$0

4% COLA

Monthly Amount	15 Yr Inflated	30 Yr Inflated	Money Lasts	5 Years	10 Years	15 Years	20 Years	30 Years
$200	$346	$624	Over 40 Yrs	$259,427	$298,213	$341,628	$389,857	$500,752
$400	$693	$1,248	Over 40 Yrs	$245,106	$263,358	$278,014	$286,656	$271,581
$600	$1,039	$1,871	31 Y & 11 M	$230,787	$228,520	$214,444	$183,539	$42,649
$800	$1,385	$2,494	23 Y & 11 M	$216,473	$193,693	$150,890	$80,449	$0
$1,000	$1,732	$3,119	19 Y & 2 M	$202,152	$158,841	$87,272	$0	$0
$1,200	$2,078	$3,743	15 Y & 11 M	$187,832	$123,997	$23,683	$0	$0
$1,400	$2,424	$4,366	13 Y & 8 M	$173,513	$89,154	$0	$0	$0

| $225,000 Balance | | | | 5% Return On Investment | | | | |

No COLA

Monthly Amount	15 Yr Inflated	30 Yr Inflated	Money Lasts	5 Years	10 Years	15 Years	20 Years	30 Years
$600	$600	$600	Over 40 Yrs	$246,385	$273,678	$308,511	$352,968	$482,123
$800	$800	$800	Over 40 Yrs	$232,792	$242,736	$255,428	$271,625	$318,683
$1,000	$1,000	$1,000	Over 40 Yrs	$219,199	$211,795	$202,344	$190,282	$155,242
$1,200	$1,200	$1,200	29 Y & 6 M	$205,606	$180,852	$149,261	$108,941	$0
$1,400	$1,400	$1,400	21 Y & 9 M	$192,012	$149,912	$96,179	$27,600	$0
$1,600	$1,600	$1,600	17 Y & 5 M	$178,419	$118,968	$43,092	$0	$0
$1,800	$1,800	$1,800	14 Y & 7 M	$164,827	$88,028	$0	$0	$0

2% COLA

Monthly Amount	15 Yr Inflated	30 Yr Inflated	Money Lasts	5 Years	10 Years	15 Years	20 Years	30 Years
$400	$528	$710	Over 40 Yrs	$258,921	$299,276	$347,538	$405,550	$560,715
$600	$792	$1,066	Over 40 Yrs	$244,801	$265,661	$287,417	$309,806	$354,777
$800	$1,056	$1,421	39 Y & 11 M	$230,680	$232,047	$227,302	$214,081	$148,921
$1,000	$1,320	$1,776	27 Y & 6 M	$216,560	$198,436	$167,190	$118,358	$0
$1,200	$1,583	$2,131	21 Y & 2 M	$202,438	$164,821	$107,079	$22,634	$0
$1,400	$1,848	$2,487	17 Y & 2 M	$188,318	$131,209	$46,957	$0	$0
$1,600	$2,111	$2,842	14 Y & 6 M	$174,197	$97,595	$0	$0	$0

3% COLA

Monthly Amount	15 Yr Inflated	30 Yr Inflated	Money Lasts	5 Years	10 Years	15 Years	20 Years	30 Years
$400	$605	$942	Over 40 Yrs	$258,380	$296,401	$339,612	$388,606	$506,415
$600	$908	$1,414	Over 40 Yrs	$243,989	$261,352	$275,537	$284,395	$273,313
$800	$1,210	$1,886	31 Y & 10 M	$229,592	$226,282	$211,424	$180,133	$40,153
$1,000	$1,513	$2,357	23 Y & 9 M	$215,204	$191,242	$147,371	$75,972	$0
$1,200	$1,815	$2,828	18 Y & 11 M	$200,812	$156,190	$83,295	$0	$0
$1,400	$2,118	$3,299	15 Y & 9 M	$186,420	$121,134	$19,209	$0	$0
$1,600	$2,420	$3,770	13 Y & 6 M	$172,029	$86,089	$0	$0	$0

4% COLA

Monthly Amount	15 Yr Inflated	30 Yr Inflated	Money Lasts	5 Years	10 Years	15 Years	20 Years	30 Years
$200	$346	$624	Over 40 Yrs	$272,494	$329,934	$399,378	$483,302	$707,136
$400	$693	$1,248	Over 40 Yrs	$257,824	$293,354	$330,966	$369,555	$441,664
$600	$1,039	$1,871	37 Y & 11 M	$243,154	$256,791	$262,599	$255,898	$176,459
$800	$1,385	$2,494	27 Y & 2 M	$228,491	$220,240	$194,252	$142,270	$0
$1,000	$1,732	$3,119	21 Y & 2 M	$213,821	$183,661	$125,834	$28,511	$0
$1,200	$2,078	$3,743	17 Y & 4 M	$199,152	$147,092	$57,447	$0	$0
$1,400	$2,424	$4,366	14 Y & 8 M	$184,482	$110,521	$0	$0	$0

| $225,000 Balance | | | | 6% Return On Investment | | | | |

No COLA

Monthly Amount	15 Yr Inflated	30 Yr Inflated	Money Lasts	5 Years	10 Years	15 Years	20 Years	30 Years
$800	$800	$800	Over 40 Yrs	$245,361	$272,609	$309,073	$357,869	$510,556
$1,000	$1,000	$1,000	Over 40 Yrs	$231,426	$240,026	$251,535	$266,936	$315,128
$1,200	$1,200	$1,200	Over 40 Yrs	$217,491	$207,442	$193,995	$176,000	$119,693
$1,400	$1,400	$1,400	25 Y & 11 M	$203,557	$174,860	$136,459	$85,070	$0
$1,600	$1,600	$1,600	19 Y & 9 M	$189,621	$142,276	$78,918	$0	$0
$1,800	$1,800	$1,800	15 Y & 11 M	$175,687	$109,694	$21,382	$0	$0
$2,000	$2,000	$2,000	13 Y & 7 M	$161,752	$77,111	$0	$0	$0

2% COLA

Monthly Amount	15 Yr Inflated	30 Yr Inflated	Money Lasts	5 Years	10 Years	15 Years	20 Years	30 Years
$600	$792	$1,066	Over 40 Yrs	$257,689	$296,914	$344,418	$402,477	$563,202
$800	$1,056	$1,421	Over 40 Yrs	$243,219	$261,571	$279,479	$296,102	$320,206
$1,000	$1,320	$1,776	33 Y & 11 M	$228,749	$226,230	$214,546	$189,734	$77,198
$1,200	$1,583	$2,131	24 Y & 4 M	$214,277	$190,889	$149,618	$83,371	$0
$1,400	$1,848	$2,487	19 Y & 2 M	$199,809	$155,549	$84,672	$0	$0
$1,600	$2,111	$2,842	15 Y & 10 M	$185,337	$120,206	$19,745	$0	$0
$1,800	$2,375	$3,197	13 Y & 6 M	$170,870	$84,878	$0	$0	$0

3% COLA

Monthly Amount	15 Yr Inflated	30 Yr Inflated	Money Lasts	5 Years	10 Years	15 Years	20 Years	30 Years
$600	$908	$1,414	Over 40 Yrs	$256,867	$292,469	$331,941	$375,291	$472,534
$800	$1,210	$1,886	39 Y & 11 M	$242,115	$255,622	$262,802	$259,780	$199,139
$1,000	$1,513	$2,357	27 Y & 7 M	$227,373	$218,807	$193,730	$144,385	$0
$1,200	$1,815	$2,828	21 Y & 2 M	$212,627	$181,981	$124,631	$28,952	$0
$1,400	$2,118	$3,299	17 Y & 3 M	$197,881	$145,150	$55,525	$0	$0
$1,600	$2,420	$3,770	14 Y & 7 M	$183,138	$108,331	$0	$0	$0
$1,800	$2,723	$4,242	12 Y & 7 M	$168,393	$71,507	$0	$0	$0

4% COLA

Monthly Amount	15 Yr Inflated	30 Yr Inflated	Money Lasts	5 Years	10 Years	15 Years	20 Years	30 Years
$400	$693	$1,248	Over 40 Yrs	$271,047	$326,149	$391,965	$470,398	$674,120
$600	$1,039	$1,871	Over 40 Yrs	$256,019	$287,762	$318,363	$344,855	$365,229
$800	$1,385	$2,494	31 Y & 11 M	$240,996	$249,385	$244,780	$219,345	$56,408
$1,000	$1,732	$3,119	23 Y & 9 M	$225,970	$210,988	$171,132	$93,704	$0
$1,200	$2,078	$3,743	18 Y & 11 M	$210,943	$172,597	$97,512	$0	$0
$1,400	$2,424	$4,366	15 Y & 10 M	$195,916	$134,204	$23,894	$0	$0
$1,600	$2,771	$4,990	13 Y & 7 M	$180,888	$95,812	$0	$0	$0

$250,000 Balance   3% Return On Investment

No COLA

Monthly Amount	15 Yr Inflated	30 Yr Inflated	Money Lasts	5 Years	10 Years	15 Years	20 Years	30 Years
$600	$600	$600	Over 40 Yrs	$251,020	$252,202	$253,572	$255,160	$259,135
$800	$800	$800	Over 40 Yrs	$238,086	$224,275	$208,265	$189,704	$143,242
$1,000	$1,000	$1,000	32 Y & 5 M	$225,154	$196,351	$162,960	$124,251	$27,354
$1,200	$1,200	$1,200	24 Y & 5 M	$212,221	$168,424	$117,651	$58,792	$0
$1,400	$1,400	$1,400	19 Y & 8 M	$199,286	$140,496	$72,343	$0	$0
$1,600	$1,600	$1,600	16 Y & 6 M	$186,353	$112,570	$27,035	$0	$0
$1,800	$1,800	$1,800	14 Y & 2 M	$173,422	$84,646	$0	$0	$0

2% COLA

Monthly Amount	15 Yr Inflated	30 Yr Inflated	Money Lasts	5 Years	10 Years	15 Years	20 Years	30 Years
$400	$528	$710	Over 40 Yrs	$262,927	$275,115	$286,157	$295,546	$306,758
$600	$792	$1,066	Over 40 Yrs	$249,483	$244,683	$234,483	$217,537	$156,668
$800	$1,056	$1,421	30 Y & 5 M	$236,037	$214,249	$182,811	$139,544	$6,649
$1,000	$1,320	$1,776	23 Y & 7 M	$222,591	$183,817	$131,142	$61,551	$0
$1,200	$1,583	$2,131	19 Y & 3 M	$209,146	$153,385	$79,476	$0	$0
$1,400	$1,848	$2,487	16 Y & 3 M	$195,701	$122,954	$27,798	$0	$0
$1,600	$2,111	$2,842	14 Y & 1 M	$182,256	$92,522	$0	$0	$0

3% COLA

Monthly Amount	15 Yr Inflated	30 Yr Inflated	Money Lasts	5 Years	10 Years	15 Years	20 Years	30 Years
$400	$605	$942	Over 40 Yrs	$262,402	$272,416	$278,963	$280,689	$262,442
$600	$908	$1,414	35 Y & 3 M	$248,696	$240,636	$223,696	$195,250	$90,170
$800	$1,210	$1,886	26 Y & 6 M	$234,981	$208,832	$168,391	$109,766	$0
$1,000	$1,513	$2,357	21 Y & 2 M	$221,275	$177,061	$113,146	$24,375	$0
$1,200	$1,815	$2,828	17 Y & 8 M	$207,567	$145,278	$57,878	$0	$0
$1,400	$2,118	$3,299	15 Y & 2 M	$193,858	$113,489	$2,599	$0	$0
$1,600	$2,420	$3,770	13 Y & 3 M	$180,151	$81,712	$0	$0	$0

4% COLA

Monthly Amount	15 Yr Inflated	30 Yr Inflated	Money Lasts	5 Years	10 Years	15 Years	20 Years	30 Years
$200	$346	$624	Over 40 Yrs	$275,840	$302,770	$330,306	$357,742	$408,020
$400	$693	$1,248	Over 40 Yrs	$261,862	$269,549	$271,092	$263,910	$209,093
$600	$1,039	$1,871	30 Y & 6 M	$247,883	$236,344	$211,917	$170,151	$10,371
$800	$1,385	$2,494	23 Y & 8 M	$233,910	$203,149	$152,760	$76,420	$0
$1,000	$1,732	$3,119	19 Y & 4 M	$219,932	$169,933	$93,546	$0	$0
$1,200	$2,078	$3,743	16 Y & 5 M	$205,953	$136,719	$34,350	$0	$0
$1,400	$2,424	$4,366	14 Y & 2 M	$191,975	$103,510	$0	$0	$0

$250,000 Balance   4% Return On Investment

No COLA

Monthly Amount	15 Yr Inflated	30 Yr Inflated	Money Lasts	5 Years	10 Years	15 Years	20 Years	30 Years
$600	$600	$600	Over 40 Yrs	$264,386	$281,888	$303,182	$329,091	$398,962
$800	$800	$800	Over 40 Yrs	$251,126	$252,497	$254,164	$256,193	$261,666
$1,000	$1,000	$1,000	Over 40 Yrs	$237,866	$223,105	$205,146	$183,296	$124,368
$1,200	$1,200	$1,200	29 Y & 2 M	$224,608	$193,714	$156,128	$110,398	$0
$1,400	$1,400	$1,400	22 Y & 5 M	$211,350	$164,326	$107,114	$37,508	$0
$1,600	$1,600	$1,600	18 Y & 3 M	$198,090	$134,934	$58,095	$0	$0
$1,800	$1,800	$1,800	15 Y & 6 M	$184,831	$105,543	$9,076	$0	$0

2% COLA

Monthly Amount	15 Yr Inflated	30 Yr Inflated	Money Lasts	5 Years	10 Years	15 Years	20 Years	30 Years
$400	$528	$710	Over 40 Yrs	$276,605	$306,105	$338,833	$375,156	$460,298
$600	$792	$1,066	Over 40 Yrs	$262,826	$274,127	$283,126	$288,825	$284,954
$800	$1,056	$1,421	36 Y & 10 M	$249,046	$242,146	$227,417	$202,506	$109,681
$1,000	$1,320	$1,776	27 Y & 1 M	$235,269	$210,170	$171,717	$116,196	$0
$1,200	$1,583	$2,131	21 Y & 6 M	$221,489	$178,193	$116,021	$29,887	$0
$1,400	$1,848	$2,487	17 Y & 10 M	$207,709	$146,211	$60,301	$0	$0
$1,600	$2,111	$2,842	15 Y & 3 M	$193,931	$114,235	$4,608	$0	$0

3% COLA

Monthly Amount	15 Yr Inflated	30 Yr Inflated	Money Lasts	5 Years	10 Years	15 Years	20 Years	30 Years
$400	$605	$942	Over 40 Yrs	$276,071	$303,320	$331,285	$359,300	$411,334
$600	$908	$1,414	Over 40 Yrs	$262,026	$269,948	$271,804	$265,039	$211,483
$800	$1,210	$1,886	30 Y & 6 M	$247,976	$236,559	$212,292	$170,738	$11,601
$1,000	$1,513	$2,357	23 Y & 8 M	$233,931	$203,197	$152,835	$76,525	$0
$1,200	$1,815	$2,828	19 Y & 4 M	$219,886	$169,826	$93,358	$0	$0
$1,400	$2,118	$3,299	16 Y & 4 M	$205,839	$136,449	$33,869	$0	$0
$1,600	$2,420	$3,770	14 Y & 2 M	$191,794	$103,084	$0	$0	$0

4% COLA

Monthly Amount	15 Yr Inflated	30 Yr Inflated	Money Lasts	5 Years	10 Years	15 Years	20 Years	30 Years
$200	$346	$624	Over 40 Yrs	$289,843	$335,219	$386,652	$444,636	$581,836
$400	$693	$1,248	Over 40 Yrs	$275,523	$300,364	$323,036	$341,433	$352,665
$600	$1,039	$1,871	35 Y & 5 M	$261,202	$265,526	$259,467	$238,317	$123,734
$800	$1,385	$2,494	26 Y & 7 M	$246,890	$230,701	$195,916	$135,230	$0
$1,000	$1,732	$3,119	21 Y & 3 M	$232,569	$195,849	$132,299	$32,021	$0
$1,200	$2,078	$3,743	17 Y & 9 M	$218,248	$161,002	$68,706	$0	$0
$1,400	$2,424	$4,366	15 Y & 3 M	$203,929	$126,159	$5,119	$0	$0

$250,000 Balance	5% Return On Investment

No COLA

Monthly Amount	15 Yr Inflated	30 Yr Inflated	Money Lasts	5 Years	10 Years	15 Years	20 Years	30 Years
$600	$600	$600	Over 40 Yrs	$278,291	$314,399	$360,483	$419,298	$590,167
$800	$800	$800	Over 40 Yrs	$264,698	$283,458	$307,401	$337,959	$426,732
$1,000	$1,000	$1,000	Over 40 Yrs	$251,106	$252,516	$254,316	$256,613	$263,287
$1,200	$1,200	$1,200	38 Y & 6 M	$237,512	$221,574	$201,232	$175,271	$99,849
$1,400	$1,400	$1,400	26 Y & 7 M	$223,919	$190,633	$148,151	$93,932	$0
$1,600	$1,600	$1,600	20 Y & 8 M	$210,326	$159,690	$95,066	$12,585	$0
$1,800	$1,800	$1,800	17 Y & 1 M	$196,734	$128,751	$41,985	$0	$0

2% COLA

Monthly Amount	15 Yr Inflated	30 Yr Inflated	Money Lasts	5 Years	10 Years	15 Years	20 Years	30 Years
$400	$528	$710	Over 40 Yrs	$290,829	$339,999	$399,512	$471,884	$668,766
$600	$792	$1,066	Over 40 Yrs	$276,707	$306,384	$339,391	$376,138	$462,824
$800	$1,056	$1,421	Over 40 Yrs	$262,587	$272,769	$279,273	$280,411	$256,967
$1,000	$1,320	$1,776	32 Y & 6 M	$248,466	$239,157	$219,162	$184,689	$51,100
$1,200	$1,583	$2,131	24 Y & 6 M	$234,345	$205,544	$159,053	$88,969	$0
$1,400	$1,848	$2,487	19 Y & 9 M	$220,225	$171,931	$98,930	$0	$0
$1,600	$2,111	$2,842	16 Y & 7 M	$206,103	$138,316	$38,823	$0	$0

3% COLA

Monthly Amount	15 Yr Inflated	30 Yr Inflated	Money Lasts	5 Years	10 Years	15 Years	20 Years	30 Years
$400	$605	$942	Over 40 Yrs	$290,287	$337,123	$391,585	$454,937	$614,462
$600	$908	$1,414	Over 40 Yrs	$275,897	$302,074	$327,510	$350,728	$381,363
$800	$1,210	$1,886	36 Y & 11 M	$261,501	$267,007	$263,400	$246,471	$148,206
$1,000	$1,513	$2,357	27 Y & 2 M	$247,111	$231,965	$199,345	$142,305	$0
$1,200	$1,815	$2,828	21 Y & 6 M	$232,719	$196,912	$135,268	$38,113	$0
$1,400	$2,118	$3,299	17 Y & 10 M	$218,327	$161,857	$71,183	$0	$0
$1,600	$2,420	$3,770	15 Y & 3 M	$203,937	$126,812	$7,119	$0	$0

4% COLA

Monthly Amount	15 Yr Inflated	30 Yr Inflated	Money Lasts	5 Years	10 Years	15 Years	20 Years	30 Years
$200	$346	$624	Over 40 Yrs	$304,401	$370,656	$451,351	$549,636	$815,186
$400	$693	$1,248	Over 40 Yrs	$289,730	$334,075	$382,937	$435,884	$549,707
$600	$1,039	$1,871	Over 40 Yrs	$275,062	$297,514	$314,573	$322,229	$284,502
$800	$1,385	$2,494	30 Y & 8 M	$260,397	$260,961	$246,223	$208,600	$19,353
$1,000	$1,732	$3,119	23 Y & 9 M	$245,728	$224,384	$177,808	$94,843	$0
$1,200	$2,078	$3,743	19 Y & 5 M	$231,059	$187,815	$109,422	$0	$0
$1,400	$2,424	$4,366	16 Y & 5 M	$216,388	$151,242	$41,032	$0	$0

| $250,000 Balance | | 6% Return On Investment | | | | | | |

No COLA

Monthly Amount	15 Yr Inflated	30 Yr Inflated	Money Lasts	5 Years	10 Years	15 Years	20 Years	30 Years
$800	$800	$800	Over 40 Yrs	$278,818	$317,383	$368,991	$438,054	$654,157
$1,000	$1,000	$1,000	Over 40 Yrs	$264,881	$284,797	$311,449	$347,116	$458,717
$1,200	$1,200	$1,200	Over 40 Yrs	$250,947	$252,215	$253,911	$256,181	$263,282
$1,400	$1,400	$1,400	34 Y & 8 M	$237,012	$219,633	$196,374	$165,248	$67,857
$1,600	$1,600	$1,600	24 Y & 5 M	$223,077	$187,049	$138,835	$74,313	$0
$1,800	$1,800	$1,800	19 Y & 3 M	$209,143	$154,468	$81,299	$0	$0
$2,000	$2,000	$2,000	15 Y & 11 M	$195,208	$121,883	$23,759	$0	$0

2% COLA

Monthly Amount	15 Yr Inflated	30 Yr Inflated	Money Lasts	5 Years	10 Years	15 Years	20 Years	30 Years
$600	$792	$1,066	Over 40 Yrs	$291,146	$341,687	$404,334	$482,657	$706,789
$800	$1,056	$1,421	Over 40 Yrs	$276,674	$306,342	$339,393	$376,282	$463,793
$1,000	$1,320	$1,776	Over 40 Yrs	$262,204	$271,002	$274,461	$269,914	$220,791
$1,200	$1,583	$2,131	29 Y & 2 M	$247,733	$235,659	$209,529	$163,544	$0
$1,400	$1,848	$2,487	22 Y & 5 M	$233,263	$200,316	$144,582	$57,146	$0
$1,600	$2,111	$2,842	18 Y & 4 M	$218,793	$164,977	$79,658	$0	$0
$1,800	$2,375	$3,197	15 Y & 7 M	$204,325	$129,647	$14,746	$0	$0

3% COLA

Monthly Amount	15 Yr Inflated	30 Yr Inflated	Money Lasts	5 Years	10 Years	15 Years	20 Years	30 Years
$600	$908	$1,414	Over 40 Yrs	$290,322	$337,239	$391,854	$455,468	$616,121
$800	$1,210	$1,886	Over 40 Yrs	$275,571	$300,393	$322,716	$339,958	$342,724
$1,000	$1,513	$2,357	32 Y & 7 M	$260,828	$263,577	$253,643	$224,563	$69,572
$1,200	$1,815	$2,828	24 Y & 7 M	$246,084	$226,753	$184,546	$109,132	$0
$1,400	$2,118	$3,299	19 Y & 10 M	$231,337	$189,922	$115,438	$0	$0
$1,600	$2,420	$3,770	16 Y & 8 M	$216,593	$153,102	$46,354	$0	$0
$1,800	$2,723	$4,242	14 Y & 4 M	$201,849	$116,281	$0	$0	$0

4% COLA

Monthly Amount	15 Yr Inflated	30 Yr Inflated	Money Lasts	5 Years	10 Years	15 Years	20 Years	30 Years
$400	$693	$1,248	Over 40 Yrs	$304,502	$370,920	$451,879	$550,575	$817,703
$600	$1,039	$1,871	Over 40 Yrs	$289,474	$332,534	$378,278	$425,036	$508,820
$800	$1,385	$2,494	36 Y & 11 M	$274,453	$294,159	$304,695	$299,525	$200,000
$1,000	$1,732	$3,119	27 Y & 3 M	$259,425	$255,760	$231,047	$173,883	$0
$1,200	$2,078	$3,743	21 Y & 7 M	$244,399	$217,366	$157,424	$48,296	$0
$1,400	$2,424	$4,366	17 Y & 11 M	$229,372	$178,975	$83,806	$0	$0
$1,600	$2,771	$4,990	15 Y & 4 M	$214,343	$140,584	$10,189	$0	$0

$275,000 Balance   3% Return On Investment

No COLA

Monthly Amount	15 Yr Inflated	30 Yr Inflated	Money Lasts	5 Years	10 Years	15 Years	20 Years	30 Years
$750	$750	$750	Over 40 Yrs	$270,301	$264,854	$258,539	$251,218	$232,893
$1,000	$1,000	$1,000	38 Y & 4 M	$254,136	$229,948	$201,908	$169,401	$88,032
$1,250	$1,250	$1,250	26 Y & 5 M	$237,969	$195,039	$145,272	$87,577	$0
$1,500	$1,500	$1,500	20 Y & 4 M	$221,802	$160,132	$88,639	$5,759	$0
$1,750	$1,750	$1,750	16 Y & 7 M	$205,636	$125,225	$32,006	$0	$0
$2,000	$2,000	$2,000	13 Y & 11 M	$189,470	$90,317	$0	$0	$0
$2,250	$2,250	$2,250	12 Y & 2 M	$173,303	$55,409	$0	$0	$0

2% COLA

Monthly Amount	15 Yr Inflated	30 Yr Inflated	Money Lasts	5 Years	10 Years	15 Years	20 Years	30 Years
$500	$660	$888	Over 40 Yrs	$285,189	$293,505	$299,286	$301,729	$292,489
$750	$990	$1,332	36 Y & 9 M	$268,381	$255,455	$234,678	$204,194	$104,847
$1,000	$1,320	$1,776	26 Y & 3 M	$251,574	$217,414	$170,090	$106,702	$0
$1,250	$1,650	$2,220	20 Y & 5 M	$234,769	$179,385	$105,512	$9,211	$0
$1,500	$1,979	$2,664	16 Y & 9 M	$217,962	$141,343	$40,930	$0	$0
$1,750	$2,309	$3,108	14 Y & 2 M	$201,157	$103,305	$0	$0	$0
$2,000	$2,639	$3,552	12 Y & 4 M	$184,351	$65,268	$0	$0	$0

3% COLA

Monthly Amount	15 Yr Inflated	30 Yr Inflated	Money Lasts	5 Years	10 Years	15 Years	20 Years	30 Years
$500	$756	$1,178	Over 40 Yrs	$284,530	$290,116	$290,262	$283,099	$236,942
$750	$1,134	$1,767	30 Y & 11 M	$267,394	$250,392	$221,191	$176,337	$21,734
$1,000	$1,513	$2,357	23 Y & 4 M	$250,257	$210,658	$152,093	$69,525	$0
$1,250	$1,891	$2,946	18 Y & 8 M	$233,120	$170,925	$83,004	$0	$0
$1,500	$2,269	$3,535	15 Y & 6 M	$215,986	$131,195	$13,911	$0	$0
$1,750	$2,647	$4,124	13 Y & 4 M	$198,851	$91,471	$0	$0	$0
$2,000	$3,025	$4,713	11 Y & 8 M	$181,712	$51,727	$0	$0	$0

4% COLA

Monthly Amount	15 Yr Inflated	30 Yr Inflated	Money Lasts	5 Years	10 Years	15 Years	20 Years	30 Years
$250	$433	$780	Over 40 Yrs	$301,328	$328,063	$354,448	$379,429	$418,936
$500	$866	$1,560	38 Y & 7 M	$283,855	$286,544	$280,444	$262,160	$170,347
$750	$1,299	$2,339	27 Y & 3 M	$266,386	$245,047	$206,497	$145,006	$0
$1,000	$1,732	$3,119	21 Y & 1 M	$248,913	$203,529	$132,492	$27,731	$0
$1,250	$2,165	$3,899	17 Y & 3 M	$231,442	$162,018	$58,507	$0	$0
$1,500	$2,598	$4,678	14 Y & 7 M	$213,969	$120,506	$0	$0	$0
$1,750	$3,031	$5,458	12 Y & 7 M	$196,495	$78,985	$0	$0	$0

$275,000 Balance   4% Return On Investment

No COLA

Monthly Amount	15 Yr Inflated	30 Yr Inflated	Money Lasts	5 Years	10 Years	15 Years	20 Years	30 Years
$750	$750	$750	Over 40 Yrs	$284,858	$296,851	$311,443	$329,196	$377,075
$1,000	$1,000	$1,000	Over 40 Yrs	$268,283	$260,111	$250,169	$238,073	$205,450
$1,250	$1,250	$1,250	32 Y & 5 M	$251,710	$223,373	$188,898	$146,954	$33,834
$1,500	$1,500	$1,500	23 Y & 4 M	$235,136	$186,634	$127,625	$55,832	$0
$1,750	$1,750	$1,750	18 Y & 5 M	$218,562	$149,895	$66,353	$0	$0
$2,000	$2,000	$2,000	15 Y & 3 M	$201,988	$113,159	$5,083	$0	$0
$2,250	$2,250	$2,250	12 Y & 11 M	$185,414	$76,420	$0	$0	$0

2% COLA

Monthly Amount	15 Yr Inflated	30 Yr Inflated	Money Lasts	5 Years	10 Years	15 Years	20 Years	30 Years
$500	$660	$888	Over 40 Yrs	$300,133	$327,130	$356,020	$386,804	$453,815
$750	$990	$1,332	Over 40 Yrs	$282,908	$287,149	$286,372	$278,869	$234,609
$1,000	$1,320	$1,776	30 Y & 9 M	$265,684	$247,176	$216,740	$170,974	$15,490
$1,250	$1,650	$2,220	22 Y & 11 M	$248,462	$207,210	$147,118	$63,075	$0
$1,500	$1,979	$2,664	18 Y & 4 M	$231,237	$167,237	$77,494	$0	$0
$1,750	$2,309	$3,108	15 Y & 4 M	$214,017	$127,270	$7,876	$0	$0
$2,000	$2,639	$3,552	13 Y & 2 M	$196,791	$87,297	$0	$0	$0

3% COLA

Monthly Amount	15 Yr Inflated	30 Yr Inflated	Money Lasts	5 Years	10 Years	15 Years	20 Years	30 Years
$500	$756	$1,178	Over 40 Yrs	$299,466	$323,635	$346,556	$366,929	$392,451
$750	$1,134	$1,767	36 Y & 11 M	$281,907	$281,924	$272,220	$249,143	$142,786
$1,000	$1,513	$2,357	26 Y & 4 M	$264,348	$240,205	$197,861	$131,307	$0
$1,250	$1,891	$2,946	20 Y & 6 M	$246,789	$198,486	$123,508	$13,491	$0
$1,500	$2,269	$3,535	16 Y & 10 M	$229,232	$156,768	$49,148	$0	$0
$1,750	$2,647	$4,124	14 Y & 3 M	$211,675	$115,059	$0	$0	$0
$2,000	$3,025	$4,713	12 Y & 4 M	$194,113	$73,328	$0	$0	$0

4% COLA

Monthly Amount	15 Yr Inflated	30 Yr Inflated	Money Lasts	5 Years	10 Years	15 Years	20 Years	30 Years
$250	$433	$780	Over 40 Yrs	$316,679	$363,510	$415,767	$473,602	$605,589
$500	$866	$1,560	Over 40 Yrs	$298,780	$319,951	$336,265	$344,628	$319,209
$750	$1,299	$2,339	31 Y & 2 M	$280,886	$276,415	$256,825	$215,780	$33,168
$1,000	$1,732	$3,119	23 Y & 5 M	$262,986	$232,855	$177,323	$86,800	$0
$1,250	$2,165	$3,899	18 Y & 9 M	$245,085	$189,298	$97,833	$0	$0
$1,500	$2,598	$4,678	15 Y & 7 M	$227,186	$145,746	$18,356	$0	$0
$1,750	$3,031	$5,458	13 Y & 5 M	$209,285	$102,182	$0	$0	$0

| $275,000 Balance | | | | | 5% Return On Investment | | | |

No COLA

Monthly Amount	15 Yr Inflated	30 Yr Inflated	Money Lasts	5 Years	10 Years	15 Years	20 Years	30 Years
$750	$750	$750	Over 40 Yrs	$300,003	$331,914	$372,642	$424,621	$575,631
$1,000	$1,000	$1,000	Over 40 Yrs	$283,014	$293,240	$306,291	$322,949	$371,342
$1,250	$1,250	$1,250	Over 40 Yrs	$266,021	$254,560	$239,935	$221,269	$167,038
$1,500	$1,500	$1,500	28 Y & 1 M	$249,029	$215,884	$173,579	$119,587	$0
$1,750	$1,750	$1,750	20 Y & 11 M	$232,037	$177,206	$107,225	$17,909	$0
$2,000	$2,000	$2,000	16 Y & 10 M	$215,048	$138,531	$40,875	$0	$0
$2,250	$2,250	$2,250	14 Y & 1 M	$198,056	$99,853	$0	$0	$0

2% COLA

Monthly Amount	15 Yr Inflated	30 Yr Inflated	Money Lasts	5 Years	10 Years	15 Years	20 Years	30 Years
$500	$660	$888	Over 40 Yrs	$315,678	$363,923	$421,444	$490,385	$673,964
$750	$990	$1,332	Over 40 Yrs	$298,026	$321,899	$346,282	$370,683	$416,505
$1,000	$1,320	$1,776	38 Y & 4 M	$280,373	$279,878	$271,134	$251,021	$159,145
$1,250	$1,650	$2,220	26 Y & 7 M	$262,725	$237,873	$196,005	$131,369	$0
$1,500	$1,979	$2,664	20 Y & 6 M	$245,074	$195,857	$120,868	$11,722	$0
$1,750	$2,309	$3,108	16 Y & 8 M	$227,424	$153,841	$45,732	$0	$0
$2,000	$2,639	$3,552	14 Y & 2 M	$209,774	$111,827	$0	$0	$0

3% COLA

Monthly Amount	15 Yr Inflated	30 Yr Inflated	Money Lasts	5 Years	10 Years	15 Years	20 Years	30 Years
$500	$756	$1,178	Over 40 Yrs	$315,000	$360,315	$411,507	$469,144	$605,911
$750	$1,134	$1,767	Over 40 Yrs	$297,009	$316,506	$331,425	$338,918	$314,683
$1,000	$1,513	$2,357	30 Y & 10 M	$279,018	$272,686	$251,317	$208,637	$23,290
$1,250	$1,891	$2,946	22 Y & 11 M	$261,028	$228,871	$171,222	$78,388	$0
$1,500	$2,269	$3,535	18 Y & 5 M	$243,039	$185,054	$91,114	$0	$0
$1,750	$2,647	$4,124	15 Y & 5 M	$225,049	$141,246	$11,037	$0	$0
$2,000	$3,025	$4,713	13 Y & 2 M	$207,056	$97,414	$0	$0	$0

4% COLA

Monthly Amount	15 Yr Inflated	30 Yr Inflated	Money Lasts	5 Years	10 Years	15 Years	20 Years	30 Years
$250	$433	$780	Over 40 Yrs	$332,641	$402,235	$486,219	$587,524	$856,829
$500	$866	$1,560	Over 40 Yrs	$314,303	$356,515	$400,716	$445,363	$525,072
$750	$1,299	$2,339	36 Y & 11 M	$295,972	$310,825	$315,284	$303,343	$193,702
$1,000	$1,732	$3,119	26 Y & 6 M	$277,636	$265,108	$229,783	$161,180	$0
$1,250	$2,165	$3,899	20 Y & 7 M	$259,298	$219,395	$144,299	$19,050	$0
$1,500	$2,598	$4,678	16 Y & 11 M	$240,962	$173,686	$58,824	$0	$0
$1,750	$3,031	$5,458	14 Y & 4 M	$222,624	$127,964	$0	$0	$0

| $275,000 Balance | | | | | 6% Return On Investment | | | |

No COLA

Monthly Amount	15 Yr Inflated	30 Yr Inflated	Money Lasts	5 Years	10 Years	15 Years	20 Years	30 Years
$1,000	$1,000	$1,000	Over 40 Yrs	$298,338	$329,570	$371,364	$427,294	$602,306
$1,250	$1,250	$1,250	Over 40 Yrs	$280,920	$288,842	$299,443	$313,630	$358,021
$1,500	$1,500	$1,500	37 Y & 11 M	$263,501	$248,113	$227,520	$199,961	$113,729
$1,750	$1,750	$1,750	24 Y & 9 M	$246,081	$207,382	$155,594	$86,290	$0
$2,000	$2,000	$2,000	18 Y & 11 M	$228,663	$166,655	$83,672	$0	$0
$2,250	$2,250	$2,250	15 Y & 6 M	$211,244	$125,926	$11,750	$0	$0
$2,500	$2,500	$2,500	13 Y & 2 M	$193,825	$85,197	$0	$0	$0

2% COLA

Monthly Amount	15 Yr Inflated	30 Yr Inflated	Money Lasts	5 Years	10 Years	15 Years	20 Years	30 Years
$750	$990	$1,332	Over 40 Yrs	$313,748	$359,950	$415,545	$483,056	$668,150
$1,000	$1,320	$1,776	Over 40 Yrs	$295,659	$315,772	$334,373	$350,090	$364,371
$1,250	$1,650	$2,220	32 Y & 5 M	$277,574	$271,606	$253,218	$217,130	$60,587
$1,500	$1,979	$2,664	23 Y & 5 M	$259,486	$227,429	$172,054	$84,176	$0
$1,750	$2,309	$3,108	18 Y & 6 M	$241,401	$183,255	$90,895	$0	$0
$2,000	$2,639	$3,552	15 Y & 4 M	$223,309	$139,075	$9,723	$0	$0
$2,250	$2,969	$3,996	13 Y & 2 M	$205,221	$94,898	$0	$0	$0

3% COLA

Monthly Amount	15 Yr Inflated	30 Yr Inflated	Money Lasts	5 Years	10 Years	15 Years	20 Years	30 Years
$750	$1,134	$1,767	Over 40 Yrs	$312,719	$354,390	$399,948	$449,080	$554,836
$1,000	$1,513	$2,357	38 Y & 5 M	$294,285	$308,351	$313,558	$304,742	$213,157
$1,250	$1,891	$2,946	26 Y & 7 M	$275,852	$262,314	$227,183	$160,437	$0
$1,500	$2,269	$3,535	20 Y & 6 M	$257,420	$216,279	$140,797	$16,109	$0
$1,750	$2,647	$4,124	16 Y & 9 M	$238,989	$170,253	$54,447	$0	$0
$2,000	$3,025	$4,713	14 Y & 2 M	$220,555	$124,205	$0	$0	$0
$2,250	$3,403	$5,302	12 Y & 4 M	$202,126	$78,186	$0	$0	$0

4% COLA

Monthly Amount	15 Yr Inflated	30 Yr Inflated	Money Lasts	5 Years	10 Years	15 Years	20 Years	30 Years
$500	$866	$1,560	Over 40 Yrs	$330,444	$396,496	$474,979	$567,953	$806,757
$750	$1,299	$2,339	Over 40 Yrs	$311,664	$348,525	$383,002	$411,079	$420,796
$1,000	$1,732	$3,119	30 Y & 11 M	$292,882	$300,533	$290,964	$254,066	$34,399
$1,250	$2,165	$3,899	23 Y & 2 M	$274,097	$252,540	$198,936	$97,077	$0
$1,500	$2,598	$4,678	18 Y & 6 M	$255,313	$204,551	$106,918	$0	$0
$1,750	$3,031	$5,458	15 Y & 5 M	$236,529	$156,555	$14,873	$0	$0
$2,000	$3,463	$6,237	13 Y & 3 M	$217,750	$108,583	$0	$0	$0

$300,000 Balance	3% Return On Investment

No COLA

Monthly Amount	15 Yr Inflated	30 Yr Inflated	Money Lasts	5 Years	10 Years	15 Years	20 Years	30 Years
$750	$750	$750	Over 40 Yrs	$299,283	$298,452	$297,490	$296,373	$293,578
$1,000	$1,000	$1,000	Over 40 Yrs	$283,117	$263,546	$240,856	$214,553	$148,711
$1,250	$1,250	$1,250	30 Y & 4 M	$266,951	$228,638	$184,222	$132,732	$3,842
$1,500	$1,500	$1,500	22 Y & 11 M	$250,784	$193,730	$127,588	$50,911	$0
$1,750	$1,750	$1,750	18 Y & 7 M	$234,618	$158,823	$70,955	$0	$0
$2,000	$2,000	$2,000	15 Y & 8 M	$218,452	$123,915	$14,320	$0	$0
$2,250	$2,250	$2,250	13 Y & 6 M	$202,285	$89,007	$0	$0	$0

2% COLA

Monthly Amount	15 Yr Inflated	30 Yr Inflated	Money Lasts	5 Years	10 Years	15 Years	20 Years	30 Years
$500	$660	$888	Over 40 Yrs	$314,171	$327,104	$338,237	$346,885	$353,176
$750	$990	$1,332	Over 40 Yrs	$297,362	$289,054	$273,629	$249,350	$165,535
$1,000	$1,320	$1,776	28 Y & 11 M	$280,556	$251,014	$209,042	$151,859	$0
$1,250	$1,650	$2,220	22 Y & 6 M	$263,752	$212,982	$144,463	$54,364	$0
$1,500	$1,979	$2,664	18 Y & 5 M	$246,944	$174,942	$79,882	$0	$0
$1,750	$2,309	$3,108	15 Y & 7 M	$230,139	$136,903	$15,300	$0	$0
$2,000	$2,639	$3,552	13 Y & 6 M	$213,331	$98,863	$0	$0	$0

3% COLA

Monthly Amount	15 Yr Inflated	30 Yr Inflated	Money Lasts	5 Years	10 Years	15 Years	20 Years	30 Years
$500	$756	$1,178	Over 40 Yrs	$313,512	$323,713	$329,211	$328,252	$297,625
$750	$1,134	$1,767	33 Y & 10 M	$296,376	$283,990	$260,139	$221,490	$82,416
$1,000	$1,513	$2,357	25 Y & 5 M	$279,238	$244,254	$191,042	$114,678	$0
$1,250	$1,891	$2,946	20 Y & 4 M	$262,103	$204,524	$121,956	$7,893	$0
$1,500	$2,269	$3,535	16 Y & 11 M	$244,968	$164,794	$52,860	$0	$0
$1,750	$2,647	$4,124	14 Y & 6 M	$227,832	$125,071	$0	$0	$0
$2,000	$3,025	$4,713	12 Y & 9 M	$210,693	$85,323	$0	$0	$0

4% COLA

Monthly Amount	15 Yr Inflated	30 Yr Inflated	Money Lasts	5 Years	10 Years	15 Years	20 Years	30 Years
$250	$433	$780	Over 40 Yrs	$330,309	$361,660	$393,397	$424,582	$479,619
$500	$866	$1,560	Over 40 Yrs	$312,837	$320,142	$319,393	$307,314	$231,030
$750	$1,299	$2,339	29 Y & 5 M	$295,369	$278,649	$245,451	$190,164	$0
$1,000	$1,732	$3,119	22 Y & 10 M	$277,895	$237,127	$171,440	$72,882	$0
$1,250	$2,165	$3,899	18 Y & 8 M	$260,423	$195,614	$97,454	$0	$0
$1,500	$2,598	$4,678	15 Y & 9 M	$242,949	$154,103	$23,474	$0	$0
$1,750	$3,031	$5,458	13 Y & 8 M	$225,477	$112,582	$0	$0	$0

$300,000 Balance   4% Return On Investment

No COLA

Monthly Amount	15 Yr Inflated	30 Yr Inflated	Money Lasts	5 Years	10 Years	15 Years	20 Years	30 Years
$750	$750	$750	Over 40 Yrs	$315,274	$333,857	$356,465	$383,973	$458,156
$1,000	$1,000	$1,000	Over 40 Yrs	$298,699	$297,116	$295,191	$292,849	$286,533
$1,250	$1,250	$1,250	39 Y & 2 M	$282,126	$260,379	$233,921	$201,731	$114,917
$1,500	$1,500	$1,500	27 Y & 1 M	$265,553	$223,643	$172,653	$110,615	$0
$1,750	$1,750	$1,750	20 Y & 11 M	$248,978	$186,902	$111,377	$19,489	$0
$2,000	$2,000	$2,000	17 Y & 3 M	$232,405	$150,164	$50,107	$0	$0
$2,250	$2,250	$2,250	14 Y & 7 M	$215,830	$113,424	$0	$0	$0

2% COLA

Monthly Amount	15 Yr Inflated	30 Yr Inflated	Money Lasts	5 Years	10 Years	15 Years	20 Years	30 Years
$500	$660	$888	Over 40 Yrs	$330,550	$364,137	$401,045	$441,584	$534,900
$750	$990	$1,332	Over 40 Yrs	$313,324	$324,154	$331,393	$333,644	$315,688
$1,000	$1,320	$1,776	34 Y & 9 M	$296,100	$284,181	$261,763	$225,751	$96,570
$1,250	$1,650	$2,220	25 Y & 8 M	$278,878	$244,218	$192,143	$117,856	$0
$1,500	$1,979	$2,664	20 Y & 5 M	$261,654	$204,244	$122,519	$9,970	$0
$1,750	$2,309	$3,108	16 Y & 11 M	$244,432	$164,274	$52,896	$0	$0
$2,000	$2,639	$3,552	14 Y & 6 M	$227,207	$124,301	$0	$0	$0

3% COLA

Monthly Amount	15 Yr Inflated	30 Yr Inflated	Money Lasts	5 Years	10 Years	15 Years	20 Years	30 Years
$500	$756	$1,178	Over 40 Yrs	$329,882	$360,640	$391,577	$421,704	$473,531
$750	$1,134	$1,767	Over 40 Yrs	$312,323	$318,929	$317,242	$303,918	$223,866
$1,000	$1,513	$2,357	29 Y & 2 M	$294,764	$277,210	$242,884	$186,082	$0
$1,250	$1,891	$2,946	22 Y & 7 M	$277,205	$235,491	$168,530	$68,268	$0
$1,500	$2,269	$3,535	18 Y & 6 M	$259,649	$193,776	$94,174	$0	$0
$1,750	$2,647	$4,124	15 Y & 8 M	$242,092	$152,067	$19,844	$0	$0
$2,000	$3,025	$4,713	13 Y & 7 M	$224,530	$110,334	$0	$0	$0

4% COLA

Monthly Amount	15 Yr Inflated	30 Yr Inflated	Money Lasts	5 Years	10 Years	15 Years	20 Years	30 Years
$250	$433	$780	Over 40 Yrs	$347,096	$400,518	$460,793	$528,383	$686,677
$500	$866	$1,560	Over 40 Yrs	$329,195	$356,955	$381,287	$399,405	$400,293
$750	$1,299	$2,339	33 Y & 11 M	$311,302	$313,422	$301,849	$270,559	$114,256
$1,000	$1,732	$3,119	25 Y & 6 M	$293,402	$269,861	$222,345	$141,576	$0
$1,250	$2,165	$3,899	20 Y & 5 M	$275,502	$226,306	$142,859	$12,629	$0
$1,500	$2,598	$4,678	16 Y & 11 M	$257,601	$182,752	$63,379	$0	$0
$1,750	$3,031	$5,458	14 Y & 7 M	$239,702	$139,190	$0	$0	$0

$300,000 Balance   5% Return On Investment

No COLA

Monthly Amount	15 Yr Inflated	30 Yr Inflated	Money Lasts	5 Years	10 Years	15 Years	20 Years	30 Years
$750	$750	$750	Over 40 Yrs	$331,911	$372,638	$424,617	$490,956	$683,685
$1,000	$1,000	$1,000	Over 40 Yrs	$314,920	$333,961	$358,263	$389,280	$479,386
$1,250	$1,250	$1,250	Over 40 Yrs	$297,928	$295,282	$291,908	$287,598	$275,081
$1,500	$1,500	$1,500	34 Y & 5 M	$280,937	$256,608	$225,555	$185,924	$70,790
$1,750	$1,750	$1,750	24 Y & 6 M	$263,946	$217,931	$159,202	$84,248	$0
$2,000	$2,000	$2,000	19 Y & 4 M	$246,954	$179,252	$92,847	$0	$0
$2,250	$2,250	$2,250	15 Y & 11 M	$229,962	$140,574	$26,489	$0	$0

2% COLA

Monthly Amount	15 Yr Inflated	30 Yr Inflated	Money Lasts	5 Years	10 Years	15 Years	20 Years	30 Years
$500	$660	$888	Over 40 Yrs	$347,585	$404,647	$473,420	$556,721	$782,020
$750	$990	$1,332	Over 40 Yrs	$329,932	$362,619	$398,252	$437,011	$524,549
$1,000	$1,320	$1,776	Over 40 Yrs	$312,280	$320,601	$323,108	$317,354	$267,196
$1,250	$1,650	$2,220	30 Y & 5 M	$294,633	$278,597	$247,980	$197,702	$9,833
$1,500	$1,979	$2,664	23 Y & 1 M	$276,982	$236,579	$172,841	$78,053	$0
$1,750	$2,309	$3,108	18 Y & 9 M	$259,330	$194,562	$97,704	$0	$0
$2,000	$2,639	$3,552	15 Y & 9 M	$241,680	$152,550	$22,568	$0	$0

3% COLA

Monthly Amount	15 Yr Inflated	30 Yr Inflated	Money Lasts	5 Years	10 Years	15 Years	20 Years	30 Years
$500	$756	$1,178	Over 40 Yrs	$346,906	$401,035	$463,476	$535,471	$713,950
$750	$1,134	$1,767	Over 40 Yrs	$328,916	$357,228	$383,398	$405,249	$422,728
$1,000	$1,513	$2,357	34 Y & 10 M	$310,925	$313,408	$303,290	$274,969	$131,338
$1,250	$1,891	$2,946	25 Y & 9 M	$292,934	$269,592	$223,192	$144,714	$0
$1,500	$2,269	$3,535	20 Y & 6 M	$274,945	$225,776	$143,087	$14,443	$0
$1,750	$2,647	$4,124	16 Y & 11 M	$256,956	$181,969	$63,011	$0	$0
$2,000	$3,025	$4,713	14 Y & 7 M	$238,964	$138,138	$0	$0	$0

4% COLA

Monthly Amount	15 Yr Inflated	30 Yr Inflated	Money Lasts	5 Years	10 Years	15 Years	20 Years	30 Years
$250	$433	$780	Over 40 Yrs	$364,547	$442,956	$538,191	$653,854	$964,874
$500	$866	$1,560	Over 40 Yrs	$346,211	$397,237	$452,689	$511,693	$633,117
$750	$1,299	$2,339	Over 40 Yrs	$327,879	$351,547	$367,256	$369,675	$301,749
$1,000	$1,732	$3,119	29 Y & 3 M	$309,542	$305,829	$281,755	$227,510	$0
$1,250	$2,165	$3,899	22 Y & 9 M	$291,205	$260,116	$196,271	$85,379	$0
$1,500	$2,598	$4,678	18 Y & 7 M	$272,869	$214,408	$110,797	$0	$0
$1,750	$3,031	$5,458	15 Y & 9 M	$254,532	$168,688	$25,294	$0	$0

> **$300,000 Balance**   **6% Return On Investment**

No COLA

Monthly Amount	15 Yr Inflated	30 Yr Inflated	Money Lasts	5 Years	10 Years	15 Years	20 Years	30 Years
$1,000	$1,000	$1,000	Over 40 Yrs	$331,792	$374,338	$431,274	$507,466	$745,881
$1,250	$1,250	$1,250	Over 40 Yrs	$314,374	$333,609	$359,352	$393,800	$501,595
$1,500	$1,500	$1,500	Over 40 Yrs	$296,956	$292,882	$287,430	$280,135	$257,306
$1,750	$1,750	$1,750	30 Y & 8 M	$279,537	$252,153	$215,507	$166,466	$13,013
$2,000	$2,000	$2,000	22 Y & 5 M	$262,118	$211,425	$143,586	$52,802	$0
$2,250	$2,250	$2,250	17 Y & 11 M	$244,699	$170,694	$71,660	$0	$0
$2,500	$2,500	$2,500	14 Y & 11 M	$227,282	$129,968	$0	$0	$0

2% COLA

Monthly Amount	15 Yr Inflated	30 Yr Inflated	Money Lasts	5 Years	10 Years	15 Years	20 Years	30 Years
$750	$990	$1,332	Over 40 Yrs	$347,204	$404,722	$475,459	$563,235	$811,739
$1,000	$1,320	$1,776	Over 40 Yrs	$329,116	$360,544	$394,288	$430,270	$507,961
$1,250	$1,650	$2,220	38 Y & 11 M	$311,029	$316,376	$313,130	$297,308	$204,173
$1,500	$1,979	$2,664	27 Y & 2 M	$292,941	$272,198	$231,965	$164,350	$0
$1,750	$2,309	$3,108	21 Y & 1 M	$274,855	$228,023	$150,804	$31,406	$0
$2,000	$2,639	$3,552	17 Y & 4 M	$256,766	$183,848	$69,637	$0	$0
$2,250	$2,969	$3,996	14 Y & 8 M	$238,677	$139,667	$0	$0	$0

3% COLA

Monthly Amount	15 Yr Inflated	30 Yr Inflated	Money Lasts	5 Years	10 Years	15 Years	20 Years	30 Years
$750	$1,134	$1,767	Over 40 Yrs	$346,173	$399,157	$459,856	$529,251	$698,408
$1,000	$1,513	$2,357	Over 40 Yrs	$327,740	$353,121	$373,471	$384,918	$356,744
$1,250	$1,891	$2,946	30 Y & 6 M	$309,307	$307,086	$287,096	$240,615	$15,189
$1,500	$2,269	$3,535	23 Y & 2 M	$290,876	$261,050	$200,711	$96,287	$0
$1,750	$2,647	$4,124	18 Y & 9 M	$272,444	$215,024	$114,360	$0	$0
$2,000	$3,025	$4,713	15 Y & 9 M	$254,009	$168,974	$27,948	$0	$0
$2,250	$3,403	$5,302	13 Y & 8 M	$235,581	$122,954	$0	$0	$0

4% COLA

Monthly Amount	15 Yr Inflated	30 Yr Inflated	Money Lasts	5 Years	10 Years	15 Years	20 Years	30 Years
$500	$866	$1,560	Over 40 Yrs	$363,899	$441,266	$534,890	$648,129	$950,336
$750	$1,299	$2,339	Over 40 Yrs	$345,121	$393,298	$442,920	$491,264	$564,394
$1,000	$1,732	$3,119	34 Y & 11 M	$326,336	$345,301	$350,873	$334,238	$177,973
$1,250	$2,165	$3,899	25 Y & 10 M	$307,552	$297,311	$258,849	$177,254	$0
$1,500	$2,598	$4,678	20 Y & 7 M	$288,768	$249,323	$166,831	$20,291	$0
$1,750	$3,031	$5,458	17 Y & 1 M	$269,984	$201,326	$74,785	$0	$0
$2,000	$3,463	$6,237	14 Y & 7 M	$251,206	$153,353	$0	$0	$0

| $325,000 Balance | | | | 3% Return On Investment | | | | |

No COLA

Monthly Amount	15 Yr Inflated	30 Yr Inflated	Money Lasts	5 Years	10 Years	15 Years	20 Years	30 Years
$750	$750	$750	Over 40 Yrs	$328,264	$332,048	$336,435	$341,521	$354,254
$1,000	$1,000	$1,000	Over 40 Yrs	$312,099	$297,142	$279,802	$259,701	$209,385
$1,250	$1,250	$1,250	34 Y & 8 M	$295,933	$262,235	$223,171	$177,885	$64,526
$1,500	$1,500	$1,500	25 Y & 10 M	$279,766	$227,327	$166,536	$96,063	$0
$1,750	$1,750	$1,750	20 Y & 9 M	$263,601	$192,422	$109,905	$14,246	$0
$2,000	$2,000	$2,000	17 Y & 4 M	$247,433	$157,512	$53,269	$0	$0
$2,250	$2,250	$2,250	14 Y & 11 M	$231,267	$122,605	$0	$0	$0

2% COLA

Monthly Amount	15 Yr Inflated	30 Yr Inflated	Money Lasts	5 Years	10 Years	15 Years	20 Years	30 Years
$500	$660	$888	Over 40 Yrs	$343,153	$360,701	$377,184	$392,035	$413,852
$750	$990	$1,332	Over 40 Yrs	$326,345	$322,651	$312,576	$294,499	$226,209
$1,000	$1,320	$1,776	31 Y & 10 M	$309,537	$284,610	$247,989	$197,009	$38,657
$1,250	$1,650	$2,220	24 Y & 8 M	$292,733	$246,581	$183,412	$99,517	$0
$1,500	$1,979	$2,664	20 Y & 1 M	$275,925	$208,539	$118,829	$2,032	$0
$1,750	$2,309	$3,108	16 Y & 11 M	$259,120	$170,501	$54,249	$0	$0
$2,000	$2,639	$3,552	14 Y & 9 M	$242,314	$132,464	$0	$0	$0

3% COLA

Monthly Amount	15 Yr Inflated	30 Yr Inflated	Money Lasts	5 Years	10 Years	15 Years	20 Years	30 Years
$500	$756	$1,178	Over 40 Yrs	$342,493	$357,309	$368,158	$373,402	$358,304
$750	$1,134	$1,767	36 Y & 8 M	$325,357	$317,587	$299,089	$266,643	$143,098
$1,000	$1,513	$2,357	27 Y & 6 M	$308,220	$277,853	$229,991	$159,831	$0
$1,250	$1,891	$2,946	21 Y & 11 M	$291,084	$238,122	$160,904	$53,044	$0
$1,500	$2,269	$3,535	18 Y & 4 M	$273,949	$198,389	$91,808	$0	$0
$1,750	$2,647	$4,124	15 Y & 9 M	$256,814	$158,667	$22,741	$0	$0
$2,000	$3,025	$4,713	13 Y & 9 M	$239,675	$118,922	$0	$0	$0

4% COLA

Monthly Amount	15 Yr Inflated	30 Yr Inflated	Money Lasts	5 Years	10 Years	15 Years	20 Years	30 Years
$250	$433	$780	Over 40 Yrs	$359,291	$395,259	$432,347	$469,736	$540,300
$500	$866	$1,560	Over 40 Yrs	$341,818	$353,738	$358,339	$352,462	$291,706
$750	$1,299	$2,339	31 Y & 6 M	$324,350	$312,244	$284,397	$235,314	$43,420
$1,000	$1,732	$3,119	24 Y & 6 M	$306,878	$270,726	$210,392	$118,038	$0
$1,250	$2,165	$3,899	20 Y & 1 M	$289,405	$229,211	$136,401	$789	$0
$1,500	$2,598	$4,678	16 Y & 11 M	$271,932	$187,700	$62,421	$0	$0
$1,750	$3,031	$5,458	14 Y & 9 M	$254,458	$146,179	$0	$0	$0

$325,000 Balance	4% Return On Investment

No COLA

Monthly Amount	15 Yr Inflated	30 Yr Inflated	Money Lasts	5 Years	10 Years	15 Years	20 Years	30 Years
$750	$750	$750	Over 40 Yrs	$345,691	$370,865	$401,493	$438,756	$539,249
$1,000	$1,000	$1,000	Over 40 Yrs	$329,116	$334,125	$340,218	$347,631	$367,623
$1,250	$1,250	$1,250	Over 40 Yrs	$312,542	$297,385	$278,944	$256,509	$196,001
$1,500	$1,500	$1,500	31 Y & 5 M	$295,970	$260,650	$217,677	$165,393	$24,389
$1,750	$1,750	$1,750	23 Y & 10 M	$279,395	$223,910	$156,402	$74,270	$0
$2,000	$2,000	$2,000	19 Y & 4 M	$262,821	$187,170	$95,129	$0	$0
$2,250	$2,250	$2,250	16 Y & 4 M	$246,246	$150,430	$33,855	$0	$0

2% COLA

Monthly Amount	15 Yr Inflated	30 Yr Inflated	Money Lasts	5 Years	10 Years	15 Years	20 Years	30 Years
$500	$660	$888	Over 40 Yrs	$360,967	$401,143	$446,068	$496,362	$615,984
$750	$990	$1,332	Over 40 Yrs	$343,740	$361,160	$376,417	$388,422	$396,771
$1,000	$1,320	$1,776	38 Y & 11 M	$326,517	$321,188	$306,788	$280,531	$177,661
$1,250	$1,650	$2,220	28 Y & 6 M	$309,295	$281,225	$237,169	$172,637	$0
$1,500	$1,979	$2,664	22 Y & 6 M	$292,070	$241,250	$167,542	$64,748	$0
$1,750	$2,309	$3,108	18 Y & 8 M	$274,849	$201,281	$97,921	$0	$0
$2,000	$2,639	$3,552	15 Y & 11 M	$257,623	$161,307	$28,290	$0	$0

3% COLA

Monthly Amount	15 Yr Inflated	30 Yr Inflated	Money Lasts	5 Years	10 Years	15 Years	20 Years	30 Years
$500	$756	$1,178	Over 40 Yrs	$360,297	$397,645	$436,601	$476,483	$554,616
$750	$1,134	$1,767	Over 40 Yrs	$342,739	$355,935	$362,266	$358,695	$304,951
$1,000	$1,513	$2,357	31 Y & 11 M	$325,181	$314,216	$287,906	$240,858	$55,137
$1,250	$1,891	$2,946	24 Y & 9 M	$307,622	$272,497	$213,554	$123,046	$0
$1,500	$2,269	$3,535	20 Y & 2 M	$290,066	$230,782	$139,196	$5,217	$0
$1,750	$2,647	$4,124	17 Y & 1 M	$272,509	$189,073	$64,869	$0	$0
$2,000	$3,025	$4,713	14 Y & 9 M	$254,947	$147,340	$0	$0	$0

4% COLA

Monthly Amount	15 Yr Inflated	30 Yr Inflated	Money Lasts	5 Years	10 Years	15 Years	20 Years	30 Years
$250	$433	$780	Over 40 Yrs	$377,512	$437,524	$505,815	$583,160	$767,762
$500	$866	$1,560	Over 40 Yrs	$359,612	$393,962	$426,311	$454,184	$481,380
$750	$1,299	$2,339	36 Y & 10 M	$341,717	$350,427	$346,872	$325,335	$195,338
$1,000	$1,732	$3,119	27 Y & 8 M	$323,819	$306,869	$267,372	$196,358	$0
$1,250	$2,165	$3,899	22 Y & 2 M	$305,918	$263,312	$187,883	$67,406	$0
$1,500	$2,598	$4,678	18 Y & 5 M	$288,018	$219,759	$108,404	$0	$0
$1,750	$3,031	$5,458	15 Y & 10 M	$270,118	$176,196	$28,898	$0	$0

$325,000 Balance   5% Return On Investment

No COLA

Monthly Amount	15 Yr Inflated	30 Yr Inflated	Money Lasts	5 Years	10 Years	15 Years	20 Years	30 Years
$750	$750	$750	Over 40 Yrs	$363,817	$413,359	$476,589	$557,287	$791,729
$1,000	$1,000	$1,000	Over 40 Yrs	$346,827	$374,683	$410,236	$455,612	$587,437
$1,250	$1,250	$1,250	Over 40 Yrs	$329,836	$336,008	$343,885	$353,937	$383,141
$1,500	$1,500	$1,500	Over 40 Yrs	$312,844	$297,329	$277,527	$252,255	$178,836
$1,750	$1,750	$1,750	28 Y & 10 M	$295,852	$258,652	$211,174	$150,578	$0
$2,000	$2,000	$2,000	22 Y & 2 M	$278,862	$219,975	$144,821	$48,902	$0
$2,250	$2,250	$2,250	18 Y & 2 M	$261,870	$181,298	$78,464	$0	$0

2% COLA

Monthly Amount	15 Yr Inflated	30 Yr Inflated	Money Lasts	5 Years	10 Years	15 Years	20 Years	30 Years
$500	$660	$888	Over 40 Yrs	$379,492	$445,369	$525,393	$623,054	$890,067
$750	$990	$1,332	Over 40 Yrs	$361,839	$403,342	$450,226	$503,343	$632,597
$1,000	$1,320	$1,776	Over 40 Yrs	$344,187	$361,323	$375,080	$383,684	$375,239
$1,250	$1,650	$2,220	34 Y & 9 M	$326,539	$319,317	$299,951	$264,032	$117,879
$1,500	$1,979	$2,664	25 Y & 11 M	$308,888	$277,301	$224,815	$144,386	$0
$1,750	$2,309	$3,108	20 Y & 10 M	$291,239	$235,288	$149,681	$24,749	$0
$2,000	$2,639	$3,552	17 Y & 5 M	$273,588	$193,273	$74,542	$0	$0

3% COLA

Monthly Amount	15 Yr Inflated	30 Yr Inflated	Money Lasts	5 Years	10 Years	15 Years	20 Years	30 Years
$500	$756	$1,178	Over 40 Yrs	$378,814	$441,760	$515,451	$601,805	$822,001
$750	$1,134	$1,767	Over 40 Yrs	$360,824	$397,952	$435,373	$471,585	$530,783
$1,000	$1,513	$2,357	39 Y & 2 M	$342,832	$354,132	$355,265	$341,304	$239,391
$1,250	$1,891	$2,946	28 Y & 7 M	$324,842	$310,314	$275,165	$211,047	$0
$1,500	$2,269	$3,535	22 Y & 7 M	$306,852	$266,498	$195,058	$80,773	$0
$1,750	$2,647	$4,124	18 Y & 9 M	$288,863	$222,691	$114,984	$0	$0
$2,000	$3,025	$4,713	15 Y & 11 M	$270,872	$178,861	$34,853	$0	$0

4% COLA

Monthly Amount	15 Yr Inflated	30 Yr Inflated	Money Lasts	5 Years	10 Years	15 Years	20 Years	30 Years
$250	$433	$780	Over 40 Yrs	$396,454	$483,678	$590,164	$720,186	$1.073 M
$500	$866	$1,560	Over 40 Yrs	$378,118	$437,960	$504,663	$578,029	$741,174
$750	$1,299	$2,339	Over 40 Yrs	$359,785	$392,268	$419,228	$436,006	$409,794
$1,000	$1,732	$3,119	32 Y & 1 M	$341,450	$346,553	$333,731	$293,846	$78,018
$1,250	$2,165	$3,899	24 Y & 10 M	$323,112	$300,839	$248,245	$151,713	$0
$1,500	$2,598	$4,678	20 Y & 3 M	$304,776	$255,130	$162,770	$9,605	$0
$1,750	$3,031	$5,458	17 Y & 2 M	$286,438	$209,410	$77,266	$0	$0

| $325,000 Balance | | | | 6% Return On Investment | | | | |

No COLA

Monthly Amount	15 Yr Inflated	30 Yr Inflated	Money Lasts	5 Years	10 Years	15 Years	20 Years	30 Years
$1,000	$1,000	$1,000	Over 40 Yrs	$365,248	$419,110	$491,190	$587,648	$889,473
$1,250	$1,250	$1,250	Over 40 Yrs	$347,831	$378,383	$419,268	$473,982	$645,184
$1,500	$1,500	$1,500	Over 40 Yrs	$330,412	$337,655	$347,347	$360,317	$400,902
$1,750	$1,750	$1,750	39 Y & 10 M	$312,993	$296,925	$275,423	$246,646	$156,605
$2,000	$2,000	$2,000	26 Y & 9 M	$295,575	$256,197	$203,500	$132,979	$0
$2,250	$2,250	$2,250	20 Y & 9 M	$278,156	$215,467	$131,576	$19,311	$0
$2,500	$2,500	$2,500	17 Y & 2 M	$260,737	$174,739	$59,654	$0	$0

2% COLA

Monthly Amount	15 Yr Inflated	30 Yr Inflated	Money Lasts	5 Years	10 Years	15 Years	20 Years	30 Years
$750	$990	$1,332	Over 40 Yrs	$380,658	$449,491	$535,369	$643,408	$955,317
$1,000	$1,320	$1,776	Over 40 Yrs	$362,571	$405,315	$454,203	$510,450	$651,551
$1,250	$1,650	$2,220	Over 40 Yrs	$344,486	$361,149	$373,045	$377,487	$347,761
$1,500	$1,979	$2,664	31 Y & 5 M	$326,398	$316,973	$291,885	$244,536	$44,045
$1,750	$2,309	$3,108	23 Y & 11 M	$308,311	$272,796	$210,720	$111,586	$0
$2,000	$2,639	$3,552	19 Y & 5 M	$290,221	$228,618	$129,550	$0	$0
$2,250	$2,969	$3,996	16 Y & 5 M	$272,133	$184,440	$48,384	$0	$0

3% COLA

Monthly Amount	15 Yr Inflated	30 Yr Inflated	Money Lasts	5 Years	10 Years	15 Years	20 Years	30 Years
$750	$1,134	$1,767	Over 40 Yrs	$379,629	$443,929	$519,770	$609,431	$842,001
$1,000	$1,513	$2,357	Over 40 Yrs	$361,195	$397,891	$433,385	$465,097	$500,331
$1,250	$1,891	$2,946	34 Y & 9 M	$342,762	$351,855	$347,008	$320,790	$158,772
$1,500	$2,269	$3,535	25 Y & 11 M	$324,331	$305,821	$260,626	$176,467	$0
$1,750	$2,647	$4,124	20 Y & 11 M	$305,899	$259,795	$174,273	$32,212	$0
$2,000	$3,025	$4,713	17 Y & 6 M	$287,465	$213,746	$87,862	$0	$0
$2,250	$3,403	$5,302	15 Y & 1 M	$269,038	$167,726	$1,519	$0	$0

4% COLA

Monthly Amount	15 Yr Inflated	30 Yr Inflated	Money Lasts	5 Years	10 Years	15 Years	20 Years	30 Years
$500	$866	$1,560	Over 40 Yrs	$397,356	$486,039	$594,809	$728,313	$1.094 M
$750	$1,299	$2,339	Over 40 Yrs	$378,576	$438,069	$502,833	$571,440	$707,977
$1,000	$1,732	$3,119	39 Y & 3 M	$359,792	$390,073	$410,788	$414,417	$321,564
$1,250	$2,165	$3,899	28 Y & 8 M	$341,008	$342,082	$318,762	$257,431	$0
$1,500	$2,598	$4,678	22 Y & 8 M	$322,224	$294,094	$226,745	$100,468	$0
$1,750	$3,031	$5,458	18 Y & 9 M	$303,439	$246,096	$134,700	$0	$0
$2,000	$3,463	$6,237	15 Y & 11 M	$284,662	$198,126	$42,716	$0	$0

$350,000 Balance　　　3% Return On Investment

No COLA

Monthly Amount	15 Yr Inflated	30 Yr Inflated	Money Lasts	5 Years	10 Years	15 Years	20 Years	30 Years
$750	$750	$750	Over 40 Yrs	$357,247	$365,648	$375,387	$386,678	$414,940
$1,000	$1,000	$1,000	Over 40 Yrs	$341,081	$330,741	$318,754	$304,858	$270,073
$1,250	$1,250	$1,250	39 Y & 7 M	$324,914	$295,832	$262,118	$223,036	$125,203
$1,500	$1,500	$1,500	28 Y & 11 M	$308,749	$260,926	$205,488	$141,218	$0
$1,750	$1,750	$1,750	22 Y & 11 M	$292,582	$226,018	$148,853	$59,397	$0
$2,000	$2,000	$2,000	19 Y & 1 M	$276,415	$191,110	$92,217	$0	$0
$2,250	$2,250	$2,250	16 Y & 5 M	$260,248	$156,202	$35,583	$0	$0

2% COLA

Monthly Amount	15 Yr Inflated	30 Yr Inflated	Money Lasts	5 Years	10 Years	15 Years	20 Years	30 Years
$500	$660	$888	Over 40 Yrs	$372,134	$394,299	$416,135	$437,189	$474,537
$750	$990	$1,332	Over 40 Yrs	$355,326	$356,250	$351,527	$339,654	$286,894
$1,000	$1,320	$1,776	34 Y & 9 M	$338,519	$318,209	$286,939	$242,163	$99,339
$1,250	$1,650	$2,220	26 Y & 10 M	$321,715	$280,178	$222,361	$144,669	$0
$1,500	$1,979	$2,664	21 Y & 10 M	$304,909	$242,139	$157,780	$47,186	$0
$1,750	$2,309	$3,108	18 Y & 5 M	$288,102	$204,098	$93,196	$0	$0
$2,000	$2,639	$3,552	15 Y & 11 M	$271,295	$166,060	$28,613	$0	$0

3% COLA

Monthly Amount	15 Yr Inflated	30 Yr Inflated	Money Lasts	5 Years	10 Years	15 Years	20 Years	30 Years
$500	$756	$1,178	Over 40 Yrs	$371,476	$390,909	$407,109	$418,557	$418,985
$750	$1,134	$1,767	39 Y & 6 M	$354,340	$351,186	$338,039	$311,797	$203,782
$1,000	$1,513	$2,357	29 Y & 8 M	$337,202	$311,450	$268,941	$204,984	$0
$1,250	$1,891	$2,946	23 Y & 9 M	$320,066	$271,719	$199,852	$98,196	$0
$1,500	$2,269	$3,535	19 Y & 9 M	$302,931	$231,988	$130,757	$0	$0
$1,750	$2,647	$4,124	16 Y & 11 M	$285,795	$192,266	$61,691	$0	$0
$2,000	$3,025	$4,713	14 Y & 10 M	$268,656	$152,517	$0	$0	$0

4% COLA

Monthly Amount	15 Yr Inflated	30 Yr Inflated	Money Lasts	5 Years	10 Years	15 Years	20 Years	30 Years
$250	$433	$780	Over 40 Yrs	$388,273	$428,857	$471,296	$514,889	$600,983
$500	$866	$1,560	Over 40 Yrs	$370,800	$387,336	$397,290	$397,618	$352,392
$750	$1,299	$2,339	33 Y & 7 M	$353,333	$345,845	$323,349	$280,469	$104,106
$1,000	$1,732	$3,119	26 Y & 2 M	$335,859	$304,324	$249,341	$163,189	$0
$1,250	$2,165	$3,899	21 Y & 5 M	$318,387	$262,811	$175,354	$45,945	$0
$1,500	$2,598	$4,678	18 Y & 2 M	$300,913	$221,298	$101,372	$0	$0
$1,750	$3,031	$5,458	15 Y & 9 M	$283,440	$179,778	$27,366	$0	$0

$350,000 Balance	4% Return On Investment

No COLA

Monthly Amount	15 Yr Inflated	30 Yr Inflated	Money Lasts	5 Years	10 Years	15 Years	20 Years	30 Years
$1,000	$1,000	$1,000	Over 40 Yrs	$359,533	$371,131	$385,242	$402,409	$448,710
$1,250	$1,250	$1,250	Over 40 Yrs	$342,959	$334,392	$323,970	$311,289	$277,092
$1,500	$1,500	$1,500	36 Y & 8 M	$326,385	$297,653	$262,696	$220,166	$105,469
$1,750	$1,750	$1,750	27 Y & 1 M	$309,812	$260,915	$201,425	$129,046	$0
$2,000	$2,000	$2,000	21 Y & 8 M	$293,237	$224,175	$140,151	$37,923	$0
$2,250	$2,250	$2,250	18 Y & 2 M	$276,662	$187,436	$78,879	$0	$0
$2,500	$2,500	$2,500	15 Y & 8 M	$260,088	$150,699	$17,609	$0	$0

2% COLA

Monthly Amount	15 Yr Inflated	30 Yr Inflated	Money Lasts	5 Years	10 Years	15 Years	20 Years	30 Years
$750	$990	$1,332	Over 40 Yrs	$374,157	$398,168	$421,442	$443,201	$477,861
$1,000	$1,320	$1,776	Over 40 Yrs	$356,933	$358,193	$351,811	$335,307	$258,742
$1,250	$1,650	$2,220	31 Y & 6 M	$339,712	$318,230	$282,189	$227,411	$39,606
$1,500	$1,979	$2,664	24 Y & 9 M	$322,487	$278,257	$212,566	$119,526	$0
$1,750	$2,309	$3,108	20 Y & 5 M	$305,264	$238,285	$142,942	$11,648	$0
$2,000	$2,639	$3,552	17 Y & 5 M	$288,040	$198,315	$73,315	$0	$0
$2,250	$2,969	$3,996	15 Y & 2 M	$270,816	$158,341	$3,688	$0	$0

3% COLA

Monthly Amount	15 Yr Inflated	30 Yr Inflated	Money Lasts	5 Years	10 Years	15 Years	20 Years	30 Years
$750	$1,134	$1,767	Over 40 Yrs	$373,155	$392,942	$407,291	$413,475	$386,037
$1,000	$1,513	$2,357	34 Y & 11 M	$355,595	$351,221	$332,929	$295,636	$136,220
$1,250	$1,891	$2,946	26 Y & 11 M	$338,037	$309,503	$258,578	$177,825	$0
$1,500	$2,269	$3,535	21 Y & 11 M	$320,482	$267,788	$184,221	$59,997	$0
$1,750	$2,647	$4,124	18 Y & 6 M	$302,924	$226,078	$109,890	$0	$0
$2,000	$3,025	$4,713	15 Y & 11 M	$285,363	$184,348	$35,507	$0	$0
$2,250	$3,403	$5,302	14 Y & 1 M	$267,809	$142,644	$0	$0	$0

4% COLA

Monthly Amount	15 Yr Inflated	30 Yr Inflated	Money Lasts	5 Years	10 Years	15 Years	20 Years	30 Years
$500	$866	$1,560	Over 40 Yrs	$390,028	$430,967	$471,333	$508,960	$562,463
$750	$1,299	$2,339	39 Y & 8 M	$372,134	$387,433	$391,896	$380,114	$276,421
$1,000	$1,732	$3,119	29 Y & 9 M	$354,233	$343,871	$312,391	$251,131	$0
$1,250	$2,165	$3,899	23 Y & 10 M	$336,334	$300,317	$232,905	$122,182	$0
$1,500	$2,598	$4,678	19 Y & 10 M	$318,433	$256,762	$153,424	$0	$0
$1,750	$3,031	$5,458	16 Y & 11 M	$300,533	$213,200	$73,918	$0	$0
$2,000	$3,463	$6,237	14 Y & 11 M	$282,641	$169,667	$0	$0	$0

$350,000 Balance	5% Return On Investment

No COLA

Monthly Amount	15 Yr Inflated	30 Yr Inflated	Money Lasts	5 Years	10 Years	15 Years	20 Years	30 Years
$1,000	$1,000	$1,000	Over 40 Yrs	$378,734	$415,407	$462,212	$521,948	$695,489
$1,250	$1,250	$1,250	Over 40 Yrs	$361,742	$376,729	$395,855	$420,267	$491,184
$1,500	$1,500	$1,500	Over 40 Yrs	$344,751	$338,051	$329,501	$318,588	$286,883
$1,750	$1,750	$1,750	34 Y & 5 M	$327,760	$299,374	$263,147	$216,910	$82,587
$2,000	$2,000	$2,000	25 Y & 6 M	$310,768	$260,697	$196,793	$115,234	$0
$2,250	$2,250	$2,250	20 Y & 7 M	$293,776	$222,020	$130,438	$13,554	$0
$2,500	$2,500	$2,500	17 Y & 4 M	$276,787	$183,345	$64,086	$0	$0

2% COLA

Monthly Amount	15 Yr Inflated	30 Yr Inflated	Money Lasts	5 Years	10 Years	15 Years	20 Years	30 Years
$750	$990	$1,332	Over 40 Yrs	$393,746	$444,064	$502,199	$569,677	$740,650
$1,000	$1,320	$1,776	Over 40 Yrs	$376,096	$402,049	$427,059	$450,024	$483,302
$1,250	$1,650	$2,220	39 Y & 8 M	$358,446	$360,040	$351,926	$330,368	$225,932
$1,500	$1,979	$2,664	29 Y & 1 M	$340,795	$318,023	$276,788	$210,720	$0
$1,750	$2,309	$3,108	23 Y & 1 M	$323,145	$276,010	$201,655	$91,083	$0
$2,000	$2,639	$3,552	19 Y & 3 M	$305,494	$233,995	$126,513	$0	$0
$2,250	$2,969	$3,996	16 Y & 6 M	$287,843	$191,977	$51,375	$0	$0

3% COLA

Monthly Amount	15 Yr Inflated	30 Yr Inflated	Money Lasts	5 Years	10 Years	15 Years	20 Years	30 Years
$750	$1,134	$1,767	Over 40 Yrs	$392,731	$438,674	$487,346	$537,918	$638,833
$1,000	$1,513	$2,357	Over 40 Yrs	$374,738	$394,853	$407,235	$407,631	$347,431
$1,250	$1,891	$2,946	31 Y & 7 M	$356,748	$351,036	$327,137	$277,378	$56,138
$1,500	$2,269	$3,535	24 Y & 10 M	$338,760	$307,221	$247,032	$147,106	$0
$1,750	$2,647	$4,124	20 Y & 6 M	$320,769	$263,412	$166,956	$16,899	$0
$2,000	$3,025	$4,713	17 Y & 5 M	$302,778	$219,582	$86,824	$0	$0
$2,250	$3,403	$5,302	15 Y & 2 M	$284,791	$175,779	$6,753	$0	$0

4% COLA

Monthly Amount	15 Yr Inflated	30 Yr Inflated	Money Lasts	5 Years	10 Years	15 Years	20 Years	30 Years
$500	$866	$1,560	Over 40 Yrs	$410,025	$478,683	$556,637	$644,362	$849,220
$750	$1,299	$2,339	Over 40 Yrs	$391,693	$432,991	$471,203	$502,339	$517,844
$1,000	$1,732	$3,119	34 Y & 11 M	$373,356	$387,273	$385,700	$360,173	$186,056
$1,250	$2,165	$3,899	26 Y & 11 M	$355,018	$341,561	$300,219	$218,047	$0
$1,500	$2,598	$4,678	21 Y & 11 M	$336,683	$295,853	$214,746	$75,941	$0
$1,750	$3,031	$5,458	18 Y & 7 M	$318,346	$250,134	$129,242	$0	$0
$2,000	$3,463	$6,237	16 Y & 1 M	$300,014	$204,440	$43,797	$0	$0

| $350,000 Balance | | | | 6% Return On Investment | | | | |

No COLA

Monthly Amount	15 Yr Inflated	30 Yr Inflated	Money Lasts	5 Years	10 Years	15 Years	20 Years	30 Years
$1,250	$1,250	$1,250	Over 40 Yrs	$381,286	$423,154	$479,183	$554,162	$788,777
$1,500	$1,500	$1,500	Over 40 Yrs	$363,868	$382,426	$407,261	$440,495	$544,489
$1,750	$1,750	$1,750	Over 40 Yrs	$346,449	$341,697	$335,337	$326,827	$300,197
$2,000	$2,000	$2,000	32 Y & 6 M	$329,030	$300,968	$263,415	$213,160	$55,909
$2,250	$2,250	$2,250	24 Y & 2 M	$311,610	$260,238	$191,490	$99,489	$0
$2,500	$2,500	$2,500	19 Y & 7 M	$294,192	$219,510	$119,568	$0	$0
$2,750	$2,750	$2,750	16 Y & 7 M	$276,774	$178,781	$47,645	$0	$0

2% COLA

Monthly Amount	15 Yr Inflated	30 Yr Inflated	Money Lasts	5 Years	10 Years	15 Years	20 Years	30 Years
$1,000	$1,320	$1,776	Over 40 Yrs	$396,027	$450,087	$514,117	$590,626	$795,138
$1,250	$1,650	$2,220	Over 40 Yrs	$377,940	$405,919	$432,959	$457,666	$491,352
$1,500	$1,979	$2,664	36 Y & 7 M	$359,852	$361,741	$351,794	$324,709	$187,623
$1,750	$2,309	$3,108	27 Y & 2 M	$341,767	$317,567	$270,635	$191,767	$0
$2,000	$2,639	$3,552	21 Y & 9 M	$323,677	$273,390	$189,466	$58,798	$0
$2,250	$2,969	$3,996	18 Y & 3 M	$305,589	$229,211	$108,297	$0	$0
$2,500	$3,299	$4,440	15 Y & 9 M	$287,503	$185,046	$27,152	$0	$0

3% COLA

Monthly Amount	15 Yr Inflated	30 Yr Inflated	Money Lasts	5 Years	10 Years	15 Years	20 Years	30 Years
$1,000	$1,513	$2,357	Over 40 Yrs	$394,651	$442,662	$493,297	$545,273	$643,913
$1,250	$1,891	$2,946	39 Y & 8 M	$376,218	$396,626	$406,922	$400,969	$302,358
$1,500	$2,269	$3,535	29 Y & 2 M	$357,787	$350,593	$320,540	$256,647	$0
$1,750	$2,647	$4,124	23 Y & 2 M	$339,356	$304,567	$234,187	$112,392	$0
$2,000	$3,025	$4,713	19 Y & 4 M	$320,921	$258,517	$147,776	$0	$0
$2,250	$3,403	$5,302	16 Y & 7 M	$302,492	$212,497	$61,431	$0	$0
$2,500	$3,782	$5,891	14 Y & 6 M	$284,059	$166,458	$0	$0	$0

4% COLA

Monthly Amount	15 Yr Inflated	30 Yr Inflated	Money Lasts	5 Years	10 Years	15 Years	20 Years	30 Years
$750	$1,299	$2,339	Over 40 Yrs	$412,033	$482,842	$562,750	$651,623	$851,572
$1,000	$1,732	$3,119	Over 40 Yrs	$393,249	$434,846	$470,705	$494,600	$465,159
$1,250	$2,165	$3,899	31 Y & 8 M	$374,464	$386,854	$378,678	$337,613	$78,835
$1,500	$2,598	$4,678	24 Y & 11 M	$355,679	$338,866	$286,661	$180,651	$0
$1,750	$3,031	$5,458	20 Y & 7 M	$336,896	$290,868	$194,613	$23,634	$0
$2,000	$3,463	$6,237	17 Y & 6 M	$318,117	$242,897	$102,628	$0	$0
$2,250	$3,896	$7,017	15 Y & 3 M	$299,332	$194,905	$10,597	$0	$0

$375,000 Balance   **3% Return On Investment**

No COLA

Monthly Amount	15 Yr Inflated	30 Yr Inflated	Money Lasts	5 Years	10 Years	15 Years	20 Years	30 Years
$750	$750	$750	Over 40 Yrs	$386,228	$399,245	$414,335	$431,830	$475,621
$1,000	$1,000	$1,000	Over 40 Yrs	$370,062	$364,339	$357,703	$350,011	$330,755
$1,250	$1,250	$1,250	Over 40 Yrs	$353,896	$329,432	$301,072	$268,193	$185,892
$1,500	$1,500	$1,500	32 Y & 5 M	$337,729	$294,522	$244,435	$186,369	$41,021
$1,750	$1,750	$1,750	25 Y & 5 M	$321,564	$259,616	$187,802	$104,550	$0
$2,000	$2,000	$2,000	20 Y & 11 M	$305,398	$224,709	$131,169	$22,730	$0
$2,250	$2,250	$2,250	17 Y & 11 M	$289,230	$189,799	$74,533	$0	$0

2% COLA

Monthly Amount	15 Yr Inflated	30 Yr Inflated	Money Lasts	5 Years	10 Years	15 Years	20 Years	30 Years
$500	$660	$888	Over 40 Yrs	$401,117	$427,896	$455,082	$482,340	$535,217
$750	$990	$1,332	Over 40 Yrs	$384,308	$389,846	$390,474	$384,804	$347,575
$1,000	$1,320	$1,776	37 Y & 9 M	$367,501	$351,808	$325,891	$287,318	$160,023
$1,250	$1,650	$2,220	28 Y & 11 M	$350,697	$313,775	$261,309	$189,820	$0
$1,500	$1,979	$2,664	23 Y & 7 M	$333,890	$275,736	$196,729	$92,339	$0
$1,750	$2,309	$3,108	19 Y & 10 M	$317,085	$237,698	$132,150	$0	$0
$2,000	$2,639	$3,552	17 Y & 2 M	$300,277	$199,658	$67,563	$0	$0

3% COLA

Monthly Amount	15 Yr Inflated	30 Yr Inflated	Money Lasts	5 Years	10 Years	15 Years	20 Years	30 Years
$500	$756	$1,178	Over 40 Yrs	$400,456	$424,504	$446,055	$463,704	$479,661
$750	$1,134	$1,767	Over 40 Yrs	$383,320	$384,781	$376,984	$356,945	$264,457
$1,000	$1,513	$2,357	31 Y & 9 M	$366,184	$345,050	$307,892	$250,139	$49,121
$1,250	$1,891	$2,946	25 Y & 5 M	$349,048	$305,318	$238,803	$143,351	$0
$1,500	$2,269	$3,535	21 Y & 2 M	$331,913	$265,586	$169,705	$36,543	$0
$1,750	$2,647	$4,124	18 Y & 2 M	$314,779	$225,865	$100,642	$0	$0
$2,000	$3,025	$4,713	15 Y & 11 M	$297,640	$186,120	$31,523	$0	$0

4% COLA

Monthly Amount	15 Yr Inflated	30 Yr Inflated	Money Lasts	5 Years	10 Years	15 Years	20 Years	30 Years
$250	$433	$780	Over 40 Yrs	$417,254	$462,455	$510,246	$560,042	$661,667
$500	$866	$1,560	Over 40 Yrs	$399,782	$420,935	$436,240	$442,771	$413,074
$750	$1,299	$2,339	35 Y & 8 M	$382,315	$379,441	$362,295	$325,618	$164,781
$1,000	$1,732	$3,119	27 Y & 10 M	$364,841	$337,921	$288,289	$208,341	$0
$1,250	$2,165	$3,899	22 Y & 10 M	$347,368	$296,407	$214,300	$91,096	$0
$1,500	$2,598	$4,678	19 Y & 4 M	$329,896	$254,896	$140,320	$0	$0
$1,750	$3,031	$5,458	16 Y & 10 M	$312,422	$213,374	$66,312	$0	$0

| $375,000 Balance | | | | | | 4% Return On Investment | | |

No COLA

Monthly Amount	15 Yr Inflated	30 Yr Inflated	Money Lasts	5 Years	10 Years	15 Years	20 Years	30 Years
$1,000	$1,000	$1,000	Over 40 Yrs	$389,949	$408,136	$430,264	$457,186	$529,792
$1,250	$1,250	$1,250	Over 40 Yrs	$373,376	$371,398	$368,992	$366,066	$358,173
$1,500	$1,500	$1,500	Over 40 Yrs	$356,801	$334,660	$307,721	$274,946	$186,555
$1,750	$1,750	$1,750	30 Y & 9 M	$340,226	$297,920	$246,448	$183,823	$14,931
$2,000	$2,000	$2,000	24 Y & 3 M	$323,653	$261,182	$185,176	$92,703	$0
$2,250	$2,250	$2,250	20 Y & 1 M	$307,079	$224,443	$123,904	$1,582	$0
$2,500	$2,500	$2,500	17 Y & 3 M	$290,505	$187,703	$62,630	$0	$0

2% COLA

Monthly Amount	15 Yr Inflated	30 Yr Inflated	Money Lasts	5 Years	10 Years	15 Years	20 Years	30 Years
$750	$990	$1,332	Over 40 Yrs	$404,573	$435,171	$466,462	$497,975	$558,939
$1,000	$1,320	$1,776	Over 40 Yrs	$387,350	$395,201	$396,835	$390,085	$339,826
$1,250	$1,650	$2,220	34 Y & 9 M	$370,128	$355,238	$327,217	$282,195	$120,700
$1,500	$1,979	$2,664	27 Y & 1 M	$352,903	$315,263	$257,590	$174,305	$0
$1,750	$2,309	$3,108	22 Y & 3 M	$335,681	$275,293	$187,968	$66,429	$0
$2,000	$2,639	$3,552	18 Y & 10 M	$318,456	$235,319	$118,337	$0	$0
$2,250	$2,969	$3,996	16 Y & 5 M	$301,233	$195,348	$48,713	$0	$0

3% COLA

Monthly Amount	15 Yr Inflated	30 Yr Inflated	Money Lasts	5 Years	10 Years	15 Years	20 Years	30 Years
$750	$1,134	$1,767	Over 40 Yrs	$403,572	$429,948	$452,313	$468,252	$467,119
$1,000	$1,513	$2,357	37 Y & 11 M	$386,012	$388,226	$377,952	$350,414	$217,306
$1,250	$1,891	$2,946	29 Y & 2 M	$368,454	$346,509	$303,600	$232,600	$0
$1,500	$2,269	$3,535	23 Y & 8 M	$350,898	$304,793	$229,243	$114,772	$0
$1,750	$2,647	$4,124	19 Y & 11 M	$333,341	$263,086	$154,916	$0	$0
$2,000	$3,025	$4,713	17 Y & 3 M	$315,780	$221,354	$80,532	$0	$0
$2,250	$3,403	$5,302	15 Y & 2 M	$298,226	$179,650	$6,207	$0	$0

4% COLA

Monthly Amount	15 Yr Inflated	30 Yr Inflated	Money Lasts	5 Years	10 Years	15 Years	20 Years	30 Years
$500	$866	$1,560	Over 40 Yrs	$420,445	$467,975	$516,359	$563,741	$643,552
$750	$1,299	$2,339	Over 40 Yrs	$402,551	$424,441	$436,920	$434,893	$357,510
$1,000	$1,732	$3,119	31 Y & 11 M	$384,650	$380,879	$357,415	$305,909	$71,096
$1,250	$2,165	$3,899	25 Y & 6 M	$366,751	$337,325	$277,931	$176,963	$0
$1,500	$2,598	$4,678	21 Y & 3 M	$348,850	$293,768	$198,447	$48,029	$0
$1,750	$3,031	$5,458	18 Y & 3 M	$330,950	$250,208	$118,945	$0	$0
$2,000	$3,463	$6,237	15 Y & 11 M	$313,057	$206,672	$39,495	$0	$0

$375,000 Balance   5% Return On Investment

No COLA

Monthly Amount	15 Yr Inflated	30 Yr Inflated	Money Lasts	5 Years	10 Years	15 Years	20 Years	30 Years
$1,000	$1,000	$1,000	Over 40 Yrs	$410,641	$456,129	$514,184	$588,279	$803,536
$1,250	$1,250	$1,250	Over 40 Yrs	$393,649	$417,450	$447,827	$486,596	$599,229
$1,500	$1,500	$1,500	Over 40 Yrs	$376,658	$378,773	$381,474	$384,921	$394,935
$1,750	$1,750	$1,750	Over 40 Yrs	$359,667	$340,096	$315,120	$283,244	$190,637
$2,000	$2,000	$2,000	29 Y & 6 M	$342,675	$301,419	$248,765	$181,563	$0
$2,250	$2,250	$2,250	23 Y & 3 M	$325,684	$262,743	$182,412	$79,888	$0
$2,500	$2,500	$2,500	19 Y & 4 M	$308,693	$224,067	$116,059	$0	$0

2% COLA

Monthly Amount	15 Yr Inflated	30 Yr Inflated	Money Lasts	5 Years	10 Years	15 Years	20 Years	30 Years
$750	$990	$1,332	Over 40 Yrs	$425,653	$484,785	$554,170	$636,005	$848,688
$1,000	$1,320	$1,776	Over 40 Yrs	$408,003	$442,771	$479,031	$516,356	$591,349
$1,250	$1,650	$2,220	Over 40 Yrs	$390,353	$400,764	$403,901	$396,701	$333,982
$1,500	$1,979	$2,664	32 Y & 6 M	$372,702	$358,746	$328,761	$277,051	$76,672
$1,750	$2,309	$3,108	25 Y & 7 M	$355,052	$316,731	$253,626	$157,412	$0
$2,000	$2,639	$3,552	21 Y & 2 M	$337,402	$274,719	$178,490	$37,760	$0
$2,250	$2,969	$3,996	17 Y & 11 M	$319,749	$232,697	$103,345	$0	$0

3% COLA

Monthly Amount	15 Yr Inflated	30 Yr Inflated	Money Lasts	5 Years	10 Years	15 Years	20 Years	30 Years
$750	$1,134	$1,767	Over 40 Yrs	$424,638	$479,396	$539,319	$604,250	$746,881
$1,000	$1,513	$2,357	Over 40 Yrs	$406,646	$435,578	$459,212	$473,969	$455,486
$1,250	$1,891	$2,946	34 Y & 10 M	$388,655	$391,758	$379,110	$343,709	$164,185
$1,500	$2,269	$3,535	27 Y & 2 M	$370,667	$347,943	$299,005	$213,438	$0
$1,750	$2,647	$4,124	22 Y & 4 M	$352,677	$304,135	$218,931	$83,235	$0
$2,000	$3,025	$4,713	18 Y & 11 M	$334,686	$260,307	$138,801	$0	$0
$2,250	$3,403	$5,302	16 Y & 6 M	$316,699	$216,503	$58,728	$0	$0

4% COLA

Monthly Amount	15 Yr Inflated	30 Yr Inflated	Money Lasts	5 Years	10 Years	15 Years	20 Years	30 Years
$500	$866	$1,560	Over 40 Yrs	$441,932	$519,404	$608,607	$710,689	$957,262
$750	$1,299	$2,339	Over 40 Yrs	$423,600	$473,713	$523,175	$568,671	$625,893
$1,000	$1,732	$3,119	37 Y & 11 M	$405,264	$427,998	$437,677	$426,512	$294,117
$1,250	$2,165	$3,899	29 Y & 3 M	$386,927	$382,284	$352,193	$284,379	$0
$1,500	$2,598	$4,678	23 Y & 9 M	$368,589	$336,574	$266,717	$142,270	$0
$1,750	$3,031	$5,458	19 Y & 11 M	$350,253	$290,856	$181,216	$0	$0
$2,000	$3,463	$6,237	17 Y & 4 M	$331,921	$245,161	$95,769	$0	$0

$375,000 Balance							6% Return On Investment	

No COLA

Monthly Amount	15 Yr Inflated	30 Yr Inflated	Money Lasts	5 Years	10 Years	15 Years	20 Years	30 Years
$1,250	$1,250	$1,250	Over 40 Yrs	$414,741	$467,925	$539,096	$634,340	$932,363
$1,500	$1,500	$1,500	Over 40 Yrs	$397,322	$427,194	$467,170	$520,667	$688,064
$1,750	$1,750	$1,750	Over 40 Yrs	$379,904	$386,467	$395,251	$407,004	$443,782
$2,000	$2,000	$2,000	Over 40 Yrs	$362,486	$345,739	$323,328	$293,336	$199,489
$2,250	$2,250	$2,250	28 Y & 5 M	$345,067	$305,011	$251,406	$179,670	$0
$2,500	$2,500	$2,500	22 Y & 5 M	$327,648	$264,280	$179,479	$65,998	$0
$2,750	$2,750	$2,750	18 Y & 8 M	$310,230	$223,553	$107,560	$0	$0

2% COLA

Monthly Amount	15 Yr Inflated	30 Yr Inflated	Money Lasts	5 Years	10 Years	15 Years	20 Years	30 Years
$1,000	$1,320	$1,776	Over 40 Yrs	$429,482	$494,857	$574,029	$670,804	$938,721
$1,250	$1,650	$2,220	Over 40 Yrs	$411,397	$450,691	$492,873	$537,844	$634,937
$1,500	$1,979	$2,664	Over 40 Yrs	$393,308	$406,512	$411,708	$404,887	$331,213
$1,750	$2,309	$3,108	30 Y & 9 M	$375,222	$362,339	$330,549	$271,944	$27,507
$2,000	$2,639	$3,552	24 Y & 4 M	$357,132	$318,160	$249,378	$138,974	$0
$2,250	$2,969	$3,996	20 Y & 2 M	$339,044	$273,983	$168,214	$6,014	$0
$2,500	$3,299	$4,440	17 Y & 4 M	$320,957	$229,814	$87,062	$0	$0

3% COLA

Monthly Amount	15 Yr Inflated	30 Yr Inflated	Money Lasts	5 Years	10 Years	15 Years	20 Years	30 Years
$1,000	$1,513	$2,357	Over 40 Yrs	$428,107	$487,435	$553,215	$625,457	$787,513
$1,250	$1,891	$2,946	Over 40 Yrs	$409,674	$441,399	$466,837	$481,148	$445,948
$1,500	$2,269	$3,535	32 Y & 6 M	$391,242	$395,364	$380,454	$336,825	$104,308
$1,750	$2,647	$4,124	25 Y & 7 M	$372,810	$349,335	$294,098	$192,565	$0
$2,000	$3,025	$4,713	21 Y & 2 M	$354,377	$303,288	$207,691	$48,196	$0
$2,250	$3,403	$5,302	18 Y & 1 M	$335,948	$257,268	$121,347	$0	$0
$2,500	$3,782	$5,891	15 Y & 9 M	$317,514	$211,230	$34,963	$0	$0

4% COLA

Monthly Amount	15 Yr Inflated	30 Yr Inflated	Money Lasts	5 Years	10 Years	15 Years	20 Years	30 Years
$750	$1,299	$2,339	Over 40 Yrs	$445,488	$527,613	$622,662	$731,799	$995,155
$1,000	$1,732	$3,119	Over 40 Yrs	$426,703	$479,615	$530,616	$574,774	$608,739
$1,250	$2,165	$3,899	34 Y & 11 M	$407,920	$431,626	$438,591	$417,789	$222,422
$1,500	$2,598	$4,678	27 Y & 3 M	$389,136	$383,636	$346,574	$260,827	$0
$1,750	$3,031	$5,458	22 Y & 5 M	$370,352	$335,642	$254,533	$103,821	$0
$2,000	$3,463	$6,237	18 Y & 11 M	$351,573	$287,669	$162,544	$0	$0
$2,250	$3,896	$7,017	16 Y & 6 M	$332,789	$239,677	$70,513	$0	$0

| $400,000 Balance | | | | | | 3% Return On Investment | | |

No COLA

Monthly Amount	15 Yr Inflated	30 Yr Inflated	Money Lasts	5 Years	10 Years	15 Years	20 Years	30 Years
$750	$750	$750	Over 40 Yrs	$415,211	$432,844	$453,286	$476,984	$536,306
$1,000	$1,000	$1,000	Over 40 Yrs	$399,044	$397,936	$396,652	$395,163	$391,436
$1,250	$1,250	$1,250	Over 40 Yrs	$382,878	$363,029	$340,019	$313,345	$246,572
$1,500	$1,500	$1,500	36 Y & 3 M	$366,712	$328,121	$283,384	$231,523	$101,703
$1,750	$1,750	$1,750	27 Y & 11 M	$350,546	$293,214	$226,751	$149,703	$0
$2,000	$2,000	$2,000	22 Y & 11 M	$334,379	$258,307	$170,118	$67,884	$0
$2,250	$2,250	$2,250	19 Y & 6 M	$318,214	$223,400	$113,485	$0	$0

2% COLA

Monthly Amount	15 Yr Inflated	30 Yr Inflated	Money Lasts	5 Years	10 Years	15 Years	20 Years	30 Years
$500	$660	$888	Over 40 Yrs	$430,099	$461,496	$494,034	$527,496	$595,901
$750	$990	$1,332	Over 40 Yrs	$413,290	$423,445	$429,424	$429,958	$408,255
$1,000	$1,320	$1,776	Over 40 Yrs	$396,482	$385,404	$364,837	$332,468	$220,702
$1,250	$1,650	$2,220	31 Y & 3 M	$379,678	$347,373	$300,258	$234,973	$33,126
$1,500	$1,979	$2,664	25 Y & 4 M	$362,872	$309,334	$235,678	$137,493	$0
$1,750	$2,309	$3,108	21 Y & 4 M	$346,066	$271,294	$171,096	$40,014	$0
$2,000	$2,639	$3,552	18 Y & 5 M	$329,258	$233,256	$106,511	$0	$0

3% COLA

Monthly Amount	15 Yr Inflated	30 Yr Inflated	Money Lasts	5 Years	10 Years	15 Years	20 Years	30 Years
$500	$756	$1,178	Over 40 Yrs	$429,439	$458,105	$485,008	$508,862	$540,349
$750	$1,134	$1,767	Over 40 Yrs	$412,303	$418,381	$415,937	$402,103	$325,146
$1,000	$1,513	$2,357	33 Y & 10 M	$395,165	$378,646	$346,837	$295,288	$109,799
$1,250	$1,891	$2,946	27 Y & 1 M	$378,029	$338,914	$277,749	$188,499	$0
$1,500	$2,269	$3,535	22 Y & 7 M	$360,895	$299,184	$208,656	$81,696	$0
$1,750	$2,647	$4,124	19 Y & 4 M	$343,759	$259,461	$139,589	$0	$0
$2,000	$3,025	$4,713	16 Y & 11 M	$326,620	$219,715	$70,468	$0	$0

4% COLA

Monthly Amount	15 Yr Inflated	30 Yr Inflated	Money Lasts	5 Years	10 Years	15 Years	20 Years	30 Years
$250	$433	$780	Over 40 Yrs	$446,237	$496,053	$549,196	$605,196	$722,348
$500	$866	$1,560	Over 40 Yrs	$428,763	$454,532	$475,188	$487,922	$473,752
$750	$1,299	$2,339	37 Y & 7 M	$411,297	$413,041	$401,248	$370,774	$225,467
$1,000	$1,732	$3,119	29 Y & 5 M	$393,823	$371,520	$327,240	$253,496	$0
$1,250	$2,165	$3,899	24 Y & 2 M	$376,350	$330,007	$253,253	$136,252	$0
$1,500	$2,598	$4,678	20 Y & 6 M	$358,877	$288,494	$179,269	$19,023	$0
$1,750	$3,031	$5,458	17 Y & 10 M	$341,404	$246,974	$105,265	$0	$0

$400,000 Balance   4% Return On Investment

No COLA

Monthly Amount	15 Yr Inflated	30 Yr Inflated	Money Lasts	5 Years	10 Years	15 Years	20 Years	30 Years
$1,000	$1,000	$1,000	Over 40 Yrs	$420,365	$445,144	$475,290	$511,967	$610,882
$1,250	$1,250	$1,250	Over 40 Yrs	$403,791	$408,404	$414,017	$420,846	$439,260
$1,500	$1,500	$1,500	Over 40 Yrs	$387,217	$371,665	$352,744	$329,724	$267,640
$1,750	$1,750	$1,750	35 Y & 1 M	$370,643	$334,927	$291,471	$238,601	$96,017
$2,000	$2,000	$2,000	27 Y & 1 M	$354,070	$298,189	$230,200	$147,482	$0
$2,250	$2,250	$2,250	22 Y & 3 M	$337,495	$261,449	$168,927	$56,360	$0
$2,500	$2,500	$2,500	18 Y & 11 M	$320,922	$224,711	$107,656	$0	$0

2% COLA

Monthly Amount	15 Yr Inflated	30 Yr Inflated	Money Lasts	5 Years	10 Years	15 Years	20 Years	30 Years
$750	$990	$1,332	Over 40 Yrs	$434,990	$472,179	$511,488	$552,757	$640,030
$1,000	$1,320	$1,776	Over 40 Yrs	$417,766	$432,206	$441,858	$444,863	$420,913
$1,250	$1,650	$2,220	38 Y & 2 M	$400,545	$392,244	$372,240	$336,972	$201,784
$1,500	$1,979	$2,664	29 Y & 6 M	$383,319	$352,268	$302,613	$229,083	$0
$1,750	$2,309	$3,108	24 Y & 1 M	$366,098	$312,299	$232,991	$121,206	$0
$2,000	$2,639	$3,552	20 Y & 5 M	$348,873	$272,327	$163,362	$13,308	$0
$2,250	$2,969	$3,996	17 Y & 8 M	$331,650	$232,355	$93,738	$0	$0

3% COLA

Monthly Amount	15 Yr Inflated	30 Yr Inflated	Money Lasts	5 Years	10 Years	15 Years	20 Years	30 Years
$750	$1,134	$1,767	Over 40 Yrs	$433,989	$466,955	$497,338	$523,032	$548,207
$1,000	$1,513	$2,357	Over 40 Yrs	$416,429	$425,233	$422,976	$405,193	$298,391
$1,250	$1,891	$2,946	31 Y & 5 M	$398,870	$383,515	$348,624	$287,379	$48,667
$1,500	$2,269	$3,535	25 Y & 6 M	$381,314	$341,799	$274,266	$169,549	$0
$1,750	$2,647	$4,124	21 Y & 5 M	$363,756	$300,090	$199,937	$51,782	$0
$2,000	$3,025	$4,713	18 Y & 6 M	$346,195	$258,358	$125,551	$0	$0
$2,250	$3,403	$5,302	16 Y & 3 M	$328,641	$216,656	$51,231	$0	$0

4% COLA

Monthly Amount	15 Yr Inflated	30 Yr Inflated	Money Lasts	5 Years	10 Years	15 Years	20 Years	30 Years
$500	$866	$1,560	Over 40 Yrs	$450,861	$504,980	$561,381	$618,517	$724,632
$750	$1,299	$2,339	Over 40 Yrs	$432,967	$461,446	$481,943	$489,671	$438,594
$1,000	$1,732	$3,119	33 Y & 11 M	$415,067	$417,885	$402,439	$360,688	$152,184
$1,250	$2,165	$3,899	27 Y & 3 M	$397,167	$374,331	$322,954	$231,741	$0
$1,500	$2,598	$4,678	22 Y & 8 M	$379,267	$330,776	$243,473	$102,810	$0
$1,750	$3,031	$5,458	19 Y & 5 M	$361,366	$287,214	$163,968	$0	$0
$2,000	$3,463	$6,237	16 Y & 11 M	$343,473	$243,677	$84,519	$0	$0

$400,000 Balance	5% Return On Investment

No COLA

Monthly Amount	15 Yr Inflated	30 Yr Inflated	Money Lasts	5 Years	10 Years	15 Years	20 Years	30 Years
$1,000	$1,000	$1,000	Over 40 Yrs	$442,547	$496,849	$566,153	$654,605	$911,575
$1,250	$1,250	$1,250	Over 40 Yrs	$425,556	$458,173	$499,801	$552,931	$707,281
$1,500	$1,500	$1,500	Over 40 Yrs	$408,565	$419,496	$433,448	$451,254	$502,982
$1,750	$1,750	$1,750	Over 40 Yrs	$391,574	$380,819	$367,093	$349,575	$298,683
$2,000	$2,000	$2,000	34 Y & 5 M	$374,583	$342,143	$300,740	$247,899	$94,386
$2,250	$2,250	$2,250	26 Y & 4 M	$357,590	$303,466	$234,386	$146,221	$0
$2,500	$2,500	$2,500	21 Y & 7 M	$340,600	$264,788	$168,031	$44,542	$0

2% COLA

Monthly Amount	15 Yr Inflated	30 Yr Inflated	Money Lasts	5 Years	10 Years	15 Years	20 Years	30 Years
$750	$990	$1,332	Over 40 Yrs	$457,560	$525,508	$606,144	$702,339	$956,742
$1,000	$1,320	$1,776	Over 40 Yrs	$439,909	$483,492	$531,003	$582,685	$699,388
$1,250	$1,650	$2,220	Over 40 Yrs	$422,261	$441,487	$455,874	$463,034	$442,030
$1,500	$1,979	$2,664	36 Y & 4 M	$404,609	$399,470	$380,737	$343,386	$184,727
$1,750	$2,309	$3,108	28 Y & 2 M	$386,959	$357,452	$305,598	$223,743	$0
$2,000	$2,639	$3,552	23 Y & 1 M	$369,309	$315,441	$230,462	$104,090	$0
$2,250	$2,969	$3,996	19 Y & 8 M	$351,656	$273,420	$155,318	$0	$0

3% COLA

Monthly Amount	15 Yr Inflated	30 Yr Inflated	Money Lasts	5 Years	10 Years	15 Years	20 Years	30 Years
$750	$1,134	$1,767	Over 40 Yrs	$456,544	$520,116	$591,289	$670,577	$854,921
$1,000	$1,513	$2,357	Over 40 Yrs	$438,553	$476,299	$511,184	$540,301	$563,535
$1,250	$1,891	$2,946	38 Y & 3 M	$420,562	$432,481	$431,085	$410,044	$272,236
$1,500	$2,269	$3,535	29 Y & 7 M	$402,574	$388,665	$350,978	$279,771	$0
$1,750	$2,647	$4,124	24 Y & 2 M	$384,583	$344,856	$270,901	$149,563	$0
$2,000	$3,025	$4,713	20 Y & 6 M	$366,592	$301,028	$190,772	$19,247	$0
$2,250	$3,403	$5,302	17 Y & 9 M	$348,606	$257,227	$110,703	$0	$0

4% COLA

Monthly Amount	15 Yr Inflated	30 Yr Inflated	Money Lasts	5 Years	10 Years	15 Years	20 Years	30 Years
$500	$866	$1,560	Over 40 Yrs	$473,839	$560,127	$660,581	$777,025	$1.065 M
$750	$1,299	$2,339	Over 40 Yrs	$455,508	$514,437	$575,150	$635,005	$733,944
$1,000	$1,732	$3,119	Over 40 Yrs	$437,170	$468,719	$489,648	$492,841	$402,160
$1,250	$2,165	$3,899	31 Y & 6 M	$418,833	$423,005	$404,163	$350,709	$70,453
$1,500	$2,598	$4,678	25 Y & 7 M	$400,497	$377,295	$318,689	$208,602	$0
$1,750	$3,031	$5,458	21 Y & 6 M	$382,160	$331,578	$233,188	$66,450	$0
$2,000	$3,463	$6,237	18 Y & 7 M	$363,828	$285,883	$147,742	$0	$0

$400,000 Balance				6% Return On Investment				

No COLA

Monthly Amount	15 Yr Inflated	30 Yr Inflated	Money Lasts	5 Years	10 Years	15 Years	20 Years	30 Years
$1,250	$1,250	$1,250	Over 40 Yrs	$448,197	$512,695	$599,008	$714,514	$1.076 M
$1,500	$1,500	$1,500	Over 40 Yrs	$430,779	$471,968	$527,089	$600,852	$831,663
$1,750	$1,750	$1,750	Over 40 Yrs	$413,360	$431,239	$455,164	$487,183	$587,370
$2,000	$2,000	$2,000	Over 40 Yrs	$395,941	$390,509	$383,240	$373,512	$343,075
$2,250	$2,250	$2,250	34 Y & 2 M	$378,522	$349,779	$311,315	$259,842	$98,778
$2,500	$2,500	$2,500	25 Y & 9 M	$361,104	$309,052	$239,396	$146,180	$0
$2,750	$2,750	$2,750	20 Y & 11 M	$343,686	$268,325	$167,475	$32,514	$0

2% COLA

Monthly Amount	15 Yr Inflated	30 Yr Inflated	Money Lasts	5 Years	10 Years	15 Years	20 Years	30 Years
$1,000	$1,320	$1,776	Over 40 Yrs	$462,938	$539,630	$633,947	$750,988	$1.082 M
$1,250	$1,650	$2,220	Over 40 Yrs	$444,853	$495,461	$552,787	$618,023	$778,528
$1,500	$1,979	$2,664	Over 40 Yrs	$426,764	$451,285	$471,624	$485,070	$474,807
$1,750	$2,309	$3,108	34 Y & 11 M	$408,678	$407,109	$390,463	$352,123	$171,096
$2,000	$2,639	$3,552	27 Y & 2 M	$390,588	$362,932	$309,293	$219,153	$0
$2,250	$2,969	$3,996	22 Y & 4 M	$372,500	$318,753	$228,126	$86,188	$0
$2,500	$3,299	$4,440	18 Y & 11 M	$354,414	$274,587	$146,978	$0	$0

3% COLA

Monthly Amount	15 Yr Inflated	30 Yr Inflated	Money Lasts	5 Years	10 Years	15 Years	20 Years	30 Years
$1,000	$1,513	$2,357	Over 40 Yrs	$461,562	$532,205	$613,126	$705,632	$931,094
$1,250	$1,891	$2,946	Over 40 Yrs	$443,131	$486,172	$526,755	$561,331	$589,543
$1,500	$2,269	$3,535	36 Y & 4 M	$424,699	$440,135	$440,367	$417,002	$247,895
$1,750	$2,647	$4,124	28 Y & 3 M	$406,267	$394,110	$354,017	$272,752	$0
$2,000	$3,025	$4,713	23 Y & 2 M	$387,832	$348,059	$267,604	$128,371	$0
$2,250	$3,403	$5,302	19 Y & 8 M	$369,404	$302,040	$181,261	$0	$0
$2,500	$3,782	$5,891	17 Y & 2 M	$350,971	$256,003	$94,879	$0	$0

4% COLA

Monthly Amount	15 Yr Inflated	30 Yr Inflated	Money Lasts	5 Years	10 Years	15 Years	20 Years	30 Years
$750	$1,299	$2,339	Over 40 Yrs	$478,943	$572,383	$682,576	$811,978	$1.139 M
$1,000	$1,732	$3,119	Over 40 Yrs	$460,160	$524,388	$590,531	$654,954	$752,329
$1,250	$2,165	$3,899	38 Y & 4 M	$441,375	$476,396	$498,507	$497,972	$366,015
$1,500	$2,598	$4,678	29 Y & 8 M	$422,591	$428,408	$406,488	$341,007	$0
$1,750	$3,031	$5,458	24 Y & 3 M	$403,807	$380,411	$314,443	$183,994	$0
$2,000	$3,463	$6,237	20 Y & 7 M	$385,029	$332,440	$222,458	$27,093	$0
$2,250	$3,896	$7,017	17 Y & 10 M	$366,244	$284,448	$130,427	$0	$0

$425,000 Balance   3% Return On Investment

No COLA

Monthly Amount	15 Yr Inflated	30 Yr Inflated	Money Lasts	5 Years	10 Years	15 Years	20 Years	30 Years
$1,000	$1,000	$1,000	Over 40 Yrs	$428,027	$431,536	$435,603	$440,318	$452,120
$1,250	$1,250	$1,250	Over 40 Yrs	$411,860	$396,628	$378,968	$358,495	$307,249
$1,500	$1,500	$1,500	Over 40 Yrs	$395,693	$361,719	$322,335	$276,677	$162,386
$1,750	$1,750	$1,750	30 Y & 11 M	$379,527	$326,812	$265,700	$194,855	$17,518
$2,000	$2,000	$2,000	25 Y & 1 M	$363,361	$291,905	$209,067	$113,035	$0
$2,250	$2,250	$2,250	21 Y & 3 M	$347,195	$256,997	$152,433	$31,215	$0
$2,500	$2,500	$2,500	18 Y & 5 M	$331,029	$222,090	$95,800	$0	$0

2% COLA

Monthly Amount	15 Yr Inflated	30 Yr Inflated	Money Lasts	5 Years	10 Years	15 Years	20 Years	30 Years
$750	$990	$1,332	Over 40 Yrs	$442,272	$457,045	$468,376	$475,115	$468,944
$1,000	$1,320	$1,776	Over 40 Yrs	$425,465	$419,003	$403,787	$377,621	$281,384
$1,250	$1,650	$2,220	33 Y & 7 M	$408,660	$380,971	$339,207	$280,126	$93,809
$1,500	$1,979	$2,664	27 Y & 2 M	$391,853	$342,931	$274,627	$182,645	$0
$1,750	$2,309	$3,108	22 Y & 10 M	$375,049	$304,894	$210,047	$85,168	$0
$2,000	$2,639	$3,552	19 Y & 8 M	$358,242	$266,855	$145,461	$0	$0
$2,250	$2,969	$3,996	17 Y & 4 M	$341,433	$228,811	$80,874	$0	$0

3% COLA

Monthly Amount	15 Yr Inflated	30 Yr Inflated	Money Lasts	5 Years	10 Years	15 Years	20 Years	30 Years
$750	$1,134	$1,767	Over 40 Yrs	$441,285	$451,978	$454,884	$447,252	$385,822
$1,000	$1,513	$2,357	35 Y & 11 M	$424,149	$412,246	$385,789	$340,443	$170,482
$1,250	$1,891	$2,946	28 Y & 9 M	$407,012	$372,515	$316,703	$233,658	$0
$1,500	$2,269	$3,535	23 Y & 11 M	$389,877	$332,783	$247,606	$126,851	$0
$1,750	$2,647	$4,124	20 Y & 7 M	$372,742	$293,060	$178,538	$20,105	$0
$2,000	$3,025	$4,713	17 Y & 11 M	$355,603	$253,315	$109,420	$0	$0
$2,250	$3,403	$5,302	15 Y & 11 M	$338,470	$213,596	$40,357	$0	$0

4% COLA

Monthly Amount	15 Yr Inflated	30 Yr Inflated	Money Lasts	5 Years	10 Years	15 Years	20 Years	30 Years
$500	$866	$1,560	Over 40 Yrs	$457,746	$488,131	$514,139	$533,077	$534,437
$750	$1,299	$2,339	39 Y & 7 M	$440,278	$446,636	$440,193	$415,924	$286,145
$1,000	$1,732	$3,119	30 Y & 11 M	$422,805	$405,116	$366,186	$298,646	$37,524
$1,250	$2,165	$3,899	25 Y & 6 M	$405,332	$363,603	$292,200	$181,403	$0
$1,500	$2,598	$4,678	21 Y & 8 M	$387,860	$322,092	$218,220	$64,177	$0
$1,750	$3,031	$5,458	18 Y & 10 M	$370,386	$280,570	$144,211	$0	$0
$2,000	$3,463	$6,237	16 Y & 8 M	$352,918	$239,075	$70,256	$0	$0

| $425,000 Balance | | | | 4% Return On Investment | | | | |

No COLA

Monthly Amount	15 Yr Inflated	30 Yr Inflated	Money Lasts	5 Years	10 Years	15 Years	20 Years	30 Years
$1,250	$1,250	$1,250	Over 40 Yrs	$434,208	$445,411	$459,041	$475,624	$520,347
$1,500	$1,500	$1,500	Over 40 Yrs	$417,634	$408,671	$397,767	$384,502	$348,725
$1,750	$1,750	$1,750	Over 40 Yrs	$401,059	$371,932	$336,494	$293,379	$177,102
$2,000	$2,000	$2,000	30 Y & 3 M	$384,486	$335,194	$275,223	$202,260	$5,484
$2,250	$2,250	$2,250	24 Y & 6 M	$367,912	$298,455	$213,950	$111,138	$0
$2,500	$2,500	$2,500	20 Y & 9 M	$351,338	$261,717	$152,679	$20,018	$0
$2,750	$2,750	$2,750	17 Y & 11 M	$334,765	$224,981	$91,410	$0	$0

2% COLA

Monthly Amount	15 Yr Inflated	30 Yr Inflated	Money Lasts	5 Years	10 Years	15 Years	20 Years	30 Years
$1,000	$1,320	$1,776	Over 40 Yrs	$448,183	$469,213	$486,883	$499,643	$502,000
$1,250	$1,650	$2,220	Over 40 Yrs	$430,960	$429,248	$417,261	$391,745	$282,860
$1,500	$1,979	$2,664	31 Y & 11 M	$413,736	$389,275	$347,636	$283,860	$63,788
$1,750	$2,309	$3,108	26 Y & 1 M	$396,514	$349,305	$278,014	$175,983	$0
$2,000	$2,639	$3,552	21 Y & 11 M	$379,290	$309,335	$208,388	$68,090	$0
$2,250	$2,969	$3,996	18 Y & 11 M	$362,065	$269,358	$138,757	$0	$0
$2,500	$3,299	$4,440	16 Y & 9 M	$344,843	$229,395	$69,147	$0	$0

3% COLA

Monthly Amount	15 Yr Inflated	30 Yr Inflated	Money Lasts	5 Years	10 Years	15 Years	20 Years	30 Years
$1,000	$1,513	$2,357	Over 40 Yrs	$446,845	$462,241	$468,001	$459,972	$379,477
$1,250	$1,891	$2,946	33 Y & 9 M	$429,287	$420,523	$393,651	$342,161	$129,756
$1,500	$2,269	$3,535	27 Y & 3 M	$411,730	$378,806	$319,291	$224,329	$0
$1,750	$2,647	$4,124	22 Y & 11 M	$394,173	$337,097	$244,960	$106,560	$0
$2,000	$3,025	$4,713	19 Y & 9 M	$376,612	$295,365	$170,578	$0	$0
$2,250	$3,403	$5,302	17 Y & 5 M	$359,057	$253,662	$96,253	$0	$0
$2,500	$3,782	$5,891	15 Y & 6 M	$341,498	$211,940	$21,894	$0	$0

4% COLA

Monthly Amount	15 Yr Inflated	30 Yr Inflated	Money Lasts	5 Years	10 Years	15 Years	20 Years	30 Years
$750	$1,299	$2,339	Over 40 Yrs	$463,384	$498,453	$526,968	$544,451	$519,684
$1,000	$1,732	$3,119	36 Y & 2 M	$445,483	$454,891	$447,462	$415,465	$233,264
$1,250	$2,165	$3,899	28 Y & 11 M	$427,583	$411,334	$367,974	$286,516	$0
$1,500	$2,598	$4,678	24 Y & 1 M	$409,683	$367,782	$288,495	$157,584	$0
$1,750	$3,031	$5,458	20 Y & 8 M	$391,783	$324,220	$208,992	$28,614	$0
$2,000	$3,463	$6,237	18 Y & 1 M	$373,888	$280,681	$129,540	$0	$0
$2,250	$3,896	$7,017	16 Y & 1 M	$355,989	$237,128	$50,052	$0	$0

$425,000 Balance	**5% Return On Investment**

No COLA

Monthly Amount	15 Yr Inflated	30 Yr Inflated	Money Lasts	5 Years	10 Years	15 Years	20 Years	30 Years
$1,250	$1,250	$1,250	Over 40 Yrs	$457,463	$498,895	$551,774	$619,263	$815,330
$1,500	$1,500	$1,500	Over 40 Yrs	$440,471	$460,218	$485,420	$517,586	$611,030
$1,750	$1,750	$1,750	Over 40 Yrs	$423,481	$421,542	$419,068	$415,909	$406,731
$2,000	$2,000	$2,000	Over 40 Yrs	$406,490	$382,866	$352,713	$314,231	$202,435
$2,250	$2,250	$2,250	29 Y & 11 M	$389,497	$344,186	$286,357	$212,550	$0
$2,500	$2,500	$2,500	24 Y & 1 M	$372,507	$305,510	$220,004	$110,874	$0
$2,750	$2,750	$2,750	20 Y & 4 M	$355,515	$266,833	$153,650	$9,197	$0

2% COLA

Monthly Amount	15 Yr Inflated	30 Yr Inflated	Money Lasts	5 Years	10 Years	15 Years	20 Years	30 Years
$1,000	$1,320	$1,776	Over 40 Yrs	$471,817	$524,215	$582,978	$649,021	$807,446
$1,250	$1,650	$2,220	Over 40 Yrs	$454,168	$482,208	$507,844	$529,361	$550,072
$1,500	$1,979	$2,664	Over 40 Yrs	$436,515	$440,190	$432,707	$409,716	$292,770
$1,750	$2,309	$3,108	30 Y & 11 M	$418,866	$398,175	$357,571	$290,076	$35,477
$2,000	$2,639	$3,552	25 Y & 3 M	$401,216	$356,162	$282,434	$170,421	$0
$2,250	$2,969	$3,996	21 Y & 4 M	$383,563	$314,142	$207,290	$50,761	$0
$2,500	$3,299	$4,440	18 Y & 6 M	$365,914	$272,137	$132,171	$0	$0

3% COLA

Monthly Amount	15 Yr Inflated	30 Yr Inflated	Money Lasts	5 Years	10 Years	15 Years	20 Years	30 Years
$1,000	$1,513	$2,357	Over 40 Yrs	$470,460	$517,020	$563,156	$606,630	$671,578
$1,250	$1,891	$2,946	Over 40 Yrs	$452,469	$473,205	$483,060	$476,380	$380,293
$1,500	$2,269	$3,535	32 Y & 2 M	$434,481	$429,387	$402,953	$346,106	$88,919
$1,750	$2,647	$4,124	26 Y & 2 M	$416,493	$385,581	$322,878	$215,900	$0
$2,000	$3,025	$4,713	22 Y & 1 M	$398,499	$341,748	$242,743	$85,576	$0
$2,250	$3,403	$5,302	19 Y & 1 M	$380,513	$297,948	$162,675	$0	$0
$2,500	$3,782	$5,891	16 Y & 10 M	$362,521	$254,127	$82,568	$0	$0

4% COLA

Monthly Amount	15 Yr Inflated	30 Yr Inflated	Money Lasts	5 Years	10 Years	15 Years	20 Years	30 Years
$750	$1,299	$2,339	Over 40 Yrs	$487,414	$555,158	$627,122	$701,336	$841,989
$1,000	$1,732	$3,119	Over 40 Yrs	$469,077	$509,441	$541,620	$559,172	$510,205
$1,250	$2,165	$3,899	33 Y & 10 M	$450,741	$463,730	$456,139	$417,045	$178,507
$1,500	$2,598	$4,678	27 Y & 5 M	$432,403	$418,018	$370,663	$274,936	$0
$1,750	$3,031	$5,458	22 Y & 11 M	$414,066	$372,300	$285,161	$132,782	$0
$2,000	$3,463	$6,237	19 Y & 10 M	$395,736	$326,608	$199,718	$0	$0
$2,250	$3,896	$7,017	17 Y & 5 M	$377,398	$280,894	$114,229	$0	$0

| $425,000 Balance | | | | | 6% Return On Investment | | | |

No COLA

Monthly Amount	15 Yr Inflated	30 Yr Inflated	Money Lasts	5 Years	10 Years	15 Years	20 Years	30 Years
$1,500	$1,500	$1,500	Over 40 Yrs	$464,234	$516,738	$587,000	$681,027	$975,245
$1,750	$1,750	$1,750	Over 40 Yrs	$446,815	$476,009	$515,077	$567,359	$730,952
$2,000	$2,000	$2,000	Over 40 Yrs	$429,397	$435,281	$443,157	$453,694	$486,670
$2,250	$2,250	$2,250	Over 40 Yrs	$411,978	$394,552	$371,232	$340,025	$242,376
$2,500	$2,500	$2,500	29 Y & 11 M	$394,561	$353,826	$299,312	$226,361	$0
$2,750	$2,750	$2,750	23 Y & 10 M	$377,142	$313,096	$227,390	$112,695	$0
$3,000	$3,000	$3,000	19 Y & 11 M	$359,723	$272,367	$155,466	$0	$0

2% COLA

Monthly Amount	15 Yr Inflated	30 Yr Inflated	Money Lasts	5 Years	10 Years	15 Years	20 Years	30 Years
$1,250	$1,650	$2,220	Over 40 Yrs	$478,308	$540,234	$612,701	$698,199	$922,108
$1,500	$1,979	$2,664	Over 40 Yrs	$460,220	$496,055	$531,537	$565,245	$618,386
$1,750	$2,309	$3,108	Over 40 Yrs	$442,134	$451,880	$450,375	$432,299	$314,682
$2,000	$2,639	$3,552	30 Y & 4 M	$424,045	$407,705	$369,210	$299,336	$10,917
$2,250	$2,969	$3,996	24 Y & 7 M	$405,955	$363,523	$288,037	$166,363	$0
$2,500	$3,299	$4,440	20 Y & 9 M	$387,869	$319,356	$206,889	$33,430	$0
$2,750	$3,629	$4,884	17 Y & 11 M	$369,782	$275,184	$125,723	$0	$0

3% COLA

Monthly Amount	15 Yr Inflated	30 Yr Inflated	Money Lasts	5 Years	10 Years	15 Years	20 Years	30 Years
$1,250	$1,891	$2,946	Over 40 Yrs	$476,585	$530,940	$586,665	$641,506	$733,122
$1,500	$2,269	$3,535	Over 40 Yrs	$458,154	$484,906	$500,282	$497,182	$391,484
$1,750	$2,647	$4,124	30 Y & 11 M	$439,722	$438,880	$413,930	$352,927	$50,073
$2,000	$3,025	$4,713	25 Y & 4 M	$421,288	$392,831	$327,518	$208,551	$0
$2,250	$3,403	$5,302	21 Y & 5 M	$402,859	$346,810	$241,172	$64,293	$0
$2,500	$3,782	$5,891	18 Y & 7 M	$384,426	$300,774	$154,793	$0	$0
$2,750	$4,160	$6,481	16 Y & 5 M	$365,993	$254,735	$68,405	$0	$0

4% COLA

Monthly Amount	15 Yr Inflated	30 Yr Inflated	Money Lasts	5 Years	10 Years	15 Years	20 Years	30 Years
$1,000	$1,732	$3,119	Over 40 Yrs	$493,615	$569,158	$650,446	$735,132	$895,913
$1,250	$2,165	$3,899	Over 40 Yrs	$474,831	$521,168	$558,420	$578,148	$509,598
$1,500	$2,598	$4,678	32 Y & 3 M	$456,047	$473,180	$466,401	$421,183	$123,351
$1,750	$3,031	$5,458	26 Y & 3 M	$437,263	$425,182	$374,355	$264,170	$0
$2,000	$3,463	$6,237	22 Y & 2 M	$418,483	$377,209	$282,369	$107,267	$0
$2,250	$3,896	$7,017	19 Y & 2 M	$399,701	$329,222	$190,343	$0	$0
$2,500	$4,329	$7,796	16 Y & 11 M	$380,916	$281,228	$98,316	$0	$0

$450,000 Balance   3% Return On Investment

No COLA

Monthly Amount	15 Yr Inflated	30 Yr Inflated	Money Lasts	5 Years	10 Years	15 Years	20 Years	30 Years
$1,000	$1,000	$1,000	Over 40 Yrs	$457,008	$465,131	$474,549	$485,467	$512,798
$1,250	$1,250	$1,250	Over 40 Yrs	$440,841	$430,223	$417,916	$403,647	$367,930
$1,500	$1,500	$1,500	Over 40 Yrs	$424,676	$395,318	$361,284	$321,830	$223,068
$1,750	$1,750	$1,750	33 Y & 11 M	$408,509	$360,409	$304,648	$240,005	$78,195
$2,000	$2,000	$2,000	27 Y & 4 M	$392,343	$325,503	$248,016	$158,188	$0
$2,250	$2,250	$2,250	22 Y & 11 M	$376,177	$290,596	$191,383	$76,369	$0
$2,500	$2,500	$2,500	19 Y & 10 M	$360,011	$255,688	$134,749	$0	$0

2% COLA

Monthly Amount	15 Yr Inflated	30 Yr Inflated	Money Lasts	5 Years	10 Years	15 Years	20 Years	30 Years
$750	$990	$1,332	Over 40 Yrs	$471,254	$490,642	$507,324	$520,265	$529,621
$1,000	$1,320	$1,776	Over 40 Yrs	$454,446	$452,600	$442,735	$422,774	$342,066
$1,250	$1,650	$2,220	35 Y & 11 M	$437,642	$414,570	$378,159	$325,281	$154,492
$1,500	$1,979	$2,664	28 Y & 11 M	$420,836	$376,530	$313,577	$227,799	$0
$1,750	$2,309	$3,108	24 Y & 4 M	$404,030	$338,490	$248,995	$130,320	$0
$2,000	$2,639	$3,552	20 Y & 11 M	$387,222	$300,452	$184,411	$32,829	$0
$2,250	$2,969	$3,996	18 Y & 5 M	$370,415	$262,409	$119,825	$0	$0

3% COLA

Monthly Amount	15 Yr Inflated	30 Yr Inflated	Money Lasts	5 Years	10 Years	15 Years	20 Years	30 Years
$750	$1,134	$1,767	Over 40 Yrs	$470,267	$485,577	$493,835	$492,408	$446,506
$1,000	$1,513	$2,357	38 Y & 1 M	$453,129	$445,842	$424,736	$385,593	$231,161
$1,250	$1,891	$2,946	30 Y & 6 M	$435,994	$406,112	$355,651	$278,809	$15,906
$1,500	$2,269	$3,535	25 Y & 5 M	$418,859	$366,381	$286,556	$172,005	$0
$1,750	$2,647	$4,124	21 Y & 9 M	$401,723	$326,657	$217,486	$65,257	$0
$2,000	$3,025	$4,713	19 Y & 1 M	$384,584	$286,912	$148,368	$0	$0
$2,250	$3,403	$5,302	16 Y & 11 M	$367,453	$247,195	$79,307	$0	$0

4% COLA

Monthly Amount	15 Yr Inflated	30 Yr Inflated	Money Lasts	5 Years	10 Years	15 Years	20 Years	30 Years
$500	$866	$1,560	Over 40 Yrs	$486,728	$521,728	$553,087	$578,228	$595,118
$750	$1,299	$2,339	Over 40 Yrs	$469,260	$480,235	$479,145	$461,079	$346,830
$1,000	$1,732	$3,119	32 Y & 7 M	$451,786	$438,715	$405,137	$343,801	$98,208
$1,250	$2,165	$3,899	26 Y & 10 M	$434,313	$397,201	$331,148	$226,553	$0
$1,500	$2,598	$4,678	22 Y & 10 M	$416,842	$355,691	$257,169	$109,331	$0
$1,750	$3,031	$5,458	19 Y & 10 M	$399,368	$314,171	$183,163	$0	$0
$2,000	$3,463	$6,237	17 Y & 7 M	$381,900	$272,672	$109,206	$0	$0

| $450,000 Balance | | | | | | 4% Return On Investment | | |

No COLA

Monthly Amount	15 Yr Inflated	30 Yr Inflated	Money Lasts	5 Years	10 Years	15 Years	20 Years	30 Years
$1,250	$1,250	$1,250	Over 40 Yrs	$464,624	$482,416	$504,065	$530,403	$601,434
$1,500	$1,500	$1,500	Over 40 Yrs	$448,051	$445,679	$442,794	$439,284	$429,814
$1,750	$1,750	$1,750	Over 40 Yrs	$431,476	$408,940	$381,522	$348,163	$258,196
$2,000	$2,000	$2,000	33 Y & 11 M	$414,902	$372,201	$320,247	$257,039	$86,571
$2,250	$2,250	$2,250	27 Y & 1 M	$398,329	$335,463	$258,977	$165,920	$0
$2,500	$2,500	$2,500	22 Y & 8 M	$381,755	$298,723	$197,703	$74,796	$0
$2,750	$2,750	$2,750	19 Y & 7 M	$365,181	$261,985	$136,431	$0	$0

2% COLA

Monthly Amount	15 Yr Inflated	30 Yr Inflated	Money Lasts	5 Years	10 Years	15 Years	20 Years	30 Years
$1,000	$1,320	$1,776	Over 40 Yrs	$478,599	$506,220	$531,906	$554,421	$583,086
$1,250	$1,650	$2,220	Over 40 Yrs	$461,376	$466,254	$462,284	$446,523	$363,945
$1,500	$1,979	$2,664	34 Y & 9 M	$444,151	$426,280	$392,658	$338,637	$144,873
$1,750	$2,309	$3,108	28 Y & 1 M	$426,931	$386,313	$323,041	$230,766	$0
$2,000	$2,639	$3,552	23 Y & 8 M	$409,705	$346,338	$253,407	$122,862	$0
$2,250	$2,969	$3,996	20 Y & 5 M	$392,481	$306,365	$183,782	$14,971	$0
$2,500	$3,299	$4,440	17 Y & 11 M	$375,259	$266,403	$114,172	$0	$0

3% COLA

Monthly Amount	15 Yr Inflated	30 Yr Inflated	Money Lasts	5 Years	10 Years	15 Years	20 Years	30 Years
$1,000	$1,513	$2,357	Over 40 Yrs	$477,262	$499,246	$513,023	$514,749	$460,561
$1,250	$1,891	$2,946	36 Y & 1 M	$459,704	$457,529	$438,674	$396,939	$210,842
$1,500	$2,269	$3,535	29 Y & 2 M	$442,147	$415,812	$364,315	$279,108	$0
$1,750	$2,647	$4,124	24 Y & 5 M	$424,590	$374,104	$289,987	$161,342	$0
$2,000	$3,025	$4,713	21 Y & 1 M	$407,028	$332,371	$215,600	$43,463	$0
$2,250	$3,403	$5,302	18 Y & 6 M	$389,474	$290,668	$141,277	$0	$0
$2,500	$3,782	$5,891	16 Y & 6 M	$371,915	$248,948	$66,921	$0	$0

4% COLA

Monthly Amount	15 Yr Inflated	30 Yr Inflated	Money Lasts	5 Years	10 Years	15 Years	20 Years	30 Years
$750	$1,299	$2,339	Over 40 Yrs	$493,800	$535,460	$571,994	$599,232	$600,771
$1,000	$1,732	$3,119	38 Y & 3 M	$475,900	$491,899	$492,490	$470,249	$314,358
$1,250	$2,165	$3,899	30 Y & 7 M	$457,999	$448,341	$412,999	$341,295	$28,012
$1,500	$2,598	$4,678	25 Y & 6 M	$440,100	$404,788	$333,521	$212,367	$0
$1,750	$3,031	$5,458	21 Y & 10 M	$422,199	$361,226	$254,014	$83,391	$0
$2,000	$3,463	$6,237	19 Y & 2 M	$404,305	$317,688	$174,563	$0	$0
$2,250	$3,896	$7,017	16 Y & 11 M	$386,405	$274,133	$95,074	$0	$0

| $450,000 Balance | | | | 5% Return On Investment | | | | |

No COLA

Monthly Amount	15 Yr Inflated	30 Yr Inflated	Money Lasts	5 Years	10 Years	15 Years	20 Years	30 Years
$1,250	$1,250	$1,250	Over 40 Yrs	$489,369	$539,616	$603,745	$685,592	$923,373
$1,500	$1,500	$1,500	Over 40 Yrs	$472,379	$500,941	$537,394	$583,919	$719,082
$1,750	$1,750	$1,750	Over 40 Yrs	$455,388	$462,265	$471,042	$482,243	$514,784
$2,000	$2,000	$2,000	Over 40 Yrs	$438,396	$423,586	$404,684	$380,560	$310,477
$2,250	$2,250	$2,250	34 Y & 5 M	$421,405	$384,909	$338,330	$278,884	$106,179
$2,500	$2,500	$2,500	26 Y & 11 M	$404,414	$346,233	$271,978	$177,207	$0
$2,750	$2,750	$2,750	22 Y & 6 M	$387,422	$307,555	$205,622	$75,527	$0

2% COLA

Monthly Amount	15 Yr Inflated	30 Yr Inflated	Money Lasts	5 Years	10 Years	15 Years	20 Years	30 Years
$1,000	$1,320	$1,776	Over 40 Yrs	$503,723	$564,936	$634,949	$715,351	$915,489
$1,250	$1,650	$2,220	Over 40 Yrs	$486,075	$522,930	$559,817	$595,695	$658,120
$1,500	$1,979	$2,664	Over 40 Yrs	$468,424	$480,914	$484,683	$476,050	$400,822
$1,750	$2,309	$3,108	34 Y & 1 M	$450,773	$438,897	$409,544	$356,408	$143,525
$2,000	$2,639	$3,552	27 Y & 6 M	$433,122	$396,884	$334,407	$236,753	$0
$2,250	$2,969	$3,996	23 Y & 1 M	$415,471	$354,866	$259,265	$117,094	$0
$2,500	$3,299	$4,440	19 Y & 11 M	$397,821	$312,860	$184,145	$0	$0

3% COLA

Monthly Amount	15 Yr Inflated	30 Yr Inflated	Money Lasts	5 Years	10 Years	15 Years	20 Years	30 Years
$1,000	$1,513	$2,357	Over 40 Yrs	$502,367	$557,743	$615,130	$672,965	$779,632
$1,250	$1,891	$2,946	Over 40 Yrs	$484,375	$513,924	$535,030	$542,707	$488,332
$1,500	$2,269	$3,535	34 Y & 10 M	$466,387	$470,110	$454,925	$412,436	$196,962
$1,750	$2,647	$4,124	28 Y & 2 M	$448,399	$426,301	$374,849	$282,229	$0
$2,000	$3,025	$4,713	23 Y & 9 M	$430,406	$382,472	$294,718	$151,911	$0
$2,250	$3,403	$5,302	20 Y & 6 M	$412,420	$338,671	$214,649	$21,704	$0
$2,500	$3,782	$5,891	17 Y & 11 M	$394,428	$294,850	$134,542	$0	$0

4% COLA

Monthly Amount	15 Yr Inflated	30 Yr Inflated	Money Lasts	5 Years	10 Years	15 Years	20 Years	30 Years
$750	$1,299	$2,339	Over 40 Yrs	$519,321	$595,881	$679,096	$767,670	$950,042
$1,000	$1,732	$3,119	Over 40 Yrs	$500,984	$550,163	$593,593	$625,504	$618,255
$1,250	$2,165	$3,899	36 Y & 3 M	$482,647	$504,451	$508,110	$483,373	$286,548
$1,500	$2,598	$4,678	29 Y & 3 M	$464,311	$458,742	$422,638	$341,269	$0
$1,750	$3,031	$5,458	24 Y & 6 M	$445,974	$413,023	$337,135	$199,115	$0
$2,000	$3,463	$6,237	21 Y & 2 M	$427,642	$367,329	$251,688	$57,060	$0
$2,250	$3,896	$7,017	18 Y & 7 M	$409,305	$321,616	$166,201	$0	$0

$450,000 Balance				6% Return On Investment				

No COLA

Monthly Amount	15 Yr Inflated	30 Yr Inflated	Money Lasts	5 Years	10 Years	15 Years	20 Years	30 Years
$1,500	$1,500	$1,500	Over 40 Yrs	$497,691	$561,511	$646,917	$761,210	$1.119 M
$1,750	$1,750	$1,750	Over 40 Yrs	$480,272	$520,782	$574,994	$647,542	$874,549
$2,000	$2,000	$2,000	Over 40 Yrs	$462,854	$480,053	$503,070	$533,872	$630,255
$2,250	$2,250	$2,250	Over 40 Yrs	$445,433	$439,322	$431,144	$420,201	$385,958
$2,500	$2,500	$2,500	35 Y & 7 M	$428,015	$398,595	$359,225	$306,538	$141,676
$2,750	$2,750	$2,750	27 Y & 2 M	$410,597	$357,868	$287,303	$192,871	$0
$3,000	$3,000	$3,000	22 Y & 5 M	$393,178	$317,137	$215,377	$79,200	$0

2% COLA

Monthly Amount	15 Yr Inflated	30 Yr Inflated	Money Lasts	5 Years	10 Years	15 Years	20 Years	30 Years
$1,250	$1,650	$2,220	Over 40 Yrs	$511,764	$585,005	$672,617	$778,382	$1.066 M
$1,500	$1,979	$2,664	Over 40 Yrs	$493,675	$540,826	$591,451	$645,425	$761,978
$1,750	$2,309	$3,108	Over 40 Yrs	$475,588	$496,651	$510,290	$512,480	$458,273
$2,000	$2,639	$3,552	33 Y & 11 M	$457,499	$452,475	$429,121	$379,509	$154,496
$2,250	$2,969	$3,996	27 Y & 2 M	$439,412	$408,296	$347,954	$246,545	$0
$2,500	$3,299	$4,440	22 Y & 9 M	$421,326	$364,131	$266,809	$113,617	$0
$2,750	$3,629	$4,884	19 Y & 8 M	$403,238	$319,954	$185,635	$0	$0

3% COLA

Monthly Amount	15 Yr Inflated	30 Yr Inflated	Money Lasts	5 Years	10 Years	15 Years	20 Years	30 Years
$1,250	$1,891	$2,946	Over 40 Yrs	$510,041	$575,713	$646,581	$721,687	$876,716
$1,500	$2,269	$3,535	Over 40 Yrs	$491,609	$529,677	$560,195	$577,358	$535,065
$1,750	$2,647	$4,124	34 Y & 2 M	$473,178	$483,651	$473,842	$433,104	$193,657
$2,000	$3,025	$4,713	27 Y & 7 M	$454,743	$437,601	$387,431	$288,727	$0
$2,250	$3,403	$5,302	23 Y & 2 M	$436,316	$391,583	$301,088	$144,475	$0
$2,500	$3,782	$5,891	19 Y & 11 M	$417,882	$345,544	$214,705	$0	$0
$2,750	$4,160	$6,481	17 Y & 8 M	$399,450	$299,508	$128,320	$0	$0

4% COLA

Monthly Amount	15 Yr Inflated	30 Yr Inflated	Money Lasts	5 Years	10 Years	15 Years	20 Years	30 Years
$1,000	$1,732	$3,119	Over 40 Yrs	$527,070	$613,928	$710,357	$815,308	$1.039 M
$1,250	$2,165	$3,899	Over 40 Yrs	$508,287	$565,940	$618,335	$658,328	$653,191
$1,500	$2,598	$4,678	34 Y & 11 M	$489,503	$517,952	$526,319	$501,367	$266,948
$1,750	$3,031	$5,458	28 Y & 3 M	$470,718	$469,953	$434,271	$344,351	$0
$2,000	$3,463	$6,237	23 Y & 9 M	$451,940	$421,982	$342,285	$187,447	$0
$2,250	$3,896	$7,017	20 Y & 7 M	$433,155	$373,992	$250,257	$30,458	$0
$2,500	$4,329	$7,796	18 Y & 1 M	$414,371	$325,997	$158,229	$0	$0

| $475,000 Balance | | | | | | 3% Return On Investment | | |

No COLA

Monthly Amount	15 Yr Inflated	30 Yr Inflated	Money Lasts	5 Years	10 Years	15 Years	20 Years	30 Years
$1,250	$1,250	$1,250	Over 40 Yrs	$469,825	$463,825	$456,868	$448,803	$428,615
$1,500	$1,500	$1,500	Over 40 Yrs	$453,656	$428,915	$400,230	$366,978	$283,741
$1,750	$1,750	$1,750	37 Y & 5 M	$437,491	$394,008	$343,599	$285,162	$138,883
$2,000	$2,000	$2,000	29 Y & 9 M	$421,325	$359,101	$286,966	$203,341	$0
$2,250	$2,250	$2,250	24 Y & 10 M	$405,158	$324,193	$230,331	$121,520	$0
$2,500	$2,500	$2,500	21 Y & 5 M	$388,992	$289,285	$173,698	$39,701	$0
$2,750	$2,750	$2,750	18 Y & 9 M	$372,826	$254,378	$117,063	$0	$0

2% COLA

Monthly Amount	15 Yr Inflated	30 Yr Inflated	Money Lasts	5 Years	10 Years	15 Years	20 Years	30 Years
$1,000	$1,320	$1,776	Over 40 Yrs	$483,429	$486,199	$481,686	$467,927	$402,746
$1,250	$1,650	$2,220	38 Y & 4 M	$466,623	$448,166	$417,106	$370,432	$215,173
$1,500	$1,979	$2,664	30 Y & 11 M	$449,816	$410,126	$352,524	$272,949	$27,656
$1,750	$2,309	$3,108	25 Y & 10 M	$433,012	$372,089	$287,944	$175,472	$0
$2,000	$2,639	$3,552	22 Y & 3 M	$416,205	$334,050	$223,360	$77,980	$0
$2,250	$2,969	$3,996	19 Y & 7 M	$399,397	$296,009	$158,775	$0	$0
$2,500	$3,299	$4,440	17 Y & 5 M	$382,592	$257,977	$94,203	$0	$0

3% COLA

Monthly Amount	15 Yr Inflated	30 Yr Inflated	Money Lasts	5 Years	10 Years	15 Years	20 Years	30 Years
$1,000	$1,513	$2,357	Over 40 Yrs	$482,112	$479,441	$463,687	$430,747	$291,843
$1,250	$1,891	$2,946	32 Y & 2 M	$464,975	$439,708	$394,598	$323,959	$76,582
$1,500	$2,269	$3,535	26 Y & 10 M	$447,840	$399,977	$325,502	$217,154	$0
$1,750	$2,647	$4,124	22 Y & 11 M	$430,705	$360,255	$256,437	$110,411	$0
$2,000	$3,025	$4,713	20 Y & 1 M	$413,566	$320,510	$187,315	$3,564	$0
$2,250	$3,403	$5,302	17 Y & 11 M	$396,434	$280,792	$118,254	$0	$0
$2,500	$3,782	$5,891	16 Y & 1 M	$379,297	$241,059	$49,162	$0	$0

4% COLA

Monthly Amount	15 Yr Inflated	30 Yr Inflated	Money Lasts	5 Years	10 Years	15 Years	20 Years	30 Years
$750	$1,299	$2,339	Over 40 Yrs	$498,242	$513,833	$518,093	$506,232	$407,511
$1,000	$1,732	$3,119	34 Y & 1 M	$480,769	$472,312	$444,084	$388,950	$158,885
$1,250	$2,165	$3,899	28 Y & 2 M	$463,296	$430,799	$370,098	$271,708	$0
$1,500	$2,598	$4,678	23 Y & 11 M	$445,823	$389,287	$296,117	$154,481	$0
$1,750	$3,031	$5,458	20 Y & 10 M	$428,349	$347,766	$222,110	$37,213	$0
$2,000	$3,463	$6,237	18 Y & 6 M	$410,882	$306,270	$148,154	$0	$0
$2,250	$3,896	$7,017	16 Y & 7 M	$393,410	$264,759	$74,166	$0	$0

$475,000 Balance		4% Return On Investment

No COLA

Monthly Amount	15 Yr Inflated	30 Yr Inflated	Money Lasts	5 Years	10 Years	15 Years	20 Years	30 Years
$1,500	$1,500	$1,500	Over 40 Yrs	$478,467	$482,685	$487,816	$494,060	$510,895
$1,750	$1,750	$1,750	Over 40 Yrs	$461,893	$445,946	$426,545	$402,940	$339,280
$2,000	$2,000	$2,000	38 Y & 2 M	$445,319	$409,207	$365,270	$311,814	$167,652
$2,250	$2,250	$2,250	29 Y & 11 M	$428,744	$372,467	$303,997	$220,693	$0
$2,500	$2,500	$2,500	24 Y & 9 M	$412,171	$335,730	$242,727	$129,575	$0
$2,750	$2,750	$2,750	21 Y & 3 M	$395,598	$298,991	$181,456	$38,456	$0
$3,000	$3,000	$3,000	18 Y & 7 M	$379,022	$262,252	$120,183	$0	$0

2% COLA

Monthly Amount	15 Yr Inflated	30 Yr Inflated	Money Lasts	5 Years	10 Years	15 Years	20 Years	30 Years
$1,250	$1,650	$2,220	Over 40 Yrs	$491,793	$503,261	$507,310	$501,304	$445,035
$1,500	$1,979	$2,664	37 Y & 7 M	$474,568	$463,286	$437,683	$393,417	$225,960
$1,750	$2,309	$3,108	30 Y & 3 M	$457,346	$423,316	$368,060	$285,539	$6,901
$2,000	$2,639	$3,552	25 Y & 4 M	$440,121	$383,345	$298,433	$177,643	$0
$2,250	$2,969	$3,996	21 Y & 10 M	$422,897	$343,370	$228,804	$69,747	$0
$2,500	$3,299	$4,440	19 Y & 2 M	$405,675	$303,408	$159,195	$0	$0
$2,750	$3,629	$4,884	17 Y & 1 M	$388,451	$263,437	$89,563	$0	$0

3% COLA

Monthly Amount	15 Yr Inflated	30 Yr Inflated	Money Lasts	5 Years	10 Years	15 Years	20 Years	30 Years
$1,250	$1,891	$2,946	38 Y & 6 M	$490,119	$494,534	$483,696	$451,714	$291,923
$1,500	$2,269	$3,535	30 Y & 11 M	$472,563	$452,818	$409,338	$333,886	$42,131
$1,750	$2,647	$4,124	25 Y & 11 M	$455,006	$411,110	$335,010	$216,119	$0
$2,000	$3,025	$4,713	22 Y & 4 M	$437,444	$369,375	$260,622	$98,239	$0
$2,250	$3,403	$5,302	19 Y & 8 M	$419,890	$327,675	$186,301	$0	$0
$2,500	$3,782	$5,891	17 Y & 6 M	$402,331	$285,955	$111,944	$0	$0
$2,750	$4,160	$6,481	15 Y & 9 M	$384,772	$244,234	$37,581	$0	$0

4% COLA

Monthly Amount	15 Yr Inflated	30 Yr Inflated	Money Lasts	5 Years	10 Years	15 Years	20 Years	30 Years
$1,000	$1,732	$3,119	Over 40 Yrs	$506,316	$528,903	$537,509	$525,021	$395,435
$1,250	$2,165	$3,899	32 Y & 4 M	$488,416	$485,348	$458,024	$396,074	$109,100
$1,500	$2,598	$4,678	26 Y & 11 M	$470,515	$441,794	$378,544	$267,143	$0
$1,750	$3,031	$5,458	23 Y & 1 M	$452,616	$398,234	$299,043	$138,175	$0
$2,000	$3,463	$6,237	20 Y & 3 M	$434,722	$354,696	$219,589	$9,293	$0
$2,250	$3,896	$7,017	17 Y & 11 M	$416,822	$311,140	$140,099	$0	$0
$2,500	$4,329	$7,796	16 Y & 2 M	$398,922	$267,583	$60,614	$0	$0

	$475,000 Balance			**5% Return On Investment**			

No COLA

Monthly Amount	15 Yr Inflated	30 Yr Inflated	Money Lasts	5 Years	10 Years	15 Years	20 Years	30 Years
$1,500	$1,500	$1,500	Over 40 Yrs	$504,285	$541,661	$589,365	$650,248	$827,124
$1,750	$1,750	$1,750	Over 40 Yrs	$487,295	$502,987	$523,014	$548,575	$622,833
$2,000	$2,000	$2,000	Over 40 Yrs	$470,304	$464,309	$456,658	$446,894	$418,529
$2,250	$2,250	$2,250	Over 40 Yrs	$453,312	$425,632	$390,305	$345,217	$214,229
$2,500	$2,500	$2,500	30 Y & 4 M	$436,322	$386,956	$323,953	$243,543	$9,938
$2,750	$2,750	$2,750	24 Y & 10 M	$419,329	$348,277	$257,595	$141,860	$0
$3,000	$3,000	$3,000	21 Y & 2 M	$402,338	$309,602	$191,244	$40,185	$0

2% COLA

Monthly Amount	15 Yr Inflated	30 Yr Inflated	Money Lasts	5 Years	10 Years	15 Years	20 Years	30 Years
$1,250	$1,650	$2,220	Over 40 Yrs	$517,981	$563,651	$611,789	$662,025	$766,165
$1,500	$1,979	$2,664	Over 40 Yrs	$500,330	$521,635	$536,655	$542,382	$508,867
$1,750	$2,309	$3,108	37 Y & 5 M	$482,681	$479,621	$461,519	$422,742	$251,579
$2,000	$2,639	$3,552	29 Y & 11 M	$465,030	$437,606	$386,379	$303,084	$0
$2,250	$2,969	$3,996	24 Y & 11 M	$447,378	$395,589	$311,240	$183,429	$0
$2,500	$3,299	$4,440	21 Y & 6 M	$429,727	$353,580	$236,114	$63,797	$0
$2,750	$3,629	$4,884	18 Y & 11 M	$412,078	$311,568	$160,974	$0	$0

3% COLA

Monthly Amount	15 Yr Inflated	30 Yr Inflated	Money Lasts	5 Years	10 Years	15 Years	20 Years	30 Years
$1,250	$1,891	$2,946	Over 40 Yrs	$516,284	$554,648	$587,004	$609,042	$596,386
$1,500	$2,269	$3,535	37 Y & 8 M	$498,295	$510,834	$506,900	$478,771	$305,018
$1,750	$2,647	$4,124	30 Y & 4 M	$480,306	$467,026	$426,825	$348,566	$13,859
$2,000	$3,025	$4,713	25 Y & 5 M	$462,313	$423,194	$346,690	$218,243	$0
$2,250	$3,403	$5,302	21 Y & 11 M	$444,327	$379,393	$266,623	$88,038	$0
$2,500	$3,782	$5,891	19 Y & 3 M	$426,336	$335,574	$186,517	$0	$0
$2,750	$4,160	$6,481	17 Y & 2 M	$408,344	$291,752	$106,405	$0	$0

4% COLA

Monthly Amount	15 Yr Inflated	30 Yr Inflated	Money Lasts	5 Years	10 Years	15 Years	20 Years	30 Years
$1,000	$1,732	$3,119	Over 40 Yrs	$532,892	$590,887	$645,568	$691,839	$726,305
$1,250	$2,165	$3,899	38 Y & 8 M	$514,554	$545,172	$560,083	$549,706	$394,599
$1,500	$2,598	$4,678	31 Y & 2 M	$496,218	$499,464	$474,611	$407,603	$62,970
$1,750	$3,031	$5,458	26 Y & 1 M	$477,880	$453,744	$389,106	$265,445	$0
$2,000	$3,463	$6,237	22 Y & 5 M	$459,550	$408,053	$303,665	$123,397	$0
$2,250	$3,896	$7,017	19 Y & 8 M	$441,212	$362,338	$218,172	$0	$0
$2,500	$4,329	$7,796	17 Y & 7 M	$422,876	$316,624	$132,692	$0	$0

| $475,000 Balance | | | | | 6% Return On Investment | | | |

No COLA

Monthly Amount	15 Yr Inflated	30 Yr Inflated	Money Lasts	5 Years	10 Years	15 Years	20 Years	30 Years
$1,750	$1,750	$1,750	Over 40 Yrs	$513,726	$565,552	$634,905	$727,715	$1.018 M
$2,000	$2,000	$2,000	Over 40 Yrs	$496,308	$524,823	$562,982	$614,048	$773,837
$2,250	$2,250	$2,250	Over 40 Yrs	$478,889	$484,094	$491,060	$500,383	$529,554
$2,500	$2,500	$2,500	Over 40 Yrs	$461,471	$443,366	$419,138	$386,715	$285,264
$2,750	$2,750	$2,750	31 Y & 4 M	$444,052	$402,637	$347,214	$273,046	$40,970
$3,000	$3,000	$3,000	25 Y & 2 M	$426,634	$361,909	$275,294	$159,383	$0
$3,250	$3,250	$3,250	21 Y & 3 M	$409,216	$321,182	$203,372	$45,714	$0

2% COLA

Monthly Amount	15 Yr Inflated	30 Yr Inflated	Money Lasts	5 Years	10 Years	15 Years	20 Years	30 Years
$1,500	$1,979	$2,664	Over 40 Yrs	$527,131	$585,598	$651,366	$725,603	$905,563
$1,750	$2,309	$3,108	Over 40 Yrs	$509,045	$541,424	$570,205	$592,659	$601,862
$2,000	$2,639	$3,552	38 Y & 1 M	$490,955	$497,245	$489,034	$459,687	$298,081
$2,250	$2,969	$3,996	29 Y & 11 M	$472,866	$453,067	$407,868	$326,724	$0
$2,500	$3,299	$4,440	24 Y & 10 M	$454,780	$408,900	$326,719	$193,791	$0
$2,750	$3,629	$4,884	21 Y & 4 M	$436,693	$364,726	$245,550	$60,821	$0
$3,000	$3,958	$5,327	18 Y & 8 M	$418,607	$320,551	$164,389	$0	$0

3% COLA

Monthly Amount	15 Yr Inflated	30 Yr Inflated	Money Lasts	5 Years	10 Years	15 Years	20 Years	30 Years
$1,500	$2,269	$3,535	Over 40 Yrs	$525,065	$574,449	$620,108	$657,535	$678,651
$1,750	$2,647	$4,124	37 Y & 6 M	$506,634	$528,423	$533,759	$513,285	$337,250
$2,000	$3,025	$4,713	29 Y & 11 M	$488,199	$482,371	$447,344	$368,906	$0
$2,250	$3,403	$5,302	24 Y & 11 M	$469,771	$436,353	$361,002	$224,652	$0
$2,500	$3,782	$5,891	21 Y & 7 M	$451,337	$390,314	$274,618	$80,337	$0
$2,750	$4,160	$6,481	18 Y & 11 M	$432,904	$344,277	$188,232	$0	$0
$3,000	$4,538	$7,070	16 Y & 11 M	$414,475	$298,247	$101,870	$0	$0

4% COLA

Monthly Amount	15 Yr Inflated	30 Yr Inflated	Money Lasts	5 Years	10 Years	15 Years	20 Years	30 Years
$1,250	$2,165	$3,899	Over 40 Yrs	$541,742	$610,710	$678,246	$738,501	$796,768
$1,500	$2,598	$4,678	37 Y & 9 M	$522,957	$562,719	$586,227	$581,537	$410,520
$1,750	$3,031	$5,458	30 Y & 5 M	$504,175	$514,725	$494,185	$424,528	$24,194
$2,000	$3,463	$6,237	25 Y & 6 M	$485,395	$466,754	$402,200	$267,626	$0
$2,250	$3,896	$7,017	21 Y & 11 M	$466,611	$418,761	$310,168	$110,633	$0
$2,500	$4,329	$7,796	19 Y & 4 M	$447,827	$370,768	$218,143	$0	$0
$2,750	$4,762	$8,576	17 Y & 3 M	$429,043	$322,778	$126,108	$0	$0

| $500,000 Balance | | | | | 3% Return On Investment | | | |

No COLA

Monthly Amount	15 Yr Inflated	30 Yr Inflated	Money Lasts	5 Years	10 Years	15 Years	20 Years	30 Years
$1,250	$1,250	$1,250	Over 40 Yrs	$498,805	$497,419	$495,815	$493,953	$489,295
$1,500	$1,500	$1,500	Over 40 Yrs	$482,640	$462,513	$439,182	$412,134	$344,427
$1,750	$1,750	$1,750	Over 40 Yrs	$466,472	$427,604	$382,546	$330,311	$199,558
$2,000	$2,000	$2,000	32 Y & 5 M	$450,306	$392,697	$325,914	$248,492	$54,693
$2,250	$2,250	$2,250	26 Y & 10 M	$434,141	$357,791	$269,281	$166,673	$0
$2,500	$2,500	$2,500	22 Y & 11 M	$417,974	$322,882	$212,645	$84,849	$0
$2,750	$2,750	$2,750	20 Y & 2 M	$401,808	$287,975	$156,013	$3,033	$0

2% COLA

Monthly Amount	15 Yr Inflated	30 Yr Inflated	Money Lasts	5 Years	10 Years	15 Years	20 Years	30 Years
$1,000	$1,320	$1,776	Over 40 Yrs	$512,410	$519,797	$520,634	$513,080	$463,429
$1,250	$1,650	$2,220	Over 40 Yrs	$495,607	$481,767	$456,057	$415,587	$275,856
$1,500	$1,979	$2,664	32 Y & 10 M	$478,799	$443,725	$391,474	$318,102	$88,341
$1,750	$2,309	$3,108	27 Y & 5 M	$461,993	$405,687	$326,895	$220,629	$0
$2,000	$2,639	$3,552	23 Y & 7 M	$445,186	$367,647	$262,308	$123,134	$0
$2,250	$2,969	$3,996	20 Y & 8 M	$428,380	$329,606	$197,722	$25,640	$0
$2,500	$3,299	$4,440	18 Y & 5 M	$411,575	$291,576	$133,156	$0	$0

3% COLA

Monthly Amount	15 Yr Inflated	30 Yr Inflated	Money Lasts	5 Years	10 Years	15 Years	20 Years	30 Years
$1,000	$1,513	$2,357	Over 40 Yrs	$511,093	$513,038	$502,635	$475,900	$352,525
$1,250	$1,891	$2,946	33 Y & 10 M	$493,957	$473,308	$433,550	$369,116	$137,271
$1,500	$2,269	$3,535	28 Y & 3 M	$476,822	$433,576	$364,452	$262,308	$0
$1,750	$2,647	$4,124	24 Y & 2 M	$459,687	$393,852	$295,385	$155,562	$0
$2,000	$3,025	$4,713	21 Y & 2 M	$442,548	$354,108	$226,266	$48,718	$0
$2,250	$3,403	$5,302	18 Y & 10 M	$425,416	$314,391	$157,205	$0	$0
$2,500	$3,782	$5,891	16 Y & 11 M	$408,278	$274,656	$88,110	$0	$0

4% COLA

Monthly Amount	15 Yr Inflated	30 Yr Inflated	Money Lasts	5 Years	10 Years	15 Years	20 Years	30 Years
$750	$1,299	$2,339	Over 40 Yrs	$527,223	$547,429	$557,039	$551,379	$468,185
$1,000	$1,732	$3,119	35 Y & 8 M	$509,750	$505,912	$483,038	$434,109	$219,575
$1,250	$2,165	$3,899	29 Y & 5 M	$492,278	$464,398	$409,048	$316,862	$0
$1,500	$2,598	$4,678	25 Y & 1 M	$474,805	$422,886	$335,067	$199,636	$0
$1,750	$3,031	$5,458	21 Y & 10 M	$457,332	$381,366	$261,061	$82,369	$0
$2,000	$3,463	$6,237	19 Y & 4 M	$439,863	$339,866	$187,102	$0	$0
$2,250	$3,896	$7,017	17 Y & 5 M	$422,392	$298,356	$113,113	$0	$0

$500,000 Balance	4% Return On Investment

No COLA

Monthly Amount	15 Yr Inflated	30 Yr Inflated	Money Lasts	5 Years	10 Years	15 Years	20 Years	30 Years
$1,500	$1,500	$1,500	Over 40 Yrs	$508,884	$519,690	$532,840	$548,838	$591,983
$1,750	$1,750	$1,750	Over 40 Yrs	$492,309	$482,951	$471,567	$457,715	$420,361
$2,000	$2,000	$2,000	Over 40 Yrs	$475,735	$446,213	$410,294	$366,593	$248,737
$2,250	$2,250	$2,250	33 Y & 1 M	$459,161	$409,473	$349,020	$275,471	$77,118
$2,500	$2,500	$2,500	27 Y & 1 M	$442,586	$372,734	$287,748	$184,349	$0
$2,750	$2,750	$2,750	22 Y & 11 M	$426,013	$335,997	$226,478	$93,231	$0
$3,000	$3,000	$3,000	20 Y & 1 M	$409,439	$299,259	$165,206	$2,110	$0

2% COLA

Monthly Amount	15 Yr Inflated	30 Yr Inflated	Money Lasts	5 Years	10 Years	15 Years	20 Years	30 Years
$1,250	$1,650	$2,220	Over 40 Yrs	$522,209	$540,265	$552,330	$556,077	$526,115
$1,500	$1,979	$2,664	Over 40 Yrs	$504,985	$500,294	$482,707	$448,195	$307,045
$1,750	$2,309	$3,108	32 Y & 5 M	$487,763	$460,323	$413,085	$340,319	$87,988
$2,000	$2,639	$3,552	27 Y & 1 M	$470,537	$420,351	$343,456	$232,421	$0
$2,250	$2,969	$3,996	23 Y & 3 M	$453,314	$380,376	$273,827	$124,524	$0
$2,500	$3,299	$4,440	20 Y & 5 M	$436,091	$340,413	$204,217	$16,658	$0
$2,750	$3,629	$4,884	18 Y & 2 M	$418,868	$300,443	$134,587	$0	$0

3% COLA

Monthly Amount	15 Yr Inflated	30 Yr Inflated	Money Lasts	5 Years	10 Years	15 Years	20 Years	30 Years
$1,250	$1,891	$2,946	Over 40 Yrs	$520,536	$531,541	$528,720	$506,493	$373,010
$1,500	$2,269	$3,535	32 Y & 11 M	$502,980	$489,825	$454,362	$388,665	$123,217
$1,750	$2,647	$4,124	27 Y & 7 M	$485,423	$448,116	$380,034	$270,898	$0
$2,000	$3,025	$4,713	23 Y & 8 M	$467,861	$406,383	$305,647	$153,019	$0
$2,250	$3,403	$5,302	20 Y & 9 M	$450,307	$364,680	$231,324	$35,248	$0
$2,500	$3,782	$5,891	18 Y & 6 M	$432,747	$322,959	$156,966	$0	$0
$2,750	$4,160	$6,481	16 Y & 8 M	$415,189	$281,240	$82,606	$0	$0

4% COLA

Monthly Amount	15 Yr Inflated	30 Yr Inflated	Money Lasts	5 Years	10 Years	15 Years	20 Years	30 Years
$1,000	$1,732	$3,119	Over 40 Yrs	$536,733	$565,910	$582,535	$579,802	$476,522
$1,250	$2,165	$3,899	33 Y & 11 M	$518,833	$522,354	$503,046	$450,851	$190,182
$1,500	$2,598	$4,678	28 Y & 4 M	$500,932	$478,800	$423,567	$321,920	$0
$1,750	$3,031	$5,458	24 Y & 4 M	$483,033	$435,239	$344,065	$192,952	$0
$2,000	$3,463	$6,237	21 Y & 3 M	$465,138	$391,701	$264,612	$64,071	$0
$2,250	$3,896	$7,017	18 Y & 11 M	$447,238	$348,146	$185,123	$0	$0
$2,500	$4,329	$7,796	16 Y & 11 M	$429,338	$304,589	$105,637	$0	$0

| $500,000 Balance | | | | | 5% Return On Investment | | | |

No COLA

Monthly Amount	15 Yr Inflated	30 Yr Inflated	Money Lasts	5 Years	10 Years	15 Years	20 Years	30 Years
$1,500	$1,500	$1,500	Over 40 Yrs	$536,193	$582,386	$641,341	$716,584	$935,179
$1,750	$1,750	$1,750	Over 40 Yrs	$519,202	$543,709	$574,986	$614,905	$730,877
$2,000	$2,000	$2,000	Over 40 Yrs	$502,210	$505,032	$508,632	$513,228	$526,577
$2,250	$2,250	$2,250	Over 40 Yrs	$485,219	$466,354	$442,278	$411,549	$322,278
$2,500	$2,500	$2,500	34 Y & 5 M	$468,229	$427,679	$375,927	$309,875	$117,985
$2,750	$2,750	$2,750	27 Y & 7 M	$451,236	$389,000	$309,569	$208,193	$0
$3,000	$3,000	$3,000	23 Y & 3 M	$434,244	$350,321	$243,213	$106,513	$0

2% COLA

Monthly Amount	15 Yr Inflated	30 Yr Inflated	Money Lasts	5 Years	10 Years	15 Years	20 Years	30 Years
$1,250	$1,650	$2,220	Over 40 Yrs	$549,889	$604,375	$663,765	$728,361	$874,219
$1,500	$1,979	$2,664	Over 40 Yrs	$532,238	$562,358	$588,627	$608,714	$616,917
$1,750	$2,309	$3,108	Over 40 Yrs	$514,587	$520,343	$513,491	$489,073	$359,624
$2,000	$2,639	$3,552	32 Y & 6 M	$496,936	$478,327	$438,351	$369,415	$102,278
$2,250	$2,969	$3,996	26 Y & 11 M	$479,285	$436,311	$363,213	$249,762	$0
$2,500	$3,299	$4,440	23 Y & 1 M	$461,636	$394,305	$288,090	$130,132	$0
$2,750	$3,629	$4,884	20 Y & 3 M	$443,985	$352,290	$212,947	$10,471	$0

3% COLA

Monthly Amount	15 Yr Inflated	30 Yr Inflated	Money Lasts	5 Years	10 Years	15 Years	20 Years	30 Years
$1,250	$1,891	$2,946	Over 40 Yrs	$548,190	$595,370	$638,978	$675,376	$704,437
$1,500	$2,269	$3,535	Over 40 Yrs	$530,201	$551,553	$558,870	$545,099	$413,061
$1,750	$2,647	$4,124	32 Y & 6 M	$512,213	$507,748	$478,798	$414,899	$121,910
$2,000	$3,025	$4,713	27 Y & 2 M	$494,220	$463,916	$398,662	$284,572	$0
$2,250	$3,403	$5,302	23 Y & 4 M	$476,233	$420,114	$318,594	$154,366	$0
$2,500	$3,782	$5,891	20 Y & 6 M	$458,242	$376,296	$238,490	$24,105	$0
$2,750	$4,160	$6,481	18 Y & 3 M	$440,251	$332,474	$158,378	$0	$0

4% COLA

Monthly Amount	15 Yr Inflated	30 Yr Inflated	Money Lasts	5 Years	10 Years	15 Years	20 Years	30 Years
$1,000	$1,732	$3,119	Over 40 Yrs	$564,798	$631,607	$697,538	$758,167	$834,350
$1,250	$2,165	$3,899	Over 40 Yrs	$546,461	$585,894	$612,056	$616,038	$502,646
$1,500	$2,598	$4,678	33 Y & 1 M	$528,125	$540,187	$526,584	$473,934	$171,018
$1,750	$3,031	$5,458	27 Y & 8 M	$509,788	$494,468	$441,081	$331,780	$0
$2,000	$3,463	$6,237	23 Y & 9 M	$491,456	$448,772	$355,632	$189,721	$0
$2,250	$3,896	$7,017	20 Y & 10 M	$473,119	$403,061	$270,146	$47,589	$0
$2,500	$4,329	$7,796	18 Y & 7 M	$454,783	$357,348	$184,667	$0	$0

$500,000 Balance	6% Return On Investment

No COLA

Monthly Amount	15 Yr Inflated	30 Yr Inflated	Money Lasts	5 Years	10 Years	15 Years	20 Years	30 Years
$1,750	$1,750	$1,750	Over 40 Yrs	$547,183	$610,324	$694,821	$807,897	$1.162 M
$2,000	$2,000	$2,000	Over 40 Yrs	$529,765	$569,597	$622,901	$694,232	$917,435
$2,250	$2,250	$2,250	Over 40 Yrs	$512,345	$528,867	$550,975	$580,561	$673,138
$2,500	$2,500	$2,500	Over 40 Yrs	$494,927	$488,139	$479,053	$466,895	$428,853
$2,750	$2,750	$2,750	36 Y & 9 M	$477,509	$447,411	$407,133	$353,230	$184,566
$3,000	$3,000	$3,000	28 Y & 5 M	$460,090	$406,681	$335,208	$239,559	$0
$3,250	$3,250	$3,250	23 Y & 7 M	$442,671	$365,952	$263,284	$125,892	$0

2% COLA

Monthly Amount	15 Yr Inflated	30 Yr Inflated	Money Lasts	5 Years	10 Years	15 Years	20 Years	30 Years
$1,500	$1,979	$2,664	Over 40 Yrs	$560,586	$630,369	$711,280	$805,783	$1.049 M
$1,750	$2,309	$3,108	Over 40 Yrs	$542,500	$586,193	$630,117	$672,835	$745,445
$2,000	$2,639	$3,552	Over 40 Yrs	$524,411	$542,017	$548,949	$539,868	$441,672
$2,250	$2,969	$3,996	32 Y & 11 M	$506,323	$497,840	$467,784	$406,905	$137,913
$2,500	$3,299	$4,440	27 Y & 2 M	$488,236	$453,672	$386,635	$273,971	$0
$2,750	$3,629	$4,884	23 Y & 1 M	$470,149	$409,496	$305,463	$140,998	$0
$3,000	$3,958	$5,327	20 Y & 2 M	$452,063	$365,323	$224,304	$8,056	$0

3% COLA

Monthly Amount	15 Yr Inflated	30 Yr Inflated	Money Lasts	5 Years	10 Years	15 Years	20 Years	30 Years
$1,500	$2,269	$3,535	Over 40 Yrs	$558,521	$619,220	$680,024	$737,717	$822,247
$1,750	$2,647	$4,124	Over 40 Yrs	$540,089	$573,193	$593,671	$593,462	$480,834
$2,000	$3,025	$4,713	32 Y & 6 M	$521,654	$527,144	$507,259	$449,085	$139,074
$2,250	$3,403	$5,302	26 Y & 11 M	$503,227	$481,127	$420,918	$304,835	$0
$2,500	$3,782	$5,891	23 Y & 2 M	$484,793	$435,086	$334,533	$160,517	$0
$2,750	$4,160	$6,481	20 Y & 4 M	$466,360	$389,047	$248,144	$16,182	$0
$3,000	$4,538	$7,070	18 Y & 1 M	$447,929	$343,016	$161,782	$0	$0

4% COLA

Monthly Amount	15 Yr Inflated	30 Yr Inflated	Money Lasts	5 Years	10 Years	15 Years	20 Years	30 Years
$1,250	$2,165	$3,899	Over 40 Yrs	$575,198	$655,481	$738,162	$818,683	$940,361
$1,500	$2,598	$4,678	Over 40 Yrs	$556,414	$607,492	$646,143	$661,718	$554,113
$1,750	$3,031	$5,458	32 Y & 7 M	$537,629	$559,494	$554,097	$504,704	$167,779
$2,000	$3,463	$6,237	27 Y & 3 M	$518,852	$511,525	$462,115	$347,806	$0
$2,250	$3,896	$7,017	23 Y & 5 M	$500,067	$463,533	$370,082	$190,811	$0
$2,500	$4,329	$7,796	20 Y & 7 M	$481,283	$415,541	$278,058	$33,841	$0
$2,750	$4,762	$8,576	18 Y & 4 M	$462,498	$367,548	$186,020	$0	$0

$525,000 Balance   3% Return On Investment

No COLA

Monthly Amount	15 Yr Inflated	30 Yr Inflated	Money Lasts	5 Years	10 Years	15 Years	20 Years	30 Years
$1,250	$1,250	$1,250	Over 40 Yrs	$527,788	$531,020	$534,767	$539,111	$549,980
$1,500	$1,500	$1,500	Over 40 Yrs	$511,621	$496,112	$478,131	$457,287	$405,109
$1,750	$1,750	$1,750	Over 40 Yrs	$495,455	$461,204	$421,498	$375,468	$260,247
$2,000	$2,000	$2,000	35 Y & 3 M	$479,289	$426,297	$364,865	$293,648	$115,378
$2,250	$2,250	$2,250	28 Y & 11 M	$463,121	$391,388	$308,230	$211,826	$0
$2,500	$2,500	$2,500	24 Y & 8 M	$446,956	$356,481	$251,596	$130,005	$0
$2,750	$2,750	$2,750	21 Y & 6 M	$430,790	$321,575	$194,964	$48,187	$0

2% COLA

Monthly Amount	15 Yr Inflated	30 Yr Inflated	Money Lasts	5 Years	10 Years	15 Years	20 Years	30 Years
$1,000	$1,320	$1,776	Over 40 Yrs	$541,393	$553,395	$559,583	$558,232	$524,110
$1,250	$1,650	$2,220	Over 40 Yrs	$524,588	$515,364	$495,006	$460,739	$336,538
$1,500	$1,979	$2,664	34 Y & 9 M	$507,780	$477,321	$430,421	$363,253	$149,018
$1,750	$2,309	$3,108	28 Y & 11 M	$490,976	$439,284	$365,843	$265,780	$0
$2,000	$2,639	$3,552	24 Y & 11 M	$474,169	$401,248	$301,261	$168,290	$0
$2,250	$2,969	$3,996	21 Y & 10 M	$457,360	$363,203	$236,671	$70,792	$0
$2,500	$3,299	$4,440	19 Y & 5 M	$440,556	$325,173	$172,103	$0	$0

3% COLA

Monthly Amount	15 Yr Inflated	30 Yr Inflated	Money Lasts	5 Years	10 Years	15 Years	20 Years	30 Years
$1,000	$1,513	$2,357	Over 40 Yrs	$540,075	$546,636	$541,585	$521,054	$413,208
$1,250	$1,891	$2,946	35 Y & 7 M	$522,939	$506,905	$472,497	$414,264	$197,947
$1,500	$2,269	$3,535	29 Y & 8 M	$505,804	$467,174	$403,401	$307,461	$0
$1,750	$2,647	$4,124	25 Y & 5 M	$488,669	$427,450	$334,333	$200,713	$0
$2,000	$3,025	$4,713	22 Y & 3 M	$471,530	$387,705	$265,214	$93,869	$0
$2,250	$3,403	$5,302	19 Y & 9 M	$454,397	$347,988	$196,152	$0	$0
$2,500	$3,782	$5,891	17 Y & 9 M	$437,260	$308,254	$127,059	$0	$0

4% COLA

Monthly Amount	15 Yr Inflated	30 Yr Inflated	Money Lasts	5 Years	10 Years	15 Years	20 Years	30 Years
$750	$1,299	$2,339	Over 40 Yrs	$556,205	$581,029	$595,992	$596,537	$528,874
$1,000	$1,732	$3,119	37 Y & 2 M	$538,733	$539,511	$521,987	$479,260	$280,253
$1,250	$2,165	$3,899	30 Y & 8 M	$521,259	$497,995	$447,998	$362,015	$31,699
$1,500	$2,598	$4,678	26 Y & 2 M	$503,787	$456,484	$374,016	$244,788	$0
$1,750	$3,031	$5,458	22 Y & 10 M	$486,313	$414,963	$300,010	$127,523	$0
$2,000	$3,463	$6,237	20 Y & 3 M	$468,846	$373,467	$226,054	$10,341	$0
$2,250	$3,896	$7,017	18 Y & 2 M	$451,373	$331,952	$152,061	$0	$0

| $525,000 Balance | | | | | 4% Return On Investment | | | |

No COLA

Monthly Amount	15 Yr Inflated	30 Yr Inflated	Money Lasts	5 Years	10 Years	15 Years	20 Years	30 Years
$1,500	$1,500	$1,500	Over 40 Yrs	$539,299	$556,696	$577,863	$603,616	$673,067
$1,750	$1,750	$1,750	Over 40 Yrs	$522,726	$519,958	$516,591	$512,494	$501,446
$2,000	$2,000	$2,000	Over 40 Yrs	$506,151	$483,219	$455,319	$421,373	$329,827
$2,250	$2,250	$2,250	36 Y & 8 M	$489,576	$446,480	$394,045	$330,251	$158,204
$2,500	$2,500	$2,500	29 Y & 7 M	$473,003	$409,741	$332,773	$239,129	$0
$2,750	$2,750	$2,750	24 Y & 11 M	$456,430	$373,003	$271,502	$148,010	$0
$3,000	$3,000	$3,000	21 Y & 8 M	$439,855	$336,264	$210,230	$56,889	$0

2% COLA

Monthly Amount	15 Yr Inflated	30 Yr Inflated	Money Lasts	5 Years	10 Years	15 Years	20 Years	30 Years
$1,250	$1,650	$2,220	Over 40 Yrs	$552,626	$577,274	$597,356	$610,858	$607,200
$1,500	$1,979	$2,664	Over 40 Yrs	$535,401	$537,300	$527,731	$502,973	$388,130
$1,750	$2,309	$3,108	34 Y & 9 M	$518,179	$497,328	$458,106	$395,093	$169,065
$2,000	$2,639	$3,552	28 Y & 11 M	$500,954	$457,357	$388,481	$287,200	$0
$2,250	$2,969	$3,996	24 Y & 9 M	$483,731	$417,384	$318,855	$179,308	$0
$2,500	$3,299	$4,440	21 Y & 8 M	$466,508	$377,421	$249,242	$71,439	$0
$2,750	$3,629	$4,884	19 Y & 4 M	$449,283	$337,447	$179,607	$0	$0

3% COLA

Monthly Amount	15 Yr Inflated	30 Yr Inflated	Money Lasts	5 Years	10 Years	15 Years	20 Years	30 Years
$1,250	$1,891	$2,946	Over 40 Yrs	$550,952	$568,547	$573,744	$561,271	$454,093
$1,500	$2,269	$3,535	34 Y & 11 M	$533,396	$526,831	$499,386	$443,444	$204,305
$1,750	$2,647	$4,124	29 Y & 2 M	$515,838	$485,121	$425,055	$325,673	$0
$2,000	$3,025	$4,713	24 Y & 11 M	$498,277	$443,390	$350,673	$207,800	$0
$2,250	$3,403	$5,302	21 Y & 11 M	$480,723	$401,686	$276,347	$90,026	$0
$2,500	$3,782	$5,891	19 Y & 6 M	$463,163	$359,966	$201,989	$0	$0
$2,750	$4,160	$6,481	17 Y & 7 M	$445,605	$318,246	$127,629	$0	$0

4% COLA

Monthly Amount	15 Yr Inflated	30 Yr Inflated	Money Lasts	5 Years	10 Years	15 Years	20 Years	30 Years
$1,000	$1,732	$3,119	Over 40 Yrs	$567,149	$602,916	$627,557	$634,578	$557,606
$1,250	$2,165	$3,899	35 Y & 9 M	$549,248	$559,360	$548,071	$505,631	$271,272
$1,500	$2,598	$4,678	29 Y & 9 M	$531,348	$515,806	$468,590	$376,698	$0
$1,750	$3,031	$5,458	25 Y & 6 M	$513,448	$472,245	$389,087	$247,729	$0
$2,000	$3,463	$6,237	22 Y & 4 M	$495,555	$428,708	$309,636	$118,850	$0
$2,250	$3,896	$7,017	19 Y & 10 M	$477,654	$385,152	$230,146	$0	$0
$2,500	$4,329	$7,796	17 Y & 10 M	$459,755	$341,594	$150,661	$0	$0

| $525,000 Balance | | | | | 5% Return On Investment | | | |

No COLA

Monthly Amount	15 Yr Inflated	30 Yr Inflated	Money Lasts	5 Years	10 Years	15 Years	20 Years	30 Years
$1,500	$1,500	$1,500	Over 40 Yrs	$568,101	$623,108	$693,314	$782,917	$1.043 M
$1,750	$1,750	$1,750	Over 40 Yrs	$551,108	$584,430	$626,958	$681,236	$838,926
$2,000	$2,000	$2,000	Over 40 Yrs	$534,118	$545,755	$560,606	$579,561	$634,628
$2,250	$2,250	$2,250	Over 40 Yrs	$517,126	$507,076	$494,251	$477,882	$430,327
$2,500	$2,500	$2,500	39 Y & 5 M	$500,135	$468,401	$427,899	$376,206	$226,030
$2,750	$2,750	$2,750	30 Y & 8 M	$483,144	$429,723	$361,542	$274,525	$21,724
$3,000	$3,000	$3,000	25 Y & 6 M	$466,152	$391,045	$295,188	$172,846	$0

2% COLA

Monthly Amount	15 Yr Inflated	30 Yr Inflated	Money Lasts	5 Years	10 Years	15 Years	20 Years	30 Years
$1,250	$1,650	$2,220	Over 40 Yrs	$581,795	$645,097	$715,737	$794,693	$982,268
$1,500	$1,979	$2,664	Over 40 Yrs	$564,144	$603,079	$640,599	$675,043	$724,958
$1,750	$2,309	$3,108	Over 40 Yrs	$546,496	$561,068	$565,468	$555,411	$467,680
$2,000	$2,639	$3,552	35 Y & 4 M	$528,844	$519,053	$490,328	$435,752	$210,335
$2,250	$2,969	$3,996	29 Y & 1 M	$511,191	$477,031	$415,184	$316,092	$0
$2,500	$3,299	$4,440	24 Y & 9 M	$493,542	$435,026	$340,062	$196,464	$0
$2,750	$3,629	$4,884	21 Y & 8 M	$475,892	$393,013	$264,921	$76,805	$0

3% COLA

Monthly Amount	15 Yr Inflated	30 Yr Inflated	Money Lasts	5 Years	10 Years	15 Years	20 Years	30 Years
$1,250	$1,891	$2,946	Over 40 Yrs	$580,098	$636,093	$690,952	$741,708	$812,482
$1,500	$2,269	$3,535	Over 40 Yrs	$562,109	$592,277	$610,845	$611,433	$521,111
$1,750	$2,647	$4,124	34 Y & 10 M	$544,120	$548,470	$530,771	$481,230	$229,954
$2,000	$3,025	$4,713	28 Y & 11 M	$526,128	$504,640	$450,638	$350,910	$0
$2,250	$3,403	$5,302	24 Y & 10 M	$508,141	$460,838	$370,569	$220,701	$0
$2,500	$3,782	$5,891	21 Y & 9 M	$490,149	$417,018	$290,463	$90,437	$0
$2,750	$4,160	$6,481	19 Y & 4 M	$472,159	$373,200	$210,355	$0	$0

4% COLA

Monthly Amount	15 Yr Inflated	30 Yr Inflated	Money Lasts	5 Years	10 Years	15 Years	20 Years	30 Years
$1,000	$1,732	$3,119	Over 40 Yrs	$596,706	$672,330	$749,512	$824,500	$942,397
$1,250	$2,165	$3,899	Over 40 Yrs	$578,368	$626,617	$664,030	$682,372	$610,697
$1,500	$2,598	$4,678	34 Y & 11 M	$560,032	$580,909	$578,555	$540,264	$279,062
$1,750	$3,031	$5,458	29 Y & 3 M	$541,694	$535,188	$493,052	$398,109	$0
$2,000	$3,463	$6,237	25 Y & 2 M	$523,364	$489,496	$407,608	$256,058	$0
$2,250	$3,896	$7,017	21 Y & 11 M	$505,027	$443,784	$322,120	$113,921	$0
$2,500	$4,329	$7,796	19 Y & 7 M	$486,689	$398,068	$236,636	$0	$0

$525,000 Balance					6% Return On Investment			

No COLA

Monthly Amount	15 Yr Inflated	30 Yr Inflated	Money Lasts	5 Years	10 Years	15 Years	20 Years	30 Years
$1,750	$1,750	$1,750	Over 40 Yrs	$580,638	$655,094	$754,733	$888,073	$1.305 M
$2,000	$2,000	$2,000	Over 40 Yrs	$563,220	$614,367	$682,813	$774,410	$1.061 M
$2,250	$2,250	$2,250	Over 40 Yrs	$545,801	$573,636	$610,887	$660,736	$816,720
$2,500	$2,500	$2,500	Over 40 Yrs	$528,383	$532,909	$538,967	$547,073	$572,437
$2,750	$2,750	$2,750	Over 40 Yrs	$510,963	$492,179	$467,042	$433,404	$328,144
$3,000	$3,000	$3,000	32 Y & 6 M	$493,544	$451,451	$395,119	$319,735	$83,852
$3,250	$3,250	$3,250	26 Y & 4 M	$476,126	$410,722	$323,196	$206,068	$0

2% COLA

Monthly Amount	15 Yr Inflated	30 Yr Inflated	Money Lasts	5 Years	10 Years	15 Years	20 Years	30 Years
$1,500	$1,979	$2,664	Over 40 Yrs	$594,042	$675,139	$771,192	$885,958	$1.193 M
$1,750	$2,309	$3,108	Over 40 Yrs	$575,957	$630,966	$690,034	$753,016	$889,034
$2,000	$2,639	$3,552	Over 40 Yrs	$557,867	$586,789	$608,865	$620,049	$585,264
$2,250	$2,969	$3,996	36 Y & 7 M	$539,778	$542,608	$527,694	$487,079	$281,494
$2,500	$3,299	$4,440	29 Y & 7 M	$521,692	$498,442	$446,546	$354,147	$0
$2,750	$3,629	$4,884	24 Y & 11 M	$503,604	$454,266	$365,374	$221,173	$0
$3,000	$3,958	$5,327	21 Y & 9 M	$485,518	$410,093	$284,216	$88,229	$0

3% COLA

Monthly Amount	15 Yr Inflated	30 Yr Inflated	Money Lasts	5 Years	10 Years	15 Years	20 Years	30 Years
$1,500	$2,269	$3,535	Over 40 Yrs	$591,976	$663,990	$739,936	$817,893	$965,829
$1,750	$2,647	$4,124	Over 40 Yrs	$573,546	$617,966	$653,587	$673,642	$624,427
$2,000	$3,025	$4,713	35 Y & 4 M	$555,111	$571,916	$567,175	$529,267	$282,667
$2,250	$3,403	$5,302	29 Y & 2 M	$536,682	$525,895	$480,829	$385,009	$0
$2,500	$3,782	$5,891	24 Y & 10 M	$518,248	$479,858	$394,448	$240,697	$0
$2,750	$4,160	$6,481	21 Y & 8 M	$499,817	$433,821	$308,063	$96,366	$0
$3,000	$4,538	$7,070	19 Y & 4 M	$481,386	$387,788	$221,696	$0	$0

4% COLA

Monthly Amount	15 Yr Inflated	30 Yr Inflated	Money Lasts	5 Years	10 Years	15 Years	20 Years	30 Years
$1,250	$2,165	$3,899	Over 40 Yrs	$608,654	$700,253	$798,076	$898,860	$1.084 M
$1,500	$2,598	$4,678	Over 40 Yrs	$589,869	$652,264	$706,059	$741,900	$697,706
$1,750	$3,031	$5,458	34 Y & 11 M	$571,086	$604,268	$614,013	$584,887	$311,374
$2,000	$3,463	$6,237	29 Y & 1 M	$552,306	$556,293	$522,024	$427,978	$0
$2,250	$3,896	$7,017	24 Y & 11 M	$533,522	$508,305	$429,997	$270,991	$0
$2,500	$4,329	$7,796	21 Y & 10 M	$514,738	$460,311	$337,971	$114,018	$0
$2,750	$4,762	$8,576	19 Y & 5 M	$495,955	$412,322	$245,937	$0	$0

| $550,000 Balance | | | | | 3% Return On Investment | | | |

No COLA

Monthly Amount	15 Yr Inflated	30 Yr Inflated	Money Lasts	5 Years	10 Years	15 Years	20 Years	30 Years
$1,250	$1,250	$1,250	Over 40 Yrs	$556,769	$564,616	$573,713	$584,259	$610,659
$1,500	$1,500	$1,500	Over 40 Yrs	$540,603	$529,710	$517,081	$502,440	$465,792
$1,750	$1,750	$1,750	Over 40 Yrs	$524,438	$494,804	$460,449	$420,622	$320,929
$2,000	$2,000	$2,000	38 Y & 4 M	$508,269	$459,892	$403,810	$338,796	$176,054
$2,250	$2,250	$2,250	31 Y & 3 M	$492,104	$424,986	$347,179	$256,979	$31,189
$2,500	$2,500	$2,500	26 Y & 5 M	$475,937	$390,078	$290,544	$175,157	$0
$2,750	$2,750	$2,750	22 Y & 11 M	$459,771	$355,170	$233,909	$93,335	$0

2% COLA

Monthly Amount	15 Yr Inflated	30 Yr Inflated	Money Lasts	5 Years	10 Years	15 Years	20 Years	30 Years
$1,000	$1,320	$1,776	Over 40 Yrs	$570,374	$586,991	$598,532	$603,385	$584,793
$1,250	$1,650	$2,220	Over 40 Yrs	$553,570	$548,962	$533,955	$505,893	$397,221
$1,500	$1,979	$2,664	36 Y & 9 M	$536,763	$510,921	$469,374	$408,409	$209,702
$1,750	$2,309	$3,108	30 Y & 8 M	$519,956	$472,881	$404,791	$310,931	$22,198
$2,000	$2,639	$3,552	26 Y & 3 M	$503,150	$434,843	$340,205	$213,437	$0
$2,250	$2,969	$3,996	22 Y & 11 M	$486,343	$396,802	$275,621	$115,946	$0
$2,500	$3,299	$4,440	20 Y & 5 M	$469,538	$358,771	$211,052	$18,479	$0

3% COLA

Monthly Amount	15 Yr Inflated	30 Yr Inflated	Money Lasts	5 Years	10 Years	15 Years	20 Years	30 Years
$1,000	$1,513	$2,357	Over 40 Yrs	$569,056	$580,233	$580,533	$566,205	$473,887
$1,250	$1,891	$2,946	37 Y & 3 M	$551,920	$540,502	$511,446	$459,418	$258,629
$1,500	$2,269	$3,535	30 Y & 11 M	$534,786	$500,773	$442,353	$352,616	$43,309
$1,750	$2,647	$4,124	26 Y & 7 M	$517,650	$461,048	$373,282	$245,867	$0
$2,000	$3,025	$4,713	23 Y & 4 M	$500,511	$421,303	$304,163	$139,021	$0
$2,250	$3,403	$5,302	20 Y & 8 M	$483,381	$381,588	$235,104	$32,276	$0
$2,500	$3,782	$5,891	18 Y & 8 M	$466,243	$341,854	$166,011	$0	$0

4% COLA

Monthly Amount	15 Yr Inflated	30 Yr Inflated	Money Lasts	5 Years	10 Years	15 Years	20 Years	30 Years
$750	$1,299	$2,339	Over 40 Yrs	$585,188	$614,626	$634,940	$641,688	$589,552
$1,000	$1,732	$3,119	38 Y & 7 M	$567,714	$573,106	$560,932	$524,410	$340,931
$1,250	$2,165	$3,899	31 Y & 11 M	$550,241	$531,592	$486,945	$407,165	$92,378
$1,500	$2,598	$4,678	27 Y & 3 M	$532,768	$490,082	$412,966	$289,942	$0
$1,750	$3,031	$5,458	23 Y & 9 M	$515,295	$448,561	$338,959	$172,673	$0
$2,000	$3,463	$6,237	21 Y & 1 M	$497,829	$407,066	$265,005	$55,496	$0
$2,250	$3,896	$7,017	18 Y & 11 M	$480,355	$365,551	$191,011	$0	$0

| $550,000 Balance | | | | 4% Return On Investment | | | | |

No COLA

Monthly Amount	15 Yr Inflated	30 Yr Inflated	Money Lasts	5 Years	10 Years	15 Years	20 Years	30 Years
$1,500	$1,500	$1,500	Over 40 Yrs	$569,716	$593,704	$622,888	$658,395	$754,156
$1,750	$1,750	$1,750	Over 40 Yrs	$553,140	$556,962	$561,612	$567,269	$582,526
$2,000	$2,000	$2,000	Over 40 Yrs	$536,568	$520,226	$500,342	$476,151	$410,911
$2,250	$2,250	$2,250	Over 40 Yrs	$519,993	$483,486	$439,067	$385,028	$239,287
$2,500	$2,500	$2,500	32 Y & 5 M	$503,419	$446,746	$377,796	$293,907	$67,669
$2,750	$2,750	$2,750	27 Y & 1 M	$486,846	$410,008	$316,524	$202,786	$0
$3,000	$3,000	$3,000	23 Y & 4 M	$470,272	$373,272	$255,255	$111,669	$0

2% COLA

Monthly Amount	15 Yr Inflated	30 Yr Inflated	Money Lasts	5 Years	10 Years	15 Years	20 Years	30 Years
$1,250	$1,650	$2,220	Over 40 Yrs	$583,042	$614,279	$642,379	$665,636	$688,287
$1,500	$1,979	$2,664	Over 40 Yrs	$565,818	$574,306	$572,755	$557,752	$469,217
$1,750	$2,309	$3,108	37 Y & 2 M	$548,595	$534,335	$503,132	$449,874	$250,155
$2,000	$2,639	$3,552	30 Y & 9 M	$531,371	$494,364	$433,504	$341,977	$31,043
$2,250	$2,969	$3,996	26 Y & 4 M	$514,147	$454,390	$363,877	$234,083	$0
$2,500	$3,299	$4,440	22 Y & 11 M	$496,925	$414,428	$294,267	$126,218	$0
$2,750	$3,629	$4,884	20 Y & 5 M	$479,700	$374,453	$224,631	$18,311	$0

3% COLA

Monthly Amount	15 Yr Inflated	30 Yr Inflated	Money Lasts	5 Years	10 Years	15 Years	20 Years	30 Years
$1,250	$1,891	$2,946	Over 40 Yrs	$581,368	$605,552	$618,766	$616,048	$535,174
$1,500	$2,269	$3,535	36 Y & 10 M	$563,813	$563,837	$544,409	$498,218	$285,382
$1,750	$2,647	$4,124	30 Y & 9 M	$546,255	$522,128	$470,081	$380,453	$35,783
$2,000	$3,025	$4,713	26 Y & 4 M	$528,694	$480,395	$395,694	$262,575	$0
$2,250	$3,403	$5,302	23 Y & 1 M	$511,140	$438,693	$321,372	$144,806	$0
$2,500	$3,782	$5,891	20 Y & 6 M	$493,580	$396,973	$247,015	$26,987	$0
$2,750	$4,160	$6,481	18 Y & 6 M	$476,022	$355,254	$172,653	$0	$0

4% COLA

Monthly Amount	15 Yr Inflated	30 Yr Inflated	Money Lasts	5 Years	10 Years	15 Years	20 Years	30 Years
$1,000	$1,732	$3,119	Over 40 Yrs	$597,564	$639,921	$672,581	$689,357	$638,693
$1,250	$2,165	$3,899	37 Y & 5 M	$579,665	$596,367	$593,096	$560,411	$352,359
$1,500	$2,598	$4,678	31 Y & 2 M	$561,764	$552,812	$513,615	$431,478	$66,075
$1,750	$3,031	$5,458	26 Y & 9 M	$543,864	$509,251	$434,111	$302,507	$0
$2,000	$3,463	$6,237	23 Y & 5 M	$525,971	$465,714	$354,659	$173,626	$0
$2,250	$3,896	$7,017	20 Y & 10 M	$508,071	$422,159	$275,171	$44,676	$0
$2,500	$4,329	$7,796	18 Y & 9 M	$490,170	$378,601	$195,684	$0	$0

| **$550,000 Balance** | | | | | **5% Return On Investment** | | | |

No COLA

Monthly Amount	15 Yr Inflated	30 Yr Inflated	Money Lasts	5 Years	10 Years	15 Years	20 Years	30 Years
$1,500	$1,500	$1,500	Over 40 Yrs	$600,008	$663,831	$745,289	$849,250	$1.151 M
$1,750	$1,750	$1,750	Over 40 Yrs	$583,016	$625,153	$678,932	$747,571	$946,977
$2,000	$2,000	$2,000	Over 40 Yrs	$566,024	$586,476	$612,578	$645,891	$742,671
$2,250	$2,250	$2,250	Over 40 Yrs	$549,032	$547,797	$546,222	$544,212	$538,372
$2,500	$2,500	$2,500	Over 40 Yrs	$532,043	$509,123	$479,871	$442,539	$334,081
$2,750	$2,750	$2,750	34 Y & 5 M	$515,051	$470,446	$413,516	$340,858	$129,774
$3,000	$3,000	$3,000	28 Y & 1 M	$498,059	$431,768	$347,162	$239,181	$0

2% COLA

Monthly Amount	15 Yr Inflated	30 Yr Inflated	Money Lasts	5 Years	10 Years	15 Years	20 Years	30 Years
$1,250	$1,650	$2,220	Over 40 Yrs	$613,703	$685,820	$767,711	$861,026	$1.090 M
$1,500	$1,979	$2,664	Over 40 Yrs	$596,051	$643,802	$692,574	$741,379	$833,013
$1,750	$2,309	$3,108	Over 40 Yrs	$578,402	$601,788	$617,439	$621,739	$575,722
$2,000	$2,639	$3,552	38 Y & 4 M	$560,750	$559,773	$542,299	$502,082	$318,379
$2,250	$2,969	$3,996	31 Y & 4 M	$543,099	$517,755	$467,159	$382,425	$61,037
$2,500	$3,299	$4,440	26 Y & 7 M	$525,450	$475,748	$392,035	$262,796	$0
$2,750	$3,629	$4,884	23 Y & 1 M	$507,799	$433,734	$316,893	$143,135	$0

3% COLA

Monthly Amount	15 Yr Inflated	30 Yr Inflated	Money Lasts	5 Years	10 Years	15 Years	20 Years	30 Years
$1,250	$1,891	$2,946	Over 40 Yrs	$612,004	$676,814	$742,924	$808,040	$920,533
$1,500	$2,269	$3,535	Over 40 Yrs	$594,017	$633,000	$662,819	$677,769	$629,164
$1,750	$2,647	$4,124	37 Y & 3 M	$576,027	$589,193	$582,744	$547,563	$338,006
$2,000	$3,025	$4,713	30 Y & 10 M	$558,034	$545,361	$502,610	$417,242	$46,529
$2,250	$3,403	$5,302	26 Y & 5 M	$540,047	$501,557	$422,538	$287,027	$0
$2,500	$3,782	$5,891	22 Y & 11 M	$522,056	$457,740	$342,436	$156,769	$0
$2,750	$4,160	$6,481	20 Y & 6 M	$504,065	$413,921	$262,326	$26,487	$0

4% COLA

Monthly Amount	15 Yr Inflated	30 Yr Inflated	Money Lasts	5 Years	10 Years	15 Years	20 Years	30 Years
$1,000	$1,732	$3,119	Over 40 Yrs	$628,612	$713,053	$801,487	$890,836	$1.050 M
$1,250	$2,165	$3,899	Over 40 Yrs	$610,275	$667,340	$716,003	$748,705	$718,748
$1,500	$2,598	$4,678	36 Y & 11 M	$591,939	$621,630	$630,527	$606,594	$387,106
$1,750	$3,031	$5,458	30 Y & 10 M	$573,602	$575,911	$545,025	$464,442	$55,402
$2,000	$3,463	$6,237	26 Y & 6 M	$555,270	$530,218	$459,581	$322,390	$0
$2,250	$3,896	$7,017	23 Y & 2 M	$536,933	$484,505	$374,092	$180,253	$0
$2,500	$4,329	$7,796	20 Y & 7 M	$518,597	$438,791	$288,610	$38,138	$0

| $550,000 Balance | | | | 6% Return On Investment | | | | |

No COLA

Monthly Amount	15 Yr Inflated	30 Yr Inflated	Money Lasts	5 Years	10 Years	15 Years	20 Years	30 Years
$1,750	$1,750	$1,750	Over 40 Yrs	$614,093	$699,865	$814,647	$968,252	$1.449 M
$2,000	$2,000	$2,000	Over 40 Yrs	$596,675	$659,137	$742,725	$854,585	$1.205 M
$2,250	$2,250	$2,250	Over 40 Yrs	$579,255	$618,406	$670,799	$740,913	$960,304
$2,500	$2,500	$2,500	Over 40 Yrs	$561,838	$577,680	$598,880	$627,251	$716,026
$2,750	$2,750	$2,750	Over 40 Yrs	$544,420	$536,951	$526,957	$513,582	$471,730
$3,000	$3,000	$3,000	37 Y & 11 M	$527,001	$496,222	$455,033	$399,912	$227,438
$3,250	$3,250	$3,250	29 Y & 7 M	$509,582	$455,493	$383,111	$286,247	$0

2% COLA

Monthly Amount	15 Yr Inflated	30 Yr Inflated	Money Lasts	5 Years	10 Years	15 Years	20 Years	30 Years
$1,500	$1,979	$2,664	Over 40 Yrs	$627,498	$719,913	$831,110	$966,143	$1.336 M
$1,750	$2,309	$3,108	Over 40 Yrs	$609,411	$675,735	$749,944	$833,191	$1.033 M
$2,000	$2,639	$3,552	Over 40 Yrs	$591,322	$631,559	$668,777	$700,225	$728,849
$2,250	$2,969	$3,996	Over 40 Yrs	$573,233	$587,380	$587,608	$567,256	$425,079
$2,500	$3,299	$4,440	32 Y & 5 M	$555,147	$543,213	$506,460	$434,323	$121,385
$2,750	$3,629	$4,884	27 Y & 2 M	$537,061	$499,041	$425,295	$301,360	$0
$3,000	$3,958	$5,327	23 Y & 5 M	$518,975	$454,867	$344,135	$168,416	$0

3% COLA

Monthly Amount	15 Yr Inflated	30 Yr Inflated	Money Lasts	5 Years	10 Years	15 Years	20 Years	30 Years
$1,500	$2,269	$3,535	Over 40 Yrs	$625,432	$708,762	$799,851	$898,073	$1.109 M
$1,750	$2,647	$4,124	Over 40 Yrs	$607,000	$662,736	$713,501	$753,822	$768,015
$2,000	$3,025	$4,713	38 Y & 5 M	$588,566	$616,687	$627,089	$609,445	$426,252
$2,250	$3,403	$5,302	31 Y & 4 M	$570,138	$570,666	$540,742	$465,187	$84,788
$2,500	$3,782	$5,891	26 Y & 7 M	$551,704	$524,629	$454,362	$320,877	$0
$2,750	$4,160	$6,481	23 Y & 2 M	$533,271	$478,591	$367,974	$176,541	$0
$3,000	$4,538	$7,070	20 Y & 6 M	$514,841	$432,559	$281,610	$32,258	$0

4% COLA

Monthly Amount	15 Yr Inflated	30 Yr Inflated	Money Lasts	5 Years	10 Years	15 Years	20 Years	30 Years
$1,250	$2,165	$3,899	Over 40 Yrs	$642,108	$745,022	$857,986	$979,036	$1.228 M
$1,500	$2,598	$4,678	Over 40 Yrs	$623,326	$697,037	$765,975	$822,080	$841,294
$1,750	$3,031	$5,458	37 Y & 4 M	$604,541	$649,039	$673,929	$665,067	$454,965
$2,000	$3,463	$6,237	30 Y & 11 M	$585,762	$601,066	$581,939	$508,159	$68,864
$2,250	$3,896	$7,017	26 Y & 6 M	$566,978	$553,076	$489,912	$351,171	$0
$2,500	$4,329	$7,796	23 Y & 2 M	$548,194	$505,084	$397,888	$194,200	$0
$2,750	$4,762	$8,576	20 Y & 7 M	$529,409	$457,089	$305,845	$37,190	$0

| $575,000 Balance | | | | 3% Return On Investment | | | | |

No COLA

Monthly Amount	15 Yr Inflated	30 Yr Inflated	Money Lasts	5 Years	10 Years	15 Years	20 Years	30 Years
$1,500	$1,500	$1,500	Over 40 Yrs	$569,584	$563,307	$556,029	$547,592	$526,473
$1,750	$1,750	$1,750	Over 40 Yrs	$553,418	$528,400	$499,395	$465,772	$381,606
$2,000	$2,000	$2,000	Over 40 Yrs	$537,253	$493,493	$442,764	$383,955	$236,744
$2,250	$2,250	$2,250	33 Y & 7 M	$521,085	$458,584	$386,128	$302,131	$91,872
$2,500	$2,500	$2,500	28 Y & 4 M	$504,919	$423,678	$329,495	$220,312	$0
$2,750	$2,750	$2,750	24 Y & 6 M	$488,754	$388,771	$272,863	$138,494	$0
$3,000	$3,000	$3,000	21 Y & 8 M	$472,586	$353,862	$216,227	$56,671	$0

2% COLA

Monthly Amount	15 Yr Inflated	30 Yr Inflated	Money Lasts	5 Years	10 Years	15 Years	20 Years	30 Years
$1,250	$1,650	$2,220	Over 40 Yrs	$582,551	$582,559	$572,902	$551,042	$457,897
$1,500	$1,979	$2,664	38 Y & 9 M	$565,744	$544,517	$508,319	$453,558	$270,383
$1,750	$2,309	$3,108	32 Y & 3 M	$548,940	$506,480	$443,740	$356,084	$82,877
$2,000	$2,639	$3,552	27 Y & 8 M	$532,132	$468,442	$379,156	$258,591	$0
$2,250	$2,969	$3,996	24 Y & 2 M	$515,324	$430,400	$314,571	$161,099	$0
$2,500	$3,299	$4,440	21 Y & 6 M	$498,520	$392,369	$250,002	$63,632	$0
$2,750	$3,629	$4,884	19 Y & 4 M	$481,714	$354,332	$185,416	$0	$0

3% COLA

Monthly Amount	15 Yr Inflated	30 Yr Inflated	Money Lasts	5 Years	10 Years	15 Years	20 Years	30 Years
$1,250	$1,891	$2,946	38 Y & 11 M	$580,902	$574,100	$550,395	$504,571	$319,312
$1,500	$2,269	$3,535	32 Y & 5 M	$563,767	$534,369	$481,300	$397,766	$103,987
$1,750	$2,647	$4,124	27 Y & 10 M	$546,633	$494,647	$412,233	$291,021	$0
$2,000	$3,025	$4,713	24 Y & 4 M	$529,494	$454,901	$343,113	$184,175	$0
$2,250	$3,403	$5,302	21 Y & 8 M	$512,361	$415,183	$274,051	$77,426	$0
$2,500	$3,782	$5,891	19 Y & 6 M	$495,224	$375,450	$204,959	$0	$0
$2,750	$4,160	$6,481	17 Y & 9 M	$478,087	$335,716	$135,859	$0	$0

4% COLA

Monthly Amount	15 Yr Inflated	30 Yr Inflated	Money Lasts	5 Years	10 Years	15 Years	20 Years	30 Years
$1,000	$1,732	$3,119	Over 40 Yrs	$596,696	$606,706	$599,885	$569,567	$401,620
$1,250	$2,165	$3,899	33 Y & 2 M	$579,224	$565,193	$525,899	$452,324	$153,066
$1,500	$2,598	$4,678	28 Y & 4 M	$561,750	$523,680	$451,914	$335,092	$0
$1,750	$3,031	$5,458	24 Y & 9 M	$544,277	$482,160	$377,908	$217,827	$0
$2,000	$3,463	$6,237	21 Y & 11 M	$526,809	$440,662	$303,952	$100,645	$0
$2,250	$3,896	$7,017	19 Y & 9 M	$509,337	$399,148	$229,959	$0	$0
$2,500	$4,329	$7,796	17 Y & 11 M	$491,864	$357,633	$155,973	$0	$0

$575,000 Balance	4% Return On Investment

No COLA

Monthly Amount	15 Yr Inflated	30 Yr Inflated	Money Lasts	5 Years	10 Years	15 Years	20 Years	30 Years
$1,750	$1,750	$1,750	Over 40 Yrs	$583,557	$593,968	$606,636	$622,048	$663,611
$2,000	$2,000	$2,000	Over 40 Yrs	$566,984	$557,229	$545,363	$530,927	$491,990
$2,250	$2,250	$2,250	Over 40 Yrs	$550,410	$520,492	$484,093	$439,809	$320,376
$2,500	$2,500	$2,500	35 Y & 7 M	$533,836	$483,754	$422,820	$348,686	$148,753
$2,750	$2,750	$2,750	29 Y & 4 M	$517,262	$447,014	$361,547	$257,564	$0
$3,000	$3,000	$3,000	25 Y & 2 M	$500,688	$410,276	$300,276	$166,445	$0
$3,250	$3,250	$3,250	21 Y & 11 M	$484,115	$373,539	$239,007	$75,326	$0

2% COLA

Monthly Amount	15 Yr Inflated	30 Yr Inflated	Money Lasts	5 Years	10 Years	15 Years	20 Years	30 Years
$1,500	$1,979	$2,664	Over 40 Yrs	$596,233	$611,312	$617,780	$612,531	$550,300
$1,750	$2,309	$3,108	39 Y & 8 M	$579,012	$571,341	$548,156	$504,653	$331,241
$2,000	$2,639	$3,552	32 Y & 8 M	$561,787	$531,371	$478,531	$396,759	$112,133
$2,250	$2,969	$3,996	27 Y & 10 M	$544,564	$491,396	$408,902	$288,863	$0
$2,500	$3,299	$4,440	24 Y & 4 M	$527,340	$451,431	$339,288	$180,992	$0
$2,750	$3,629	$4,884	21 Y & 7 M	$510,117	$411,461	$269,657	$73,092	$0
$3,000	$3,958	$5,327	19 Y & 5 M	$492,895	$371,493	$200,037	$0	$0

3% COLA

Monthly Amount	15 Yr Inflated	30 Yr Inflated	Money Lasts	5 Years	10 Years	15 Years	20 Years	30 Years
$1,500	$2,269	$3,535	38 Y & 11 M	$594,229	$600,844	$589,435	$553,001	$366,475
$1,750	$2,647	$4,124	32 Y & 5 M	$576,671	$559,134	$515,104	$435,231	$116,868
$2,000	$3,025	$4,713	27 Y & 9 M	$559,110	$517,402	$440,718	$317,354	$0
$2,250	$3,403	$5,302	24 Y & 3 M	$541,556	$475,699	$366,394	$199,581	$0
$2,500	$3,782	$5,891	21 Y & 7 M	$523,997	$433,979	$292,038	$81,763	$0
$2,750	$4,160	$6,481	19 Y & 5 M	$506,439	$392,260	$217,677	$0	$0
$3,000	$4,538	$7,070	17 Y & 8 M	$488,882	$350,546	$143,337	$0	$0

4% COLA

Monthly Amount	15 Yr Inflated	30 Yr Inflated	Money Lasts	5 Years	10 Years	15 Years	20 Years	30 Years
$1,250	$2,165	$3,899	39 Y & 1 M	$610,081	$633,372	$638,119	$615,188	$433,442
$1,500	$2,598	$4,678	32 Y & 7 M	$592,181	$589,819	$558,639	$486,257	$147,163
$1,750	$3,031	$5,458	27 Y & 11 M	$574,280	$546,256	$479,134	$357,284	$0
$2,000	$3,463	$6,237	24 Y & 6 M	$556,387	$502,720	$399,683	$228,405	$0
$2,250	$3,896	$7,017	21 Y & 9 M	$538,486	$459,163	$320,191	$99,450	$0
$2,500	$4,329	$7,796	19 Y & 7 M	$520,586	$415,605	$240,706	$0	$0
$2,750	$4,762	$8,576	17 Y & 10 M	$502,687	$372,050	$161,209	$0	$0

$575,000 Balance	5% Return On Investment

No COLA

Monthly Amount	15 Yr Inflated	30 Yr Inflated	Money Lasts	5 Years	10 Years	15 Years	20 Years	30 Years
$1,750	$1,750	$1,750	Over 40 Yrs	$614,923	$665,875	$730,905	$813,901	$1.055 M
$2,000	$2,000	$2,000	Over 40 Yrs	$597,931	$627,197	$664,550	$712,223	$850,721
$2,250	$2,250	$2,250	Over 40 Yrs	$580,940	$588,522	$598,199	$610,549	$646,427
$2,500	$2,500	$2,500	Over 40 Yrs	$563,949	$549,844	$531,842	$508,867	$442,121
$2,750	$2,750	$2,750	38 Y & 11 M	$546,957	$511,167	$465,488	$407,189	$237,821
$3,000	$3,000	$3,000	30 Y & 11 M	$529,967	$472,491	$399,137	$305,516	$33,530
$3,250	$3,250	$3,250	26 Y & 1 M	$512,975	$433,813	$332,781	$203,835	$0

2% COLA

Monthly Amount	15 Yr Inflated	30 Yr Inflated	Money Lasts	5 Years	10 Years	15 Years	20 Years	30 Years
$1,500	$1,979	$2,664	Over 40 Yrs	$627,958	$684,524	$744,546	$807,710	$941,062
$1,750	$2,309	$3,108	Over 40 Yrs	$610,310	$642,512	$669,415	$688,075	$683,778
$2,000	$2,639	$3,552	Over 40 Yrs	$592,658	$600,496	$594,273	$568,415	$426,428
$2,250	$2,969	$3,996	33 Y & 9 M	$575,005	$558,476	$519,130	$448,755	$169,083
$2,500	$3,299	$4,440	28 Y & 5 M	$557,356	$516,470	$444,008	$329,128	$0
$2,750	$3,629	$4,884	24 Y & 8 M	$539,707	$474,458	$368,868	$209,470	$0
$3,000	$3,958	$5,327	21 Y & 9 M	$522,057	$432,443	$293,732	$89,829	$0

3% COLA

Monthly Amount	15 Yr Inflated	30 Yr Inflated	Money Lasts	5 Years	10 Years	15 Years	20 Years	30 Years
$1,500	$2,269	$3,535	Over 40 Yrs	$625,924	$673,723	$714,793	$744,102	$737,213
$1,750	$2,647	$4,124	39 Y & 9 M	$607,934	$629,915	$634,717	$613,896	$446,056
$2,000	$3,025	$4,713	32 Y & 9 M	$589,942	$586,087	$554,587	$483,579	$154,587
$2,250	$3,403	$5,302	27 Y & 11 M	$571,956	$542,283	$474,516	$353,366	$0
$2,500	$3,782	$5,891	24 Y & 5 M	$553,963	$498,462	$394,409	$223,101	$0
$2,750	$4,160	$6,481	21 Y & 8 M	$535,973	$454,644	$314,300	$92,821	$0
$3,000	$4,538	$7,070	19 Y & 5 M	$517,986	$410,832	$234,216	$0	$0

4% COLA

Monthly Amount	15 Yr Inflated	30 Yr Inflated	Money Lasts	5 Years	10 Years	15 Years	20 Years	30 Years
$1,250	$2,165	$3,899	Over 40 Yrs	$642,183	$708,064	$767,978	$815,040	$826,797
$1,500	$2,598	$4,678	39 Y & 1 M	$623,845	$662,353	$682,502	$672,930	$495,159
$1,750	$3,031	$5,458	32 Y & 6 M	$605,509	$616,634	$597,000	$530,776	$163,452
$2,000	$3,463	$6,237	27 Y & 10 M	$587,177	$570,940	$511,553	$388,720	$0
$2,250	$3,896	$7,017	24 Y & 4 M	$568,841	$525,230	$426,069	$246,590	$0
$2,500	$4,329	$7,796	21 Y & 8 M	$550,503	$479,514	$340,585	$104,473	$0
$2,750	$4,762	$8,576	19 Y & 6 M	$532,166	$433,799	$255,089	$0	$0

| $575,000 Balance | | | | | 6% Return On Investment | | | |

No COLA

Monthly Amount	15 Yr Inflated	30 Yr Inflated	Money Lasts	5 Years	10 Years	15 Years	20 Years	30 Years
$2,000	$2,000	$2,000	Over 40 Yrs	$630,131	$703,909	$802,640	$934,763	$1.348 M
$2,250	$2,250	$2,250	Over 40 Yrs	$612,712	$663,180	$730,718	$821,098	$1.104 M
$2,500	$2,500	$2,500	Over 40 Yrs	$595,294	$622,452	$658,795	$707,430	$859,613
$2,750	$2,750	$2,750	Over 40 Yrs	$577,875	$581,723	$586,871	$593,761	$615,320
$3,000	$3,000	$3,000	Over 40 Yrs	$560,456	$540,993	$514,948	$480,094	$371,032
$3,250	$3,250	$3,250	33 Y & 8 M	$543,038	$500,265	$443,026	$366,427	$126,743
$3,500	$3,500	$3,500	27 Y & 5 M	$525,619	$459,536	$371,102	$252,757	$0

2% COLA

Monthly Amount	15 Yr Inflated	30 Yr Inflated	Money Lasts	5 Years	10 Years	15 Years	20 Years	30 Years
$1,750	$2,309	$3,108	Over 40 Yrs	$642,867	$720,507	$809,858	$913,369	$1.176 M
$2,000	$2,639	$3,552	Over 40 Yrs	$624,778	$676,331	$728,691	$780,402	$872,433
$2,250	$2,969	$3,996	Over 40 Yrs	$606,690	$632,152	$647,525	$647,439	$568,674
$2,500	$3,299	$4,440	35 Y & 6 M	$588,603	$587,986	$566,377	$514,507	$264,981
$2,750	$3,629	$4,884	29 Y & 5 M	$570,515	$543,809	$485,204	$381,532	$0
$3,000	$3,958	$5,327	25 Y & 3 M	$552,429	$499,636	$404,046	$248,590	$0
$3,250	$4,288	$5,772	22 Y & 2 M	$534,337	$455,447	$322,855	$115,585	$0

3% COLA

Monthly Amount	15 Yr Inflated	30 Yr Inflated	Money Lasts	5 Years	10 Years	15 Years	20 Years	30 Years
$1,750	$2,647	$4,124	Over 40 Yrs	$640,456	$707,507	$773,413	$833,996	$911,594
$2,000	$3,025	$4,713	Over 40 Yrs	$622,021	$661,457	$687,001	$689,620	$569,835
$2,250	$3,403	$5,302	33 Y & 9 M	$603,594	$615,439	$600,659	$545,370	$228,385
$2,500	$3,782	$5,891	28 Y & 6 M	$585,160	$569,399	$514,273	$401,050	$0
$2,750	$4,160	$6,481	24 Y & 8 M	$566,728	$523,364	$427,890	$256,722	$0
$3,000	$4,538	$7,070	21 Y & 10 M	$548,297	$477,331	$341,525	$112,438	$0
$3,250	$4,916	$7,659	19 Y & 7 M	$529,866	$431,306	$255,165	$0	$0

4% COLA

Monthly Amount	15 Yr Inflated	30 Yr Inflated	Money Lasts	5 Years	10 Years	15 Years	20 Years	30 Years
$1,500	$2,598	$4,678	Over 40 Yrs	$656,780	$741,807	$825,886	$902,255	$984,877
$1,750	$3,031	$5,458	39 Y & 10 M	$637,996	$693,808	$733,839	$745,241	$598,543
$2,000	$3,463	$6,237	32 Y & 11 M	$619,218	$645,838	$641,857	$588,342	$212,461
$2,250	$3,896	$7,017	27 Y & 11 M	$600,434	$597,848	$549,827	$431,351	$0
$2,500	$4,329	$7,796	24 Y & 6 M	$581,649	$549,853	$457,798	$274,373	$0
$2,750	$4,762	$8,576	21 Y & 8 M	$562,866	$501,863	$365,764	$117,375	$0
$3,000	$5,195	$9,356	19 Y & 6 M	$544,081	$453,866	$273,718	$0	$0

$600,000 Balance   3% Return On Investment

No COLA

Monthly Amount	15 Yr Inflated	30 Yr Inflated	Money Lasts	5 Years	10 Years	15 Years	20 Years	30 Years
$1,500	$1,500	$1,500	Over 40 Yrs	$598,567	$596,906	$594,980	$592,747	$587,157
$1,750	$1,750	$1,750	Over 40 Yrs	$582,401	$561,999	$538,347	$510,926	$442,289
$2,000	$2,000	$2,000	Over 40 Yrs	$566,234	$527,090	$481,711	$429,105	$297,422
$2,250	$2,250	$2,250	36 Y & 3 M	$550,068	$492,183	$425,077	$347,284	$152,554
$2,500	$2,500	$2,500	30 Y & 4 M	$533,902	$457,276	$368,444	$265,464	$7,686
$2,750	$2,750	$2,750	26 Y & 1 M	$517,734	$422,365	$311,807	$183,640	$0
$3,000	$3,000	$3,000	22 Y & 11 M	$501,569	$387,460	$255,176	$101,823	$0

2% COLA

Monthly Amount	15 Yr Inflated	30 Yr Inflated	Money Lasts	5 Years	10 Years	15 Years	20 Years	30 Years
$1,250	$1,650	$2,220	Over 40 Yrs	$611,534	$616,158	$611,854	$596,199	$518,585
$1,500	$1,979	$2,664	Over 40 Yrs	$594,727	$578,119	$547,274	$498,718	$331,072
$1,750	$2,309	$3,108	33 Y & 11 M	$577,921	$540,078	$482,689	$401,236	$143,560
$2,000	$2,639	$3,552	28 Y & 11 M	$561,114	$502,039	$418,105	$303,745	$0
$2,250	$2,969	$3,996	25 Y & 4 M	$544,306	$463,997	$353,520	$206,252	$0
$2,500	$3,299	$4,440	22 Y & 6 M	$527,501	$425,965	$288,947	$108,780	$0
$2,750	$3,629	$4,884	20 Y & 3 M	$510,695	$387,928	$224,361	$11,285	$0

3% COLA

Monthly Amount	15 Yr Inflated	30 Yr Inflated	Money Lasts	5 Years	10 Years	15 Years	20 Years	30 Years
$1,250	$1,891	$2,946	Over 40 Yrs	$609,886	$607,700	$589,348	$549,728	$379,999
$1,500	$2,269	$3,535	33 Y & 10 M	$592,751	$567,970	$520,251	$442,922	$164,671
$1,750	$2,647	$4,124	28 Y & 11 M	$575,615	$528,245	$451,182	$336,175	$0
$2,000	$3,025	$4,713	25 Y & 5 M	$558,476	$488,500	$382,063	$229,328	$0
$2,250	$3,403	$5,302	22 Y & 7 M	$541,344	$448,783	$313,002	$122,581	$0
$2,500	$3,782	$5,891	20 Y & 4 M	$524,206	$409,049	$243,908	$15,785	$0
$2,750	$4,160	$6,481	18 Y & 6 M	$507,069	$369,313	$174,807	$0	$0

4% COLA

Monthly Amount	15 Yr Inflated	30 Yr Inflated	Money Lasts	5 Years	10 Years	15 Years	20 Years	30 Years
$1,000	$1,732	$3,119	Over 40 Yrs	$625,677	$640,301	$638,830	$614,716	$462,296
$1,250	$2,165	$3,899	34 Y & 5 M	$608,204	$598,787	$564,843	$497,471	$213,741
$1,500	$2,598	$4,678	29 Y & 5 M	$590,732	$557,277	$490,864	$380,246	$0
$1,750	$3,031	$5,458	25 Y & 8 M	$573,260	$515,758	$416,857	$262,979	$0
$2,000	$3,463	$6,237	22 Y & 10 M	$555,792	$474,261	$342,903	$145,800	$0
$2,250	$3,896	$7,017	20 Y & 6 M	$538,318	$432,746	$268,908	$28,548	$0
$2,500	$4,329	$7,796	18 Y & 8 M	$520,846	$391,231	$194,922	$0	$0

| **$600,000 Balance** | | | | **4% Return On Investment** | | | | |

No COLA

Monthly Amount	15 Yr Inflated	30 Yr Inflated	Money Lasts	5 Years	10 Years	15 Years	20 Years	30 Years
$1,750	$1,750	$1,750	Over 40 Yrs	$613,974	$630,976	$651,662	$676,829	$744,700
$2,000	$2,000	$2,000	Over 40 Yrs	$597,400	$594,237	$590,388	$585,707	$573,079
$2,250	$2,250	$2,250	Over 40 Yrs	$580,826	$557,498	$529,116	$494,586	$401,459
$2,500	$2,500	$2,500	39 Y & 2 M	$564,252	$520,759	$467,843	$403,464	$229,840
$2,750	$2,750	$2,750	31 Y & 10 M	$547,679	$484,022	$406,573	$312,345	$58,223
$3,000	$3,000	$3,000	27 Y & 1 M	$531,104	$447,281	$345,298	$221,222	$0
$3,250	$3,250	$3,250	23 Y & 7 M	$514,531	$410,544	$284,028	$130,102	$0

2% COLA

Monthly Amount	15 Yr Inflated	30 Yr Inflated	Money Lasts	5 Years	10 Years	15 Years	20 Years	30 Years
$1,500	$1,979	$2,664	Over 40 Yrs	$626,650	$648,318	$662,802	$667,308	$631,386
$1,750	$2,309	$3,108	Over 40 Yrs	$609,428	$608,347	$593,179	$559,431	$412,326
$2,000	$2,639	$3,552	34 Y & 9 M	$592,204	$568,377	$523,554	$451,537	$193,218
$2,250	$2,969	$3,996	29 Y & 6 M	$574,980	$528,403	$453,926	$343,641	$0
$2,500	$3,299	$4,440	25 Y & 8 M	$557,757	$488,440	$384,314	$235,774	$0
$2,750	$3,629	$4,884	22 Y & 9 M	$540,533	$448,466	$314,678	$127,866	$0
$3,000	$3,958	$5,327	20 Y & 5 M	$523,312	$408,499	$245,061	$19,995	$0

3% COLA

Monthly Amount	15 Yr Inflated	30 Yr Inflated	Money Lasts	5 Years	10 Years	15 Years	20 Years	30 Years
$1,500	$2,269	$3,535	Over 40 Yrs	$624,644	$637,846	$634,453	$607,771	$447,548
$1,750	$2,647	$4,124	33 Y & 11 M	$607,087	$596,140	$560,127	$490,009	$197,951
$2,000	$3,025	$4,713	29 Y & 2 M	$589,526	$554,408	$485,742	$372,133	$0
$2,250	$3,403	$5,302	25 Y & 6 M	$571,971	$512,704	$411,417	$254,359	$0
$2,500	$3,782	$5,891	22 Y & 7 M	$554,413	$470,985	$337,062	$136,542	$0
$2,750	$4,160	$6,481	20 Y & 4 M	$536,855	$429,265	$262,700	$18,703	$0
$3,000	$4,538	$7,070	18 Y & 6 M	$519,298	$387,550	$188,358	$0	$0

4% COLA

Monthly Amount	15 Yr Inflated	30 Yr Inflated	Money Lasts	5 Years	10 Years	15 Years	20 Years	30 Years
$1,250	$2,165	$3,899	Over 40 Yrs	$640,497	$670,377	$683,140	$669,961	$514,520
$1,500	$2,598	$4,678	33 Y & 11 M	$622,597	$626,825	$603,662	$541,034	$228,246
$1,750	$3,031	$5,458	29 Y & 2 M	$604,697	$583,263	$524,158	$412,062	$0
$2,000	$3,463	$6,237	25 Y & 6 M	$586,804	$539,726	$444,706	$283,183	$0
$2,250	$3,896	$7,017	22 Y & 8 M	$568,903	$496,171	$365,218	$154,232	$0
$2,500	$4,329	$7,796	20 Y & 5 M	$551,003	$452,611	$285,729	$25,292	$0
$2,750	$4,762	$8,576	18 Y & 7 M	$533,103	$409,055	$206,232	$0	$0

| $600,000 Balance | | | | 5% Return On Investment | | | | |

No COLA

Monthly Amount	15 Yr Inflated	30 Yr Inflated	Money Lasts	5 Years	10 Years	15 Years	20 Years	30 Years
$1,750	$1,750	$1,750	Over 40 Yrs	$646,830	$706,598	$782,879	$880,235	$1.163 M
$2,000	$2,000	$2,000	Over 40 Yrs	$629,839	$667,921	$716,526	$778,559	$958,775
$2,250	$2,250	$2,250	Over 40 Yrs	$612,846	$629,242	$650,167	$676,874	$754,464
$2,500	$2,500	$2,500	Over 40 Yrs	$595,856	$590,568	$583,817	$575,202	$550,172
$2,750	$2,750	$2,750	Over 40 Yrs	$578,865	$551,890	$517,463	$473,525	$345,876
$3,000	$3,000	$3,000	34 Y & 5 M	$561,873	$513,213	$451,110	$371,847	$141,575
$3,250	$3,250	$3,250	28 Y & 6 M	$544,882	$474,536	$384,754	$270,168	$0

2% COLA

Monthly Amount	15 Yr Inflated	30 Yr Inflated	Money Lasts	5 Years	10 Years	15 Years	20 Years	30 Years
$1,500	$1,979	$2,664	Over 40 Yrs	$659,865	$725,247	$796,520	$874,042	$1.049 M
$1,750	$2,309	$3,108	Over 40 Yrs	$642,216	$683,232	$721,385	$754,405	$791,821
$2,000	$2,639	$3,552	Over 40 Yrs	$624,565	$641,219	$646,249	$634,752	$534,485
$2,250	$2,969	$3,996	36 Y & 4 M	$606,912	$599,199	$571,104	$515,090	$277,135
$2,500	$3,299	$4,440	30 Y & 5 M	$589,264	$557,194	$495,984	$395,465	$19,858
$2,750	$3,629	$4,884	26 Y & 3 M	$571,613	$515,178	$420,837	$275,798	$0
$3,000	$3,958	$5,327	23 Y & 1 M	$553,964	$473,167	$345,706	$156,163	$0

3% COLA

Monthly Amount	15 Yr Inflated	30 Yr Inflated	Money Lasts	5 Years	10 Years	15 Years	20 Years	30 Years
$1,500	$2,269	$3,535	Over 40 Yrs	$657,831	$714,445	$766,765	$810,433	$845,260
$1,750	$2,647	$4,124	Over 40 Yrs	$639,840	$670,634	$686,686	$680,221	$554,090
$2,000	$3,025	$4,713	34 Y & 10 M	$621,848	$626,807	$606,558	$549,907	$262,627
$2,250	$3,403	$5,302	29 Y & 7 M	$603,862	$583,005	$526,489	$419,699	$0
$2,500	$3,782	$5,891	25 Y & 9 M	$585,869	$539,182	$446,379	$289,429	$0
$2,750	$4,160	$6,481	22 Y & 10 M	$567,879	$495,365	$366,273	$159,151	$0
$3,000	$4,538	$7,070	20 Y & 6 M	$549,892	$451,553	$286,186	$28,919	$0

4% COLA

Monthly Amount	15 Yr Inflated	30 Yr Inflated	Money Lasts	5 Years	10 Years	15 Years	20 Years	30 Years
$1,250	$2,165	$3,899	Over 40 Yrs	$674,089	$748,785	$819,950	$881,369	$934,843
$1,500	$2,598	$4,678	Over 40 Yrs	$655,753	$703,075	$734,475	$739,262	$603,208
$1,750	$3,031	$5,458	34 Y & 2 M	$637,416	$657,357	$648,973	$597,107	$271,498
$2,000	$3,463	$6,237	29 Y & 3 M	$619,084	$611,662	$563,526	$455,052	$0
$2,250	$3,896	$7,017	25 Y & 7 M	$600,747	$565,950	$478,039	$312,918	$0
$2,500	$4,329	$7,796	22 Y & 9 M	$582,410	$520,236	$392,558	$170,804	$0
$2,750	$4,762	$8,576	20 Y & 5 M	$564,074	$474,523	$307,065	$28,659	$0

| $600,000 Balance | | | | 6% Return On Investment | | | | |

No COLA

Monthly Amount	15 Yr Inflated	30 Yr Inflated	Money Lasts	5 Years	10 Years	15 Years	20 Years	30 Years
$2,000	$2,000	$2,000	Over 40 Yrs	$663,587	$748,680	$862,555	$1.015 M	$1.492 M
$2,250	$2,250	$2,250	Over 40 Yrs	$646,167	$707,951	$790,631	$901,276	$1.247 M
$2,500	$2,500	$2,500	Over 40 Yrs	$628,749	$667,221	$718,706	$787,604	$1.003 M
$2,750	$2,750	$2,750	Over 40 Yrs	$611,331	$626,494	$646,787	$673,942	$758,913
$3,000	$3,000	$3,000	Over 40 Yrs	$593,913	$585,766	$574,864	$560,276	$514,627
$3,250	$3,250	$3,250	38 Y & 11 M	$576,495	$545,039	$502,942	$446,609	$270,337
$3,500	$3,500	$3,500	30 Y & 8 M	$559,074	$504,306	$431,014	$332,933	$26,030

2% COLA

Monthly Amount	15 Yr Inflated	30 Yr Inflated	Money Lasts	5 Years	10 Years	15 Years	20 Years	30 Years
$1,750	$2,309	$3,108	Over 40 Yrs	$676,323	$765,280	$869,776	$993,553	$1.320 M
$2,000	$2,639	$3,552	Over 40 Yrs	$658,233	$721,101	$788,604	$860,580	$1.016 M
$2,250	$2,969	$3,996	Over 40 Yrs	$640,145	$676,924	$707,438	$727,615	$712,255
$2,500	$3,299	$4,440	38 Y & 11 M	$622,059	$632,757	$626,290	$594,683	$408,566
$2,750	$3,629	$4,884	31 Y & 10 M	$603,972	$588,582	$545,119	$461,711	$104,774
$3,000	$3,958	$5,327	27 Y & 2 M	$585,885	$544,407	$463,958	$328,767	$0
$3,250	$4,288	$5,772	23 Y & 8 M	$567,792	$500,217	$382,768	$195,760	$0

3% COLA

Monthly Amount	15 Yr Inflated	30 Yr Inflated	Money Lasts	5 Years	10 Years	15 Years	20 Years	30 Years
$1,750	$2,647	$4,124	Over 40 Yrs	$673,912	$752,277	$833,325	$914,174	$1.055 M
$2,000	$3,025	$4,713	Over 40 Yrs	$655,477	$706,227	$746,913	$769,795	$713,416
$2,250	$3,403	$5,302	36 Y & 4 M	$637,049	$660,209	$660,572	$625,545	$371,967
$2,500	$3,782	$5,891	30 Y & 6 M	$618,616	$614,172	$574,190	$481,232	$30,412
$2,750	$4,160	$6,481	26 Y & 4 M	$600,183	$568,133	$487,801	$336,896	$0
$3,000	$4,538	$7,070	23 Y & 2 M	$581,752	$522,101	$401,438	$192,614	$0
$3,250	$4,916	$7,659	20 Y & 9 M	$563,321	$476,075	$315,076	$48,332	$0

4% COLA

Monthly Amount	15 Yr Inflated	30 Yr Inflated	Money Lasts	5 Years	10 Years	15 Years	20 Years	30 Years
$1,500	$2,598	$4,678	Over 40 Yrs	$690,236	$786,576	$885,797	$982,430	$1.128 M
$1,750	$3,031	$5,458	Over 40 Yrs	$671,452	$738,581	$793,755	$825,421	$742,130
$2,000	$3,463	$6,237	34 Y & 11 M	$652,673	$690,608	$701,768	$668,517	$356,042
$2,250	$3,896	$7,017	29 Y & 8 M	$633,888	$642,616	$609,737	$511,523	$0
$2,500	$4,329	$7,796	25 Y & 10 M	$615,106	$594,626	$517,714	$354,556	$0
$2,750	$4,762	$8,576	22 Y & 11 M	$596,321	$546,634	$425,677	$197,552	$0
$3,000	$5,195	$9,356	20 Y & 7 M	$577,537	$498,637	$333,630	$40,521	$0

$625,000 Balance   3% Return On Investment

No COLA

Monthly Amount	15 Yr Inflated	30 Yr Inflated	Money Lasts	5 Years	10 Years	15 Years	20 Years	30 Years
$1,500	$1,500	$1,500	Over 40 Yrs	$627,547	$630,500	$633,924	$637,894	$647,832
$1,800	$1,800	$1,800	Over 40 Yrs	$608,150	$588,615	$565,968	$539,715	$473,996
$2,100	$2,100	$2,100	Over 40 Yrs	$588,749	$546,723	$498,005	$441,527	$300,153
$2,400	$2,400	$2,400	34 Y & 9 M	$569,350	$504,836	$430,046	$343,344	$126,312
$2,700	$2,700	$2,700	28 Y & 7 M	$549,950	$462,948	$362,087	$245,161	$0
$3,000	$3,000	$3,000	24 Y & 5 M	$530,550	$421,058	$294,127	$146,978	$0
$3,300	$3,300	$3,300	21 Y & 4 M	$511,152	$379,171	$226,168	$48,795	$0

2% COLA

Monthly Amount	15 Yr Inflated	30 Yr Inflated	Money Lasts	5 Years	10 Years	15 Years	20 Years	30 Years
$1,200	$1,583	$2,131	Over 40 Yrs	$643,874	$657,354	$663,714	$660,853	$616,811
$1,500	$1,979	$2,664	Over 40 Yrs	$623,708	$611,714	$586,219	$543,865	$391,747
$1,800	$2,375	$3,197	34 Y & 5 M	$603,540	$566,067	$508,722	$426,892	$166,740
$2,100	$2,771	$3,729	28 Y & 9 M	$583,375	$520,424	$431,224	$309,905	$0
$2,400	$3,167	$4,262	24 Y & 8 M	$563,205	$474,776	$353,722	$192,916	$0
$2,700	$3,563	$4,795	21 Y & 8 M	$543,037	$429,132	$276,230	$75,946	$0
$3,000	$3,958	$5,327	19 Y & 3 M	$522,873	$383,489	$198,730	$0	$0

3% COLA

Monthly Amount	15 Yr Inflated	30 Yr Inflated	Money Lasts	5 Years	10 Years	15 Years	20 Years	30 Years
$1,200	$1,815	$2,828	Over 40 Yrs	$642,295	$649,246	$642,115	$616,247	$483,766
$1,500	$2,269	$3,535	35 Y & 3 M	$621,731	$601,565	$559,198	$488,071	$225,347
$1,800	$2,723	$4,242	29 Y & 5 M	$601,170	$553,898	$476,317	$359,967	$0
$2,100	$3,176	$4,949	25 Y & 2 M	$580,604	$506,211	$393,391	$231,791	$0
$2,400	$3,630	$5,656	22 Y & 1 M	$560,041	$458,532	$310,477	$103,626	$0
$2,700	$4,084	$6,362	19 Y & 7 M	$539,480	$410,863	$227,595	$0	$0
$3,000	$4,538	$7,070	17 Y & 8 M	$518,917	$363,184	$144,681	$0	$0

4% COLA

Monthly Amount	15 Yr Inflated	30 Yr Inflated	Money Lasts	5 Years	10 Years	15 Years	20 Years	30 Years
$900	$1,558	$2,807	Over 40 Yrs	$661,649	$690,510	$707,391	$706,792	$622,452
$1,200	$2,078	$3,743	36 Y & 10 M	$640,682	$640,689	$618,589	$566,076	$324,144
$1,500	$2,598	$4,678	30 Y & 6 M	$619,714	$590,876	$529,813	$425,399	$25,925
$1,800	$3,117	$5,614	25 Y & 11 M	$598,746	$541,054	$441,015	$284,701	$0
$2,100	$3,636	$6,549	22 Y & 8 M	$577,784	$491,258	$352,268	$144,079	$0
$2,400	$4,156	$7,485	20 Y & 1 M	$556,816	$441,428	$263,444	$3,319	$0
$2,700	$4,676	$8,420	17 Y & 11 M	$535,848	$391,613	$174,666	$0	$0

| $625,000 Balance | | | | | 4% Return On Investment | | | |

No COLA

Monthly Amount	15 Yr Inflated	30 Yr Inflated	Money Lasts	5 Years	10 Years	15 Years	20 Years	30 Years
$1,800	$1,800	$1,800	Over 40 Yrs	$641,076	$660,634	$684,430	$713,381	$791,459
$2,100	$2,100	$2,100	Over 40 Yrs	$621,187	$616,548	$610,904	$604,037	$585,516
$2,400	$2,400	$2,400	Over 40 Yrs	$601,299	$572,463	$537,379	$494,694	$379,577
$2,700	$2,700	$2,700	35 Y & 11 M	$581,409	$528,374	$463,848	$385,343	$173,623
$3,000	$3,000	$3,000	29 Y & 2 M	$561,521	$484,288	$390,324	$276,002	$0
$3,300	$3,300	$3,300	24 Y & 8 M	$541,632	$440,201	$316,796	$166,655	$0
$3,600	$3,600	$3,600	21 Y & 5 M	$521,743	$396,116	$243,271	$57,312	$0

2% COLA

Monthly Amount	15 Yr Inflated	30 Yr Inflated	Money Lasts	5 Years	10 Years	15 Years	20 Years	30 Years
$1,500	$1,979	$2,664	Over 40 Yrs	$657,066	$685,323	$707,825	$722,085	$712,469
$1,800	$2,375	$3,197	Over 40 Yrs	$636,398	$637,359	$624,279	$592,632	$449,596
$2,100	$2,771	$3,729	34 Y & 4 M	$615,732	$589,396	$540,729	$463,163	$186,670
$2,400	$3,167	$4,262	28 Y & 7 M	$595,060	$541,427	$457,173	$333,686	$0
$2,700	$3,563	$4,795	24 Y & 6 M	$574,395	$493,468	$373,635	$204,241	$0
$3,000	$3,958	$5,327	21 Y & 6 M	$553,728	$445,505	$290,085	$74,773	$0
$3,300	$4,354	$5,860	19 Y & 1 M	$533,058	$397,538	$206,528	$0	$0

3% COLA

Monthly Amount	15 Yr Inflated	30 Yr Inflated	Money Lasts	5 Years	10 Years	15 Years	20 Years	30 Years
$1,500	$2,269	$3,535	Over 40 Yrs	$655,061	$674,854	$679,479	$662,552	$528,639
$1,800	$2,723	$4,242	34 Y & 7 M	$633,993	$624,805	$590,285	$521,222	$229,078
$2,100	$3,176	$4,949	28 Y & 10 M	$612,921	$574,733	$501,040	$379,810	$0
$2,400	$3,630	$5,656	24 Y & 9 M	$591,852	$524,672	$411,812	$238,417	$0
$2,700	$4,084	$6,362	21 Y & 9 M	$570,783	$474,617	$322,613	$97,089	$0
$3,000	$4,538	$7,070	19 Y & 4 M	$549,715	$424,558	$233,386	$0	$0
$3,300	$4,992	$7,777	17 Y & 5 M	$528,644	$374,499	$144,163	$0	$0

4% COLA

Monthly Amount	15 Yr Inflated	30 Yr Inflated	Money Lasts	5 Years	10 Years	15 Years	20 Years	30 Years
$1,200	$2,078	$3,743	Over 40 Yrs	$674,493	$716,093	$744,057	$750,531	$652,882
$1,500	$2,598	$4,678	35 Y & 5 M	$653,014	$663,832	$648,687	$595,812	$309,329
$1,800	$3,117	$5,614	29 Y & 6 M	$631,534	$611,561	$553,292	$441,072	$0
$2,100	$3,636	$6,549	25 Y & 4 M	$610,060	$559,316	$457,951	$286,412	$0
$2,400	$4,156	$7,485	22 Y & 2 M	$588,580	$507,036	$362,529	$131,606	$0
$2,700	$4,676	$8,420	19 Y & 8 M	$567,099	$454,772	$267,154	$0	$0
$3,000	$5,195	$9,356	17 Y & 9 M	$545,619	$402,501	$171,751	$0	$0

$625,000 Balance   **5% Return On Investment**

No COLA

Monthly Amount	15 Yr Inflated	30 Yr Inflated	Money Lasts	5 Years	10 Years	15 Years	20 Years	30 Years
$1,800	$1,800	$1,800	Over 40 Yrs	$675,339	$739,586	$821,581	$926,231	$1.230 M
$2,100	$2,100	$2,100	Over 40 Yrs	$654,949	$693,171	$741,955	$804,217	$985,098
$2,400	$2,400	$2,400	Over 40 Yrs	$634,560	$646,760	$662,331	$682,204	$739,939
$2,700	$2,700	$2,700	Over 40 Yrs	$614,170	$600,347	$582,705	$560,190	$494,783
$3,000	$3,000	$3,000	38 Y & 6 M	$593,780	$553,934	$503,080	$438,177	$249,619
$3,300	$3,300	$3,300	30 Y & 2 M	$573,391	$507,525	$423,460	$316,169	$4,468
$3,600	$3,600	$3,600	25 Y & 1 M	$553,001	$461,111	$343,833	$194,153	$0

2% COLA

Monthly Amount	15 Yr Inflated	30 Yr Inflated	Money Lasts	5 Years	10 Years	15 Years	20 Years	30 Years
$1,500	$1,979	$2,664	Over 40 Yrs	$691,771	$765,969	$848,493	$940,375	$1.157 M
$1,800	$2,375	$3,197	Over 40 Yrs	$670,593	$715,554	$758,334	$796,810	$848,412
$2,100	$2,771	$3,729	Over 40 Yrs	$649,411	$665,134	$668,164	$653,220	$539,596
$2,400	$3,167	$4,262	34 Y & 10 M	$628,230	$614,719	$578,002	$509,641	$230,796
$2,700	$3,563	$4,795	28 Y & 9 M	$607,050	$564,304	$487,846	$366,077	$0
$3,000	$3,958	$5,327	24 Y & 6 M	$585,871	$513,889	$397,679	$222,497	$0
$3,300	$4,354	$5,860	21 Y & 5 M	$564,689	$463,470	$307,510	$78,902	$0

3% COLA

Monthly Amount	15 Yr Inflated	30 Yr Inflated	Money Lasts	5 Years	10 Years	15 Years	20 Years	30 Years
$1,500	$2,269	$3,535	Over 40 Yrs	$689,738	$755,168	$818,740	$876,767	$953,312
$1,800	$2,723	$4,242	Over 40 Yrs	$668,152	$702,600	$722,649	$720,508	$603,877
$2,100	$3,176	$4,949	34 Y & 5 M	$646,560	$650,008	$626,507	$564,165	$254,220
$2,400	$3,630	$5,656	28 Y & 8 M	$624,972	$597,427	$530,382	$407,840	$0
$2,700	$4,084	$6,362	24 Y & 7 M	$603,387	$544,857	$434,287	$251,585	$0
$3,000	$4,538	$7,070	21 Y & 6 M	$581,799	$492,276	$338,160	$95,254	$0
$3,300	$4,992	$7,777	19 Y & 2 M	$560,208	$439,695	$242,039	$0	$0

4% COLA

Monthly Amount	15 Yr Inflated	30 Yr Inflated	Money Lasts	5 Years	10 Years	15 Years	20 Years	30 Years
$1,200	$2,078	$3,743	Over 40 Yrs	$709,664	$798,649	$889,017	$976,131	$1.109 M
$1,500	$2,598	$4,678	Over 40 Yrs	$687,659	$743,796	$786,446	$805,591	$711,252
$1,800	$3,117	$5,614	34 Y & 8 M	$665,656	$688,940	$683,858	$635,035	$313,278
$2,100	$3,636	$6,549	28 Y & 11 M	$643,657	$634,106	$581,321	$464,565	$0
$2,400	$4,156	$7,485	24 Y & 11 M	$621,653	$579,239	$478,703	$293,937	$0
$2,700	$4,676	$8,420	21 Y & 10 M	$599,649	$524,387	$376,133	$123,416	$0
$3,000	$5,195	$9,356	19 Y & 5 M	$577,645	$469,530	$273,539	$0	$0

| $625,000 Balance | | | | | | 6% Return On Investment | | |

No COLA

Monthly Amount	15 Yr Inflated	30 Yr Inflated	Money Lasts	5 Years	10 Years	15 Years	20 Years	30 Years
$2,100	$2,100	$2,100	Over 40 Yrs	$690,075	$777,159	$893,699	$1.050 M	$1.538 M
$2,400	$2,400	$2,400	Over 40 Yrs	$669,173	$728,286	$807,393	$913,256	$1.245 M
$2,700	$2,700	$2,700	Over 40 Yrs	$648,271	$679,411	$721,084	$776,853	$951,356
$3,000	$3,000	$3,000	Over 40 Yrs	$627,367	$630,536	$634,776	$640,451	$658,208
$3,300	$3,300	$3,300	Over 40 Yrs	$606,466	$581,662	$548,469	$504,049	$365,057
$3,600	$3,600	$3,600	31 Y & 9 M	$585,563	$532,787	$462,161	$367,648	$71,911
$3,900	$3,900	$3,900	25 Y & 10 M	$564,660	$483,912	$375,853	$231,245	$0

2% COLA

Monthly Amount	15 Yr Inflated	30 Yr Inflated	Money Lasts	5 Years	10 Years	15 Years	20 Years	30 Years
$1,800	$2,375	$3,197	Over 40 Yrs	$706,159	$801,214	$913,454	$1.047 M	$1.403 M
$2,100	$2,771	$3,729	Over 40 Yrs	$684,456	$748,206	$816,058	$887,583	$1.038 M
$2,400	$3,167	$4,262	Over 40 Yrs	$662,748	$695,193	$718,657	$728,025	$673,603
$2,700	$3,563	$4,795	35 Y & 11 M	$641,044	$642,186	$621,269	$568,494	$309,167
$3,000	$3,958	$5,327	29 Y & 2 M	$619,341	$589,179	$523,873	$408,946	$0
$3,300	$4,354	$5,860	24 Y & 8 M	$597,633	$536,164	$426,467	$249,375	$0
$3,600	$4,750	$6,393	21 Y & 6 M	$575,929	$483,153	$329,070	$89,824	$0

3% COLA

Monthly Amount	15 Yr Inflated	30 Yr Inflated	Money Lasts	5 Years	10 Years	15 Years	20 Years	30 Years
$1,800	$2,723	$4,242	Over 40 Yrs	$703,684	$787,848	$875,973	$965,495	$1.130 M
$2,100	$3,176	$4,949	Over 40 Yrs	$681,562	$732,592	$772,296	$792,287	$720,462
$2,400	$3,630	$5,656	34 Y & 10 M	$659,443	$677,350	$668,637	$619,099	$310,516
$2,700	$4,084	$6,362	28 Y & 9 M	$637,327	$622,118	$565,015	$445,993	$0
$3,000	$4,538	$7,070	24 Y & 7 M	$615,208	$566,871	$461,349	$272,790	$0
$3,300	$4,992	$7,777	21 Y & 6 M	$593,088	$511,633	$357,702	$99,624	$0
$3,600	$5,445	$8,484	19 Y & 1 M	$570,969	$456,391	$254,052	$0	$0

4% COLA

Monthly Amount	15 Yr Inflated	30 Yr Inflated	Money Lasts	5 Years	10 Years	15 Years	20 Years	30 Years
$1,500	$2,598	$4,678	Over 40 Yrs	$723,692	$831,350	$945,716	$1.063 M	$1.272 M
$1,800	$3,117	$5,614	Over 40 Yrs	$701,151	$773,756	$835,271	$874,223	$808,532
$2,100	$3,636	$6,549	34 Y & 6 M	$678,616	$716,190	$724,887	$685,933	$345,200
$2,400	$4,156	$7,485	28 Y & 9 M	$656,075	$658,588	$614,415	$497,473	$0
$2,700	$4,676	$8,420	24 Y & 8 M	$633,534	$601,002	$503,995	$309,126	$0
$3,000	$5,195	$9,356	21 Y & 7 M	$610,992	$543,408	$393,546	$120,704	$0
$3,300	$5,714	$10,291	19 Y & 3 M	$588,457	$485,842	$283,171	$0	$0

$650,000 Balance   3% Return On Investment

No COLA

Monthly Amount	15 Yr Inflated	30 Yr Inflated	Money Lasts	5 Years	10 Years	15 Years	20 Years	30 Years
$1,500	$1,500	$1,500	Over 40 Yrs	$656,530	$664,101	$672,878	$683,052	$708,520
$1,800	$1,800	$1,800	Over 40 Yrs	$637,130	$622,211	$604,915	$584,863	$534,673
$2,100	$2,100	$2,100	Over 40 Yrs	$617,731	$580,324	$536,958	$486,685	$360,841
$2,400	$2,400	$2,400	37 Y & 3 M	$598,332	$538,435	$468,998	$388,501	$187,001
$2,700	$2,700	$2,700	30 Y & 5 M	$578,932	$496,544	$401,034	$290,312	$13,155
$3,000	$3,000	$3,000	25 Y & 10 M	$559,532	$454,655	$333,074	$192,128	$0
$3,300	$3,300	$3,300	22 Y & 6 M	$540,133	$412,766	$265,113	$93,943	$0

2% COLA

Monthly Amount	15 Yr Inflated	30 Yr Inflated	Money Lasts	5 Years	10 Years	15 Years	20 Years	30 Years
$1,200	$1,583	$2,131	Over 40 Yrs	$672,856	$690,951	$702,662	$706,004	$677,489
$1,500	$1,979	$2,664	Over 40 Yrs	$652,690	$645,313	$625,169	$589,019	$452,430
$1,800	$2,375	$3,197	36 Y & 1 M	$632,522	$599,666	$547,672	$472,044	$227,421
$2,100	$2,771	$3,729	30 Y & 1 M	$612,355	$554,019	$470,171	$355,056	$2,365
$2,400	$3,167	$4,262	25 Y & 10 M	$592,186	$508,373	$392,671	$238,068	$0
$2,700	$3,563	$4,795	22 Y & 7 M	$572,020	$462,730	$315,179	$121,099	$0
$3,000	$3,958	$5,327	20 Y & 1 M	$551,854	$417,087	$237,679	$4,115	$0

3% COLA

Monthly Amount	15 Yr Inflated	30 Yr Inflated	Money Lasts	5 Years	10 Years	15 Years	20 Years	30 Years
$1,200	$1,815	$2,828	Over 40 Yrs	$671,277	$682,843	$681,063	$661,398	$544,448
$1,500	$2,269	$3,535	36 Y & 8 M	$650,714	$635,163	$598,147	$533,224	$286,029
$1,800	$2,723	$4,242	30 Y & 7 M	$630,153	$587,498	$515,269	$405,122	$27,814
$2,100	$3,176	$4,949	26 Y & 3 M	$609,586	$539,807	$432,340	$276,942	$0
$2,400	$3,630	$5,656	22 Y & 11 M	$589,023	$492,129	$349,425	$148,778	$0
$2,700	$4,084	$6,362	20 Y & 5 M	$568,462	$444,460	$266,544	$20,680	$0
$3,000	$4,538	$7,070	18 Y & 4 M	$547,899	$396,781	$183,629	$0	$0

4% COLA

Monthly Amount	15 Yr Inflated	30 Yr Inflated	Money Lasts	5 Years	10 Years	15 Years	20 Years	30 Years
$900	$1,558	$2,807	Over 40 Yrs	$690,631	$724,107	$746,337	$751,939	$683,126
$1,200	$2,078	$3,743	38 Y & 1 M	$669,663	$674,287	$657,539	$611,231	$384,829
$1,500	$2,598	$4,678	31 Y & 6 M	$648,696	$624,473	$568,761	$470,552	$86,605
$1,800	$3,117	$5,614	26 Y & 11 M	$627,728	$574,653	$479,965	$329,855	$0
$2,100	$3,636	$6,549	23 Y & 6 M	$606,766	$524,855	$391,215	$189,231	$0
$2,400	$4,156	$7,485	20 Y & 10 M	$585,799	$475,027	$302,395	$48,474	$0
$2,700	$4,676	$8,420	18 Y & 8 M	$564,831	$425,214	$213,620	$0	$0

$650,000 Balance   4% Return On Investment

No COLA

Monthly Amount	15 Yr Inflated	30 Yr Inflated	Money Lasts	5 Years	10 Years	15 Years	20 Years	30 Years
$1,800	$1,800	$1,800	Over 40 Yrs	$671,492	$697,642	$729,456	$768,162	$872,547
$2,100	$2,100	$2,100	Over 40 Yrs	$651,603	$653,554	$655,928	$658,816	$666,606
$2,400	$2,400	$2,400	Over 40 Yrs	$631,715	$609,468	$582,402	$549,471	$460,658
$2,700	$2,700	$2,700	39 Y & 5 M	$611,826	$565,380	$508,873	$440,123	$254,713
$3,000	$3,000	$3,000	31 Y & 5 M	$591,936	$521,293	$435,345	$330,776	$48,764
$3,300	$3,300	$3,300	26 Y & 4 M	$572,048	$477,209	$361,821	$221,434	$0
$3,600	$3,600	$3,600	22 Y & 9 M	$552,159	$433,120	$288,292	$112,087	$0

2% COLA

Monthly Amount	15 Yr Inflated	30 Yr Inflated	Money Lasts	5 Years	10 Years	15 Years	20 Years	30 Years
$1,500	$1,979	$2,664	Over 40 Yrs	$687,482	$722,329	$752,847	$776,862	$793,553
$1,800	$2,375	$3,197	Over 40 Yrs	$666,815	$674,366	$669,303	$647,411	$530,684
$2,100	$2,771	$3,729	36 Y & 4 M	$646,147	$626,401	$585,751	$517,940	$267,757
$2,400	$3,167	$4,262	30 Y & 2 M	$625,477	$578,434	$502,197	$388,465	$4,820
$2,700	$3,563	$4,795	25 Y & 9 M	$604,809	$530,472	$418,656	$259,014	$0
$3,000	$3,958	$5,327	22 Y & 6 M	$584,144	$482,510	$335,107	$129,550	$0
$3,300	$4,354	$5,860	19 Y & 11 M	$563,473	$434,543	$251,551	$0	$0

3% COLA

Monthly Amount	15 Yr Inflated	30 Yr Inflated	Money Lasts	5 Years	10 Years	15 Years	20 Years	30 Years
$1,500	$2,269	$3,535	Over 40 Yrs	$685,477	$711,861	$724,504	$717,332	$609,725
$1,800	$2,723	$4,242	36 Y & 3 M	$664,410	$661,812	$635,309	$576,001	$310,162
$2,100	$3,176	$4,949	30 Y & 3 M	$643,338	$611,740	$546,065	$434,590	$10,398
$2,400	$3,630	$5,656	25 Y & 11 M	$622,268	$561,678	$456,834	$293,194	$0
$2,700	$4,084	$6,362	22 Y & 8 M	$601,200	$511,626	$367,638	$151,870	$0
$3,000	$4,538	$7,070	20 Y & 2 M	$580,130	$461,564	$278,408	$10,468	$0
$3,300	$4,992	$7,777	18 Y & 2 M	$559,060	$411,504	$189,184	$0	$0

4% COLA

Monthly Amount	15 Yr Inflated	30 Yr Inflated	Money Lasts	5 Years	10 Years	15 Years	20 Years	30 Years
$1,200	$2,078	$3,743	Over 40 Yrs	$704,910	$753,100	$789,083	$805,312	$733,969
$1,500	$2,598	$4,678	36 Y & 10 M	$683,431	$700,839	$693,713	$650,595	$390,422
$1,800	$3,117	$5,614	30 Y & 9 M	$661,950	$648,566	$598,314	$495,849	$46,872
$2,100	$3,636	$6,549	26 Y & 4 M	$640,476	$596,321	$502,972	$341,188	$0
$2,400	$4,156	$7,485	22 Y & 11 M	$618,996	$544,042	$407,551	$186,381	$0
$2,700	$4,676	$8,420	20 Y & 6 M	$597,515	$491,776	$312,176	$31,675	$0
$3,000	$5,195	$9,356	18 Y & 5 M	$576,036	$439,507	$216,775	$0	$0

| $650,000 Balance | | | | 5% Return On Investment | | | | |

No COLA

Monthly Amount	15 Yr Inflated	30 Yr Inflated	Money Lasts	5 Years	10 Years	15 Years	20 Years	30 Years
$1,800	$1,800	$1,800	Over 40 Yrs	$707,246	$780,307	$873,553	$992,563	$1.338 M
$2,100	$2,100	$2,100	Over 40 Yrs	$686,856	$733,894	$793,928	$870,549	$1.093 M
$2,400	$2,400	$2,400	Over 40 Yrs	$666,466	$687,481	$714,303	$748,535	$847,986
$2,700	$2,700	$2,700	Over 40 Yrs	$646,077	$641,071	$634,681	$626,525	$602,831
$3,000	$3,000	$3,000	Over 40 Yrs	$625,687	$594,657	$555,054	$504,509	$357,668
$3,300	$3,300	$3,300	33 Y & 1 M	$605,299	$548,248	$475,434	$382,503	$112,521
$3,600	$3,600	$3,600	27 Y & 2 M	$584,908	$501,832	$395,804	$260,483	$0

2% COLA

Monthly Amount	15 Yr Inflated	30 Yr Inflated	Money Lasts	5 Years	10 Years	15 Years	20 Years	30 Years
$1,500	$1,979	$2,664	Over 40 Yrs	$723,681	$806,694	$900,468	$1.007 M	$1.265 M
$1,800	$2,375	$3,197	Over 40 Yrs	$702,499	$756,276	$810,308	$863,143	$956,465
$2,100	$2,771	$3,729	Over 40 Yrs	$681,319	$705,857	$720,138	$719,553	$647,647
$2,400	$3,167	$4,262	37 Y & 4 M	$660,137	$655,441	$629,975	$575,973	$338,844
$2,700	$3,563	$4,795	30 Y & 7 M	$638,957	$605,027	$539,820	$432,411	$30,114
$3,000	$3,958	$5,327	25 Y & 11 M	$617,778	$554,611	$449,652	$288,827	$0
$3,300	$4,354	$5,860	22 Y & 7 M	$596,596	$504,192	$359,483	$145,233	$0

3% COLA

Monthly Amount	15 Yr Inflated	30 Yr Inflated	Money Lasts	5 Years	10 Years	15 Years	20 Years	30 Years
$1,500	$2,269	$3,535	Over 40 Yrs	$721,644	$795,890	$870,713	$943,100	$1.061 M
$1,800	$2,723	$4,242	Over 40 Yrs	$700,059	$743,322	$774,621	$786,838	$711,920
$2,100	$3,176	$4,949	36 Y & 5 M	$678,468	$690,731	$678,481	$630,499	$362,272
$2,400	$3,630	$5,656	30 Y & 3 M	$656,879	$638,149	$582,352	$474,169	$12,642
$2,700	$4,084	$6,362	25 Y & 10 M	$635,293	$585,578	$486,259	$317,917	$0
$3,000	$4,538	$7,070	22 Y & 7 M	$613,706	$532,998	$390,133	$161,585	$0
$3,300	$4,992	$7,777	20 Y & 1 M	$592,117	$480,419	$294,013	$5,273	$0

4% COLA

Monthly Amount	15 Yr Inflated	30 Yr Inflated	Money Lasts	5 Years	10 Years	15 Years	20 Years	30 Years
$1,200	$2,078	$3,743	Over 40 Yrs	$741,571	$839,372	$940,991	$1.042 M	$1.217 M
$1,500	$2,598	$4,678	Over 40 Yrs	$719,568	$784,522	$838,423	$871,928	$819,307
$1,800	$3,117	$5,614	36 Y & 4 M	$697,563	$729,662	$735,831	$701,368	$421,328
$2,100	$3,636	$6,549	30 Y & 4 M	$675,564	$674,830	$633,296	$530,898	$23,505
$2,400	$4,156	$7,485	25 Y & 11 M	$653,559	$619,960	$530,675	$360,269	$0
$2,700	$4,676	$8,420	22 Y & 9 M	$631,556	$565,109	$428,106	$189,749	$0
$3,000	$5,195	$9,356	20 Y & 3 M	$609,551	$510,252	$325,510	$19,157	$0

| $650,000 Balance | | | | | 6% Return On Investment | | | |

No COLA

Monthly Amount	15 Yr Inflated	30 Yr Inflated	Money Lasts	5 Years	10 Years	15 Years	20 Years	30 Years
$2,100	$2,100	$2,100	Over 40 Yrs	$723,531	$821,931	$953,612	$1.130 M	$1.681 M
$2,400	$2,400	$2,400	Over 40 Yrs	$702,627	$773,055	$867,303	$993,429	$1.388 M
$2,700	$2,700	$2,700	Over 40 Yrs	$681,726	$724,181	$780,997	$857,029	$1.095 M
$3,000	$3,000	$3,000	Over 40 Yrs	$660,823	$675,307	$694,689	$720,626	$801,789
$3,300	$3,300	$3,300	Over 40 Yrs	$639,921	$626,433	$608,383	$584,227	$508,645
$3,600	$3,600	$3,600	35 Y & 11 M	$619,018	$577,558	$522,074	$447,823	$215,490
$3,900	$3,900	$3,900	28 Y & 5 M	$598,116	$528,684	$435,769	$311,428	$0

2% COLA

Monthly Amount	15 Yr Inflated	30 Yr Inflated	Money Lasts	5 Years	10 Years	15 Years	20 Years	30 Years
$1,800	$2,375	$3,197	Over 40 Yrs	$739,616	$845,988	$973,371	$1.127 M	$1.546 M
$2,100	$2,771	$3,729	Over 40 Yrs	$717,911	$792,976	$875,970	$967,759	$1.182 M
$2,400	$3,167	$4,262	Over 40 Yrs	$696,204	$739,965	$778,573	$808,207	$817,196
$2,700	$3,563	$4,795	39 Y & 4 M	$674,499	$686,956	$681,181	$648,669	$452,752
$3,000	$3,958	$5,327	31 Y & 5 M	$652,797	$633,950	$583,788	$489,126	$88,273
$3,300	$4,354	$5,860	26 Y & 5 M	$631,089	$580,937	$486,383	$329,557	$0
$3,600	$4,750	$6,393	22 Y & 10 M	$609,384	$527,925	$388,984	$170,002	$0

3% COLA

Monthly Amount	15 Yr Inflated	30 Yr Inflated	Money Lasts	5 Years	10 Years	15 Years	20 Years	30 Years
$1,800	$2,723	$4,242	Over 40 Yrs	$737,139	$832,618	$935,887	$1.046 M	$1.274 M
$2,100	$3,176	$4,949	Over 40 Yrs	$715,016	$777,362	$832,209	$872,463	$864,044
$2,400	$3,630	$5,656	37 Y & 4 M	$692,898	$722,118	$728,547	$699,272	$454,093
$2,700	$4,084	$6,362	30 Y & 7 M	$670,782	$666,888	$624,927	$526,167	$44,392
$3,000	$4,538	$7,070	25 Y & 11 M	$648,664	$611,645	$521,268	$352,972	$0
$3,300	$4,992	$7,777	22 Y & 8 M	$626,543	$556,403	$417,615	$179,803	$0
$3,600	$5,445	$8,484	20 Y & 2 M	$604,426	$501,164	$313,966	$6,642	$0

4% COLA

Monthly Amount	15 Yr Inflated	30 Yr Inflated	Money Lasts	5 Years	10 Years	15 Years	20 Years	30 Years
$1,500	$2,598	$4,678	Over 40 Yrs	$757,147	$876,120	$1.006 M	$1.143 M	$1.416 M
$1,800	$3,117	$5,614	Over 40 Yrs	$734,606	$818,527	$895,186	$954,403	$952,122
$2,100	$3,636	$6,549	36 Y & 6 M	$712,070	$760,958	$784,797	$766,107	$488,780
$2,400	$4,156	$7,485	30 Y & 4 M	$689,531	$703,359	$674,329	$577,652	$25,033
$2,700	$4,676	$8,420	25 Y & 11 M	$666,989	$645,773	$563,910	$389,306	$0
$3,000	$5,195	$9,356	22 Y & 8 M	$644,448	$588,178	$453,457	$200,877	$0
$3,300	$5,714	$10,291	20 Y & 2 M	$621,913	$530,613	$343,086	$12,622	$0

$675,000 Balance	3% Return On Investment

No COLA

Monthly Amount	15 Yr Inflated	30 Yr Inflated	Money Lasts	5 Years	10 Years	15 Years	20 Years	30 Years
$1,600	$1,600	$1,600	Over 40 Yrs	$679,046	$683,735	$689,172	$695,474	$711,251
$2,000	$2,000	$2,000	Over 40 Yrs	$653,180	$627,883	$598,557	$564,562	$479,465
$2,400	$2,400	$2,400	39 Y & 11 M	$627,314	$572,032	$507,946	$433,652	$247,682
$2,800	$2,800	$2,800	30 Y & 6 M	$601,446	$516,178	$417,329	$302,735	$15,886
$3,200	$3,200	$3,200	24 Y & 10 M	$575,582	$460,327	$326,716	$171,824	$0
$3,600	$3,600	$3,600	20 Y & 11 M	$549,715	$404,475	$236,103	$40,913	$0
$4,000	$4,000	$4,000	18 Y & 3 M	$523,849	$348,622	$145,489	$0	$0

2% COLA

Monthly Amount	15 Yr Inflated	30 Yr Inflated	Money Lasts	5 Years	10 Years	15 Years	20 Years	30 Years
$1,200	$1,583	$2,131	Over 40 Yrs	$701,838	$724,550	$741,613	$751,159	$738,174
$1,600	$2,111	$2,842	Over 40 Yrs	$674,946	$663,684	$638,270	$595,159	$438,069
$2,000	$2,639	$3,552	33 Y & 4 M	$648,060	$602,834	$534,953	$439,202	$138,057
$2,400	$3,167	$4,262	26 Y & 11 M	$621,168	$541,971	$431,621	$283,222	$0
$2,800	$3,694	$4,972	22 Y & 8 M	$594,280	$481,117	$328,301	$127,267	$0
$3,200	$4,222	$5,683	19 Y & 6 M	$567,390	$420,253	$224,959	$0	$0
$3,600	$4,750	$6,393	17 Y & 2 M	$540,499	$359,390	$121,625	$0	$0

3% COLA

Monthly Amount	15 Yr Inflated	30 Yr Inflated	Money Lasts	5 Years	10 Years	15 Years	20 Years	30 Years
$1,200	$1,815	$2,828	Over 40 Yrs	$700,259	$716,441	$720,012	$706,551	$605,128
$1,600	$2,420	$3,770	35 Y & 9 M	$672,841	$652,874	$609,476	$535,697	$260,704
$2,000	$3,025	$4,713	28 Y & 7 M	$645,421	$589,293	$498,910	$364,786	$0
$2,400	$3,630	$5,656	23 Y & 10 M	$618,005	$525,728	$388,375	$193,931	$0
$2,800	$4,235	$6,598	20 Y & 5 M	$590,590	$462,170	$277,857	$23,110	$0
$3,200	$4,841	$7,541	17 Y & 10 M	$563,169	$398,585	$167,284	$0	$0
$3,600	$5,445	$8,484	15 Y & 11 M	$535,754	$335,028	$56,769	$0	$0

4% COLA

Monthly Amount	15 Yr Inflated	30 Yr Inflated	Money Lasts	5 Years	10 Years	15 Years	20 Years	30 Years
$800	$1,385	$2,494	Over 40 Yrs	$726,601	$774,313	$814,895	$844,017	$843,285
$1,200	$2,078	$3,743	39 Y & 4 M	$698,645	$707,884	$696,486	$656,382	$445,506
$1,600	$2,771	$4,990	30 Y & 10 M	$670,689	$641,465	$578,110	$468,804	$47,900
$2,000	$3,463	$6,237	25 Y & 4 M	$642,736	$575,053	$459,748	$281,256	$0
$2,400	$4,156	$7,485	21 Y & 6 M	$614,781	$508,625	$341,343	$93,626	$0
$2,800	$4,849	$8,732	18 Y & 9 M	$586,823	$442,204	$222,972	$0	$0
$3,200	$5,541	$9,980	16 Y & 7 M	$558,872	$375,794	$104,605	$0	$0

| $675,000 Balance | | | | | | 4% Return On Investment | | |

No COLA

Monthly Amount	15 Yr Inflated	30 Yr Inflated	Money Lasts	5 Years	10 Years	15 Years	20 Years	30 Years
$2,000	$2,000	$2,000	Over 40 Yrs	$688,650	$705,257	$725,461	$750,042	$816,337
$2,400	$2,400	$2,400	Over 40 Yrs	$662,130	$646,472	$627,422	$604,246	$541,742
$2,800	$2,800	$2,800	39 Y & 7 M	$635,613	$587,694	$529,391	$458,457	$267,155
$3,200	$3,200	$3,200	29 Y & 10 M	$609,094	$528,910	$431,353	$312,661	$0
$3,600	$3,600	$3,600	24 Y & 3 M	$582,576	$470,129	$333,319	$166,870	$0
$4,000	$4,000	$4,000	20 Y & 6 M	$556,058	$411,346	$235,282	$21,073	$0
$4,400	$4,400	$4,400	17 Y & 9 M	$529,540	$352,566	$137,250	$0	$0

2% COLA

Monthly Amount	15 Yr Inflated	30 Yr Inflated	Money Lasts	5 Years	10 Years	15 Years	20 Years	30 Years
$1,600	$2,111	$2,842	Over 40 Yrs	$711,008	$743,338	$770,008	$788,469	$786,973
$2,000	$2,639	$3,552	Over 40 Yrs	$683,452	$679,393	$658,622	$615,869	$436,473
$2,400	$3,167	$4,262	31 Y & 9 M	$655,893	$615,440	$547,221	$443,244	$85,908
$2,800	$3,694	$4,972	25 Y & 10 M	$628,339	$551,496	$435,838	$270,650	$0
$3,200	$4,222	$5,683	21 Y & 10 M	$600,781	$487,539	$324,428	$98,012	$0
$3,600	$4,750	$6,393	18 Y & 10 M	$573,222	$423,582	$213,022	$0	$0
$4,000	$5,278	$7,104	16 Y & 8 M	$545,663	$359,623	$101,607	$0	$0

3% COLA

Monthly Amount	15 Yr Inflated	30 Yr Inflated	Money Lasts	5 Years	10 Years	15 Years	20 Years	30 Years
$1,600	$2,420	$3,770	Over 40 Yrs	$708,871	$732,187	$739,803	$725,021	$591,027
$2,000	$3,025	$4,713	33 Y & 5 M	$680,775	$665,427	$620,813	$536,467	$191,321
$2,400	$3,630	$5,656	27 Y & 1 M	$652,685	$598,686	$501,861	$347,976	$0
$2,800	$4,235	$6,598	22 Y & 9 M	$624,594	$531,950	$382,923	$159,517	$0
$3,200	$4,841	$7,541	19 Y & 7 M	$596,497	$465,185	$263,924	$0	$0
$3,600	$5,445	$8,484	17 Y & 3 M	$568,407	$398,451	$144,988	$0	$0
$4,000	$6,050	$9,426	15 Y & 5 M	$540,314	$331,702	$26,026	$0	$0

4% COLA

Monthly Amount	15 Yr Inflated	30 Yr Inflated	Money Lasts	5 Years	10 Years	15 Years	20 Years	30 Years
$1,200	$2,078	$3,743	Over 40 Yrs	$735,327	$790,107	$834,107	$860,091	$815,057
$1,600	$2,771	$4,990	35 Y & 10 M	$706,685	$720,418	$706,930	$653,782	$356,995
$2,000	$3,463	$6,237	28 Y & 8 M	$678,052	$650,744	$579,778	$447,520	$0
$2,400	$4,156	$7,485	23 Y & 11 M	$649,412	$581,048	$452,574	$241,159	$0
$2,800	$4,849	$8,732	20 Y & 6 M	$620,772	$511,362	$325,408	$34,879	$0
$3,200	$5,541	$9,980	17 Y & 11 M	$592,138	$441,686	$198,248	$0	$0
$3,600	$6,234	$11,227	15 Y & 11 M	$563,498	$371,998	$71,072	$0	$0

| $675,000 Balance | | | | | 5% Return On Investment | | | |

No COLA

Monthly Amount	15 Yr Inflated	30 Yr Inflated	Money Lasts	5 Years	10 Years	15 Years	20 Years	30 Years
$2,000	$2,000	$2,000	Over 40 Yrs	$725,560	$790,089	$872,445	$977,555	$1.283 M
$2,400	$2,400	$2,400	Over 40 Yrs	$698,375	$728,207	$766,280	$814,872	$956,043
$2,800	$2,800	$2,800	Over 40 Yrs	$671,187	$666,321	$660,111	$652,187	$629,162
$3,200	$3,200	$3,200	39 Y & 11 M	$644,002	$604,439	$553,946	$489,502	$302,281
$3,600	$3,600	$3,600	29 Y & 6 M	$616,816	$542,556	$447,779	$326,816	$0
$4,000	$4,000	$4,000	23 Y & 9 M	$589,629	$480,671	$341,611	$164,132	$0
$4,400	$4,400	$4,400	20 Y & 1 M	$562,443	$418,787	$235,442	$1,443	$0

2% COLA

Monthly Amount	15 Yr Inflated	30 Yr Inflated	Money Lasts	5 Years	10 Years	15 Years	20 Years	30 Years
$1,600	$2,111	$2,842	Over 40 Yrs	$748,524	$830,598	$922,370	$1.025 M	$1.270 M
$2,000	$2,639	$3,552	Over 40 Yrs	$720,286	$763,385	$802,165	$833,746	$858,625
$2,400	$3,167	$4,262	39 Y & 11 M	$692,044	$696,162	$681,945	$642,301	$446,886
$2,800	$3,694	$4,972	30 Y & 7 M	$663,806	$628,948	$561,742	$450,891	$35,228
$3,200	$4,222	$5,683	24 Y & 11 M	$635,564	$561,719	$441,511	$259,433	$0
$3,600	$4,750	$6,393	21 Y & 2 M	$607,322	$494,495	$321,289	$67,981	$0
$4,000	$5,278	$7,104	18 Y & 4 M	$579,081	$427,266	$201,055	$0	$0

3% COLA

Monthly Amount	15 Yr Inflated	30 Yr Inflated	Money Lasts	5 Years	10 Years	15 Years	20 Years	30 Years
$1,600	$2,420	$3,770	Over 40 Yrs	$746,355	$819,091	$890,660	$957,363	$1.053 M
$2,000	$3,025	$4,713	Over 40 Yrs	$717,569	$748,973	$762,475	$748,902	$586,768
$2,400	$3,630	$5,656	31 Y & 10 M	$688,786	$678,871	$634,325	$540,502	$120,690
$2,800	$4,235	$6,598	25 Y & 11 M	$660,004	$608,777	$506,194	$332,140	$0
$3,200	$4,841	$7,541	21 Y & 10 M	$631,218	$538,656	$378,002	$123,663	$0
$3,600	$5,445	$8,484	18 Y & 11 M	$602,434	$468,562	$249,869	$0	$0
$4,000	$6,050	$9,426	16 Y & 8 M	$573,652	$398,456	$121,713	$0	$0

4% COLA

Monthly Amount	15 Yr Inflated	30 Yr Inflated	Money Lasts	5 Years	10 Years	15 Years	20 Years	30 Years
$1,200	$2,078	$3,743	Over 40 Yrs	$773,478	$880,094	$992,965	$1.109 M	$1.325 M
$1,600	$2,771	$4,990	Over 40 Yrs	$744,139	$806,957	$856,197	$881,406	$794,713
$2,000	$3,463	$6,237	33 Y & 7 M	$714,806	$733,831	$719,448	$654,052	$264,145
$2,400	$4,156	$7,485	27 Y & 2 M	$685,466	$660,682	$582,647	$426,600	$0
$2,800	$4,849	$8,732	22 Y & 10 M	$656,128	$587,547	$445,887	$199,236	$0
$3,200	$5,541	$9,980	19 Y & 8 M	$626,794	$514,422	$309,135	$0	$0
$3,600	$6,234	$11,227	17 Y & 4 M	$597,455	$441,281	$172,363	$0	$0

$675,000 Balance	6% Return On Investment

No COLA

Monthly Amount	15 Yr Inflated	30 Yr Inflated	Money Lasts	5 Years	10 Years	15 Years	20 Years	30 Years
$2,400	$2,400	$2,400	Over 40 Yrs	$736,083	$817,826	$927,217	$1.074 M	$1.532 M
$2,800	$2,800	$2,800	Over 40 Yrs	$708,214	$752,661	$812,142	$891,742	$1.141 M
$3,200	$3,200	$3,200	Over 40 Yrs	$680,344	$687,496	$697,067	$709,874	$749,949
$3,600	$3,600	$3,600	Over 40 Yrs	$652,474	$622,329	$581,988	$528,004	$359,082
$4,000	$4,000	$4,000	29 Y & 5 M	$624,604	$557,162	$466,911	$346,135	$0
$4,400	$4,400	$4,400	23 Y & 6 M	$596,735	$491,998	$351,837	$164,270	$0
$4,800	$4,800	$4,800	19 Y & 9 M	$568,865	$426,833	$236,761	$0	$0

2% COLA

Monthly Amount	15 Yr Inflated	30 Yr Inflated	Money Lasts	5 Years	10 Years	15 Years	20 Years	30 Years
$2,000	$2,639	$3,552	Over 40 Yrs	$758,601	$855,418	$968,350	$1.101 M	$1.447 M
$2,400	$3,167	$4,262	Over 40 Yrs	$729,660	$784,736	$838,485	$888,381	$960,774
$2,800	$3,694	$4,972	39 Y & 5 M	$700,722	$714,062	$708,637	$675,677	$474,847
$3,200	$4,222	$5,683	29 Y & 10 M	$671,781	$643,380	$578,767	$462,930	$0
$3,600	$4,750	$6,393	24 Y & 4 M	$642,840	$572,697	$448,900	$250,183	$0
$4,000	$5,278	$7,104	20 Y & 7 M	$613,901	$502,011	$319,020	$37,414	$0
$4,400	$5,806	$7,814	17 Y & 10 M	$584,958	$431,327	$189,156	$0	$0

3% COLA

Monthly Amount	15 Yr Inflated	30 Yr Inflated	Money Lasts	5 Years	10 Years	15 Years	20 Years	30 Years
$2,000	$3,025	$4,713	Over 40 Yrs	$755,844	$840,542	$926,657	$1.010 M	$1.144 M
$2,400	$3,630	$5,656	39 Y & 11 M	$726,354	$766,892	$788,465	$779,455	$597,687
$2,800	$4,235	$6,598	30 Y & 8 M	$696,867	$693,251	$650,293	$548,619	$51,305
$3,200	$4,841	$7,541	24 Y & 11 M	$667,371	$619,577	$512,052	$317,650	$0
$3,600	$5,445	$8,484	21 Y & 2 M	$637,881	$545,934	$373,878	$86,818	$0
$4,000	$6,050	$9,426	18 Y & 5 M	$608,389	$472,276	$235,676	$0	$0
$4,400	$6,655	$10,369	16 Y & 3 M	$578,899	$398,627	$97,480	$0	$0

4% COLA

Monthly Amount	15 Yr Inflated	30 Yr Inflated	Money Lasts	5 Years	10 Years	15 Years	20 Years	30 Years
$1,600	$2,771	$4,990	Over 40 Yrs	$783,090	$901,695	$1.029 M	$1.160 M	$1.405 M
$2,000	$3,463	$6,237	Over 40 Yrs	$753,039	$824,920	$881,507	$909,048	$786,795
$2,400	$4,156	$7,485	31 Y & 11 M	$722,986	$748,129	$734,242	$657,828	$168,615
$2,800	$4,849	$8,732	25 Y & 11 M	$692,931	$671,348	$587,014	$406,693	$0
$3,200	$5,541	$9,980	21 Y & 11 M	$662,882	$594,576	$439,793	$155,552	$0
$3,600	$6,234	$11,227	18 Y & 11 M	$632,828	$517,792	$292,557	$0	$0
$4,000	$6,927	$12,475	16 Y & 9 M	$602,774	$441,004	$145,301	$0	$0

$700,000 Balance   3% Return On Investment

No COLA

Monthly Amount	15 Yr Inflated	30 Yr Inflated	Money Lasts	5 Years	10 Years	15 Years	20 Years	30 Years
$1,600	$1,600	$1,600	Over 40 Yrs	$708,027	$717,333	$728,121	$740,627	$771,934
$2,000	$2,000	$2,000	Over 40 Yrs	$682,160	$661,481	$637,507	$609,714	$540,145
$2,400	$2,400	$2,400	Over 40 Yrs	$656,296	$605,631	$546,895	$478,805	$308,362
$2,800	$2,800	$2,800	32 Y & 5 M	$630,429	$549,777	$456,279	$347,889	$76,570
$3,200	$3,200	$3,200	26 Y & 3 M	$604,563	$493,926	$365,668	$216,980	$0
$3,600	$3,600	$3,600	22 Y & 1 M	$578,697	$438,074	$275,052	$86,067	$0
$4,000	$4,000	$4,000	19 Y & 1 M	$552,831	$382,222	$184,439	$0	$0

2% COLA

Monthly Amount	15 Yr Inflated	30 Yr Inflated	Money Lasts	5 Years	10 Years	15 Years	20 Years	30 Years
$1,200	$1,583	$2,131	Over 40 Yrs	$730,819	$758,147	$780,562	$796,312	$798,855
$1,600	$2,111	$2,842	Over 40 Yrs	$703,929	$697,284	$677,221	$640,315	$498,753
$2,000	$2,639	$3,552	34 Y & 9 M	$677,041	$636,432	$573,903	$484,357	$198,743
$2,400	$3,167	$4,262	28 Y & 1 M	$650,150	$575,569	$470,568	$328,372	$0
$2,800	$3,694	$4,972	23 Y & 7 M	$623,263	$514,715	$367,249	$172,417	$0
$3,200	$4,222	$5,683	20 Y & 4 M	$596,372	$453,850	$263,906	$16,422	$0
$3,600	$4,750	$6,393	17 Y & 10 M	$569,481	$392,987	$160,574	$0	$0

3% COLA

Monthly Amount	15 Yr Inflated	30 Yr Inflated	Money Lasts	5 Years	10 Years	15 Years	20 Years	30 Years
$1,200	$1,815	$2,828	Over 40 Yrs	$729,240	$750,038	$758,961	$751,702	$665,808
$1,600	$2,420	$3,770	36 Y & 11 M	$701,824	$686,474	$648,427	$580,849	$321,386
$2,000	$3,025	$4,713	29 Y & 8 M	$674,403	$622,892	$537,861	$409,942	$0
$2,400	$3,630	$5,656	24 Y & 8 M	$646,986	$559,324	$427,324	$239,084	$0
$2,800	$4,235	$6,598	21 Y & 2 M	$619,573	$495,769	$316,810	$68,267	$0
$3,200	$4,841	$7,541	18 Y & 6 M	$592,151	$432,184	$206,236	$0	$0
$3,600	$5,445	$8,484	16 Y & 6 M	$564,736	$368,628	$95,721	$0	$0

4% COLA

Monthly Amount	15 Yr Inflated	30 Yr Inflated	Money Lasts	5 Years	10 Years	15 Years	20 Years	30 Years
$800	$1,385	$2,494	Over 40 Yrs	$755,584	$807,911	$853,844	$889,168	$903,963
$1,200	$2,078	$3,743	Over 40 Yrs	$727,627	$741,483	$735,438	$701,537	$506,191
$1,600	$2,771	$4,990	31 Y & 10 M	$699,670	$675,062	$617,060	$513,958	$108,583
$2,000	$3,463	$6,237	26 Y & 2 M	$671,720	$608,654	$498,700	$326,414	$0
$2,400	$4,156	$7,485	22 Y & 3 M	$643,762	$542,223	$380,293	$138,780	$0
$2,800	$4,849	$8,732	19 Y & 4 M	$615,806	$475,804	$261,923	$0	$0
$3,200	$5,541	$9,980	17 Y & 2 M	$587,855	$409,394	$143,558	$0	$0

$700,000 Balance   4% Return On Investment

No COLA

Monthly Amount	15 Yr Inflated	30 Yr Inflated	Money Lasts	5 Years	10 Years	15 Years	20 Years	30 Years
$2,000	$2,000	$2,000	Over 40 Yrs	$719,066	$742,262	$770,484	$804,820	$897,422
$2,400	$2,400	$2,400	Over 40 Yrs	$692,547	$683,480	$672,448	$659,027	$622,830
$2,800	$2,800	$2,800	Over 40 Yrs	$666,029	$624,697	$574,412	$513,232	$348,236
$3,200	$3,200	$3,200	31 Y & 11 M	$639,511	$565,916	$476,377	$367,440	$73,647
$3,600	$3,600	$3,600	25 Y & 9 M	$612,991	$507,133	$378,339	$221,642	$0
$4,000	$4,000	$4,000	21 Y & 8 M	$586,475	$448,353	$280,306	$75,851	$0
$4,400	$4,400	$4,400	18 Y & 9 M	$559,956	$389,570	$182,271	$0	$0

2% COLA

Monthly Amount	15 Yr Inflated	30 Yr Inflated	Money Lasts	5 Years	10 Years	15 Years	20 Years	30 Years
$1,600	$2,111	$2,842	Over 40 Yrs	$741,424	$780,345	$815,034	$843,251	$868,063
$2,000	$2,639	$3,552	Over 40 Yrs	$713,868	$716,399	$703,645	$670,646	$517,553
$2,400	$3,167	$4,262	33 Y & 5 M	$686,310	$652,446	$592,244	$498,022	$166,991
$2,800	$3,694	$4,972	27 Y & 1 M	$658,756	$588,502	$480,860	$325,426	$0
$3,200	$4,222	$5,683	22 Y & 10 M	$631,197	$524,544	$369,451	$152,788	$0
$3,600	$4,750	$6,393	19 Y & 9 M	$603,638	$460,588	$258,046	$0	$0
$4,000	$5,278	$7,104	17 Y & 5 M	$576,080	$396,630	$146,632	$0	$0

3% COLA

Monthly Amount	15 Yr Inflated	30 Yr Inflated	Money Lasts	5 Years	10 Years	15 Years	20 Years	30 Years
$1,600	$2,420	$3,770	Over 40 Yrs	$739,288	$769,193	$784,827	$779,800	$672,112
$2,000	$3,025	$4,713	34 Y & 11 M	$711,192	$702,433	$665,837	$591,246	$272,406
$2,400	$3,630	$5,656	28 Y & 3 M	$683,100	$635,688	$546,880	$402,750	$0
$2,800	$4,235	$6,598	23 Y & 8 M	$655,010	$568,954	$427,944	$214,291	$0
$3,200	$4,841	$7,541	20 Y & 5 M	$626,914	$502,191	$308,947	$25,723	$0
$3,600	$5,445	$8,484	17 Y & 11 M	$598,824	$435,457	$190,011	$0	$0
$4,000	$6,050	$9,426	15 Y & 11 M	$570,729	$368,706	$71,047	$0	$0

4% COLA

Monthly Amount	15 Yr Inflated	30 Yr Inflated	Money Lasts	5 Years	10 Years	15 Years	20 Years	30 Years
$1,200	$2,078	$3,743	Over 40 Yrs	$765,743	$827,113	$879,130	$914,868	$896,142
$1,600	$2,771	$4,990	37 Y & 3 M	$737,102	$757,424	$751,954	$708,561	$438,081
$2,000	$3,463	$6,237	29 Y & 9 M	$708,469	$687,752	$624,804	$502,300	$0
$2,400	$4,156	$7,485	24 Y & 10 M	$679,829	$618,053	$497,596	$295,934	$0
$2,800	$4,849	$8,732	21 Y & 3 M	$651,189	$548,368	$370,430	$89,656	$0
$3,200	$5,541	$9,980	18 Y & 7 M	$622,554	$478,691	$243,269	$0	$0
$3,600	$6,234	$11,227	16 Y & 7 M	$593,914	$409,002	$116,093	$0	$0

| $700,000 Balance | | | | | | | 5% Return On Investment | |

No COLA

Monthly Amount	15 Yr Inflated	30 Yr Inflated	Money Lasts	5 Years	10 Years	15 Years	20 Years	30 Years
$2,000	$2,000	$2,000	Over 40 Yrs	$757,466	$830,810	$924,418	$1.044 M	$1.391 M
$2,400	$2,400	$2,400	Over 40 Yrs	$730,281	$768,928	$818,251	$881,202	$1.064 M
$2,800	$2,800	$2,800	Over 40 Yrs	$703,094	$707,043	$712,084	$718,517	$737,205
$3,200	$3,200	$3,200	Over 40 Yrs	$675,908	$645,159	$605,916	$555,831	$410,325
$3,600	$3,600	$3,600	32 Y & 1 M	$648,722	$583,277	$499,750	$393,148	$83,447
$4,000	$4,000	$4,000	25 Y & 6 M	$621,537	$521,395	$393,586	$230,464	$0
$4,400	$4,400	$4,400	21 Y & 4 M	$594,350	$459,511	$287,418	$67,779	$0

2% COLA

Monthly Amount	15 Yr Inflated	30 Yr Inflated	Money Lasts	5 Years	10 Years	15 Years	20 Years	30 Years
$1,600	$2,111	$2,842	Over 40 Yrs	$780,430	$871,321	$974,344	$1.091 M	$1.378 M
$2,000	$2,639	$3,552	Over 40 Yrs	$752,192	$804,106	$854,137	$900,074	$966,667
$2,400	$3,167	$4,262	Over 40 Yrs	$723,951	$736,885	$733,920	$708,636	$554,937
$2,800	$3,694	$4,972	32 Y & 6 M	$695,712	$669,668	$613,712	$517,218	$143,269
$3,200	$4,222	$5,683	26 Y & 4 M	$667,471	$602,442	$493,485	$325,766	$0
$3,600	$4,750	$6,393	22 Y & 3 M	$639,229	$535,217	$373,262	$134,313	$0
$4,000	$5,278	$7,104	19 Y & 3 M	$610,988	$467,989	$253,029	$0	$0

3% COLA

Monthly Amount	15 Yr Inflated	30 Yr Inflated	Money Lasts	5 Years	10 Years	15 Years	20 Years	30 Years
$1,600	$2,420	$3,770	Over 40 Yrs	$778,264	$859,815	$942,636	$1.024 M	$1.161 M
$2,000	$3,025	$4,713	Over 40 Yrs	$749,477	$789,696	$814,449	$815,235	$694,819
$2,400	$3,630	$5,656	33 Y & 6 M	$720,694	$719,595	$686,300	$606,836	$228,742
$2,800	$4,235	$6,598	27 Y & 2 M	$691,913	$649,503	$558,171	$398,478	$0
$3,200	$4,841	$7,541	22 Y & 11 M	$663,125	$579,377	$429,974	$189,995	$0
$3,600	$5,445	$8,484	19 Y & 9 M	$634,344	$509,287	$301,845	$0	$0
$4,000	$6,050	$9,426	17 Y & 5 M	$605,558	$439,177	$173,684	$0	$0

4% COLA

Monthly Amount	15 Yr Inflated	30 Yr Inflated	Money Lasts	5 Years	10 Years	15 Years	20 Years	30 Years
$1,200	$2,078	$3,743	Over 40 Yrs	$805,386	$920,816	$1.045 M	$1.175 M	$1.433 M
$1,600	$2,771	$4,990	Over 40 Yrs	$776,046	$847,678	$908,169	$947,738	$902,760
$2,000	$3,463	$6,237	34 Y & 11 M	$746,712	$774,552	$771,419	$720,382	$372,190
$2,400	$4,156	$7,485	28 Y & 4 M	$717,373	$701,404	$634,619	$492,931	$0
$2,800	$4,849	$8,732	23 Y & 9 M	$688,034	$628,269	$497,861	$265,568	$0
$3,200	$5,541	$9,980	20 Y & 6 M	$658,701	$555,142	$361,106	$38,190	$0
$3,600	$6,234	$11,227	17 Y & 11 M	$629,362	$482,002	$224,335	$0	$0

$700,000 Balance   6% Return On Investment

No COLA

Monthly Amount	15 Yr Inflated	30 Yr Inflated	Money Lasts	5 Years	10 Years	15 Years	20 Years	30 Years
$2,400	$2,400	$2,400	Over 40 Yrs	$769,539	$862,598	$987,131	$1.154 M	$1.675 M
$2,800	$2,800	$2,800	Over 40 Yrs	$741,670	$797,434	$872,058	$971,920	$1.284 M
$3,200	$3,200	$3,200	Over 40 Yrs	$713,801	$732,269	$756,983	$790,056	$893,542
$3,600	$3,600	$3,600	Over 40 Yrs	$685,929	$667,100	$641,903	$608,183	$502,673
$4,000	$4,000	$4,000	32 Y & 6 M	$658,060	$601,935	$526,827	$426,317	$111,810
$4,400	$4,400	$4,400	25 Y & 5 M	$630,189	$536,767	$411,748	$244,445	$0
$4,800	$4,800	$4,800	21 Y & 2 M	$602,320	$471,603	$296,674	$62,579	$0

2% COLA

Monthly Amount	15 Yr Inflated	30 Yr Inflated	Money Lasts	5 Years	10 Years	15 Years	20 Years	30 Years
$2,000	$2,639	$3,552	Over 40 Yrs	$792,056	$900,186	$1.028 M	$1.181 M	$1.590 M
$2,400	$3,167	$4,262	Over 40 Yrs	$763,116	$829,507	$898,400	$968,562	$1.104 M
$2,800	$3,694	$4,972	Over 40 Yrs	$734,176	$758,832	$768,548	$755,851	$618,425
$3,200	$4,222	$5,683	31 Y & 11 M	$705,237	$688,150	$638,679	$543,106	$132,421
$3,600	$4,750	$6,393	25 Y & 10 M	$676,295	$617,466	$508,810	$330,357	$0
$4,000	$5,278	$7,104	21 Y & 9 M	$647,355	$546,781	$378,934	$117,594	$0
$4,400	$5,806	$7,814	18 Y & 10 M	$618,413	$476,098	$249,069	$0	$0

3% COLA

Monthly Amount	15 Yr Inflated	30 Yr Inflated	Money Lasts	5 Years	10 Years	15 Years	20 Years	30 Years
$2,000	$3,025	$4,713	Over 40 Yrs	$789,299	$885,311	$986,568	$1.091 M	$1.288 M
$2,400	$3,630	$5,656	Over 40 Yrs	$759,809	$811,662	$848,378	$859,634	$741,279
$2,800	$4,235	$6,598	32 Y & 7 M	$730,321	$738,022	$710,208	$628,799	$194,893
$3,200	$4,841	$7,541	26 Y & 5 M	$700,827	$664,349	$571,969	$397,833	$0
$3,600	$5,445	$8,484	22 Y & 3 M	$671,336	$590,703	$433,789	$166,991	$0
$4,000	$6,050	$9,426	19 Y & 4 M	$641,845	$517,047	$295,590	$0	$0
$4,400	$6,655	$10,369	16 Y & 11 M	$612,353	$443,395	$157,389	$0	$0

4% COLA

Monthly Amount	15 Yr Inflated	30 Yr Inflated	Money Lasts	5 Years	10 Years	15 Years	20 Years	30 Years
$1,600	$2,771	$4,990	Over 40 Yrs	$816,544	$946,465	$1.089 M	$1.240 M	$1.548 M
$2,000	$3,463	$6,237	Over 40 Yrs	$786,496	$869,695	$941,426	$989,233	$930,394
$2,400	$4,156	$7,485	33 Y & 7 M	$756,442	$792,901	$794,157	$738,007	$312,204
$2,800	$4,849	$8,732	27 Y & 3 M	$726,387	$716,119	$646,927	$486,872	$0
$3,200	$5,541	$9,980	22 Y & 11 M	$696,339	$639,349	$499,708	$235,732	$0
$3,600	$6,234	$11,227	19 Y & 10 M	$666,282	$562,560	$352,466	$0	$0
$4,000	$6,927	$12,475	17 Y & 6 M	$636,228	$485,775	$205,213	$0	$0

$725,000 Balance   3% Return On Investment

No COLA

Monthly Amount	15 Yr Inflated	30 Yr Inflated	Money Lasts	5 Years	10 Years	15 Years	20 Years	30 Years
$1,600	$1,600	$1,600	Over 40 Yrs	$737,010	$750,931	$767,070	$785,780	$832,612
$2,000	$2,000	$2,000	Over 40 Yrs	$711,143	$695,080	$676,457	$654,869	$600,828
$2,400	$2,400	$2,400	Over 40 Yrs	$685,277	$639,227	$585,842	$523,954	$369,039
$2,800	$2,800	$2,800	34 Y & 5 M	$659,410	$583,374	$495,227	$393,041	$137,249
$3,200	$3,200	$3,200	27 Y & 8 M	$633,545	$527,523	$404,615	$262,130	$0
$3,600	$3,600	$3,600	23 Y & 3 M	$607,679	$471,671	$314,001	$131,218	$0
$4,000	$4,000	$4,000	19 Y & 11 M	$581,813	$415,818	$223,386	$0	$0

2% COLA

Monthly Amount	15 Yr Inflated	30 Yr Inflated	Money Lasts	5 Years	10 Years	15 Years	20 Years	30 Years
$1,200	$1,583	$2,131	Over 40 Yrs	$759,802	$791,747	$819,513	$841,465	$859,537
$1,600	$2,111	$2,842	Over 40 Yrs	$732,910	$730,880	$716,168	$685,464	$559,432
$2,000	$2,639	$3,552	36 Y & 3 M	$706,023	$670,029	$612,850	$529,507	$259,420
$2,400	$3,167	$4,262	29 Y & 3 M	$679,132	$609,167	$509,518	$373,526	$0
$2,800	$3,694	$4,972	24 Y & 6 M	$652,244	$548,312	$406,198	$217,571	$0
$3,200	$4,222	$5,683	21 Y & 2 M	$625,353	$487,448	$302,858	$61,579	$0
$3,600	$4,750	$6,393	18 Y & 7 M	$598,463	$426,585	$199,522	$0	$0

3% COLA

Monthly Amount	15 Yr Inflated	30 Yr Inflated	Money Lasts	5 Years	10 Years	15 Years	20 Years	30 Years
$1,200	$1,815	$2,828	Over 40 Yrs	$758,222	$783,636	$797,909	$796,855	$726,491
$1,600	$2,420	$3,770	38 Y & 4 M	$730,805	$720,070	$687,376	$626,003	$382,069
$2,000	$3,025	$4,713	30 Y & 8 M	$703,384	$656,488	$576,807	$455,090	$37,516
$2,400	$3,630	$5,656	25 Y & 7 M	$675,969	$592,924	$466,275	$284,237	$0
$2,800	$4,235	$6,598	21 Y & 11 M	$648,554	$529,365	$355,756	$113,414	$0
$3,200	$4,841	$7,541	19 Y & 2 M	$621,134	$465,782	$245,185	$0	$0
$3,600	$5,445	$8,484	17 Y & 1 M	$593,717	$402,223	$134,666	$0	$0

4% COLA

Monthly Amount	15 Yr Inflated	30 Yr Inflated	Money Lasts	5 Years	10 Years	15 Years	20 Years	30 Years
$800	$1,385	$2,494	Over 40 Yrs	$784,565	$841,510	$892,795	$934,323	$964,646
$1,200	$2,078	$3,743	Over 40 Yrs	$756,608	$775,079	$774,384	$746,686	$566,869
$1,600	$2,771	$4,990	32 Y & 9 M	$728,652	$708,660	$656,007	$559,108	$169,260
$2,000	$3,463	$6,237	26 Y & 11 M	$700,700	$642,249	$537,647	$371,562	$0
$2,400	$4,156	$7,485	22 Y & 11 M	$672,744	$575,820	$419,242	$183,932	$0
$2,800	$4,849	$8,732	19 Y & 11 M	$644,788	$509,401	$300,872	$0	$0
$3,200	$5,541	$9,980	17 Y & 8 M	$616,835	$442,990	$182,505	$0	$0

$725,000 Balance	4% Return On Investment

No COLA

Monthly Amount	15 Yr Inflated	30 Yr Inflated	Money Lasts	5 Years	10 Years	15 Years	20 Years	30 Years
$2,000	$2,000	$2,000	Over 40 Yrs	$749,482	$779,267	$815,506	$859,596	$978,503
$2,400	$2,400	$2,400	Over 40 Yrs	$722,963	$720,485	$717,470	$713,803	$703,911
$2,800	$2,800	$2,800	Over 40 Yrs	$696,446	$661,704	$619,436	$568,011	$429,322
$3,200	$3,200	$3,200	34 Y & 5 M	$669,926	$602,921	$521,400	$422,218	$154,732
$3,600	$3,600	$3,600	27 Y & 5 M	$643,408	$544,139	$423,364	$276,422	$0
$4,000	$4,000	$4,000	22 Y & 11 M	$616,891	$485,359	$325,330	$130,630	$0
$4,400	$4,400	$4,400	19 Y & 9 M	$590,372	$426,576	$227,293	$0	$0

2% COLA

Monthly Amount	15 Yr Inflated	30 Yr Inflated	Money Lasts	5 Years	10 Years	15 Years	20 Years	30 Years
$1,600	$2,111	$2,842	Over 40 Yrs	$771,840	$817,351	$860,056	$898,026	$949,144
$2,000	$2,639	$3,552	Over 40 Yrs	$744,285	$753,406	$748,669	$725,424	$598,636
$2,400	$3,167	$4,262	35 Y & 1 M	$716,727	$689,453	$637,270	$552,803	$248,080
$2,800	$3,694	$4,972	28 Y & 4 M	$689,172	$625,507	$525,884	$380,205	$0
$3,200	$4,222	$5,683	23 Y & 10 M	$661,614	$561,553	$414,478	$207,571	$0
$3,600	$4,750	$6,393	20 Y & 7 M	$634,055	$497,595	$303,071	$34,934	$0
$4,000	$5,278	$7,104	18 Y & 2 M	$606,496	$433,635	$191,653	$0	$0

3% COLA

Monthly Amount	15 Yr Inflated	30 Yr Inflated	Money Lasts	5 Years	10 Years	15 Years	20 Years	30 Years
$1,600	$2,420	$3,770	Over 40 Yrs	$769,704	$806,198	$829,850	$834,578	$753,198
$2,000	$3,025	$4,713	36 Y & 5 M	$741,608	$739,439	$710,861	$646,024	$353,489
$2,400	$3,630	$5,656	29 Y & 4 M	$713,516	$672,695	$591,905	$457,527	$0
$2,800	$4,235	$6,598	24 Y & 8 M	$685,427	$605,961	$472,967	$269,069	$0
$3,200	$4,841	$7,541	21 Y & 3 M	$657,331	$539,198	$353,972	$80,503	$0
$3,600	$5,445	$8,484	18 Y & 8 M	$629,240	$472,463	$235,035	$0	$0
$4,000	$6,050	$9,426	16 Y & 7 M	$601,146	$405,714	$116,073	$0	$0

4% COLA

Monthly Amount	15 Yr Inflated	30 Yr Inflated	Money Lasts	5 Years	10 Years	15 Years	20 Years	30 Years
$1,200	$2,078	$3,743	Over 40 Yrs	$796,159	$864,118	$924,152	$969,643	$977,221
$1,600	$2,771	$4,990	38 Y & 6 M	$767,519	$794,433	$796,982	$763,344	$519,173
$2,000	$3,463	$6,237	30 Y & 10 M	$738,886	$724,757	$669,827	$557,077	$61,177
$2,400	$4,156	$7,485	25 Y & 8 M	$710,244	$655,059	$542,620	$350,713	$0
$2,800	$4,849	$8,732	21 Y & 11 M	$681,604	$585,374	$415,454	$144,435	$0
$3,200	$5,541	$9,980	19 Y & 3 M	$652,971	$515,699	$288,295	$0	$0
$3,600	$6,234	$11,227	17 Y & 2 M	$624,331	$446,010	$161,118	$0	$0

| $725,000 Balance | | 5% Return On Investment | | | | | | |

No COLA

Monthly Amount	15 Yr Inflated	30 Yr Inflated	Money Lasts	5 Years	10 Years	15 Years	20 Years	30 Years
$2,000	$2,000	$2,000	Over 40 Yrs	$789,374	$871,533	$976,392	$1.110 M	$1.499 M
$2,400	$2,400	$2,400	Over 40 Yrs	$762,188	$809,649	$870,223	$947,533	$1.172 M
$2,800	$2,800	$2,800	Over 40 Yrs	$735,002	$747,767	$764,059	$784,852	$845,262
$3,200	$3,200	$3,200	Over 40 Yrs	$707,816	$685,883	$657,891	$622,165	$518,375
$3,600	$3,600	$3,600	34 Y & 11 M	$680,630	$624,001	$551,725	$459,482	$191,501
$4,000	$4,000	$4,000	27 Y & 5 M	$653,444	$562,117	$445,559	$296,797	$0
$4,400	$4,400	$4,400	22 Y & 9 M	$626,257	$500,234	$339,393	$134,115	$0

2% COLA

Monthly Amount	15 Yr Inflated	30 Yr Inflated	Money Lasts	5 Years	10 Years	15 Years	20 Years	30 Years
$1,600	$2,111	$2,842	Over 40 Yrs	$812,338	$912,044	$1.026 M	$1.158 M	$1.486 M
$2,000	$2,639	$3,552	Over 40 Yrs	$784,100	$844,831	$906,113	$966,412	$1.075 M
$2,400	$3,167	$4,262	Over 40 Yrs	$755,857	$777,605	$785,891	$774,966	$662,984
$2,800	$3,694	$4,972	34 Y & 6 M	$727,619	$710,391	$665,688	$583,556	$251,329
$3,200	$4,222	$5,683	27 Y & 9 M	$699,377	$643,163	$545,455	$392,093	$0
$3,600	$4,750	$6,393	23 Y & 4 M	$671,136	$575,939	$425,233	$200,642	$0
$4,000	$5,278	$7,104	20 Y & 2 M	$642,895	$508,712	$305,003	$9,176	$0

3% COLA

Monthly Amount	15 Yr Inflated	30 Yr Inflated	Money Lasts	5 Years	10 Years	15 Years	20 Years	30 Years
$1,600	$2,420	$3,770	Over 40 Yrs	$810,170	$900,536	$994,608	$1.090 M	$1.269 M
$2,000	$3,025	$4,713	Over 40 Yrs	$781,384	$830,418	$866,423	$881,569	$802,872
$2,400	$3,630	$5,656	35 Y & 2 M	$752,601	$760,317	$738,273	$673,168	$336,792
$2,800	$4,235	$6,598	28 Y & 5 M	$723,819	$690,223	$610,140	$464,804	$0
$3,200	$4,841	$7,541	23 Y & 11 M	$695,033	$620,102	$481,950	$256,332	$0
$3,600	$5,445	$8,484	20 Y & 8 M	$666,250	$550,008	$353,816	$47,971	$0
$4,000	$6,050	$9,426	18 Y & 2 M	$637,466	$479,901	$225,659	$0	$0

4% COLA

Monthly Amount	15 Yr Inflated	30 Yr Inflated	Money Lasts	5 Years	10 Years	15 Years	20 Years	30 Years
$1,200	$2,078	$3,743	Over 40 Yrs	$837,292	$961,538	$1.097 M	$1.241 M	$1.541 M
$1,600	$2,771	$4,990	Over 40 Yrs	$807,953	$888,402	$960,144	$1.014 M	$1.011 M
$2,000	$3,463	$6,237	36 Y & 6 M	$778,620	$815,275	$823,394	$786,717	$480,243
$2,400	$4,156	$7,485	29 Y & 6 M	$749,281	$742,127	$686,593	$559,263	$0
$2,800	$4,849	$8,732	24 Y & 9 M	$719,942	$668,992	$549,835	$331,902	$0
$3,200	$5,541	$9,980	21 Y & 4 M	$690,608	$595,864	$413,079	$104,522	$0
$3,600	$6,234	$11,227	18 Y & 9 M	$661,268	$522,723	$276,308	$0	$0

$725,000 Balance					6% Return On Investment			

No COLA

Monthly Amount	15 Yr Inflated	30 Yr Inflated	Money Lasts	5 Years	10 Years	15 Years	20 Years	30 Years
$2,400	$2,400	$2,400	Over 40 Yrs	$802,995	$907,371	$1.047 M	$1.234 M	$1.819 M
$2,800	$2,800	$2,800	Over 40 Yrs	$775,126	$842,206	$931,973	$1.052 M	$1.428 M
$3,200	$3,200	$3,200	Over 40 Yrs	$747,255	$777,036	$816,891	$870,226	$1.037 M
$3,600	$3,600	$3,600	Over 40 Yrs	$719,386	$711,872	$701,817	$688,362	$646,259
$4,000	$4,000	$4,000	36 Y & 5 M	$691,516	$646,707	$586,741	$506,493	$255,395
$4,400	$4,400	$4,400	27 Y & 8 M	$663,646	$581,542	$471,666	$324,629	$0
$4,800	$4,800	$4,800	22 Y & 8 M	$635,777	$516,377	$356,592	$142,764	$0

2% COLA

Monthly Amount	15 Yr Inflated	30 Yr Inflated	Money Lasts	5 Years	10 Years	15 Years	20 Years	30 Years
$2,000	$2,639	$3,552	Over 40 Yrs	$825,511	$944,957	$1.088 M	$1.261 M	$1.734 M
$2,400	$3,167	$4,262	Over 40 Yrs	$796,571	$874,278	$958,313	$1.049 M	$1.248 M
$2,800	$3,694	$4,972	Over 40 Yrs	$767,633	$803,604	$828,465	$836,034	$762,021
$3,200	$4,222	$5,683	34 Y & 5 M	$738,692	$732,921	$698,593	$623,283	$276,007
$3,600	$4,750	$6,393	27 Y & 5 M	$709,751	$662,237	$568,723	$410,534	$0
$4,000	$5,278	$7,104	22 Y & 11 M	$680,811	$591,554	$438,849	$197,774	$0
$4,400	$5,806	$7,814	19 Y & 10 M	$651,869	$520,868	$308,980	$0	$0

3% COLA

Monthly Amount	15 Yr Inflated	30 Yr Inflated	Money Lasts	5 Years	10 Years	15 Years	20 Years	30 Years
$2,000	$3,025	$4,713	Over 40 Yrs	$822,756	$930,086	$1.046 M	$1.171 M	$1.431 M
$2,400	$3,630	$5,656	Over 40 Yrs	$793,265	$856,434	$908,293	$939,812	$884,865
$2,800	$4,235	$6,598	34 Y & 6 M	$763,777	$782,793	$770,121	$708,976	$338,478
$3,200	$4,841	$7,541	27 Y & 10 M	$734,282	$709,119	$631,881	$478,009	$0
$3,600	$5,445	$8,484	23 Y & 5 M	$704,792	$635,476	$493,706	$247,174	$0
$4,000	$6,050	$9,426	20 Y & 3 M	$675,301	$561,821	$355,508	$16,291	$0
$4,400	$6,655	$10,369	17 Y & 10 M	$645,809	$488,166	$217,302	$0	$0

4% COLA

Monthly Amount	15 Yr Inflated	30 Yr Inflated	Money Lasts	5 Years	10 Years	15 Years	20 Years	30 Years
$1,600	$2,771	$4,990	Over 40 Yrs	$850,001	$991,237	$1.149 M	$1.321 M	$1.692 M
$2,000	$3,463	$6,237	Over 40 Yrs	$819,952	$914,465	$1.001 M	$1.069 M	$1.074 M
$2,400	$4,156	$7,485	35 Y & 3 M	$789,897	$837,673	$854,071	$818,186	$455,794
$2,800	$4,849	$8,732	28 Y & 6 M	$759,842	$760,890	$706,841	$567,050	$0
$3,200	$5,541	$9,980	23 Y & 11 M	$729,793	$684,119	$559,622	$315,909	$0
$3,600	$6,234	$11,227	20 Y & 9 M	$699,738	$607,333	$412,382	$64,756	$0
$4,000	$6,927	$12,475	18 Y & 3 M	$669,685	$530,548	$265,131	$0	$0

$750,000 Balance	3% Return On Investment

No COLA

Monthly Amount	15 Yr Inflated	30 Yr Inflated	Money Lasts	5 Years	10 Years	15 Years	20 Years	30 Years
$1,600	$1,600	$1,600	Over 40 Yrs	$765,990	$784,527	$806,017	$830,930	$893,292
$2,000	$2,000	$2,000	Over 40 Yrs	$740,126	$728,678	$715,407	$700,023	$661,513
$2,400	$2,400	$2,400	Over 40 Yrs	$714,259	$672,826	$624,793	$569,109	$429,724
$2,800	$2,800	$2,800	36 Y & 6 M	$688,393	$616,973	$534,177	$438,194	$197,931
$3,200	$3,200	$3,200	29 Y & 2 M	$662,527	$561,123	$443,566	$307,286	$0
$3,600	$3,600	$3,600	24 Y & 5 M	$636,661	$505,270	$352,951	$176,373	$0
$4,000	$4,000	$4,000	20 Y & 11 M	$610,794	$449,417	$262,337	$45,459	$0

2% COLA

Monthly Amount	15 Yr Inflated	30 Yr Inflated	Money Lasts	5 Years	10 Years	15 Years	20 Years	30 Years
$1,200	$1,583	$2,131	Over 40 Yrs	$788,783	$825,344	$858,461	$886,617	$920,220
$1,600	$2,111	$2,842	Over 40 Yrs	$761,893	$764,481	$755,122	$730,624	$620,122
$2,000	$2,639	$3,552	37 Y & 9 M	$735,005	$703,627	$651,802	$574,664	$320,108
$2,400	$3,167	$4,262	30 Y & 5 M	$708,114	$642,765	$548,467	$418,680	$20,034
$2,800	$3,694	$4,972	25 Y & 6 M	$681,227	$581,912	$445,149	$262,724	$0
$3,200	$4,222	$5,683	21 Y & 11 M	$654,336	$521,045	$341,805	$106,727	$0
$3,600	$4,750	$6,393	19 Y & 3 M	$627,445	$460,183	$238,471	$0	$0

3% COLA

Monthly Amount	15 Yr Inflated	30 Yr Inflated	Money Lasts	5 Years	10 Years	15 Years	20 Years	30 Years
$1,200	$1,815	$2,828	Over 40 Yrs	$787,204	$817,236	$836,861	$842,010	$787,174
$1,600	$2,420	$3,770	39 Y & 8 M	$759,787	$753,668	$726,324	$671,153	$442,746
$2,000	$3,025	$4,713	31 Y & 9 M	$732,366	$690,087	$615,758	$500,246	$98,203
$2,400	$3,630	$5,656	26 Y & 6 M	$704,950	$626,521	$505,223	$329,390	$0
$2,800	$4,235	$6,598	22 Y & 8 M	$677,536	$562,966	$394,710	$158,574	$0
$3,200	$4,841	$7,541	19 Y & 10 M	$650,114	$499,378	$284,132	$0	$0
$3,600	$5,445	$8,484	17 Y & 8 M	$622,699	$435,822	$173,616	$0	$0

4% COLA

Monthly Amount	15 Yr Inflated	30 Yr Inflated	Money Lasts	5 Years	10 Years	15 Years	20 Years	30 Years
$800	$1,385	$2,494	Over 40 Yrs	$813,547	$875,108	$931,745	$979,477	$1.025 M
$1,200	$2,078	$3,743	Over 40 Yrs	$785,591	$808,678	$813,335	$791,841	$627,553
$1,600	$2,771	$4,990	33 Y & 9 M	$757,635	$742,260	$694,959	$604,264	$229,948
$2,000	$3,463	$6,237	27 Y & 10 M	$729,683	$675,848	$576,598	$416,718	$0
$2,400	$4,156	$7,485	23 Y & 8 M	$701,726	$609,419	$458,193	$229,087	$0
$2,800	$4,849	$8,732	20 Y & 7 M	$673,769	$542,999	$339,820	$41,528	$0
$3,200	$5,541	$9,980	18 Y & 3 M	$645,818	$476,589	$221,455	$0	$0

| $750,000 Balance | | | | | 4% Return On Investment | | | |

No COLA

Monthly Amount	15 Yr Inflated	30 Yr Inflated	Money Lasts	5 Years	10 Years	15 Years	20 Years	30 Years
$2,000	$2,000	$2,000	Over 40 Yrs	$779,898	$816,275	$860,532	$914,377	$1.060 M
$2,400	$2,400	$2,400	Over 40 Yrs	$753,380	$757,492	$762,496	$768,584	$785,000
$2,800	$2,800	$2,800	Over 40 Yrs	$726,861	$698,709	$664,457	$622,785	$510,400
$3,200	$3,200	$3,200	37 Y & 1 M	$700,343	$639,929	$566,425	$476,996	$235,816
$3,600	$3,600	$3,600	29 Y & 2 M	$673,824	$581,146	$468,388	$331,201	$0
$4,000	$4,000	$4,000	24 Y & 3 M	$647,308	$522,366	$370,356	$185,411	$0
$4,400	$4,400	$4,400	20 Y & 10 M	$620,788	$463,582	$272,317	$39,614	$0

2% COLA

Monthly Amount	15 Yr Inflated	30 Yr Inflated	Money Lasts	5 Years	10 Years	15 Years	20 Years	30 Years
$1,600	$2,111	$2,842	Over 40 Yrs	$802,257	$854,356	$905,079	$952,803	$1.030 M
$2,000	$2,639	$3,552	Over 40 Yrs	$774,701	$790,412	$793,693	$780,203	$679,725
$2,400	$3,167	$4,262	36 Y & 10 M	$747,143	$726,459	$682,293	$607,578	$329,161
$2,800	$3,694	$4,972	29 Y & 8 M	$719,589	$662,516	$570,912	$434,988	$0
$3,200	$4,222	$5,683	24 Y & 11 M	$692,030	$598,557	$459,498	$262,345	$0
$3,600	$4,750	$6,393	21 Y & 6 M	$664,471	$534,600	$348,093	$89,709	$0
$4,000	$5,278	$7,104	18 Y & 10 M	$636,913	$470,642	$236,679	$0	$0

3% COLA

Monthly Amount	15 Yr Inflated	30 Yr Inflated	Money Lasts	5 Years	10 Years	15 Years	20 Years	30 Years
$1,600	$2,420	$3,770	Over 40 Yrs	$800,120	$843,204	$874,872	$889,354	$834,281
$2,000	$3,025	$4,713	37 Y & 11 M	$772,025	$776,447	$755,888	$700,806	$434,580
$2,400	$3,630	$5,656	30 Y & 7 M	$743,933	$709,703	$636,930	$512,307	$35,008
$2,800	$4,235	$6,598	25 Y & 7 M	$715,843	$642,969	$517,995	$323,853	$0
$3,200	$4,841	$7,541	21 Y & 11 M	$687,747	$576,204	$398,995	$135,280	$0
$3,600	$5,445	$8,484	19 Y & 4 M	$659,655	$509,469	$280,059	$0	$0
$4,000	$6,050	$9,426	17 Y & 3 M	$631,563	$442,721	$161,097	$0	$0

4% COLA

Monthly Amount	15 Yr Inflated	30 Yr Inflated	Money Lasts	5 Years	10 Years	15 Years	20 Years	30 Years
$1,200	$2,078	$3,743	Over 40 Yrs	$826,575	$901,125	$969,178	$1.024 M	$1.058 M
$1,600	$2,771	$4,990	39 Y & 10 M	$797,935	$831,438	$842,003	$818,120	$600,255
$2,000	$3,463	$6,237	31 Y & 11 M	$769,301	$761,761	$714,847	$611,850	$142,255
$2,400	$4,156	$7,485	26 Y & 7 M	$740,661	$692,065	$587,644	$405,492	$0
$2,800	$4,849	$8,732	22 Y & 9 M	$712,021	$622,379	$460,476	$199,211	$0
$3,200	$5,541	$9,980	19 Y & 11 M	$683,387	$552,705	$333,318	$0	$0
$3,600	$6,234	$11,227	17 Y & 9 M	$654,746	$483,015	$206,141	$0	$0

| $750,000 Balance | | | | | 5% Return On Investment | | | |

No COLA

Monthly Amount	15 Yr Inflated	30 Yr Inflated	Money Lasts	5 Years	10 Years	15 Years	20 Years	30 Years
$2,000	$2,000	$2,000	Over 40 Yrs	$821,280	$912,254	$1.028 M	$1.177 M	$1.607 M
$2,400	$2,400	$2,400	Over 40 Yrs	$794,095	$850,373	$922,200	$1.014 M	$1.280 M
$2,800	$2,800	$2,800	Over 40 Yrs	$766,908	$788,488	$816,030	$851,183	$953,303
$3,200	$3,200	$3,200	Over 40 Yrs	$739,722	$726,605	$709,864	$688,498	$626,424
$3,600	$3,600	$3,600	38 Y & 6 M	$712,536	$664,722	$603,697	$525,812	$299,546
$4,000	$4,000	$4,000	29 Y & 6 M	$685,351	$602,841	$497,534	$363,134	$0
$4,400	$4,400	$4,400	24 Y & 3 M	$658,163	$540,955	$391,365	$200,445	$0

2% COLA

Monthly Amount	15 Yr Inflated	30 Yr Inflated	Money Lasts	5 Years	10 Years	15 Years	20 Years	30 Years
$1,600	$2,111	$2,842	Over 40 Yrs	$844,244	$952,765	$1.078 M	$1.224 M	$1.594 M
$2,000	$2,639	$3,552	Over 40 Yrs	$816,006	$885,552	$958,084	$1.033 M	$1.183 M
$2,400	$3,167	$4,262	Over 40 Yrs	$787,765	$818,329	$837,866	$841,300	$771,035
$2,800	$3,694	$4,972	36 Y & 7 M	$759,526	$751,113	$717,661	$649,888	$359,374
$3,200	$4,222	$5,683	29 Y & 3 M	$731,285	$683,888	$597,433	$458,433	$0
$3,600	$4,750	$6,393	24 Y & 6 M	$703,043	$616,662	$477,208	$266,977	$0
$4,000	$5,278	$7,104	21 Y & 2 M	$674,801	$549,432	$356,972	$75,504	$0

3% COLA

Monthly Amount	15 Yr Inflated	30 Yr Inflated	Money Lasts	5 Years	10 Years	15 Years	20 Years	30 Years
$1,600	$2,420	$3,770	Over 40 Yrs	$842,078	$941,259	$1.047 M	$1.156 M	$1.377 M
$2,000	$3,025	$4,713	Over 40 Yrs	$813,290	$871,139	$918,394	$947,898	$910,912
$2,400	$3,630	$5,656	36 Y & 11 M	$784,507	$801,038	$790,245	$739,499	$444,836
$2,800	$4,235	$6,598	29 Y & 9 M	$755,726	$730,946	$662,114	$531,138	$0
$3,200	$4,841	$7,541	24 Y & 11 M	$726,939	$660,823	$533,921	$322,660	$0
$3,600	$5,445	$8,484	21 Y & 6 M	$698,157	$590,731	$405,790	$114,306	$0
$4,000	$6,050	$9,426	18 Y & 11 M	$669,372	$520,621	$277,629	$0	$0

4% COLA

Monthly Amount	15 Yr Inflated	30 Yr Inflated	Money Lasts	5 Years	10 Years	15 Years	20 Years	30 Years
$1,200	$2,078	$3,743	Over 40 Yrs	$869,200	$1.002 M	$1.149 M	$1.308 M	$1.649 M
$1,600	$2,771	$4,990	Over 40 Yrs	$839,860	$929,124	$1.012 M	$1.080 M	$1.119 M
$2,000	$3,463	$6,237	37 Y & 11 M	$810,526	$855,996	$875,366	$853,048	$588,291
$2,400	$4,156	$7,485	30 Y & 8 M	$781,188	$782,850	$738,567	$625,598	$57,505
$2,800	$4,849	$8,732	25 Y & 8 M	$751,848	$709,711	$601,805	$398,230	$0
$3,200	$5,541	$9,980	22 Y & 2 M	$722,515	$636,587	$465,052	$170,855	$0
$3,600	$6,234	$11,227	19 Y & 5 M	$693,176	$563,448	$328,284	$0	$0

$750,000 Balance — 6% Return On Investment

No COLA

Monthly Amount	15 Yr Inflated	30 Yr Inflated	Money Lasts	5 Years	10 Years	15 Years	20 Years	30 Years
$2,400	$2,400	$2,400	Over 40 Yrs	$836,450	$952,140	$1.107 M	$1.314 M	$1.962 M
$2,800	$2,800	$2,800	Over 40 Yrs	$808,581	$886,975	$991,884	$1.132 M	$1.572 M
$3,200	$3,200	$3,200	Over 40 Yrs	$780,711	$821,809	$876,807	$950,406	$1.181 M
$3,600	$3,600	$3,600	Over 40 Yrs	$752,840	$756,641	$761,728	$768,536	$789,838
$4,000	$4,000	$4,000	Over 40 Yrs	$724,972	$691,478	$646,657	$586,674	$398,983
$4,400	$4,400	$4,400	30 Y & 2 M	$697,102	$626,312	$531,580	$404,806	$8,122
$4,800	$4,800	$4,800	24 Y & 5 M	$669,231	$561,144	$416,500	$222,934	$0

2% COLA

Monthly Amount	15 Yr Inflated	30 Yr Inflated	Money Lasts	5 Years	10 Years	15 Years	20 Years	30 Years
$2,000	$2,639	$3,552	Over 40 Yrs	$858,967	$989,729	$1.148 M	$1.342 M	$1.878 M
$2,400	$3,167	$4,262	Over 40 Yrs	$830,027	$919,050	$1.018 M	$1.129 M	$1.392 M
$2,800	$3,694	$4,972	Over 40 Yrs	$801,088	$848,376	$888,379	$916,213	$905,612
$3,200	$4,222	$5,683	36 Y & 11 M	$772,148	$777,692	$758,506	$703,462	$419,592
$3,600	$4,750	$6,393	29 Y & 2 M	$743,208	$707,011	$628,642	$490,718	$0
$4,000	$5,278	$7,104	24 Y & 4 M	$714,267	$636,326	$498,764	$277,953	$0
$4,400	$5,806	$7,814	20 Y & 10 M	$685,326	$565,642	$368,900	$65,227	$0

3% COLA

Monthly Amount	15 Yr Inflated	30 Yr Inflated	Money Lasts	5 Years	10 Years	15 Years	20 Years	30 Years
$2,000	$3,025	$4,713	Over 40 Yrs	$856,210	$974,855	$1.106 M	$1.251 M	$1.575 M
$2,400	$3,630	$5,656	Over 40 Yrs	$826,721	$901,205	$968,206	$1.020 M	$1.028 M
$2,800	$4,235	$6,598	36 Y & 7 M	$797,233	$827,564	$830,034	$789,154	$482,067
$3,200	$4,841	$7,541	29 Y & 4 M	$767,738	$753,890	$691,794	$558,186	$0
$3,600	$5,445	$8,484	24 Y & 7 M	$738,248	$680,247	$553,620	$327,352	$0
$4,000	$6,050	$9,426	21 Y & 2 M	$708,756	$606,590	$415,419	$96,465	$0
$4,400	$6,655	$10,369	18 Y & 8 M	$679,265	$532,938	$277,219	$0	$0

4% COLA

Monthly Amount	15 Yr Inflated	30 Yr Inflated	Money Lasts	5 Years	10 Years	15 Years	20 Years	30 Years
$1,600	$2,771	$4,990	Over 40 Yrs	$883,456	$1.036 M	$1.208 M	$1.401 M	$1.835 M
$2,000	$3,463	$6,237	Over 40 Yrs	$853,408	$959,236	$1.061 M	$1.150 M	$1.218 M
$2,400	$4,156	$7,485	36 Y & 11 M	$823,353	$882,445	$913,988	$898,369	$599,390
$2,800	$4,849	$8,732	29 Y & 10 M	$793,298	$805,661	$766,756	$647,230	$0
$3,200	$5,541	$9,980	25 Y & 1 M	$763,249	$728,890	$619,535	$396,086	$0
$3,600	$6,234	$11,227	21 Y & 7 M	$733,194	$652,104	$472,296	$144,935	$0
$4,000	$6,927	$12,475	18 Y & 11 M	$703,140	$575,318	$325,042	$0	$0

| $800,000 Balance | | | | | 3% Return On Investment | | | |

No COLA

Monthly Amount	15 Yr Inflated	30 Yr Inflated	Money Lasts	5 Years	10 Years	15 Years	20 Years	30 Years
$2,000	$2,000	$2,000	Over 40 Yrs	$798,089	$795,873	$793,304	$790,326	$782,871
$2,400	$2,400	$2,400	Over 40 Yrs	$772,222	$740,020	$702,690	$659,414	$551,084
$2,800	$2,800	$2,800	Over 40 Yrs	$746,357	$684,170	$612,078	$528,504	$319,302
$3,200	$3,200	$3,200	32 Y & 5 M	$720,490	$628,317	$521,463	$397,590	$87,512
$3,600	$3,600	$3,600	26 Y & 10 M	$694,625	$572,465	$430,850	$266,678	$0
$4,000	$4,000	$4,000	22 Y & 11 M	$668,758	$516,613	$340,235	$135,765	$0
$4,400	$4,400	$4,400	20 Y & 2 M	$642,892	$460,762	$249,622	$4,854	$0

2% COLA

Monthly Amount	15 Yr Inflated	30 Yr Inflated	Money Lasts	5 Years	10 Years	15 Years	20 Years	30 Years
$1,600	$2,111	$2,842	Over 40 Yrs	$819,856	$831,675	$833,018	$820,926	$741,481
$2,000	$2,639	$3,552	Over 40 Yrs	$792,968	$770,822	$729,698	$664,966	$441,465
$2,400	$3,167	$4,262	32 Y & 10 M	$766,077	$709,960	$626,366	$508,985	$141,399
$2,800	$3,694	$4,972	27 Y & 5 M	$739,190	$649,107	$523,047	$353,030	$0
$3,200	$4,222	$5,683	23 Y & 7 M	$712,299	$588,242	$419,705	$197,036	$0
$3,600	$4,750	$6,393	20 Y & 8 M	$685,409	$527,379	$316,370	$41,046	$0
$4,000	$5,278	$7,104	18 Y & 5 M	$658,518	$466,513	$213,024	$0	$0

3% COLA

Monthly Amount	15 Yr Inflated	30 Yr Inflated	Money Lasts	5 Years	10 Years	15 Years	20 Years	30 Years
$1,600	$2,420	$3,770	Over 40 Yrs	$817,752	$820,867	$804,226	$761,465	$564,118
$2,000	$3,025	$4,713	33 Y & 10 M	$790,330	$757,283	$693,657	$590,552	$219,567
$2,400	$3,630	$5,656	28 Y & 3 M	$762,914	$693,719	$583,124	$419,699	$0
$2,800	$4,235	$6,598	24 Y & 2 M	$735,499	$630,161	$472,606	$248,877	$0
$3,200	$4,841	$7,541	21 Y & 2 M	$708,079	$566,575	$362,032	$77,953	$0
$3,600	$5,445	$8,484	18 Y & 10 M	$680,662	$503,017	$251,514	$0	$0
$4,000	$6,050	$9,426	16 Y & 11 M	$653,245	$439,446	$140,973	$0	$0

4% COLA

Monthly Amount	15 Yr Inflated	30 Yr Inflated	Money Lasts	5 Years	10 Years	15 Years	20 Years	30 Years
$1,200	$2,078	$3,743	Over 40 Yrs	$843,554	$875,873	$891,231	$882,144	$748,912
$1,600	$2,771	$4,990	35 Y & 8 M	$815,598	$809,455	$772,857	$694,568	$351,309
$2,000	$3,463	$6,237	29 Y & 5 M	$787,646	$743,042	$654,492	$507,017	$0
$2,400	$4,156	$7,485	25 Y & 1 M	$759,690	$676,615	$536,091	$319,392	$0
$2,800	$4,849	$8,732	21 Y & 10 M	$731,734	$610,196	$417,721	$131,837	$0
$3,200	$5,541	$9,980	19 Y & 4 M	$703,782	$543,785	$299,353	$0	$0
$3,600	$6,234	$11,227	17 Y & 5 M	$675,825	$477,363	$180,976	$0	$0

$800,000 Balance   4% Return On Investment

No COLA

Monthly Amount	15 Yr Inflated	30 Yr Inflated	Money Lasts	5 Years	10 Years	15 Years	20 Years	30 Years
$2,400	$2,400	$2,400	Over 40 Yrs	$814,213	$831,505	$852,543	$878,139	$947,170
$2,800	$2,800	$2,800	Over 40 Yrs	$787,694	$772,722	$754,506	$732,343	$672,574
$3,200	$3,200	$3,200	Over 40 Yrs	$761,175	$713,939	$656,470	$586,549	$397,980
$3,600	$3,600	$3,600	33 Y & 1 M	$734,658	$655,159	$558,436	$440,758	$123,392
$4,000	$4,000	$4,000	27 Y & 1 M	$708,139	$596,377	$460,401	$294,965	$0
$4,400	$4,400	$4,400	22 Y & 11 M	$681,622	$537,596	$362,367	$149,174	$0
$4,800	$4,800	$4,800	20 Y & 1 M	$655,103	$478,813	$264,330	$3,378	$0

2% COLA

Monthly Amount	15 Yr Inflated	30 Yr Inflated	Money Lasts	5 Years	10 Years	15 Years	20 Years	30 Years
$2,000	$2,639	$3,552	Over 40 Yrs	$835,535	$864,426	$883,742	$889,761	$841,896
$2,400	$3,167	$4,262	Over 40 Yrs	$807,974	$800,469	$772,338	$717,132	$491,328
$2,800	$3,694	$4,972	32 Y & 5 M	$780,421	$736,525	$660,954	$544,538	$140,834
$3,200	$4,222	$5,683	27 Y & 1 M	$752,863	$672,569	$549,546	$371,903	$0
$3,600	$4,750	$6,393	23 Y & 3 M	$725,304	$608,613	$438,141	$199,266	$0
$4,000	$5,278	$7,104	20 Y & 5 M	$697,746	$544,654	$326,726	$26,615	$0
$4,400	$5,806	$7,814	18 Y & 2 M	$670,189	$480,700	$215,328	$0	$0

3% COLA

Monthly Amount	15 Yr Inflated	30 Yr Inflated	Money Lasts	5 Years	10 Years	15 Years	20 Years	30 Years
$2,000	$3,025	$4,713	Over 40 Yrs	$832,856	$850,455	$845,929	$810,355	$596,739
$2,400	$3,630	$5,656	32 Y & 11 M	$804,766	$783,715	$726,976	$621,863	$197,176
$2,800	$4,235	$6,598	27 Y & 7 M	$776,676	$716,980	$608,041	$433,408	$0
$3,200	$4,841	$7,541	23 Y & 8 M	$748,579	$650,216	$489,041	$244,836	$0
$3,600	$5,445	$8,484	20 Y & 9 M	$720,488	$583,481	$370,105	$56,383	$0
$4,000	$6,050	$9,426	18 Y & 6 M	$692,396	$516,734	$251,145	$0	$0
$4,400	$6,655	$10,369	16 Y & 8 M	$664,303	$449,989	$132,182	$0	$0

4% COLA

Monthly Amount	15 Yr Inflated	30 Yr Inflated	Money Lasts	5 Years	10 Years	15 Years	20 Years	30 Years
$1,600	$2,771	$4,990	Over 40 Yrs	$858,767	$905,450	$932,051	$927,676	$762,427
$2,000	$3,463	$6,237	33 Y & 11 M	$830,133	$835,773	$804,894	$721,407	$304,428
$2,400	$4,156	$7,485	28 Y & 4 M	$801,494	$766,079	$677,693	$515,051	$0
$2,800	$4,849	$8,732	24 Y & 4 M	$772,853	$696,393	$550,525	$308,769	$0
$3,200	$5,541	$9,980	21 Y & 3 M	$744,220	$626,718	$423,366	$102,481	$0
$3,600	$6,234	$11,227	18 Y & 11 M	$715,580	$557,027	$296,187	$0	$0
$4,000	$6,927	$12,475	16 Y & 11 M	$686,939	$487,336	$168,995	$0	$0

$800,000 Balance   **5% Return On Investment**

No COLA

Monthly Amount	15 Yr Inflated	30 Yr Inflated	Money Lasts	5 Years	10 Years	15 Years	20 Years	30 Years
$2,400	$2,400	$2,400	Over 40 Yrs	$857,909	$931,816	$1.026 M	$1.147 M	$1.496 M
$2,800	$2,800	$2,800	Over 40 Yrs	$830,722	$869,932	$919,975	$983,846	$1.169 M
$3,200	$3,200	$3,200	Over 40 Yrs	$803,537	$808,052	$813,814	$821,166	$842,526
$3,600	$3,600	$3,600	Over 40 Yrs	$776,350	$746,167	$707,644	$658,478	$515,643
$4,000	$4,000	$4,000	34 Y & 5 M	$749,164	$684,283	$601,477	$495,793	$188,764
$4,400	$4,400	$4,400	27 Y & 7 M	$721,978	$622,400	$495,311	$333,111	$0
$4,800	$4,800	$4,800	23 Y & 3 M	$694,792	$560,518	$389,145	$170,425	$0

2% COLA

Monthly Amount	15 Yr Inflated	30 Yr Inflated	Money Lasts	5 Years	10 Years	15 Years	20 Years	30 Years
$2,000	$2,639	$3,552	Over 40 Yrs	$879,821	$966,998	$1.062 M	$1.165 M	$1.399 M
$2,400	$3,167	$4,262	Over 40 Yrs	$851,580	$899,776	$941,815	$973,968	$987,138
$2,800	$3,694	$4,972	Over 40 Yrs	$823,341	$832,559	$821,609	$782,555	$575,475
$3,200	$4,222	$5,683	32 Y & 6 M	$795,098	$765,330	$701,374	$591,090	$163,724
$3,600	$4,750	$6,393	26 Y & 11 M	$766,856	$698,103	$581,151	$399,638	$0
$4,000	$5,278	$7,104	23 Y & 1 M	$738,615	$630,878	$460,920	$208,171	$0
$4,400	$5,806	$7,814	20 Y & 3 M	$710,374	$563,652	$340,700	$16,738	$0

3% COLA

Monthly Amount	15 Yr Inflated	30 Yr Inflated	Money Lasts	5 Years	10 Years	15 Years	20 Years	30 Years
$2,000	$3,025	$4,713	Over 40 Yrs	$877,104	$952,586	$1.022 M	$1.081 M	$1.127 M
$2,400	$3,630	$5,656	Over 40 Yrs	$848,321	$882,482	$894,190	$872,163	$660,932
$2,800	$4,235	$6,598	32 Y & 6 M	$819,540	$812,390	$766,061	$663,803	$194,953
$3,200	$4,841	$7,541	27 Y & 2 M	$790,753	$742,268	$637,867	$455,324	$0
$3,600	$5,445	$8,484	23 Y & 4 M	$761,971	$672,175	$509,736	$246,970	$0
$4,000	$6,050	$9,426	20 Y & 6 M	$733,186	$602,067	$381,578	$38,562	$0
$4,400	$6,655	$10,369	18 Y & 3 M	$704,402	$531,964	$253,419	$0	$0

4% COLA

Monthly Amount	15 Yr Inflated	30 Yr Inflated	Money Lasts	5 Years	10 Years	15 Years	20 Years	30 Years
$1,600	$2,771	$4,990	Over 40 Yrs	$903,674	$1.011 M	$1.116 M	$1.213 M	$1.335 M
$2,000	$3,463	$6,237	Over 40 Yrs	$874,341	$937,441	$979,312	$985,713	$804,388
$2,400	$4,156	$7,485	33 Y & 1 M	$845,001	$864,294	$842,513	$758,261	$273,599
$2,800	$4,849	$8,732	27 Y & 8 M	$815,662	$791,157	$705,752	$530,895	$0
$3,200	$5,541	$9,980	23 Y & 9 M	$786,330	$718,033	$569,002	$303,524	$0
$3,600	$6,234	$11,227	20 Y & 10 M	$756,990	$644,893	$432,230	$76,141	$0
$4,000	$6,927	$12,475	18 Y & 7 M	$727,651	$571,751	$295,444	$0	$0

$800,000 Balance   6% Return On Investment

No COLA

Monthly Amount	15 Yr Inflated	30 Yr Inflated	Money Lasts	5 Years	10 Years	15 Years	20 Years	30 Years
$2,800	$2,800	$2,800	Over 40 Yrs	$875,492	$976,519	$1.112 M	$1.293 M	$1.859 M
$3,200	$3,200	$3,200	Over 40 Yrs	$847,622	$911,352	$996,636	$1.111 M	$1.468 M
$3,600	$3,600	$3,600	Over 40 Yrs	$819,752	$846,185	$881,559	$928,897	$1.077 M
$4,000	$4,000	$4,000	Over 40 Yrs	$791,883	$781,020	$766,482	$747,028	$686,158
$4,400	$4,400	$4,400	36 Y & 9 M	$764,013	$715,854	$651,405	$565,158	$295,287
$4,800	$4,800	$4,800	28 Y & 5 M	$736,143	$650,689	$536,331	$383,294	$0
$5,200	$5,200	$5,200	23 Y & 7 M	$708,274	$585,523	$421,255	$201,425	$0

2% COLA

Monthly Amount	15 Yr Inflated	30 Yr Inflated	Money Lasts	5 Years	10 Years	15 Years	20 Years	30 Years
$2,400	$3,167	$4,262	Over 40 Yrs	$896,938	$1.009 M	$1.138 M	$1.289 M	$1.679 M
$2,800	$3,694	$4,972	Over 40 Yrs	$868,000	$937,918	$1.008 M	$1.077 M	$1.193 M
$3,200	$4,222	$5,683	Over 40 Yrs	$839,059	$867,236	$878,337	$863,823	$706,776
$3,600	$4,750	$6,393	32 Y & 11 M	$810,118	$796,551	$748,467	$651,071	$220,702
$4,000	$5,278	$7,104	27 Y & 2 M	$781,178	$725,866	$618,590	$438,307	$0
$4,400	$5,806	$7,814	23 Y & 1 M	$752,237	$655,184	$488,728	$225,585	$0
$4,800	$6,334	$8,524	20 Y & 2 M	$723,296	$584,499	$358,851	$12,830	$0

3% COLA

Monthly Amount	15 Yr Inflated	30 Yr Inflated	Money Lasts	5 Years	10 Years	15 Years	20 Years	30 Years
$2,400	$3,630	$5,656	Over 40 Yrs	$893,631	$990,745	$1.088 M	$1.180 M	$1.316 M
$2,800	$4,235	$6,598	Over 40 Yrs	$864,144	$917,106	$949,862	$949,510	$769,237
$3,200	$4,841	$7,541	32 Y & 6 M	$834,650	$843,434	$811,624	$718,546	$222,530
$3,600	$5,445	$8,484	26 Y & 11 M	$805,159	$769,790	$673,450	$487,712	$0
$4,000	$6,050	$9,426	23 Y & 2 M	$775,667	$696,132	$535,246	$256,820	$0
$4,400	$6,655	$10,369	20 Y & 4 M	$746,176	$622,479	$397,043	$25,921	$0
$4,800	$7,260	$11,312	18 Y & 1 M	$716,686	$548,830	$258,858	$0	$0

4% COLA

Monthly Amount	15 Yr Inflated	30 Yr Inflated	Money Lasts	5 Years	10 Years	15 Years	20 Years	30 Years
$2,000	$3,463	$6,237	Over 40 Yrs	$920,318	$1.049 M	$1.181 M	$1.310 M	$1.505 M
$2,400	$4,156	$7,485	Over 40 Yrs	$890,265	$971,987	$1.034 M	$1.059 M	$886,559
$2,800	$4,849	$8,732	32 Y & 7 M	$860,210	$895,206	$886,587	$807,590	$268,603
$3,200	$5,541	$9,980	27 Y & 3 M	$830,161	$818,433	$739,364	$556,446	$0
$3,600	$6,234	$11,227	23 Y & 5 M	$800,105	$741,647	$592,125	$305,293	$0
$4,000	$6,927	$12,475	20 Y & 7 M	$770,051	$664,860	$444,870	$54,092	$0
$4,400	$7,619	$13,722	18 Y & 4 M	$740,002	$588,090	$297,666	$0	$0

$850,000 Balance				3% Return On Investment				

No COLA

Monthly Amount	15 Yr Inflated	30 Yr Inflated	Money Lasts	5 Years	10 Years	15 Years	20 Years	30 Years
$2,000	$2,000	$2,000	Over 40 Yrs	$856,052	$863,068	$871,201	$880,630	$904,232
$2,400	$2,400	$2,400	Over 40 Yrs	$830,187	$807,218	$780,590	$749,722	$672,452
$2,800	$2,800	$2,800	Over 40 Yrs	$804,320	$751,365	$689,976	$618,808	$440,662
$3,200	$3,200	$3,200	35 Y & 11 M	$778,454	$695,513	$599,360	$487,894	$208,874
$3,600	$3,600	$3,600	29 Y & 6 M	$752,589	$639,662	$508,748	$356,984	$0
$4,000	$4,000	$4,000	25 Y & 1 M	$726,722	$583,809	$418,134	$226,072	$0
$4,400	$4,400	$4,400	21 Y & 11 M	$700,855	$527,956	$327,519	$95,158	$0

2% COLA

Monthly Amount	15 Yr Inflated	30 Yr Inflated	Money Lasts	5 Years	10 Years	15 Years	20 Years	30 Years
$1,600	$2,111	$2,842	Over 40 Yrs	$877,820	$898,871	$910,917	$911,232	$862,845
$2,000	$2,639	$3,552	Over 40 Yrs	$850,932	$838,018	$807,596	$755,270	$562,826
$2,400	$3,167	$4,262	35 Y & 3 M	$824,041	$777,157	$704,264	$599,290	$262,761
$2,800	$3,694	$4,972	29 Y & 5 M	$797,154	$716,302	$600,945	$443,334	$0
$3,200	$4,222	$5,683	25 Y & 3 M	$770,263	$655,439	$497,605	$287,344	$0
$3,600	$4,750	$6,393	22 Y & 2 M	$743,373	$594,576	$394,270	$131,353	$0
$4,000	$5,278	$7,104	19 Y & 8 M	$716,482	$533,709	$290,924	$0	$0

3% COLA

Monthly Amount	15 Yr Inflated	30 Yr Inflated	Money Lasts	5 Years	10 Years	15 Years	20 Years	30 Years
$1,600	$2,420	$3,770	Over 40 Yrs	$875,715	$888,062	$882,124	$851,770	$685,480
$2,000	$3,025	$4,713	35 Y & 11 M	$848,294	$824,478	$771,554	$680,857	$340,930
$2,400	$3,630	$5,656	29 Y & 11 M	$820,877	$760,913	$661,021	$510,003	$0
$2,800	$4,235	$6,598	25 Y & 8 M	$793,464	$697,358	$550,505	$339,182	$0
$3,200	$4,841	$7,541	22 Y & 6 M	$766,042	$633,770	$439,930	$168,258	$0
$3,600	$5,445	$8,484	19 Y & 11 M	$738,626	$570,213	$329,414	$0	$0
$4,000	$6,050	$9,426	17 Y & 11 M	$711,209	$506,643	$218,873	$0	$0

4% COLA

Monthly Amount	15 Yr Inflated	30 Yr Inflated	Money Lasts	5 Years	10 Years	15 Years	20 Years	30 Years
$1,200	$2,078	$3,743	Over 40 Yrs	$901,518	$943,070	$969,131	$972,451	$870,277
$1,600	$2,771	$4,990	37 Y & 6 M	$873,562	$876,649	$850,753	$784,871	$472,667
$2,000	$3,463	$6,237	30 Y & 11 M	$845,610	$810,240	$732,393	$597,325	$75,107
$2,400	$4,156	$7,485	26 Y & 5 M	$817,653	$743,809	$613,986	$409,695	$0
$2,800	$4,849	$8,732	23 Y & 1 M	$789,697	$677,392	$495,619	$222,142	$0
$3,200	$5,541	$9,980	20 Y & 5 M	$761,746	$610,982	$377,254	$34,574	$0
$3,600	$6,234	$11,227	18 Y & 4 M	$733,788	$544,558	$258,873	$0	$0

$850,000 Balance   4% Return On Investment

No COLA

Monthly Amount	15 Yr Inflated	30 Yr Inflated	Money Lasts	5 Years	10 Years	15 Years	20 Years	30 Years
$2,400	$2,400	$2,400	Over 40 Yrs	$875,044	$905,515	$942,587	$987,691	$1.109 M
$2,800	$2,800	$2,800	Over 40 Yrs	$848,527	$846,735	$844,554	$841,901	$834,746
$3,200	$3,200	$3,200	Over 40 Yrs	$822,008	$787,951	$746,517	$696,106	$560,152
$3,600	$3,600	$3,600	37 Y & 8 M	$795,490	$729,171	$648,483	$550,313	$285,561
$4,000	$4,000	$4,000	30 Y & 3 M	$768,972	$670,389	$550,449	$404,522	$10,973
$4,400	$4,400	$4,400	25 Y & 6 M	$742,454	$611,608	$452,413	$258,728	$0
$4,800	$4,800	$4,800	22 Y & 1 M	$715,935	$552,824	$354,374	$112,930	$0

2% COLA

Monthly Amount	15 Yr Inflated	30 Yr Inflated	Money Lasts	5 Years	10 Years	15 Years	20 Years	30 Years
$2,000	$2,639	$3,552	Over 40 Yrs	$896,366	$938,436	$973,785	$999,312	$1.004 M
$2,400	$3,167	$4,262	Over 40 Yrs	$868,808	$874,483	$862,387	$826,691	$653,502
$2,800	$3,694	$4,972	35 Y & 4 M	$841,253	$810,537	$751,000	$654,094	$303,006
$3,200	$4,222	$5,683	29 Y & 4 M	$813,695	$746,581	$639,592	$481,456	$0
$3,600	$4,750	$6,393	25 Y & 2 M	$786,137	$682,626	$528,188	$308,822	$0
$4,000	$5,278	$7,104	21 Y & 11 M	$758,577	$618,664	$416,770	$136,168	$0
$4,400	$5,806	$7,814	19 Y & 7 M	$731,020	$554,711	$305,373	$0	$0

3% COLA

Monthly Amount	15 Yr Inflated	30 Yr Inflated	Money Lasts	5 Years	10 Years	15 Years	20 Years	30 Years
$2,000	$3,025	$4,713	Over 40 Yrs	$893,689	$924,468	$935,977	$919,913	$758,914
$2,400	$3,630	$5,656	35 Y & 5 M	$865,599	$857,727	$817,025	$731,422	$359,351
$2,800	$4,235	$6,598	29 Y & 6 M	$837,509	$790,993	$698,089	$542,964	$0
$3,200	$4,841	$7,541	25 Y & 4 M	$809,412	$724,227	$579,089	$354,392	$0
$3,600	$5,445	$8,484	22 Y & 3 M	$781,321	$657,493	$460,153	$165,941	$0
$4,000	$6,050	$9,426	19 Y & 9 M	$753,228	$590,744	$341,190	$0	$0
$4,400	$6,655	$10,369	17 Y & 10 M	$725,135	$524,000	$222,228	$0	$0

4% COLA

Monthly Amount	15 Yr Inflated	30 Yr Inflated	Money Lasts	5 Years	10 Years	15 Years	20 Years	30 Years
$1,600	$2,771	$4,990	Over 40 Yrs	$919,601	$979,463	$1.022 M	$1.037 M	$924,598
$2,000	$3,463	$6,237	36 Y & 2 M	$890,967	$909,788	$894,944	$830,966	$466,602
$2,400	$4,156	$7,485	30 Y & 2 M	$862,326	$840,089	$767,737	$624,603	$8,400
$2,800	$4,849	$8,732	25 Y & 10 M	$833,686	$770,405	$640,572	$418,325	$0
$3,200	$5,541	$9,980	22 Y & 7 M	$805,052	$700,728	$513,410	$212,032	$0
$3,600	$6,234	$11,227	20 Y & 1 M	$776,412	$631,039	$386,235	$5,738	$0
$4,000	$6,927	$12,475	18 Y & 1 M	$747,772	$561,348	$259,044	$0	$0

| $850,000 Balance | | | | 5% Return On Investment | | | | |

No COLA

Monthly Amount	15 Yr Inflated	30 Yr Inflated	Money Lasts	5 Years	10 Years	15 Years	20 Years	30 Years
$2,400	$2,400	$2,400	Over 40 Yrs	$921,722	$1.013 M	$1.130 M	$1.279 M	$1.712 M
$2,800	$2,800	$2,800	Over 40 Yrs	$894,536	$951,377	$1.024 M	$1.117 M	$1.385 M
$3,200	$3,200	$3,200	Over 40 Yrs	$867,351	$889,495	$917,758	$953,829	$1.059 M
$3,600	$3,600	$3,600	Over 40 Yrs	$840,164	$827,611	$811,591	$791,144	$731,740
$4,000	$4,000	$4,000	Over 40 Yrs	$812,978	$765,727	$705,422	$628,456	$404,858
$4,400	$4,400	$4,400	31 Y & 7 M	$785,792	$703,846	$599,258	$465,775	$77,983
$4,800	$4,800	$4,800	26 Y & 1 M	$758,607	$641,963	$493,092	$303,091	$0

2% COLA

Monthly Amount	15 Yr Inflated	30 Yr Inflated	Money Lasts	5 Years	10 Years	15 Years	20 Years	30 Years
$2,000	$2,639	$3,552	Over 40 Yrs	$943,635	$1.048 M	$1.166 M	$1.298 M	$1.615 M
$2,400	$3,167	$4,262	Over 40 Yrs	$915,393	$981,219	$1.046 M	$1.107 M	$1.203 M
$2,800	$3,694	$4,972	Over 40 Yrs	$887,154	$914,001	$925,551	$915,214	$791,562
$3,200	$4,222	$5,683	35 Y & 11 M	$858,913	$846,776	$805,324	$723,760	$379,829
$3,600	$4,750	$6,393	29 Y & 7 M	$830,671	$779,551	$685,102	$532,310	$0
$4,000	$5,278	$7,104	25 Y & 3 M	$802,430	$712,323	$564,866	$340,834	$0
$4,400	$5,806	$7,814	21 Y & 11 M	$774,190	$645,098	$444,647	$149,405	$0

3% COLA

Monthly Amount	15 Yr Inflated	30 Yr Inflated	Money Lasts	5 Years	10 Years	15 Years	20 Years	30 Years
$2,000	$3,025	$4,713	Over 40 Yrs	$940,918	$1.034 M	$1.126 M	$1.213 M	$1.343 M
$2,400	$3,630	$5,656	Over 40 Yrs	$912,135	$963,927	$998,138	$1.005 M	$877,031
$2,800	$4,235	$6,598	35 Y & 5 M	$883,354	$893,835	$870,006	$796,469	$411,052
$3,200	$4,841	$7,541	29 Y & 5 M	$854,567	$823,712	$741,812	$587,988	$0
$3,600	$5,445	$8,484	25 Y & 3 M	$825,785	$753,620	$613,685	$379,639	$0
$4,000	$6,050	$9,426	22 Y & 1 M	$797,000	$683,511	$485,524	$171,228	$0
$4,400	$6,655	$10,369	19 Y & 8 M	$768,216	$613,409	$357,366	$0	$0

4% COLA

Monthly Amount	15 Yr Inflated	30 Yr Inflated	Money Lasts	5 Years	10 Years	15 Years	20 Years	30 Years
$1,600	$2,771	$4,990	Over 40 Yrs	$967,489	$1.092 M	$1.220 M	$1.346 M	$1.551 M
$2,000	$3,463	$6,237	Over 40 Yrs	$938,156	$1.019 M	$1.083 M	$1.118 M	$1.020 M
$2,400	$4,156	$7,485	35 Y & 6 M	$908,816	$945,740	$946,462	$890,929	$489,702
$2,800	$4,849	$8,732	29 Y & 8 M	$879,477	$872,604	$809,702	$663,565	$0
$3,200	$5,541	$9,980	25 Y & 5 M	$850,144	$799,478	$672,948	$436,188	$0
$3,600	$6,234	$11,227	22 Y & 4 M	$820,804	$726,336	$536,174	$208,802	$0
$4,000	$6,927	$12,475	19 Y & 10 M	$791,465	$653,195	$399,389	$0	$0

$850,000 Balance   6% Return On Investment

No COLA

Monthly Amount	15 Yr Inflated	30 Yr Inflated	Money Lasts	5 Years	10 Years	15 Years	20 Years	30 Years
$2,800	$2,800	$2,800	Over 40 Yrs	$942,404	$1.066 M	$1.232 M	$1.453 M	$2.146 M
$3,200	$3,200	$3,200	Over 40 Yrs	$914,534	$1.001 M	$1.116 M	$1.271 M	$1.755 M
$3,600	$3,600	$3,600	Over 40 Yrs	$886,663	$935,727	$1.001 M	$1.089 M	$1.364 M
$4,000	$4,000	$4,000	Over 40 Yrs	$858,795	$870,565	$886,315	$907,391	$973,341
$4,400	$4,400	$4,400	Over 40 Yrs	$830,925	$805,399	$771,237	$725,522	$582,475
$4,800	$4,800	$4,800	33 Y & 9 M	$803,054	$740,230	$656,157	$543,649	$191,602
$5,200	$5,200	$5,200	27 Y & 1 M	$775,185	$675,064	$541,081	$361,780	$0

2% COLA

Monthly Amount	15 Yr Inflated	30 Yr Inflated	Money Lasts	5 Years	10 Years	15 Years	20 Years	30 Years
$2,400	$3,167	$4,262	Over 40 Yrs	$963,850	$1.098 M	$1.258 M	$1.450 M	$1.966 M
$2,800	$3,694	$4,972	Over 40 Yrs	$934,912	$1.027 M	$1.128 M	$1.237 M	$1.480 M
$3,200	$4,222	$5,683	Over 40 Yrs	$905,971	$956,777	$998,162	$1.024 M	$993,942
$3,600	$4,750	$6,393	37 Y & 7 M	$877,030	$886,094	$868,296	$811,430	$507,881
$4,000	$5,278	$7,104	30 Y & 4 M	$848,088	$815,407	$738,415	$598,661	$21,798
$4,400	$5,806	$7,814	25 Y & 7 M	$819,147	$744,724	$608,551	$385,935	$0
$4,800	$6,334	$8,524	22 Y & 2 M	$790,207	$674,043	$478,682	$173,190	$0

3% COLA

Monthly Amount	15 Yr Inflated	30 Yr Inflated	Money Lasts	5 Years	10 Years	15 Years	20 Years	30 Years
$2,400	$3,630	$5,656	Over 40 Yrs	$960,543	$1.080 M	$1.208 M	$1.341 M	$1.603 M
$2,800	$4,235	$6,598	Over 40 Yrs	$931,054	$1.007 M	$1.070 M	$1.110 M	$1.056 M
$3,200	$4,841	$7,541	36 Y & 1 M	$901,561	$932,976	$931,451	$878,901	$509,703
$3,600	$5,445	$8,484	29 Y & 8 M	$872,071	$859,333	$793,277	$648,068	$0
$4,000	$6,050	$9,426	25 Y & 4 M	$842,578	$785,674	$655,073	$417,176	$0
$4,400	$6,655	$10,369	22 Y & 1 M	$813,087	$712,022	$516,873	$186,281	$0
$4,800	$7,260	$11,312	19 Y & 7 M	$783,597	$638,373	$378,687	$0	$0

4% COLA

Monthly Amount	15 Yr Inflated	30 Yr Inflated	Money Lasts	5 Years	10 Years	15 Years	20 Years	30 Years
$2,000	$3,463	$6,237	Over 40 Yrs	$987,230	$1.138 M	$1.301 M	$1.470 M	$1.792 M
$2,400	$4,156	$7,485	Over 40 Yrs	$957,175	$1.062 M	$1.154 M	$1.219 M	$1.174 M
$2,800	$4,849	$8,732	35 Y & 6 M	$927,121	$984,747	$1.006 M	$967,944	$555,772
$3,200	$5,541	$9,980	29 Y & 6 M	$897,072	$907,976	$859,193	$716,804	$0
$3,600	$6,234	$11,227	25 Y & 4 M	$867,016	$831,188	$711,951	$465,647	$0
$4,000	$6,927	$12,475	22 Y & 2 M	$836,963	$754,405	$564,702	$214,454	$0
$4,400	$7,619	$13,722	19 Y & 8 M	$806,914	$677,635	$417,495	$0	$0

| $900,000 Balance | | | | 3% Return On Investment | | | | |

No COLA

Monthly Amount	15 Yr Inflated	30 Yr Inflated	Money Lasts	5 Years	10 Years	15 Years	20 Years	30 Years
$2,000	$2,000	$2,000	Over 40 Yrs	$914,016	$930,264	$949,100	$970,935	$1.026 M
$2,500	$2,500	$2,500	Over 40 Yrs	$881,684	$860,452	$835,837	$807,302	$735,872
$3,000	$3,000	$3,000	Over 40 Yrs	$849,351	$790,635	$722,566	$643,657	$446,130
$3,500	$3,500	$3,500	33 Y & 11 M	$817,018	$720,819	$609,298	$480,015	$156,394
$4,000	$4,000	$4,000	27 Y & 4 M	$784,685	$651,004	$496,029	$316,373	$0
$4,500	$4,500	$4,500	22 Y & 11 M	$752,353	$581,189	$382,764	$152,734	$0
$5,000	$5,000	$5,000	19 Y & 10 M	$720,020	$511,375	$269,497	$0	$0

2% COLA

Monthly Amount	15 Yr Inflated	30 Yr Inflated	Money Lasts	5 Years	10 Years	15 Years	20 Years	30 Years
$1,500	$1,979	$2,664	Over 40 Yrs	$942,509	$981,292	$1.015 M	$1.041 M	$1.059 M
$2,000	$2,639	$3,552	Over 40 Yrs	$908,896	$905,214	$885,495	$845,577	$684,189
$2,500	$3,299	$4,440	35 Y & 11 M	$875,284	$829,142	$756,341	$650,620	$309,148
$3,000	$3,958	$5,327	28 Y & 11 M	$841,671	$753,064	$627,171	$455,642	$0
$3,500	$4,618	$6,215	24 Y & 4 M	$808,058	$676,987	$498,004	$260,661	$0
$4,000	$5,278	$7,104	20 Y & 11 M	$774,445	$600,903	$368,819	$65,651	$0
$4,500	$5,938	$7,991	18 Y & 5 M	$740,831	$524,825	$239,648	$0	$0

3% COLA

Monthly Amount	15 Yr Inflated	30 Yr Inflated	Money Lasts	5 Years	10 Years	15 Years	20 Years	30 Years
$1,500	$2,269	$3,535	Over 40 Yrs	$940,532	$971,143	$987,640	$984,754	$892,847
$2,000	$3,025	$4,713	38 Y & 1 M	$906,257	$891,672	$849,450	$771,160	$462,289
$2,500	$3,782	$5,891	30 Y & 6 M	$871,988	$812,223	$711,297	$557,618	$31,839
$3,000	$4,538	$7,070	25 Y & 5 M	$837,718	$732,762	$573,124	$344,039	$0
$3,500	$5,294	$8,248	21 Y & 9 M	$803,443	$653,293	$434,932	$130,443	$0
$4,000	$6,050	$9,426	19 Y & 1 M	$769,173	$573,838	$296,771	$0	$0
$4,500	$6,807	$10,605	16 Y & 11 M	$734,899	$494,377	$158,598	$0	$0

4% COLA

Monthly Amount	15 Yr Inflated	30 Yr Inflated	Money Lasts	5 Years	10 Years	15 Years	20 Years	30 Years
$1,000	$1,732	$3,119	Over 40 Yrs	$973,460	$1.043 M	$1.106 M	$1.157 M	$1.190 M
$1,500	$2,598	$4,678	Over 40 Yrs	$938,514	$960,452	$958,253	$922,078	$693,419
$2,000	$3,463	$6,237	32 Y & 7 M	$903,574	$877,436	$810,293	$687,634	$196,475
$2,500	$4,329	$7,796	26 Y & 10 M	$868,629	$794,407	$662,313	$453,152	$0
$3,000	$5,195	$9,356	22 Y & 10 M	$833,681	$711,370	$514,306	$218,608	$0
$3,500	$6,061	$10,915	19 Y & 10 M	$798,742	$628,362	$366,368	$0	$0
$4,000	$6,927	$12,475	17 Y & 7 M	$763,796	$545,330	$218,378	$0	$0

$900,000 Balance					4% Return On Investment			

No COLA

Monthly Amount	15 Yr Inflated	30 Yr Inflated	Money Lasts	5 Years	10 Years	15 Years	20 Years	30 Years
$2,500	$2,500	$2,500	Over 40 Yrs	$929,248	$964,833	$1.008 M	$1.061 M	$1.203 M
$3,000	$3,000	$3,000	Over 40 Yrs	$896,100	$891,356	$885,583	$878,558	$859,615
$3,500	$3,500	$3,500	Over 40 Yrs	$862,952	$817,878	$763,038	$696,317	$516,378
$4,000	$4,000	$4,000	33 Y & 11 M	$829,805	$744,401	$640,496	$514,077	$173,141
$4,500	$4,500	$4,500	27 Y & 1 M	$796,657	$670,924	$517,950	$331,834	$0
$5,000	$5,000	$5,000	22 Y & 8 M	$763,509	$597,447	$395,407	$149,593	$0
$5,500	$5,500	$5,500	19 Y & 7 M	$730,360	$523,967	$272,860	$0	$0

2% COLA

Monthly Amount	15 Yr Inflated	30 Yr Inflated	Money Lasts	5 Years	10 Years	15 Years	20 Years	30 Years
$2,000	$2,639	$3,552	Over 40 Yrs	$957,199	$1.012 M	$1.064 M	$1.109 M	$1.166 M
$2,500	$3,299	$4,440	Over 40 Yrs	$922,753	$932,512	$924,596	$893,109	$728,072
$3,000	$3,958	$5,327	34 Y & 9 M	$888,307	$852,571	$785,342	$677,331	$289,906
$3,500	$4,618	$6,215	28 Y & 1 M	$853,859	$772,628	$646,090	$461,545	$0
$4,000	$5,278	$7,104	23 Y & 8 M	$819,411	$692,679	$506,822	$245,730	$0
$4,500	$5,938	$7,991	20 Y & 5 M	$784,962	$612,734	$367,562	$29,935	$0
$5,000	$6,597	$8,879	17 Y & 11 M	$750,518	$532,802	$228,336	$0	$0

3% COLA

Monthly Amount	15 Yr Inflated	30 Yr Inflated	Money Lasts	5 Years	10 Years	15 Years	20 Years	30 Years
$2,000	$3,025	$4,713	Over 40 Yrs	$954,522	$998,480	$1.026 M	$1.029 M	$921,081
$2,500	$3,782	$5,891	36 Y & 1 M	$919,408	$915,057	$877,344	$793,877	$421,710
$3,000	$4,538	$7,070	29 Y & 2 M	$884,293	$831,623	$728,642	$558,246	$0
$3,500	$5,294	$8,248	24 Y & 5 M	$849,175	$748,182	$579,923	$322,597	$0
$4,000	$6,050	$9,426	21 Y & 1 M	$814,060	$664,755	$431,235	$86,994	$0
$4,500	$6,807	$10,605	18 Y & 6 M	$778,942	$581,324	$282,540	$0	$0
$5,000	$7,563	$11,783	16 Y & 6 M	$743,828	$497,888	$133,824	$0	$0

4% COLA

Monthly Amount	15 Yr Inflated	30 Yr Inflated	Money Lasts	5 Years	10 Years	15 Years	20 Years	30 Years
$1,500	$2,598	$4,678	Over 40 Yrs	$987,593	$1.071 M	$1.144 M	$1.198 M	$1.201 M
$2,000	$3,463	$6,237	38 Y & 3 M	$951,800	$983,799	$984,989	$940,520	$628,764
$2,500	$4,329	$7,796	30 Y & 7 M	$916,000	$896,687	$826,015	$682,633	$56,183
$3,000	$5,195	$9,356	25 Y & 6 M	$880,199	$809,568	$667,011	$424,680	$0
$3,500	$6,061	$10,915	21 Y & 10 M	$844,405	$722,476	$508,078	$166,869	$0
$4,000	$6,927	$12,475	19 Y & 2 M	$808,605	$635,362	$349,092	$0	$0
$4,500	$7,792	$14,034	16 Y & 11 M	$772,810	$548,263	$190,153	$0	$0

$900,000 Balance   5% Return On Investment

No COLA

Monthly Amount	15 Yr Inflated	30 Yr Inflated	Money Lasts	5 Years	10 Years	15 Years	20 Years	30 Years
$2,500	$2,500	$2,500	Over 40 Yrs	$978,741	$1.079 M	$1.207 M	$1.371 M	$1.847 M
$3,000	$3,000	$3,000	Over 40 Yrs	$944,758	$1.002 M	$1.075 M	$1.168 M	$1.438 M
$3,500	$3,500	$3,500	Over 40 Yrs	$910,775	$924,527	$942,078	$964,479	$1.030 M
$4,000	$4,000	$4,000	Over 40 Yrs	$876,793	$847,175	$809,373	$761,127	$620,964
$4,500	$4,500	$4,500	34 Y & 5 M	$842,811	$769,821	$676,665	$557,771	$212,366
$5,000	$5,000	$5,000	26 Y & 11 M	$808,827	$692,464	$543,952	$354,411	$0
$5,500	$5,500	$5,500	22 Y & 6 M	$774,845	$615,111	$411,247	$151,058	$0

2% COLA

Monthly Amount	15 Yr Inflated	30 Yr Inflated	Money Lasts	5 Years	10 Years	15 Years	20 Years	30 Years
$2,000	$2,639	$3,552	Over 40 Yrs	$1.007 M	$1.130 M	$1.270 M	$1.431 M	$1.831 M
$2,500	$3,299	$4,440	Over 40 Yrs	$972,149	$1.046 M	$1.120 M	$1.191 M	$1.316 M
$3,000	$3,958	$5,327	Over 40 Yrs	$936,848	$961,834	$969,384	$952,151	$801,805
$3,500	$4,618	$6,215	34 Y & 1 M	$901,545	$877,801	$819,103	$712,838	$287,101
$4,000	$5,278	$7,104	27 Y & 6 M	$866,245	$793,767	$668,812	$473,500	$0
$4,500	$5,938	$7,991	23 Y & 1 M	$830,941	$709,737	$518,533	$234,189	$0
$5,000	$6,597	$8,879	19 Y & 11 M	$795,644	$625,718	$368,281	$0	$0

3% COLA

Monthly Amount	15 Yr Inflated	30 Yr Inflated	Money Lasts	5 Years	10 Years	15 Years	20 Years	30 Years
$2,000	$3,025	$4,713	Over 40 Yrs	$1.005 M	$1.115 M	$1.230 M	$1.346 M	$1.559 M
$2,500	$3,782	$5,891	Over 40 Yrs	$968,755	$1.028 M	$1.070 M	$1.085 M	$976,709
$3,000	$4,538	$7,070	34 Y & 10 M	$932,776	$940,221	$909,865	$824,909	$394,050
$3,500	$5,294	$8,248	28 Y & 2 M	$896,793	$852,580	$749,649	$564,373	$0
$4,000	$6,050	$9,426	23 Y & 9 M	$860,814	$764,957	$589,472	$303,894	$0
$4,500	$6,807	$10,605	20 Y & 6 M	$824,834	$677,328	$429,282	$43,391	$0
$5,000	$7,563	$11,783	17 Y & 11 M	$788,854	$589,692	$269,069	$0	$0

4% COLA

Monthly Amount	15 Yr Inflated	30 Yr Inflated	Money Lasts	5 Years	10 Years	15 Years	20 Years	30 Years
$1,500	$2,598	$4,678	Over 40 Yrs	$1.039 M	$1.192 M	$1.358 M	$1.535 M	$1.900 M
$2,000	$3,463	$6,237	Over 40 Yrs	$1.002 M	$1.100 M	$1.187 M	$1.251 M	$1.237 M
$2,500	$4,329	$7,796	36 Y & 3 M	$965,296	$1.009 M	$1.016 M	$966,795	$573,271
$3,000	$5,195	$9,356	29 Y & 3 M	$928,621	$917,473	$845,240	$682,478	$0
$3,500	$6,061	$10,915	24 Y & 6 M	$891,953	$826,068	$674,316	$398,313	$0
$4,000	$6,927	$12,475	21 Y & 2 M	$855,279	$734,641	$503,338	$114,041	$0
$4,500	$7,792	$14,034	18 Y & 7 M	$818,611	$643,231	$332,407	$0	$0

| $900,000 Balance | | | | | 6% Return On Investment | | | |

No COLA

Monthly Amount	15 Yr Inflated	30 Yr Inflated	Money Lasts	5 Years	10 Years	15 Years	20 Years	30 Years
$3,000	$3,000	$3,000	Over 40 Yrs	$995,379	$1.123 M	$1.294 M	$1.522 M	$2.238 M
$3,500	$3,500	$3,500	Over 40 Yrs	$960,541	$1.042 M	$1.150 M	$1.295 M	$1.749 M
$4,000	$4,000	$4,000	Over 40 Yrs	$925,706	$960,105	$1.006 M	$1.068 M	$1.261 M
$4,500	$4,500	$4,500	Over 40 Yrs	$890,869	$878,648	$862,294	$840,410	$771,929
$5,000	$5,000	$5,000	35 Y & 7 M	$856,031	$797,191	$718,448	$613,072	$283,344
$5,500	$5,500	$5,500	27 Y & 2 M	$821,194	$715,733	$574,604	$385,739	$0
$6,000	$6,000	$6,000	22 Y & 5 M	$786,355	$634,274	$430,754	$158,399	$0

2% COLA

Monthly Amount	15 Yr Inflated	30 Yr Inflated	Money Lasts	5 Years	10 Years	15 Years	20 Years	30 Years
$2,500	$3,299	$4,440	Over 40 Yrs	$1.024 M	$1.170 M	$1.345 M	$1.557 M	$2.132 M
$3,000	$3,958	$5,327	Over 40 Yrs	$987,353	$1.082 M	$1.183 M	$1.291 M	$1.524 M
$3,500	$4,618	$6,215	Over 40 Yrs	$951,175	$993,306	$1.021 M	$1.025 M	$916,590
$4,000	$5,278	$7,104	33 Y & 11 M	$915,000	$904,950	$858,243	$759,017	$308,973
$4,500	$5,938	$7,991	27 Y & 2 M	$878,823	$816,597	$695,908	$493,087	$0
$5,000	$6,597	$8,879	22 Y & 9 M	$842,651	$728,259	$533,607	$227,228	$0
$5,500	$7,257	$9,767	19 Y & 8 M	$806,477	$639,905	$371,264	$0	$0

3% COLA

Monthly Amount	15 Yr Inflated	30 Yr Inflated	Money Lasts	5 Years	10 Years	15 Years	20 Years	30 Years
$2,500	$3,782	$5,891	Over 40 Yrs	$1.020 M	$1.151 M	$1.293 M	$1.443 M	$1.753 M
$3,000	$4,538	$7,070	Over 40 Yrs	$983,221	$1.059 M	$1.120 M	$1.155 M	$1.070 M
$3,500	$5,294	$8,248	34 Y & 1 M	$946,354	$967,282	$947,642	$866,124	$387,097
$4,000	$6,050	$9,426	27 Y & 7 M	$909,491	$875,218	$774,904	$577,538	$0
$4,500	$6,807	$10,605	23 Y & 2 M	$872,625	$783,150	$602,157	$288,930	$0
$5,000	$7,563	$11,783	19 Y & 11 M	$835,762	$691,080	$429,394	$0	$0
$5,500	$8,319	$12,961	17 Y & 8 M	$798,899	$599,015	$256,655	$0	$0

4% COLA

Monthly Amount	15 Yr Inflated	30 Yr Inflated	Money Lasts	5 Years	10 Years	15 Years	20 Years	30 Years
$2,000	$3,463	$6,237	Over 40 Yrs	$1.054 M	$1.228 M	$1.421 M	$1.631 M	$2.079 M
$2,500	$4,329	$7,796	Over 40 Yrs	$1.017 M	$1.132 M	$1.237 M	$1.317 M	$1.307 M
$3,000	$5,195	$9,356	34 Y & 11 M	$979,004	$1.036 M	$1.053 M	$1.003 M	$533,770
$3,500	$6,061	$10,915	28 Y & 3 M	$941,442	$939,932	$868,595	$688,799	$0
$4,000	$6,927	$12,475	23 Y & 9 M	$903,873	$843,943	$684,523	$374,802	$0
$4,500	$7,792	$14,034	20 Y & 7 M	$866,311	$747,980	$500,516	$60,933	$0
$5,000	$8,659	$15,594	18 Y & 1 M	$828,744	$651,993	$316,434	$0	$0

$950,000 Balance	3% Return On Investment

No COLA

Monthly Amount	15 Yr Inflated	30 Yr Inflated	Money Lasts	5 Years	10 Years	15 Years	20 Years	30 Years
$2,000	$2,000	$2,000	Over 40 Yrs	$971,980	$997,460	$1.027 M	$1.061 M	$1.147 M
$2,500	$2,500	$2,500	Over 40 Yrs	$939,647	$927,646	$913,732	$897,603	$857,230
$3,000	$3,000	$3,000	Over 40 Yrs	$907,314	$857,830	$800,465	$733,962	$567,493
$3,500	$3,500	$3,500	37 Y & 5 M	$874,982	$788,016	$687,198	$570,323	$277,762
$4,000	$4,000	$4,000	29 Y & 9 M	$842,649	$718,199	$573,928	$406,679	$0
$4,500	$4,500	$4,500	24 Y & 10 M	$810,317	$648,386	$460,664	$243,042	$0
$5,000	$5,000	$5,000	21 Y & 5 M	$777,985	$578,572	$347,397	$79,402	$0

2% COLA

Monthly Amount	15 Yr Inflated	30 Yr Inflated	Money Lasts	5 Years	10 Years	15 Years	20 Years	30 Years
$1,500	$1,979	$2,664	Over 40 Yrs	$1.000 M	$1.048 M	$1.093 M	$1.131 M	$1.181 M
$2,000	$2,639	$3,552	Over 40 Yrs	$966,859	$972,409	$963,392	$935,880	$805,549
$2,500	$3,299	$4,440	38 Y & 4 M	$933,248	$896,338	$834,240	$740,925	$430,510
$3,000	$3,958	$5,327	30 Y & 11 M	$899,636	$820,261	$705,069	$545,947	$55,456
$3,500	$4,618	$6,215	25 Y & 10 M	$866,021	$744,182	$575,901	$350,965	$0
$4,000	$5,278	$7,104	22 Y & 3 M	$832,409	$668,100	$446,718	$155,956	$0
$4,500	$5,938	$7,991	19 Y & 7 M	$798,794	$592,020	$317,546	$0	$0

3% COLA

Monthly Amount	15 Yr Inflated	30 Yr Inflated	Money Lasts	5 Years	10 Years	15 Years	20 Years	30 Years
$1,500	$2,269	$3,535	Over 40 Yrs	$998,495	$1.038 M	$1.066 M	$1.075 M	$1.014 M
$2,000	$3,025	$4,713	Over 40 Yrs	$964,220	$958,867	$927,347	$861,463	$583,648
$2,500	$3,782	$5,891	32 Y & 2 M	$929,952	$879,419	$789,196	$647,925	$153,205
$3,000	$4,538	$7,070	26 Y & 10 M	$895,682	$799,957	$651,021	$434,343	$0
$3,500	$5,294	$8,248	22 Y & 11 M	$861,407	$720,489	$512,830	$220,747	$0
$4,000	$6,050	$9,426	20 Y & 1 M	$827,136	$641,032	$374,666	$7,191	$0
$4,500	$6,807	$10,605	17 Y & 11 M	$792,862	$561,573	$236,497	$0	$0

4% COLA

Monthly Amount	15 Yr Inflated	30 Yr Inflated	Money Lasts	5 Years	10 Years	15 Years	20 Years	30 Years
$1,000	$1,732	$3,119	Over 40 Yrs	$1.031 M	$1.111 M	$1.184 M	$1.247 M	$1.312 M
$1,500	$2,598	$4,678	Over 40 Yrs	$996,478	$1.028 M	$1.036 M	$1.012 M	$814,783
$2,000	$3,463	$6,237	34 Y & 1 M	$961,538	$944,632	$888,191	$777,939	$317,836
$2,500	$4,329	$7,796	28 Y & 2 M	$926,592	$861,602	$740,212	$543,458	$0
$3,000	$5,195	$9,356	23 Y & 11 M	$891,645	$778,566	$592,206	$308,915	$0
$3,500	$6,061	$10,915	20 Y & 10 M	$856,705	$695,556	$444,265	$74,506	$0
$4,000	$6,927	$12,475	18 Y & 6 M	$821,760	$612,528	$296,279	$0	$0

$950,000 Balance				4% Return On Investment				

No COLA

Monthly Amount	15 Yr Inflated	30 Yr Inflated	Money Lasts	5 Years	10 Years	15 Years	20 Years	30 Years
$2,500	$2,500	$2,500	Over 40 Yrs	$990,081	$1.039 M	$1.098 M	$1.170 M	$1.365 M
$3,000	$3,000	$3,000	Over 40 Yrs	$956,932	$965,367	$975,628	$988,113	$1.022 M
$3,500	$3,500	$3,500	Over 40 Yrs	$923,785	$891,890	$853,086	$805,874	$678,550
$4,000	$4,000	$4,000	38 Y & 2 M	$890,638	$818,415	$730,545	$623,636	$335,314
$4,500	$4,500	$4,500	29 Y & 11 M	$857,489	$744,936	$607,997	$441,390	$0
$5,000	$5,000	$5,000	24 Y & 9 M	$824,341	$671,458	$485,452	$259,148	$0
$5,500	$5,500	$5,500	21 Y & 3 M	$791,193	$597,982	$362,909	$76,907	$0

2% COLA

Monthly Amount	15 Yr Inflated	30 Yr Inflated	Money Lasts	5 Years	10 Years	15 Years	20 Years	30 Years
$2,000	$2,639	$3,552	Over 40 Yrs	$1.018 M	$1.086 M	$1.154 M	$1.218 M	$1.328 M
$2,500	$3,299	$4,440	Over 40 Yrs	$983,585	$1.007 M	$1.015 M	$1.003 M	$890,240
$3,000	$3,958	$5,327	37 Y & 7 M	$949,140	$926,584	$875,390	$786,888	$452,078
$3,500	$4,618	$6,215	30 Y & 3 M	$914,691	$846,638	$736,136	$571,100	$13,845
$4,000	$5,278	$7,104	25 Y & 4 M	$880,244	$766,691	$596,867	$355,284	$0
$4,500	$5,938	$7,991	21 Y & 10 M	$845,795	$686,746	$457,610	$139,493	$0
$5,000	$6,597	$8,879	19 Y & 2 M	$811,351	$606,815	$318,383	$0	$0

3% COLA

Monthly Amount	15 Yr Inflated	30 Yr Inflated	Money Lasts	5 Years	10 Years	15 Years	20 Years	30 Years
$2,000	$3,025	$4,713	Over 40 Yrs	$1.015 M	$1.072 M	$1.116 M	$1.139 M	$1.083 M
$2,500	$3,782	$5,891	38 Y & 6 M	$980,242	$989,071	$967,393	$903,436	$583,886
$3,000	$4,538	$7,070	30 Y & 11 M	$945,127	$905,636	$818,690	$667,804	$84,368
$3,500	$5,294	$8,248	25 Y & 11 M	$910,007	$822,194	$669,972	$432,155	$0
$4,000	$6,050	$9,426	22 Y & 4 M	$874,893	$738,769	$521,286	$196,553	$0
$4,500	$6,807	$10,605	19 Y & 8 M	$839,775	$655,336	$372,586	$0	$0
$5,000	$7,563	$11,783	17 Y & 6 M	$804,660	$571,899	$223,870	$0	$0

4% COLA

Monthly Amount	15 Yr Inflated	30 Yr Inflated	Money Lasts	5 Years	10 Years	15 Years	20 Years	30 Years
$1,500	$2,598	$4,678	Over 40 Yrs	$1.048 M	$1.145 M	$1.234 M	$1.308 M	$1.363 M
$2,000	$3,463	$6,237	Over 40 Yrs	$1.013 M	$1.058 M	$1.075 M	$1.050 M	$790,939
$2,500	$4,329	$7,796	32 Y & 4 M	$976,831	$970,698	$916,061	$792,188	$218,350
$3,000	$5,195	$9,356	26 Y & 11 M	$941,031	$883,579	$757,056	$534,231	$0
$3,500	$6,061	$10,915	23 Y & 1 M	$905,238	$796,488	$598,124	$276,424	$0
$4,000	$6,927	$12,475	20 Y & 3 M	$869,437	$709,372	$439,137	$18,511	$0
$4,500	$7,792	$14,034	17 Y & 11 M	$833,643	$622,278	$280,202	$0	$0

$950,000 Balance   5% Return On Investment

No COLA

Monthly Amount	15 Yr Inflated	30 Yr Inflated	Money Lasts	5 Years	10 Years	15 Years	20 Years	30 Years
$2,500	$2,500	$2,500	Over 40 Yrs	$1.043 M	$1.161 M	$1.311 M	$1.504 M	$2.063 M
$3,000	$3,000	$3,000	Over 40 Yrs	$1.009 M	$1.083 M	$1.179 M	$1.301 M	$1.654 M
$3,500	$3,500	$3,500	Over 40 Yrs	$974,589	$1.006 M	$1.046 M	$1.097 M	$1.246 M
$4,000	$4,000	$4,000	Over 40 Yrs	$940,607	$928,618	$913,316	$893,788	$837,053
$4,500	$4,500	$4,500	Over 40 Yrs	$906,624	$851,263	$780,609	$690,432	$428,455
$5,000	$5,000	$5,000	30 Y & 4 M	$872,641	$773,910	$647,901	$487,078	$19,859
$5,500	$5,500	$5,500	24 Y & 10 M	$838,660	$696,557	$515,195	$283,725	$0

2% COLA

Monthly Amount	15 Yr Inflated	30 Yr Inflated	Money Lasts	5 Years	10 Years	15 Years	20 Years	30 Years
$2,000	$2,639	$3,552	Over 40 Yrs	$1.071 M	$1.211 M	$1.374 M	$1.563 M	$2.047 M
$2,500	$3,299	$4,440	Over 40 Yrs	$1.036 M	$1.127 M	$1.224 M	$1.324 M	$1.533 M
$3,000	$3,958	$5,327	Over 40 Yrs	$1.001 M	$1.043 M	$1.073 M	$1.085 M	$1.018 M
$3,500	$4,618	$6,215	37 Y & 5 M	$965,360	$959,248	$923,052	$845,505	$503,201
$4,000	$5,278	$7,104	29 Y & 11 M	$930,059	$875,214	$772,762	$606,170	$0
$4,500	$5,938	$7,991	24 Y & 11 M	$894,756	$791,182	$622,478	$366,851	$0
$5,000	$6,597	$8,879	21 Y & 6 M	$859,458	$707,164	$472,230	$127,607	$0

3% COLA

Monthly Amount	15 Yr Inflated	30 Yr Inflated	Money Lasts	5 Years	10 Years	15 Years	20 Years	30 Years
$2,000	$3,025	$4,713	Over 40 Yrs	$1.069 M	$1.197 M	$1.334 M	$1.479 M	$1.775 M
$2,500	$3,782	$5,891	Over 40 Yrs	$1.033 M	$1.109 M	$1.174 M	$1.218 M	$1.193 M
$3,000	$4,538	$7,070	37 Y & 8 M	$996,589	$1.022 M	$1.014 M	$957,571	$610,144
$3,500	$5,294	$8,248	30 Y & 4 M	$960,608	$934,027	$853,599	$697,042	$27,505
$4,000	$6,050	$9,426	25 Y & 5 M	$924,628	$846,400	$693,415	$436,554	$0
$4,500	$6,807	$10,605	21 Y & 11 M	$888,648	$758,772	$533,228	$176,056	$0
$5,000	$7,563	$11,783	19 Y & 3 M	$852,668	$671,136	$373,016	$0	$0

4% COLA

Monthly Amount	15 Yr Inflated	30 Yr Inflated	Money Lasts	5 Years	10 Years	15 Years	20 Years	30 Years
$1,500	$2,598	$4,678	Over 40 Yrs	$1.102 M	$1.273 M	$1.462 M	$1.668 M	$2.116 M
$2,000	$3,463	$6,237	Over 40 Yrs	$1.066 M	$1.182 M	$1.291 M	$1.384 M	$1.453 M
$2,500	$4,329	$7,796	38 Y & 8 M	$1.029 M	$1.090 M	$1.120 M	$1.099 M	$789,367
$3,000	$5,195	$9,356	31 Y & 2 M	$992,435	$998,918	$949,186	$815,142	$125,841
$3,500	$6,061	$10,915	26 Y & 1 M	$955,767	$907,512	$778,261	$530,977	$0
$4,000	$6,927	$12,475	22 Y & 5 M	$919,092	$816,084	$607,282	$246,704	$0
$4,500	$7,792	$14,034	19 Y & 8 M	$882,425	$724,675	$436,353	$0	$0

| $950,000 Balance | | | | 6% Return On Investment | | | | |

No COLA

Monthly Amount	15 Yr Inflated	30 Yr Inflated	Money Lasts	5 Years	10 Years	15 Years	20 Years	30 Years
$3,000	$3,000	$3,000	Over 40 Yrs	$1.062 M	$1.213 M	$1.414 M	$1.683 M	$2.525 M
$3,500	$3,500	$3,500	Over 40 Yrs	$1.027 M	$1.131 M	$1.270 M	$1.455 M	$2.036 M
$4,000	$4,000	$4,000	Over 40 Yrs	$992,616	$1.050 M	$1.126 M	$1.228 M	$1.548 M
$4,500	$4,500	$4,500	Over 40 Yrs	$957,780	$968,192	$982,125	$1.001 M	$1.059 M
$5,000	$5,000	$5,000	Over 40 Yrs	$922,942	$886,734	$838,278	$773,433	$570,525
$5,500	$5,500	$5,500	31 Y & 4 M	$888,105	$805,276	$694,432	$546,098	$81,947
$6,000	$6,000	$6,000	25 Y & 2 M	$853,267	$723,818	$550,585	$318,761	$0

2% COLA

Monthly Amount	15 Yr Inflated	30 Yr Inflated	Money Lasts	5 Years	10 Years	15 Years	20 Years	30 Years
$2,500	$3,299	$4,440	Over 40 Yrs	$1.090 M	$1.260 M	$1.465 M	$1.717 M	$2.419 M
$3,000	$3,958	$5,327	Over 40 Yrs	$1.054 M	$1.171 M	$1.303 M	$1.451 M	$1.811 M
$3,500	$4,618	$6,215	Over 40 Yrs	$1.018 M	$1.083 M	$1.140 M	$1.185 M	$1.204 M
$4,000	$5,278	$7,104	38 Y & 1 M	$981,911	$994,494	$978,073	$919,376	$596,153
$4,500	$5,938	$7,991	29 Y & 11 M	$945,733	$906,138	$815,734	$653,441	$0
$5,000	$6,597	$8,879	24 Y & 10 M	$909,563	$817,801	$653,435	$387,586	$0
$5,500	$7,257	$9,767	21 Y & 4 M	$873,387	$729,445	$491,087	$121,619	$0

3% COLA

Monthly Amount	15 Yr Inflated	30 Yr Inflated	Money Lasts	5 Years	10 Years	15 Years	20 Years	30 Years
$2,500	$3,782	$5,891	Over 40 Yrs	$1.087 M	$1.241 M	$1.413 M	$1.604 M	$2.041 M
$3,000	$4,538	$7,070	Over 40 Yrs	$1.050 M	$1.149 M	$1.240 M	$1.315 M	$1.357 M
$3,500	$5,294	$8,248	37 Y & 6 M	$1.013 M	$1.057 M	$1.067 M	$1.026 M	$674,267
$4,000	$6,050	$9,426	29 Y & 11 M	$976,402	$964,762	$894,733	$737,897	$0
$4,500	$6,807	$10,605	24 Y & 11 M	$939,536	$872,693	$721,985	$449,286	$0
$5,000	$7,563	$11,783	21 Y & 7 M	$902,673	$780,622	$549,222	$160,651	$0
$5,500	$8,319	$12,961	18 Y & 11 M	$865,811	$688,558	$376,484	$0	$0

4% COLA

Monthly Amount	15 Yr Inflated	30 Yr Inflated	Money Lasts	5 Years	10 Years	15 Years	20 Years	30 Years
$2,000	$3,463	$6,237	Over 40 Yrs	$1.121 M	$1.317 M	$1.541 M	$1.791 M	$2.366 M
$2,500	$4,329	$7,796	Over 40 Yrs	$1.083 M	$1.221 M	$1.357 M	$1.477 M	$1.594 M
$3,000	$5,195	$9,356	37 Y & 9 M	$1.046 M	$1.125 M	$1.172 M	$1.163 M	$820,953
$3,500	$6,061	$10,915	30 Y & 5 M	$1.008 M	$1.029 M	$988,419	$849,149	$48,645
$4,000	$6,927	$12,475	25 Y & 6 M	$970,784	$933,486	$804,353	$535,161	$0
$4,500	$7,792	$14,034	21 Y & 11 M	$933,223	$837,522	$620,342	$221,288	$0
$5,000	$8,659	$15,594	19 Y & 4 M	$895,655	$741,536	$436,264	$0	$0

| $1,000,000 Balance | | 3% Return On Investment | | | | | | |

No COLA

Monthly Amount	15 Yr Inflated	30 Yr Inflated	Money Lasts	5 Years	10 Years	15 Years	20 Years	30 Years
$2,400	$2,400	$2,400	Over 40 Yrs	$1.004 M	$1.009 M	$1.014 M	$1.021 M	$1.037 M
$3,000	$3,000	$3,000	Over 40 Yrs	$965,279	$925,027	$878,365	$824,269	$688,860
$3,600	$3,600	$3,600	38 Y & 11 M	$926,480	$841,250	$742,445	$627,902	$341,180
$4,200	$4,200	$4,200	29 Y & 11 M	$887,680	$757,470	$606,522	$431,531	$0
$4,800	$4,800	$4,800	24 Y & 5 M	$848,882	$673,694	$470,603	$235,164	$0
$5,400	$5,400	$5,400	20 Y & 8 M	$810,081	$589,913	$334,679	$38,792	$0
$6,000	$6,000	$6,000	17 Y & 11 M	$771,282	$506,135	$198,758	$0	$0

2% COLA

Monthly Amount	15 Yr Inflated	30 Yr Inflated	Money Lasts	5 Years	10 Years	15 Years	20 Years	30 Years
$1,800	$2,375	$3,197	Over 40 Yrs	$1.038 M	$1.070 M	$1.093 M	$1.104 M	$1.077 M
$2,400	$3,167	$4,262	Over 40 Yrs	$997,932	$978,743	$937,959	$870,207	$626,849
$3,000	$3,958	$5,327	32 Y & 10 M	$957,600	$887,458	$782,969	$636,254	$176,820
$3,600	$4,750	$6,393	26 Y & 7 M	$917,263	$796,161	$627,961	$402,265	$0
$4,200	$5,542	$7,459	22 Y & 4 M	$876,926	$704,862	$472,946	$168,270	$0
$4,800	$6,334	$8,524	19 Y & 3 M	$836,592	$613,568	$317,943	$0	$0
$5,400	$7,125	$9,590	16 Y & 11 M	$796,257	$522,280	$162,949	$0	$0

3% COLA

Monthly Amount	15 Yr Inflated	30 Yr Inflated	Money Lasts	5 Years	10 Years	15 Years	20 Years	30 Years
$1,800	$2,723	$4,242	Over 40 Yrs	$1.036 M	$1.058 M	$1.061 M	$1.037 M	$877,356
$2,400	$3,630	$5,656	35 Y & 3 M	$994,769	$962,500	$894,715	$780,917	$360,591
$3,000	$4,538	$7,070	28 Y & 3 M	$953,645	$867,153	$728,919	$524,648	$0
$3,600	$5,445	$8,484	23 Y & 6 M	$912,517	$771,799	$563,106	$268,357	$0
$4,200	$6,353	$9,898	20 Y & 2 M	$871,393	$676,450	$397,303	$12,075	$0
$4,800	$7,260	$11,312	17 Y & 8 M	$830,265	$581,097	$231,494	$0	$0
$5,400	$8,168	$12,726	15 Y & 8 M	$789,142	$485,747	$65,685	$0	$0

4% COLA

Monthly Amount	15 Yr Inflated	30 Yr Inflated	Money Lasts	5 Years	10 Years	15 Years	20 Years	30 Years
$1,200	$2,078	$3,743	Over 40 Yrs	$1.075 M	$1.145 M	$1.203 M	$1.243 M	$1.234 M
$1,800	$3,117	$5,614	38 Y & 11 M	$1.033 M	$1.045 M	$1.025 M	$961,993	$637,941
$2,400	$4,156	$7,485	30 Y & 6 M	$991,545	$945,398	$847,684	$680,613	$41,467
$3,000	$5,195	$9,356	25 Y & 1 M	$949,610	$845,764	$670,107	$399,225	$0
$3,600	$6,234	$11,227	21 Y & 4 M	$907,679	$746,145	$492,566	$117,917	$0
$4,200	$7,273	$13,098	18 Y & 6 M	$865,745	$646,510	$314,985	$0	$0
$4,800	$8,312	$14,969	16 Y & 5 M	$823,815	$546,892	$137,444	$0	$0

$1,000,000 Balance   4% Return On Investment

No COLA

Monthly Amount	15 Yr Inflated	30 Yr Inflated	Money Lasts	5 Years	10 Years	15 Years	20 Years	30 Years
$3,000	$3,000	$3,000	Over 40 Yrs	$1.018 M	$1.039 M	$1.066 M	$1.098 M	$1.184 M
$3,600	$3,600	$3,600	Over 40 Yrs	$977,988	$951,208	$918,624	$878,982	$772,071
$4,200	$4,200	$4,200	38 Y & 5 M	$938,211	$863,034	$771,570	$660,290	$360,181
$4,800	$4,800	$4,800	29 Y & 2 M	$898,434	$774,863	$624,521	$441,606	$0
$5,400	$5,400	$5,400	23 Y & 9 M	$858,656	$686,688	$477,463	$222,911	$0
$6,000	$6,000	$6,000	20 Y & 1 M	$818,878	$598,515	$330,411	$4,220	$0
$6,600	$6,600	$6,600	17 Y & 6 M	$779,102	$510,344	$183,360	$0	$0

2% COLA

Monthly Amount	15 Yr Inflated	30 Yr Inflated	Money Lasts	5 Years	10 Years	15 Years	20 Years	30 Years
$2,400	$3,167	$4,262	Over 40 Yrs	$1.051 M	$1.097 M	$1.133 M	$1.155 M	$1.140 M
$3,000	$3,958	$5,327	Over 40 Yrs	$1.010 M	$1.001 M	$965,436	$896,441	$614,242
$3,600	$4,750	$6,393	31 Y & 2 M	$968,634	$904,660	$798,328	$637,488	$88,337
$4,200	$5,542	$7,459	25 Y & 5 M	$927,297	$808,725	$631,212	$378,529	$0
$4,800	$6,334	$8,524	21 Y & 6 M	$885,959	$712,790	$464,104	$119,589	$0
$5,400	$7,125	$9,590	18 Y & 7 M	$844,624	$616,865	$297,008	$0	$0
$6,000	$7,917	$10,655	16 Y & 5 M	$803,288	$520,933	$129,906	$0	$0

3% COLA

Monthly Amount	15 Yr Inflated	30 Yr Inflated	Money Lasts	5 Years	10 Years	15 Years	20 Years	30 Years
$2,400	$3,630	$5,656	Over 40 Yrs	$1.048 M	$1.080 M	$1.087 M	$1.060 M	$845,859
$3,000	$4,538	$7,070	32 Y & 11 M	$1.006 M	$979,650	$908,739	$777,362	$246,543
$3,600	$5,445	$8,484	26 Y & 8 M	$963,819	$879,530	$730,295	$494,610	$0
$4,200	$6,353	$9,898	22 Y & 5 M	$921,681	$779,414	$551,859	$211,865	$0
$4,800	$7,260	$11,312	19 Y & 4 M	$879,540	$679,293	$373,418	$0	$0
$5,400	$8,168	$12,726	16 Y & 11 M	$837,403	$579,177	$194,977	$0	$0
$6,000	$9,076	$14,139	15 Y & 2 M	$795,260	$479,048	$16,521	$0	$0

4% COLA

Monthly Amount	15 Yr Inflated	30 Yr Inflated	Money Lasts	5 Years	10 Years	15 Years	20 Years	30 Years
$1,800	$3,117	$5,614	Over 40 Yrs	$1.088 M	$1.167 M	$1.229 M	$1.263 M	$1.182 M
$2,400	$4,156	$7,485	35 Y & 5 M	$1.045 M	$1.062 M	$1.038 M	$953,273	$494,914
$3,000	$5,195	$9,356	28 Y & 4 M	$1.002 M	$957,592	$847,105	$643,791	$0
$3,600	$6,234	$11,227	23 Y & 8 M	$958,910	$853,076	$656,376	$334,406	$0
$4,200	$7,273	$13,098	20 Y & 3 M	$915,950	$748,540	$465,599	$24,920	$0
$4,800	$8,312	$14,969	17 Y & 9 M	$872,996	$644,024	$274,864	$0	$0
$5,400	$9,351	$16,841	15 Y & 9 M	$830,035	$539,481	$84,070	$0	$0

| $1,000,000 Balance | | 5% Return On Investment | | | | | | |

No COLA

Monthly Amount	15 Yr Inflated	30 Yr Inflated	Money Lasts	5 Years	10 Years	15 Years	20 Years	30 Years
$3,000	$3,000	$3,000	Over 40 Yrs	$1.072 M	$1.165 M	$1.283 M	$1.433 M	$1.870 M
$3,600	$3,600	$3,600	Over 40 Yrs	$1.032 M	$1.072 M	$1.123 M	$1.189 M	$1.380 M
$4,200	$4,200	$4,200	Over 40 Yrs	$990,827	$979,119	$964,178	$945,108	$889,705
$4,800	$4,800	$4,800	38 Y & 6 M	$950,048	$886,296	$804,932	$701,087	$399,398
$5,400	$5,400	$5,400	28 Y & 8 M	$909,269	$793,470	$645,680	$457,056	$0
$6,000	$6,000	$6,000	23 Y & 3 M	$868,491	$700,649	$486,434	$213,036	$0
$6,600	$6,600	$6,600	19 Y & 8 M	$827,711	$607,823	$327,183	$0	$0

2% COLA

Monthly Amount	15 Yr Inflated	30 Yr Inflated	Money Lasts	5 Years	10 Years	15 Years	20 Years	30 Years
$2,400	$3,167	$4,262	Over 40 Yrs	$1.107 M	$1.226 M	$1.358 M	$1.505 M	$1.852 M
$3,000	$3,958	$5,327	Over 40 Yrs	$1.064 M	$1.125 M	$1.177 M	$1.217 M	$1.234 M
$3,600	$4,750	$6,393	39 Y & 1 M	$1.022 M	$1.024 M	$996,938	$930,298	$616,330
$4,200	$5,542	$7,459	29 Y & 11 M	$979,752	$923,044	$816,592	$643,108	$0
$4,800	$6,334	$8,524	24 Y & 6 M	$937,389	$822,206	$636,258	$355,946	$0
$5,400	$7,125	$9,590	20 Y & 9 M	$895,031	$721,378	$455,935	$68,782	$0
$6,000	$7,917	$10,655	17 Y & 11 M	$852,668	$620,538	$275,600	$0	$0

3% COLA

Monthly Amount	15 Yr Inflated	30 Yr Inflated	Money Lasts	5 Years	10 Years	15 Years	20 Years	30 Years
$2,400	$3,630	$5,656	Over 40 Yrs	$1.104 M	$1.208 M	$1.310 M	$1.403 M	$1.525 M
$3,000	$4,538	$7,070	Over 40 Yrs	$1.060 M	$1.103 M	$1.118 M	$1.090 M	$826,246
$3,600	$5,445	$8,484	31 Y & 3 M	$1.017 M	$997,954	$925,521	$777,627	$127,114
$4,200	$6,353	$9,898	25 Y & 6 M	$974,053	$892,801	$733,296	$465,031	$0
$4,800	$7,260	$11,312	21 Y & 6 M	$930,876	$787,642	$541,060	$152,415	$0
$5,400	$8,168	$12,726	18 Y & 8 M	$887,702	$682,489	$348,828	$0	$0
$6,000	$9,076	$14,139	16 Y & 6 M	$844,523	$577,321	$156,577	$0	$0

4% COLA

Monthly Amount	15 Yr Inflated	30 Yr Inflated	Money Lasts	5 Years	10 Years	15 Years	20 Years	30 Years
$1,800	$3,117	$5,614	Over 40 Yrs	$1.144 M	$1.300 M	$1.463 M	$1.630 M	$1.934 M
$2,400	$4,156	$7,485	Over 40 Yrs	$1.100 M	$1.190 M	$1.258 M	$1.289 M	$1.138 M
$3,000	$5,195	$9,356	33 Y & 1 M	$1.056 M	$1.080 M	$1.053 M	$947,808	$341,939
$3,600	$6,234	$11,227	26 Y & 9 M	$1.012 M	$970,671	$848,015	$606,799	$0
$4,200	$7,273	$13,098	22 Y & 6 M	$968,238	$860,960	$642,845	$265,675	$0
$4,800	$8,312	$14,969	19 Y & 5 M	$924,234	$751,267	$437,720	$0	$0
$5,400	$9,351	$16,841	17 Y & 1 M	$880,225	$641,547	$232,531	$0	$0

$1,000,000 Balance   6% Return On Investment

No COLA

Monthly Amount	15 Yr Inflated	30 Yr Inflated	Money Lasts	5 Years	10 Years	15 Years	20 Years	30 Years
$3,600	$3,600	$3,600	Over 40 Yrs	$1.087 M	$1.204 M	$1.361 M	$1.570 M	$2.226 M
$4,200	$4,200	$4,200	Over 40 Yrs	$1.046 M	$1.107 M	$1.188 M	$1.298 M	$1.639 M
$4,800	$4,800	$4,800	Over 40 Yrs	$1.004 M	$1.009 M	$1.016 M	$1.025 M	$1.053 M
$5,400	$5,400	$5,400	39 Y & 5 M	$961,983	$911,107	$843,024	$751,914	$466,824
$6,000	$6,000	$6,000	28 Y & 5 M	$920,178	$813,360	$670,413	$479,118	$0
$6,600	$6,600	$6,600	22 Y & 10 M	$878,374	$715,611	$497,798	$206,315	$0
$7,200	$7,200	$7,200	19 Y & 3 M	$836,569	$617,862	$325,183	$0	$0

2% COLA

Monthly Amount	15 Yr Inflated	30 Yr Inflated	Money Lasts	5 Years	10 Years	15 Years	20 Years	30 Years
$3,000	$3,958	$5,327	Over 40 Yrs	$1.121 M	$1.261 M	$1.423 M	$1.612 M	$2.098 M
$3,600	$4,750	$6,393	Over 40 Yrs	$1.078 M	$1.155 M	$1.228 M	$1.293 M	$1.369 M
$4,200	$5,542	$7,459	38 Y & 4 M	$1.034 M	$1.049 M	$1.033 M	$973,366	$640,344
$4,800	$6,334	$8,524	29 Y & 2 M	$990,941	$942,670	$838,166	$654,260	$0
$5,400	$7,125	$9,590	23 Y & 10 M	$947,532	$836,654	$643,376	$335,156	$0
$6,000	$7,917	$10,655	20 Y & 2 M	$904,121	$730,630	$448,578	$16,055	$0
$6,600	$8,709	$11,721	17 Y & 7 M	$860,710	$624,602	$253,758	$0	$0

3% COLA

Monthly Amount	15 Yr Inflated	30 Yr Inflated	Money Lasts	5 Years	10 Years	15 Years	20 Years	30 Years
$3,000	$4,538	$7,070	Over 40 Yrs	$1.117 M	$1.238 M	$1.360 M	$1.475 M	$1.645 M
$3,600	$5,445	$8,484	39 Y & 1 M	$1.073 M	$1.128 M	$1.153 M	$1.129 M	$824,857
$4,200	$6,353	$9,898	30 Y & 1 M	$1.029 M	$1.017 M	$945,467	$782,814	$5,115
$4,800	$7,260	$11,312	24 Y & 7 M	$984,331	$907,001	$738,170	$436,483	$0
$5,400	$8,168	$12,726	20 Y & 10 M	$940,096	$796,521	$530,872	$90,150	$0
$6,000	$9,076	$14,139	18 Y & 1 M	$895,856	$686,030	$323,556	$0	$0
$6,600	$9,983	$15,553	15 Y & 11 M	$851,622	$575,559	$116,278	$0	$0

4% COLA

Monthly Amount	15 Yr Inflated	30 Yr Inflated	Money Lasts	5 Years	10 Years	15 Years	20 Years	30 Years
$2,400	$4,156	$7,485	Over 40 Yrs	$1.158 M	$1.330 M	$1.513 M	$1.700 M	$2.035 M
$3,000	$5,195	$9,356	Over 40 Yrs	$1.113 M	$1.215 M	$1.292 M	$1.323 M	$1.108 M
$3,600	$6,234	$11,227	31 Y & 4 M	$1.068 M	$1.100 M	$1.071 M	$946,720	$181,308
$4,200	$7,273	$13,098	25 Y & 7 M	$1.023 M	$984,639	$850,566	$569,943	$0
$4,800	$8,312	$14,969	21 Y & 7 M	$977,593	$869,478	$629,741	$193,265	$0
$5,400	$9,351	$16,841	18 Y & 9 M	$932,511	$754,291	$408,850	$0	$0
$6,000	$10,390	$18,712	16 Y & 6 M	$887,435	$639,132	$188,025	$0	$0

$1,050,000 Balance   3% Return On Investment

No COLA

Monthly Amount	15 Yr Inflated	30 Yr Inflated	Money Lasts	5 Years	10 Years	15 Years	20 Years	30 Years
$2,400	$2,400	$2,400	Over 40 Yrs	$1.062 M	$1.076 M	$1.092 M	$1.111 M	$1.158 M
$3,000	$3,000	$3,000	Over 40 Yrs	$1.023 M	$992,221	$956,261	$914,573	$810,220
$3,600	$3,600	$3,600	Over 40 Yrs	$984,443	$908,445	$820,343	$718,207	$462,541
$4,200	$4,200	$4,200	32 Y & 5 M	$945,643	$824,665	$684,417	$521,834	$114,854
$4,800	$4,800	$4,800	26 Y & 3 M	$906,845	$740,889	$548,502	$325,472	$0
$5,400	$5,400	$5,400	22 Y & 1 M	$868,046	$657,110	$412,578	$129,098	$0
$6,000	$6,000	$6,000	19 Y & 1 M	$829,246	$573,332	$276,658	$0	$0

2% COLA

Monthly Amount	15 Yr Inflated	30 Yr Inflated	Money Lasts	5 Years	10 Years	15 Years	20 Years	30 Years
$1,800	$2,375	$3,197	Over 40 Yrs	$1.096 M	$1.137 M	$1.171 M	$1.194 M	$1.198 M
$2,400	$3,167	$4,262	Over 40 Yrs	$1.056 M	$1.046 M	$1.016 M	$960,510	$748,211
$3,000	$3,958	$5,327	34 Y & 9 M	$1.016 M	$954,654	$860,868	$726,561	$298,186
$3,600	$4,750	$6,393	28 Y & 1 M	$975,228	$863,358	$705,862	$492,574	$0
$4,200	$5,542	$7,459	23 Y & 7 M	$934,890	$772,058	$550,844	$258,576	$0
$4,800	$6,334	$8,524	20 Y & 4 M	$894,555	$680,764	$395,842	$24,606	$0
$5,400	$7,125	$9,590	17 Y & 10 M	$854,221	$589,476	$240,847	$0	$0

3% COLA

Monthly Amount	15 Yr Inflated	30 Yr Inflated	Money Lasts	5 Years	10 Years	15 Years	20 Years	30 Years
$1,800	$2,723	$4,242	Over 40 Yrs	$1.094 M	$1.125 M	$1.138 M	$1.128 M	$998,721
$2,400	$3,630	$5,656	36 Y & 11 M	$1.053 M	$1.030 M	$972,614	$871,224	$481,954
$3,000	$4,538	$7,070	29 Y & 8 M	$1.012 M	$934,347	$806,817	$614,954	$0
$3,600	$5,445	$8,484	24 Y & 8 M	$970,481	$838,996	$641,006	$358,665	$0
$4,200	$6,353	$9,898	21 Y & 2 M	$929,357	$743,646	$475,201	$102,379	$0
$4,800	$7,260	$11,312	18 Y & 6 M	$888,230	$648,294	$309,394	$0	$0
$5,400	$8,168	$12,726	16 Y & 6 M	$847,105	$552,942	$143,582	$0	$0

4% COLA

Monthly Amount	15 Yr Inflated	30 Yr Inflated	Money Lasts	5 Years	10 Years	15 Years	20 Years	30 Years
$1,200	$2,078	$3,743	Over 40 Yrs	$1.133 M	$1.212 M	$1.281 M	$1.334 M	$1.356 M
$1,800	$3,117	$5,614	Over 40 Yrs	$1.091 M	$1.112 M	$1.103 M	$1.052 M	$759,300
$2,400	$4,156	$7,485	31 Y & 10 M	$1.050 M	$1.013 M	$925,583	$770,920	$162,834
$3,000	$5,195	$9,356	26 Y & 2 M	$1.008 M	$912,959	$748,001	$489,524	$0
$3,600	$6,234	$11,227	22 Y & 3 M	$965,645	$813,343	$570,468	$208,226	$0
$4,200	$7,273	$13,098	19 Y & 4 M	$923,708	$713,705	$392,882	$0	$0
$4,800	$8,312	$14,969	17 Y & 2 M	$881,778	$614,087	$215,341	$0	$0

$1,050,000 Balance   4% Return On Investment

No COLA

Monthly Amount	15 Yr Inflated	30 Yr Inflated	Money Lasts	5 Years	10 Years	15 Years	20 Years	30 Years
$3,000	$3,000	$3,000	Over 40 Yrs	$1.079 M	$1.113 M	$1.156 M	$1.207 M	$1.346 M
$3,600	$3,600	$3,600	Over 40 Yrs	$1.039 M	$1.025 M	$1.009 M	$988,536	$934,239
$4,200	$4,200	$4,200	Over 40 Yrs	$999,043	$937,048	$861,620	$769,850	$522,356
$4,800	$4,800	$4,800	31 Y & 11 M	$959,266	$848,875	$714,567	$551,161	$110,470
$5,400	$5,400	$5,400	25 Y & 9 M	$919,488	$760,701	$567,512	$332,467	$0
$6,000	$6,000	$6,000	21 Y & 8 M	$879,710	$672,526	$420,455	$113,772	$0
$6,600	$6,600	$6,600	18 Y & 9 M	$839,933	$584,354	$273,405	$0	$0

2% COLA

Monthly Amount	15 Yr Inflated	30 Yr Inflated	Money Lasts	5 Years	10 Years	15 Years	20 Years	30 Years
$2,400	$3,167	$4,262	Over 40 Yrs	$1.112 M	$1.171 M	$1.223 M	$1.265 M	$1.302 M
$3,000	$3,958	$5,327	Over 40 Yrs	$1.071 M	$1.075 M	$1.055 M	$1.006 M	$776,413
$3,600	$4,750	$6,393	33 Y & 5 M	$1.029 M	$978,674	$888,378	$747,048	$250,513
$4,200	$5,542	$7,459	27 Y & 1 M	$988,130	$882,738	$721,261	$488,088	$0
$4,800	$6,334	$8,524	22 Y & 10 M	$946,793	$786,805	$554,155	$229,151	$0
$5,400	$7,125	$9,590	19 Y & 9 M	$905,458	$690,880	$387,059	$0	$0
$6,000	$7,917	$10,655	17 Y & 5 M	$864,121	$594,945	$219,953	$0	$0

3% COLA

Monthly Amount	15 Yr Inflated	30 Yr Inflated	Money Lasts	5 Years	10 Years	15 Years	20 Years	30 Years
$2,400	$3,630	$5,656	Over 40 Yrs	$1.109 M	$1.154 M	$1.177 M	$1.170 M	$1.008 M
$3,000	$4,538	$7,070	34 Y & 11 M	$1.067 M	$1.054 M	$998,785	$886,917	$408,709
$3,600	$5,445	$8,484	28 Y & 3 M	$1.025 M	$953,543	$820,343	$604,167	$0
$4,200	$6,353	$9,898	23 Y & 8 M	$982,513	$853,425	$641,905	$321,421	$0
$4,800	$7,260	$11,312	20 Y & 5 M	$940,373	$753,306	$463,465	$38,667	$0
$5,400	$8,168	$12,726	17 Y & 11 M	$898,237	$653,190	$285,025	$0	$0
$6,000	$9,076	$14,139	15 Y & 11 M	$856,094	$553,061	$106,568	$0	$0

4% COLA

Monthly Amount	15 Yr Inflated	30 Yr Inflated	Money Lasts	5 Years	10 Years	15 Years	20 Years	30 Years
$1,800	$3,117	$5,614	Over 40 Yrs	$1.149 M	$1.241 M	$1.319 M	$1.372 M	$1.344 M
$2,400	$4,156	$7,485	37 Y & 3 M	$1.106 M	$1.136 M	$1.128 M	$1.063 M	$657,086
$3,000	$5,195	$9,356	29 Y & 9 M	$1.063 M	$1.032 M	$937,150	$753,343	$0
$3,600	$6,234	$11,227	24 Y & 10 M	$1.020 M	$927,090	$746,427	$443,967	$0
$4,200	$7,273	$13,098	21 Y & 3 M	$976,782	$822,551	$555,643	$134,470	$0
$4,800	$8,312	$14,969	18 Y & 7 M	$933,828	$718,035	$364,909	$0	$0
$5,400	$9,351	$16,841	16 Y & 7 M	$890,868	$613,494	$174,118	$0	$0

$1,050,000 Balance   5% Return On Investment

No COLA

Monthly Amount	15 Yr Inflated	30 Yr Inflated	Money Lasts	5 Years	10 Years	15 Years	20 Years	30 Years
$3,000	$3,000	$3,000	Over 40 Yrs	$1.136 M	$1.246 M	$1.387 M	$1.566 M	$2.086 M
$3,600	$3,600	$3,600	Over 40 Yrs	$1.095 M	$1.153 M	$1.227 M	$1.322 M	$1.596 M
$4,200	$4,200	$4,200	Over 40 Yrs	$1.055 M	$1.061 M	$1.068 M	$1.078 M	$1.106 M
$4,800	$4,800	$4,800	Over 40 Yrs	$1.014 M	$967,742	$908,877	$833,750	$615,492
$5,400	$5,400	$5,400	32 Y & 1 M	$973,083	$874,916	$749,627	$589,722	$125,170
$6,000	$6,000	$6,000	25 Y & 6 M	$932,305	$782,092	$590,379	$345,698	$0
$6,600	$6,600	$6,600	21 Y & 4 M	$891,524	$689,265	$431,126	$101,667	$0

2% COLA

Monthly Amount	15 Yr Inflated	30 Yr Inflated	Money Lasts	5 Years	10 Years	15 Years	20 Years	30 Years
$2,400	$3,167	$4,262	Over 40 Yrs	$1.171 M	$1.307 M	$1.462 M	$1.637 M	$2.068 M
$3,000	$3,958	$5,327	Over 40 Yrs	$1.128 M	$1.206 M	$1.281 M	$1.350 M	$1.450 M
$3,600	$4,750	$6,393	Over 40 Yrs	$1.086 M	$1.105 M	$1.101 M	$1.063 M	$832,431
$4,200	$5,542	$7,459	32 Y & 6 M	$1.044 M	$1.004 M	$920,542	$775,777	$214,796
$4,800	$6,334	$8,524	26 Y & 4 M	$1.001 M	$903,649	$740,201	$488,606	$0
$5,400	$7,125	$9,590	22 Y & 3 M	$958,844	$802,821	$559,880	$201,446	$0
$6,000	$7,917	$10,655	19 Y & 3 M	$916,482	$701,982	$379,546	$0	$0

3% COLA

Monthly Amount	15 Yr Inflated	30 Yr Inflated	Money Lasts	5 Years	10 Years	15 Years	20 Years	30 Years
$2,400	$3,630	$5,656	Over 40 Yrs	$1.167 M	$1.290 M	$1.414 M	$1.535 M	$1.741 M
$3,000	$4,538	$7,070	Over 40 Yrs	$1.124 M	$1.185 M	$1.222 M	$1.223 M	$1.042 M
$3,600	$5,445	$8,484	33 Y & 6 M	$1.081 M	$1.079 M	$1.029 M	$910,294	$343,212
$4,200	$6,353	$9,898	27 Y & 2 M	$1.038 M	$974,244	$837,239	$597,691	$0
$4,800	$7,260	$11,312	22 Y & 11 M	$994,690	$869,088	$645,008	$285,081	$0
$5,400	$8,168	$12,726	19 Y & 9 M	$951,516	$763,933	$452,774	$0	$0
$6,000	$9,076	$14,139	17 Y & 5 M	$908,337	$658,768	$260,525	$0	$0

4% COLA

Monthly Amount	15 Yr Inflated	30 Yr Inflated	Money Lasts	5 Years	10 Years	15 Years	20 Years	30 Years
$1,800	$3,117	$5,614	Over 40 Yrs	$1.208 M	$1.381 M	$1.567 M	$1.763 M	$2.150 M
$2,400	$4,156	$7,485	Over 40 Yrs	$1.164 M	$1.272 M	$1.362 M	$1.422 M	$1.354 M
$3,000	$5,195	$9,356	34 Y & 11 M	$1.120 M	$1.162 M	$1.157 M	$1.080 M	$558,044
$3,600	$6,234	$11,227	28 Y & 4 M	$1.076 M	$1.052 M	$951,961	$739,463	$0
$4,200	$7,273	$13,098	23 Y & 9 M	$1.032 M	$942,404	$746,791	$398,340	$0
$4,800	$8,312	$14,969	20 Y & 6 M	$988,047	$832,709	$541,662	$57,306	$0
$5,400	$9,351	$16,841	17 Y & 11 M	$944,039	$722,993	$336,480	$0	$0

$1,050,000 Balance   6% Return On Investment

No COLA

Monthly Amount	15 Yr Inflated	30 Yr Inflated	Money Lasts	5 Years	10 Years	15 Years	20 Years	30 Years
$3,600	$3,600	$3,600	Over 40 Yrs	$1.154 M	$1.294 M	$1.481 M	$1.731 M	$2.513 M
$4,200	$4,200	$4,200	Over 40 Yrs	$1.113 M	$1.196 M	$1.308 M	$1.458 M	$1.927 M
$4,800	$4,800	$4,800	Over 40 Yrs	$1.071 M	$1.098 M	$1.135 M	$1.185 M	$1.340 M
$5,400	$5,400	$5,400	Over 40 Yrs	$1.029 M	$1.001 M	$962,854	$912,273	$754,003
$6,000	$6,000	$6,000	32 Y & 6 M	$987,090	$902,901	$790,238	$639,470	$167,704
$6,600	$6,600	$6,600	25 Y & 5 M	$945,285	$805,154	$617,625	$366,670	$0
$7,200	$7,200	$7,200	21 Y & 2 M	$903,480	$707,405	$445,011	$93,869	$0

2% COLA

Monthly Amount	15 Yr Inflated	30 Yr Inflated	Money Lasts	5 Years	10 Years	15 Years	20 Years	30 Years
$3,000	$3,958	$5,327	Over 40 Yrs	$1.188 M	$1.350 M	$1.542 M	$1.772 M	$2.386 M
$3,600	$4,750	$6,393	Over 40 Yrs	$1.145 M	$1.244 M	$1.348 M	$1.453 M	$1.657 M
$4,200	$5,542	$7,459	Over 40 Yrs	$1.101 M	$1.138 M	$1.153 M	$1.134 M	$927,520
$4,800	$6,334	$8,524	31 Y & 11 M	$1.058 M	$1.032 M	$957,991	$814,614	$198,524
$5,400	$7,125	$9,590	25 Y & 10 M	$1.014 M	$926,196	$763,203	$495,512	$0
$6,000	$7,917	$10,655	21 Y & 9 M	$971,032	$820,170	$568,402	$176,407	$0
$6,600	$8,709	$11,721	18 Y & 10 M	$927,621	$714,145	$373,587	$0	$0

3% COLA

Monthly Amount	15 Yr Inflated	30 Yr Inflated	Money Lasts	5 Years	10 Years	15 Years	20 Years	30 Years
$3,000	$4,538	$7,070	Over 40 Yrs	$1.184 M	$1.328 M	$1.480 M	$1.636 M	$1.932 M
$3,600	$5,445	$8,484	Over 40 Yrs	$1.140 M	$1.218 M	$1.273 M	$1.289 M	$1.112 M
$4,200	$6,353	$9,898	32 Y & 7 M	$1.095 M	$1.107 M	$1.065 M	$943,173	$292,297
$4,800	$7,260	$11,312	26 Y & 5 M	$1.051 M	$996,542	$857,997	$596,839	$0
$5,400	$8,168	$12,726	22 Y & 3 M	$1.007 M	$886,064	$650,700	$250,507	$0
$6,000	$9,076	$14,139	19 Y & 4 M	$962,769	$775,575	$443,388	$0	$0
$6,600	$9,983	$15,553	16 Y & 11 M	$918,532	$665,101	$236,106	$0	$0

4% COLA

Monthly Amount	15 Yr Inflated	30 Yr Inflated	Money Lasts	5 Years	10 Years	15 Years	20 Years	30 Years
$2,400	$4,156	$7,485	Over 40 Yrs	$1.225 M	$1.420 M	$1.633 M	$1.861 M	$2.322 M
$3,000	$5,195	$9,356	Over 40 Yrs	$1.180 M	$1.305 M	$1.412 M	$1.484 M	$1.395 M
$3,600	$6,234	$11,227	33 Y & 7 M	$1.135 M	$1.189 M	$1.191 M	$1.107 M	$468,488
$4,200	$7,273	$13,098	27 Y & 3 M	$1.090 M	$1.074 M	$970,393	$730,301	$0
$4,800	$8,312	$14,969	22 Y & 11 M	$1.045 M	$959,018	$749,564	$353,617	$0
$5,400	$9,351	$16,841	19 Y & 10 M	$999,422	$843,832	$528,677	$0	$0
$6,000	$10,390	$18,712	17 Y & 6 M	$954,345	$728,673	$307,850	$0	$0

$1,100,000 Balance	3% Return On Investment

No COLA

Monthly Amount	15 Yr Inflated	30 Yr Inflated	Money Lasts	5 Years	10 Years	15 Years	20 Years	30 Years
$2,400	$2,400	$2,400	Over 40 Yrs	$1.120 M	$1.143 M	$1.170 M	$1.201 M	$1.279 M
$3,000	$3,000	$3,000	Over 40 Yrs	$1.081 M	$1.059 M	$1.034 M	$1.005 M	$931,585
$3,600	$3,600	$3,600	Over 40 Yrs	$1.042 M	$975,639	$898,237	$808,508	$583,897
$4,200	$4,200	$4,200	35 Y & 1 M	$1.004 M	$891,859	$762,315	$612,138	$236,214
$4,800	$4,800	$4,800	28 Y & 2 M	$964,808	$808,083	$626,395	$415,771	$0
$5,400	$5,400	$5,400	23 Y & 7 M	$926,009	$724,306	$490,476	$219,404	$0
$6,000	$6,000	$6,000	20 Y & 4 M	$887,211	$640,529	$354,557	$23,038	$0

2% COLA

Monthly Amount	15 Yr Inflated	30 Yr Inflated	Money Lasts	5 Years	10 Years	15 Years	20 Years	30 Years
$1,800	$2,375	$3,197	Over 40 Yrs	$1.154 M	$1.204 M	$1.249 M	$1.285 M	$1.320 M
$2,400	$3,167	$4,262	Over 40 Yrs	$1.114 M	$1.113 M	$1.094 M	$1.051 M	$869,573
$3,000	$3,958	$5,327	36 Y & 9 M	$1.074 M	$1.022 M	$938,766	$816,866	$419,549
$3,600	$4,750	$6,393	29 Y & 8 M	$1.033 M	$930,554	$783,761	$582,880	$0
$4,200	$5,542	$7,459	24 Y & 10 M	$992,855	$839,256	$628,745	$348,883	$0
$4,800	$6,334	$8,524	21 Y & 5 M	$952,518	$747,958	$473,740	$114,911	$0
$5,400	$7,125	$9,590	18 Y & 9 M	$912,184	$656,671	$318,743	$0	$0

3% COLA

Monthly Amount	15 Yr Inflated	30 Yr Inflated	Money Lasts	5 Years	10 Years	15 Years	20 Years	30 Years
$1,800	$2,723	$4,242	Over 40 Yrs	$1.152 M	$1.192 M	$1.216 M	$1.218 M	$1.120 M
$2,400	$3,630	$5,656	38 Y & 9 M	$1.111 M	$1.097 M	$1.051 M	$961,530	$603,320
$3,000	$4,538	$7,070	30 Y & 11 M	$1.070 M	$1.002 M	$884,715	$705,259	$86,707
$3,600	$5,445	$8,484	25 Y & 10 M	$1.028 M	$906,191	$718,903	$448,969	$0
$4,200	$6,353	$9,898	22 Y & 2 M	$987,320	$810,841	$553,098	$192,684	$0
$4,800	$7,260	$11,312	19 Y & 5 M	$946,193	$715,488	$387,290	$0	$0
$5,400	$8,168	$12,726	17 Y & 3 M	$905,069	$620,139	$221,482	$0	$0

4% COLA

Monthly Amount	15 Yr Inflated	30 Yr Inflated	Money Lasts	5 Years	10 Years	15 Years	20 Years	30 Years
$1,200	$2,078	$3,743	Over 40 Yrs	$1.191 M	$1.279 M	$1.359 M	$1.424 M	$1.477 M
$1,800	$3,117	$5,614	Over 40 Yrs	$1.149 M	$1.179 M	$1.181 M	$1.143 M	$880,670
$2,400	$4,156	$7,485	33 Y & 1 M	$1.107 M	$1.080 M	$1.003 M	$861,224	$284,194
$3,000	$5,195	$9,356	27 Y & 3 M	$1.066 M	$980,153	$825,899	$579,829	$0
$3,600	$6,234	$11,227	23 Y & 2 M	$1.024 M	$880,539	$648,367	$298,534	$0
$4,200	$7,273	$13,098	20 Y & 2 M	$981,672	$780,901	$470,781	$17,129	$0
$4,800	$8,312	$14,969	17 Y & 10 M	$939,743	$681,284	$293,241	$0	$0

$1,100,000 Balance   4% Return On Investment

No COLA

Monthly Amount	15 Yr Inflated	30 Yr Inflated	Money Lasts	5 Years	10 Years	15 Years	20 Years	30 Years
$3,000	$3,000	$3,000	Over 40 Yrs	$1.139 M	$1.187 M	$1.246 M	$1.317 M	$1.508 M
$3,600	$3,600	$3,600	Over 40 Yrs	$1.100 M	$1.099 M	$1.099 M	$1.098 M	$1.096 M
$4,200	$4,200	$4,200	Over 40 Yrs	$1.060 M	$1.011 M	$951,668	$879,408	$684,529
$4,800	$4,800	$4,800	35 Y & 3 M	$1.020 M	$922,885	$804,611	$660,713	$272,637
$5,400	$5,400	$5,400	27 Y & 11 M	$980,321	$834,714	$657,561	$442,026	$0
$6,000	$6,000	$6,000	23 Y & 4 M	$940,543	$746,540	$510,505	$223,332	$0
$6,600	$6,600	$6,600	20 Y & 1 M	$900,766	$658,369	$363,455	$4,646	$0

2% COLA

Monthly Amount	15 Yr Inflated	30 Yr Inflated	Money Lasts	5 Years	10 Years	15 Years	20 Years	30 Years
$2,400	$3,167	$4,262	Over 40 Yrs	$1.173 M	$1.245 M	$1.313 M	$1.374 M	$1.464 M
$3,000	$3,958	$5,327	Over 40 Yrs	$1.132 M	$1.149 M	$1.146 M	$1.116 M	$938,593
$3,600	$4,750	$6,393	35 Y & 8 M	$1.090 M	$1.053 M	$978,425	$856,605	$412,683
$4,200	$5,542	$7,459	28 Y & 10 M	$1.049 M	$956,753	$811,310	$597,645	$0
$4,800	$6,334	$8,524	24 Y & 2 M	$1.008 M	$860,816	$644,201	$338,705	$0
$5,400	$7,125	$9,590	20 Y & 10 M	$966,291	$764,892	$477,107	$79,769	$0
$6,000	$7,917	$10,655	18 Y & 4 M	$924,954	$668,958	$310,001	$0	$0

3% COLA

Monthly Amount	15 Yr Inflated	30 Yr Inflated	Money Lasts	5 Years	10 Years	15 Years	20 Years	30 Years
$2,400	$3,630	$5,656	Over 40 Yrs	$1.170 M	$1.228 M	$1.267 M	$1.279 M	$1.170 M
$3,000	$4,538	$7,070	36 Y & 11 M	$1.128 M	$1.128 M	$1.089 M	$996,470	$570,873
$3,600	$5,445	$8,484	29 Y & 9 M	$1.085 M	$1.028 M	$910,389	$713,722	$0
$4,200	$6,353	$9,898	24 Y & 11 M	$1.043 M	$927,437	$731,952	$430,977	$0
$4,800	$7,260	$11,312	21 Y & 6 M	$1.001 M	$827,319	$553,513	$148,223	$0
$5,400	$8,168	$12,726	18 Y & 10 M	$959,069	$727,201	$375,071	$0	$0
$6,000	$9,076	$14,139	16 Y & 10 M	$916,927	$627,074	$196,618	$0	$0

4% COLA

Monthly Amount	15 Yr Inflated	30 Yr Inflated	Money Lasts	5 Years	10 Years	15 Years	20 Years	30 Years
$1,800	$3,117	$5,614	Over 40 Yrs	$1.209 M	$1.315 M	$1.409 M	$1.482 M	$1.506 M
$2,400	$4,156	$7,485	38 Y & 11 M	$1.166 M	$1.210 M	$1.218 M	$1.172 M	$819,253
$3,000	$5,195	$9,356	31 Y & 2 M	$1.124 M	$1.106 M	$1.027 M	$862,906	$132,082
$3,600	$6,234	$11,227	25 Y & 11 M	$1.081 M	$1.001 M	$836,472	$553,522	$0
$4,200	$7,273	$13,098	22 Y & 3 M	$1.038 M	$896,563	$645,690	$244,027	$0
$4,800	$8,312	$14,969	19 Y & 6 M	$994,661	$792,048	$454,958	$0	$0
$5,400	$9,351	$16,841	17 Y & 4 M	$951,700	$687,504	$264,162	$0	$0

$1,100,000 Balance	5% Return On Investment

No COLA

Monthly Amount	15 Yr Inflated	30 Yr Inflated	Money Lasts	5 Years	10 Years	15 Years	20 Years	30 Years
$3,000	$3,000	$3,000	Over 40 Yrs	$1.200 M	$1.328 M	$1.491 M	$1.698 M	$2.303 M
$3,600	$3,600	$3,600	Over 40 Yrs	$1.159 M	$1.235 M	$1.331 M	$1.454 M	$1.812 M
$4,200	$4,200	$4,200	Over 40 Yrs	$1.118 M	$1.142 M	$1.172 M	$1.210 M	$1.322 M
$4,800	$4,800	$4,800	Over 40 Yrs	$1.078 M	$1.049 M	$1.013 M	$966,412	$831,587
$5,400	$5,400	$5,400	36 Y & 2 M	$1.037 M	$956,360	$853,572	$722,386	$341,266
$6,000	$6,000	$6,000	28 Y & 1 M	$996,119	$863,537	$694,325	$478,362	$0
$6,600	$6,600	$6,600	23 Y & 3 M	$955,339	$770,710	$535,072	$234,332	$0

2% COLA

Monthly Amount	15 Yr Inflated	30 Yr Inflated	Money Lasts	5 Years	10 Years	15 Years	20 Years	30 Years
$2,400	$3,167	$4,262	Over 40 Yrs	$1.234 M	$1.388 M	$1.565 M	$1.770 M	$2.284 M
$3,000	$3,958	$5,327	Over 40 Yrs	$1.192 M	$1.288 M	$1.385 M	$1.483 M	$1.666 M
$3,600	$4,750	$6,393	Over 40 Yrs	$1.150 M	$1.187 M	$1.205 M	$1.196 M	$1.049 M
$4,200	$5,542	$7,459	35 Y & 2 M	$1.107 M	$1.086 M	$1.024 M	$908,442	$430,896
$4,800	$6,334	$8,524	28 Y & 3 M	$1.065 M	$985,094	$844,147	$621,270	$0
$5,400	$7,125	$9,590	23 Y & 9 M	$1.023 M	$884,267	$663,828	$334,112	$0
$6,000	$7,917	$10,655	20 Y & 6 M	$980,295	$783,426	$483,490	$46,944	$0

3% COLA

Monthly Amount	15 Yr Inflated	30 Yr Inflated	Money Lasts	5 Years	10 Years	15 Years	20 Years	30 Years
$2,400	$3,630	$5,656	Over 40 Yrs	$1.231 M	$1.371 M	$1.518 M	$1.668 M	$1.958 M
$3,000	$4,538	$7,070	Over 40 Yrs	$1.188 M	$1.266 M	$1.326 M	$1.356 M	$1.258 M
$3,600	$5,445	$8,484	35 Y & 9 M	$1.145 M	$1.161 M	$1.133 M	$1.043 M	$559,312
$4,200	$6,353	$9,898	28 Y & 11 M	$1.102 M	$1.056 M	$941,185	$730,355	$0
$4,800	$7,260	$11,312	24 Y & 3 M	$1.059 M	$950,534	$748,955	$417,745	$0
$5,400	$8,168	$12,726	20 Y & 11 M	$1.015 M	$845,379	$556,722	$105,135	$0
$6,000	$9,076	$14,139	18 Y & 5 M	$972,151	$740,211	$364,470	$0	$0

4% COLA

Monthly Amount	15 Yr Inflated	30 Yr Inflated	Money Lasts	5 Years	10 Years	15 Years	20 Years	30 Years
$1,800	$3,117	$5,614	Over 40 Yrs	$1.272 M	$1.463 M	$1.671 M	$1.895 M	$2.366 M
$2,400	$4,156	$7,485	Over 40 Yrs	$1.228 M	$1.353 M	$1.466 M	$1.554 M	$1.570 M
$3,000	$5,195	$9,356	36 Y & 11 M	$1.184 M	$1.243 M	$1.261 M	$1.213 M	$774,135
$3,600	$6,234	$11,227	29 Y & 10 M	$1.140 M	$1.134 M	$1.056 M	$872,127	$0
$4,200	$7,273	$13,098	24 Y & 11 M	$1.096 M	$1.024 M	$850,735	$531,003	$0
$4,800	$8,312	$14,969	21 Y & 7 M	$1.052 M	$914,155	$645,610	$189,973	$0
$5,400	$9,351	$16,841	18 Y & 11 M	$1.008 M	$804,437	$440,425	$0	$0

$1,100,000 Balance	6% Return On Investment

No COLA

Monthly Amount	15 Yr Inflated	30 Yr Inflated	Money Lasts	5 Years	10 Years	15 Years	20 Years	30 Years
$3,600	$3,600	$3,600	Over 40 Yrs	$1.221 M	$1.383 M	$1.601 M	$1.891 M	$2.800 M
$4,200	$4,200	$4,200	Over 40 Yrs	$1.179 M	$1.286 M	$1.428 M	$1.618 M	$2.214 M
$4,800	$4,800	$4,800	Over 40 Yrs	$1.138 M	$1.188 M	$1.255 M	$1.345 M	$1.627 M
$5,400	$5,400	$5,400	Over 40 Yrs	$1.096 M	$1.090 M	$1.083 M	$1.073 M	$1.041 M
$6,000	$6,000	$6,000	37 Y & 11 M	$1.054 M	$992,443	$910,066	$799,827	$454,881
$6,600	$6,600	$6,600	28 Y & 5 M	$1.012 M	$894,696	$737,454	$527,028	$0
$7,200	$7,200	$7,200	23 Y & 3 M	$970,391	$796,944	$564,834	$254,219	$0

2% COLA

Monthly Amount	15 Yr Inflated	30 Yr Inflated	Money Lasts	5 Years	10 Years	15 Years	20 Years	30 Years
$3,000	$3,958	$5,327	Over 40 Yrs	$1.255 M	$1.440 M	$1.662 M	$1.932 M	$2.673 M
$3,600	$4,750	$6,393	Over 40 Yrs	$1.212 M	$1.334 M	$1.467 M	$1.613 M	$1.944 M
$4,200	$5,542	$7,459	Over 40 Yrs	$1.168 M	$1.228 M	$1.273 M	$1.294 M	$1.215 M
$4,800	$6,334	$8,524	35 Y & 3 M	$1.125 M	$1.122 M	$1.078 M	$974,975	$485,708
$5,400	$7,125	$9,590	27 Y & 11 M	$1.081 M	$1.016 M	$883,030	$655,867	$0
$6,000	$7,917	$10,655	23 Y & 5 M	$1.038 M	$909,714	$688,233	$336,767	$0
$6,600	$8,709	$11,721	20 Y & 2 M	$994,533	$803,688	$493,417	$17,616	$0

3% COLA

Monthly Amount	15 Yr Inflated	30 Yr Inflated	Money Lasts	5 Years	10 Years	15 Years	20 Years	30 Years
$3,000	$4,538	$7,070	Over 40 Yrs	$1.251 M	$1.418 M	$1.600 M	$1.796 M	$2.219 M
$3,600	$5,445	$8,484	Over 40 Yrs	$1.207 M	$1.307 M	$1.392 M	$1.450 M	$1.399 M
$4,200	$6,353	$9,898	35 Y & 3 M	$1.162 M	$1.197 M	$1.185 M	$1.104 M	$579,471
$4,800	$7,260	$11,312	28 Y & 4 M	$1.118 M	$1.086 M	$977,824	$757,194	$0
$5,400	$8,168	$12,726	23 Y & 9 M	$1.074 M	$975,608	$770,530	$410,865	$0
$6,000	$9,076	$14,139	20 Y & 6 M	$1.030 M	$865,115	$563,211	$64,509	$0
$6,600	$9,983	$15,553	18 Y & 1 M	$985,444	$754,643	$355,933	$0	$0

4% COLA

Monthly Amount	15 Yr Inflated	30 Yr Inflated	Money Lasts	5 Years	10 Years	15 Years	20 Years	30 Years
$2,400	$4,156	$7,485	Over 40 Yrs	$1.292 M	$1.509 M	$1.753 M	$2.021 M	$2.610 M
$3,000	$5,195	$9,356	Over 40 Yrs	$1.247 M	$1.394 M	$1.532 M	$1.644 M	$1.682 M
$3,600	$6,234	$11,227	35 Y & 10 M	$1.202 M	$1.279 M	$1.311 M	$1.267 M	$755,657
$4,200	$7,273	$13,098	28 Y & 11 M	$1.156 M	$1.164 M	$1.090 M	$890,653	$0
$4,800	$8,312	$14,969	24 Y & 4 M	$1.111 M	$1.049 M	$869,393	$513,975	$0
$5,400	$9,351	$16,841	20 Y & 11 M	$1.066 M	$933,377	$648,508	$137,173	$0
$6,000	$10,390	$18,712	18 Y & 6 M	$1.021 M	$818,215	$427,679	$0	$0

$1,150,000 Balance   3% Return On Investment

No COLA

Monthly Amount	15 Yr Inflated	30 Yr Inflated	Money Lasts	5 Years	10 Years	15 Years	20 Years	30 Years
$3,000	$3,000	$3,000	Over 40 Yrs	$1.139 M	$1.127 M	$1.112 M	$1.095 M	$1.053 M
$3,750	$3,750	$3,750	Over 40 Yrs	$1.091 M	$1.022 M	$942,156	$849,722	$618,342
$4,500	$4,500	$4,500	33 Y & 7 M	$1.042 M	$917,169	$772,256	$604,263	$183,743
$5,250	$5,250	$5,250	26 Y & 3 M	$993,673	$812,446	$602,354	$358,801	$0
$6,000	$6,000	$6,000	21 Y & 8 M	$945,174	$707,723	$432,453	$113,340	$0
$6,750	$6,750	$6,750	18 Y & 5 M	$896,675	$603,002	$262,554	$0	$0
$7,500	$7,500	$7,500	16 Y & 1 M	$848,176	$498,279	$92,651	$0	$0

2% COLA

Monthly Amount	15 Yr Inflated	30 Yr Inflated	Money Lasts	5 Years	10 Years	15 Years	20 Years	30 Years
$2,250	$2,969	$3,996	Over 40 Yrs	$1.182 M	$1.203 M	$1.210 M	$1.200 M	$1.103 M
$3,000	$3,958	$5,327	38 Y & 9 M	$1.131 M	$1.089 M	$1.017 M	$907,172	$540,911
$3,750	$4,948	$6,659	29 Y & 9 M	$1.081 M	$974,924	$822,897	$614,672	$0
$4,500	$5,938	$7,991	24 Y & 2 M	$1.031 M	$860,803	$629,138	$322,190	$0
$5,250	$6,927	$9,323	20 Y & 4 M	$980,233	$746,694	$435,401	$29,744	$0
$6,000	$7,917	$10,655	17 Y & 7 M	$929,813	$632,572	$241,641	$0	$0
$6,750	$8,907	$11,987	15 Y & 6 M	$879,396	$518,463	$47,898	$0	$0

3% COLA

Monthly Amount	15 Yr Inflated	30 Yr Inflated	Money Lasts	5 Years	10 Years	15 Years	20 Years	30 Years
$2,250	$3,403	$5,302	Over 40 Yrs	$1.179 M	$1.188 M	$1.170 M	$1.116 M	$853,913
$3,000	$4,538	$7,070	32 Y & 5 M	$1.128 M	$1.069 M	$962,611	$795,561	$208,068
$3,750	$5,672	$8,837	25 Y & 11 M	$1.076 M	$949,550	$755,358	$475,223	$0
$4,500	$6,807	$10,605	21 Y & 8 M	$1.025 M	$830,355	$548,088	$154,840	$0
$5,250	$7,941	$12,372	18 Y & 7 M	$973,312	$711,169	$340,830	$0	$0
$6,000	$9,076	$14,139	16 Y & 3 M	$921,903	$591,972	$133,556	$0	$0
$6,750	$10,210	$15,907	14 Y & 5 M	$870,496	$472,782	$0	$0	$0

4% COLA

Monthly Amount	15 Yr Inflated	30 Yr Inflated	Money Lasts	5 Years	10 Years	15 Years	20 Years	30 Years
$1,500	$2,598	$4,678	Over 40 Yrs	$1.228 M	$1.296 M	$1.348 M	$1.374 M	$1.300 M
$2,250	$3,896	$7,017	36 Y & 4 M	$1.176 M	$1.172 M	$1.126 M	$1.022 M	$554,761
$3,000	$5,195	$9,356	28 Y & 4 M	$1.124 M	$1.047 M	$903,799	$670,136	$0
$3,750	$6,494	$11,695	23 Y & 3 M	$1.071 M	$922,820	$681,858	$318,470	$0
$4,500	$7,792	$14,034	19 Y & 9 M	$1.019 M	$798,295	$459,925	$0	$0
$5,250	$9,091	$16,373	17 Y & 2 M	$966,255	$673,749	$237,937	$0	$0
$6,000	$10,390	$18,712	15 Y & 2 M	$913,841	$549,220	$15,997	$0	$0

$1,150,000 Balance   4% Return On Investment

No COLA

Monthly Amount	15 Yr Inflated	30 Yr Inflated	Money Lasts	5 Years	10 Years	15 Years	20 Years	30 Years
$3,750	$3,750	$3,750	Over 40 Yrs	$1.151 M	$1.151 M	$1.152 M	$1.153 M	$1.156 M
$4,500	$4,500	$4,500	Over 40 Yrs	$1.101 M	$1.041 M	$968,185	$879,614	$640,748
$5,250	$5,250	$5,250	32 Y & 1 M	$1.051 M	$930,768	$784,370	$606,253	$125,890
$6,000	$6,000	$6,000	25 Y & 2 M	$1.001 M	$820,552	$600,552	$332,889	$0
$6,750	$6,750	$6,750	20 Y & 9 M	$951,654	$710,336	$416,735	$59,525	$0
$7,500	$7,500	$7,500	17 Y & 9 M	$901,932	$600,118	$232,918	$0	$0
$8,250	$8,250	$8,250	15 Y & 6 M	$852,211	$489,904	$49,102	$0	$0

2% COLA

Monthly Amount	15 Yr Inflated	30 Yr Inflated	Money Lasts	5 Years	10 Years	15 Years	20 Years	30 Years
$3,000	$3,958	$5,327	Over 40 Yrs	$1.192 M	$1.223 M	$1.236 M	$1.225 M	$1.101 M
$3,750	$4,948	$6,659	35 Y & 10 M	$1.141 M	$1.103 M	$1.027 M	$901,403	$443,371
$4,500	$5,938	$7,991	27 Y & 10 M	$1.089 M	$982,794	$817,797	$577,714	$0
$5,250	$6,927	$9,323	22 Y & 10 M	$1.037 M	$862,888	$608,934	$254,066	$0
$6,000	$7,917	$10,655	19 Y & 5 M	$985,787	$742,972	$400,052	$0	$0
$6,750	$8,907	$11,987	16 Y & 10 M	$934,118	$623,063	$191,178	$0	$0
$7,500	$9,896	$13,319	14 Y & 11 M	$882,445	$503,146	$0	$0	$0

3% COLA

Monthly Amount	15 Yr Inflated	30 Yr Inflated	Money Lasts	5 Years	10 Years	15 Years	20 Years	30 Years
$3,000	$4,538	$7,070	38 Y & 11 M	$1.188 M	$1.202 M	$1.179 M	$1.106 M	$733,048
$3,750	$5,672	$8,837	29 Y & 11 M	$1.136 M	$1.077 M	$955,834	$752,610	$0
$4,500	$6,807	$10,605	24 Y & 3 M	$1.083 M	$951,386	$732,776	$399,154	$0
$5,250	$7,941	$12,372	20 Y & 5 M	$1.030 M	$826,240	$509,726	$45,708	$0
$6,000	$9,076	$14,139	17 Y & 8 M	$977,760	$701,085	$286,663	$0	$0
$6,750	$10,210	$15,907	15 Y & 7 M	$925,087	$575,938	$63,607	$0	$0
$7,500	$11,344	$17,675	13 Y & 11 M	$872,414	$450,796	$0	$0	$0

4% COLA

Monthly Amount	15 Yr Inflated	30 Yr Inflated	Money Lasts	5 Years	10 Years	15 Years	20 Years	30 Years
$2,250	$3,896	$7,017	Over 40 Yrs	$1.238 M	$1.310 M	$1.356 M	$1.359 M	$1.153 M
$3,000	$5,195	$9,356	32 Y & 7 M	$1.184 M	$1.180 M	$1.117 M	$972,460	$294,247
$3,750	$6,494	$11,695	26 Y & 1 M	$1.131 M	$1.049 M	$878,816	$585,691	$0
$4,500	$7,792	$14,034	21 Y & 9 M	$1.077 M	$918,326	$640,390	$198,923	$0
$5,250	$9,091	$16,373	18 Y & 8 M	$1.023 M	$787,653	$401,906	$0	$0
$6,000	$10,390	$18,712	16 Y & 4 M	$969,579	$657,001	$163,473	$0	$0
$6,750	$11,689	$21,051	14 Y & 6 M	$915,880	$526,336	$0	$0	$0

$1,150,000 Balance   5% Return On Investment

No COLA

Monthly Amount	15 Yr Inflated	30 Yr Inflated	Money Lasts	5 Years	10 Years	15 Years	20 Years	30 Years
$3,750	$3,750	$3,750	Over 40 Yrs	$1.213 M	$1.293 M	$1.395 M	$1.526 M	$1.906 M
$4,500	$4,500	$4,500	Over 40 Yrs	$1.162 M	$1.177 M	$1.196 M	$1.221 M	$1.293 M
$5,250	$5,250	$5,250	Over 40 Yrs	$1.111 M	$1.061 M	$997,331	$916,058	$679,945
$6,000	$6,000	$6,000	30 Y & 11 M	$1.060 M	$944,979	$798,267	$611,022	$67,042
$6,750	$6,750	$6,750	24 Y & 3 M	$1.009 M	$828,950	$599,209	$305,993	$0
$7,500	$7,500	$7,500	19 Y & 11 M	$957,985	$712,918	$400,145	$0	$0
$8,250	$8,250	$8,250	17 Y & 2 M	$907,010	$596,887	$201,083	$0	$0

2% COLA

Monthly Amount	15 Yr Inflated	30 Yr Inflated	Money Lasts	5 Years	10 Years	15 Years	20 Years	30 Years
$3,000	$3,958	$5,327	Over 40 Yrs	$1.256 M	$1.369 M	$1.489 M	$1.615 M	$1.882 M
$3,750	$4,948	$6,659	Over 40 Yrs	$1.203 M	$1.243 M	$1.264 M	$1.256 M	$1.110 M
$4,500	$5,938	$7,991	33 Y & 9 M	$1.150 M	$1.117 M	$1.038 M	$897,511	$338,152
$5,250	$6,927	$9,323	26 Y & 5 M	$1.097 M	$990,921	$812,861	$538,574	$0
$6,000	$7,917	$10,655	21 Y & 9 M	$1.044 M	$864,873	$587,439	$179,611	$0
$6,750	$8,907	$11,987	18 Y & 7 M	$991,161	$738,835	$362,032	$0	$0
$7,500	$9,896	$13,319	16 Y & 2 M	$938,207	$612,788	$136,616	$0	$0

3% COLA

Monthly Amount	15 Yr Inflated	30 Yr Inflated	Money Lasts	5 Years	10 Years	15 Years	20 Years	30 Years
$3,000	$4,538	$7,070	Over 40 Yrs	$1.252 M	$1.347 M	$1.430 M	$1.488 M	$1.475 M
$3,750	$5,672	$8,837	35 Y & 11 M	$1.198 M	$1.216 M	$1.189 M	$1.097 M	$600,716
$4,500	$6,807	$10,605	27 Y & 11 M	$1.144 M	$1.085 M	$949,012	$706,712	$0
$5,250	$7,941	$12,372	22 Y & 11 M	$1.090 M	$953,106	$708,720	$315,941	$0
$6,000	$9,076	$14,139	19 Y & 5 M	$1.036 M	$821,656	$468,417	$0	$0
$6,750	$10,210	$15,907	16 Y & 11 M	$981,996	$690,211	$228,118	$0	$0
$7,500	$11,344	$17,675	14 Y & 11 M	$928,029	$558,772	$0	$0	$0

4% COLA

Monthly Amount	15 Yr Inflated	30 Yr Inflated	Money Lasts	5 Years	10 Years	15 Years	20 Years	30 Years
$2,250	$3,896	$7,017	Over 40 Yrs	$1.303 M	$1.462 M	$1.621 M	$1.772 M	$1.985 M
$3,000	$5,195	$9,356	38 Y & 11 M	$1.248 M	$1.325 M	$1.365 M	$1.346 M	$990,235
$3,750	$6,494	$11,695	29 Y & 11 M	$1.193 M	$1.188 M	$1.109 M	$919,497	$0
$4,500	$7,792	$14,034	24 Y & 4 M	$1.138 M	$1.050 M	$852,138	$493,193	$0
$5,250	$9,091	$16,373	20 Y & 6 M	$1.083 M	$913,310	$595,662	$66,768	$0
$6,000	$10,390	$18,712	17 Y & 9 M	$1.028 M	$776,189	$339,243	$0	$0
$6,750	$11,689	$21,051	15 Y & 7 M	$972,656	$639,056	$82,788	$0	$0

| $1,150,000 Balance | | | | 6% Return On Investment | | | | |

No COLA

Monthly Amount	15 Yr Inflated	30 Yr Inflated	Money Lasts	5 Years	10 Years	15 Years	20 Years	30 Years
$4,500	$4,500	$4,500	Over 40 Yrs	$1.225 M	$1.326 M	$1.461 M	$1.642 M	$2.208 M
$5,250	$5,250	$5,250	Over 40 Yrs	$1.173 M	$1.204 M	$1.246 M	$1.301 M	$1.475 M
$6,000	$6,000	$6,000	Over 40 Yrs	$1.121 M	$1.082 M	$1.030 M	$960,186	$742,059
$6,750	$6,750	$6,750	30 Y & 2 M	$1.069 M	$959,801	$814,128	$619,185	$9,191
$7,500	$7,500	$7,500	23 Y & 5 M	$1.016 M	$837,615	$598,360	$278,182	$0
$8,250	$8,250	$8,250	19 Y & 5 M	$964,145	$715,429	$382,591	$0	$0
$9,000	$9,000	$9,000	16 Y & 8 M	$911,890	$593,244	$166,825	$0	$0

2% COLA

Monthly Amount	15 Yr Inflated	30 Yr Inflated	Money Lasts	5 Years	10 Years	15 Years	20 Years	30 Years
$3,750	$4,948	$6,659	Over 40 Yrs	$1.268 M	$1.397 M	$1.539 M	$1.694 M	$2.049 M
$4,500	$5,938	$7,991	Over 40 Yrs	$1.213 M	$1.264 M	$1.295 M	$1.295 M	$1.137 M
$5,250	$6,927	$9,323	32 Y & 1 M	$1.159 M	$1.132 M	$1.052 M	$896,015	$226,105
$6,000	$7,917	$10,655	25 Y & 3 M	$1.105 M	$999,256	$808,059	$497,120	$0
$6,750	$8,907	$11,987	20 Y & 10 M	$1.051 M	$866,739	$564,576	$98,250	$0
$7,500	$9,896	$13,319	17 Y & 10 M	$996,328	$734,207	$321,075	$0	$0
$8,250	$10,886	$14,651	15 Y & 7 M	$942,065	$601,678	$77,572	$0	$0

3% COLA

Monthly Amount	15 Yr Inflated	30 Yr Inflated	Money Lasts	5 Years	10 Years	15 Years	20 Years	30 Years
$3,750	$5,672	$8,837	Over 40 Yrs	$1.262 M	$1.369 M	$1.460 M	$1.524 M	$1.482 M
$4,500	$6,807	$10,605	33 Y & 9 M	$1.207 M	$1.231 M	$1.201 M	$1.091 M	$456,745
$5,250	$7,941	$12,372	26 Y & 5 M	$1.152 M	$1.093 M	$942,176	$657,795	$0
$6,000	$9,076	$14,139	21 Y & 10 M	$1.097 M	$954,658	$683,041	$224,868	$0
$6,750	$10,210	$15,907	18 Y & 7 M	$1.041 M	$816,557	$423,911	$0	$0
$7,500	$11,344	$17,675	16 Y & 3 M	$986,000	$678,462	$164,804	$0	$0
$8,250	$12,479	$19,441	14 Y & 5 M	$930,705	$540,359	$0	$0	$0

4% COLA

Monthly Amount	15 Yr Inflated	30 Yr Inflated	Money Lasts	5 Years	10 Years	15 Years	20 Years	30 Years
$3,000	$5,195	$9,356	Over 40 Yrs	$1.314 M	$1.484 M	$1.652 M	$1.804 M	$1.970 M
$3,750	$6,494	$11,695	35 Y & 11 M	$1.257 M	$1.340 M	$1.376 M	$1.334 M	$811,024
$4,500	$7,792	$14,034	27 Y & 11 M	$1.201 M	$1.196 M	$1.100 M	$862,716	$0
$5,250	$9,091	$16,373	22 Y & 11 M	$1.145 M	$1.052 M	$823,550	$391,718	$0
$6,000	$10,390	$18,712	19 Y & 6 M	$1.088 M	$907,758	$547,507	$0	$0
$6,750	$11,689	$21,051	16 Y & 11 M	$1.032 M	$763,790	$271,423	$0	$0
$7,500	$12,988	$23,390	14 Y & 11 M	$975,469	$619,820	$0	$0	$0

$1,200,000 Balance   3% Return On Investment

No COLA

Monthly Amount	15 Yr Inflated	30 Yr Inflated	Money Lasts	5 Years	10 Years	15 Years	20 Years	30 Years
$3,000	$3,000	$3,000	Over 40 Yrs	$1.197 M	$1.194 M	$1.190 M	$1.185 M	$1.174 M
$3,750	$3,750	$3,750	Over 40 Yrs	$1.149 M	$1.089 M	$1.020 M	$940,033	$739,713
$4,500	$4,500	$4,500	36 Y & 3 M	$1.100 M	$984,364	$850,154	$694,568	$305,107
$5,250	$5,250	$5,250	27 Y & 11 M	$1.052 M	$879,642	$680,254	$449,109	$0
$6,000	$6,000	$6,000	22 Y & 11 M	$1.003 M	$774,920	$510,354	$203,649	$0
$6,750	$6,750	$6,750	19 Y & 6 M	$954,640	$670,198	$340,454	$0	$0
$7,500	$7,500	$7,500	16 Y & 11 M	$906,140	$565,474	$170,550	$0	$0

2% COLA

Monthly Amount	15 Yr Inflated	30 Yr Inflated	Money Lasts	5 Years	10 Years	15 Years	20 Years	30 Years
$2,250	$2,969	$3,996	Over 40 Yrs	$1.240 M	$1.270 M	$1.288 M	$1.290 M	$1.225 M
$3,000	$3,958	$5,327	Over 40 Yrs	$1.189 M	$1.156 M	$1.095 M	$997,472	$662,267
$3,750	$4,948	$6,659	31 Y & 3 M	$1.139 M	$1.042 M	$900,793	$704,975	$99,575
$4,500	$5,938	$7,991	25 Y & 4 M	$1.089 M	$927,999	$707,038	$412,497	$0
$5,250	$6,927	$9,323	21 Y & 4 M	$1.038 M	$813,890	$513,300	$120,050	$0
$6,000	$7,917	$10,655	18 Y & 5 M	$987,776	$699,767	$319,537	$0	$0
$6,750	$8,907	$11,987	16 Y & 3 M	$937,360	$585,659	$125,796	$0	$0

3% COLA

Monthly Amount	15 Yr Inflated	30 Yr Inflated	Money Lasts	5 Years	10 Years	15 Years	20 Years	30 Years
$2,250	$3,403	$5,302	Over 40 Yrs	$1.237 M	$1.255 M	$1.248 M	$1.206 M	$975,275
$3,000	$4,538	$7,070	33 Y & 10 M	$1.185 M	$1.136 M	$1.041 M	$885,869	$329,433
$3,750	$5,672	$8,837	27 Y & 1 M	$1.134 M	$1.017 M	$833,257	$565,528	$0
$4,500	$6,807	$10,605	22 Y & 7 M	$1.083 M	$897,552	$625,987	$245,146	$0
$5,250	$7,941	$12,372	19 Y & 4 M	$1.031 M	$778,364	$418,728	$0	$0
$6,000	$9,076	$14,139	16 Y & 11 M	$979,866	$659,168	$211,455	$0	$0
$6,750	$10,210	$15,907	15 Y & 1 M	$928,461	$539,980	$4,189	$0	$0

4% COLA

Monthly Amount	15 Yr Inflated	30 Yr Inflated	Money Lasts	5 Years	10 Years	15 Years	20 Years	30 Years
$1,500	$2,598	$4,678	Over 40 Yrs	$1.286 M	$1.364 M	$1.426 M	$1.464 M	$1.422 M
$2,250	$3,896	$7,017	37 Y & 7 M	$1.234 M	$1.239 M	$1.204 M	$1.112 M	$676,119
$3,000	$5,195	$9,356	29 Y & 5 M	$1.181 M	$1.115 M	$981,697	$760,442	$0
$3,750	$6,494	$11,695	24 Y & 2 M	$1.129 M	$990,016	$759,757	$408,777	$0
$4,500	$7,792	$14,034	20 Y & 6 M	$1.077 M	$865,491	$537,825	$57,118	$0
$5,250	$9,091	$16,373	17 Y & 10 M	$1.024 M	$740,944	$315,835	$0	$0
$6,000	$10,390	$18,712	15 Y & 9 M	$971,805	$616,416	$93,896	$0	$0

| $1,200,000 Balance | | | 4% Return On Investment | | | | | |

No COLA

Monthly Amount	15 Yr Inflated	30 Yr Inflated	Money Lasts	5 Years	10 Years	15 Years	20 Years	30 Years
$3,750	$3,750	$3,750	Over 40 Yrs	$1.211 M	$1.225 M	$1.242 M	$1.263 M	$1.318 M
$4,500	$4,500	$4,500	Over 40 Yrs	$1.162 M	$1.115 M	$1.058 M	$989,172	$802,920
$5,250	$5,250	$5,250	35 Y & 1 M	$1.112 M	$1.005 M	$874,416	$715,808	$288,058
$6,000	$6,000	$6,000	27 Y & 1 M	$1.062 M	$894,564	$690,600	$442,445	$0
$6,750	$6,750	$6,750	22 Y & 3 M	$1.012 M	$784,347	$506,781	$169,080	$0
$7,500	$7,500	$7,500	18 Y & 11 M	$962,765	$674,133	$322,968	$0	$0
$8,250	$8,250	$8,250	16 Y & 6 M	$913,044	$563,917	$139,151	$0	$0

2% COLA

Monthly Amount	15 Yr Inflated	30 Yr Inflated	Money Lasts	5 Years	10 Years	15 Years	20 Years	30 Years
$3,000	$3,958	$5,327	Over 40 Yrs	$1.253 M	$1.297 M	$1.326 M	$1.335 M	$1.263 M
$3,750	$4,948	$6,659	38 Y & 2 M	$1.202 M	$1.177 M	$1.117 M	$1.011 M	$605,545
$4,500	$5,938	$7,991	29 Y & 6 M	$1.150 M	$1.057 M	$907,844	$687,270	$0
$5,250	$6,927	$9,323	24 Y & 1 M	$1.098 M	$936,898	$698,978	$363,617	$0
$6,000	$7,917	$10,655	20 Y & 5 M	$1.047 M	$816,981	$490,095	$39,944	$0
$6,750	$8,907	$11,987	17 Y & 8 M	$994,950	$697,074	$281,224	$0	$0
$7,500	$9,896	$13,319	15 Y & 8 M	$943,277	$577,159	$72,345	$0	$0

3% COLA

Monthly Amount	15 Yr Inflated	30 Yr Inflated	Money Lasts	5 Years	10 Years	15 Years	20 Years	30 Years
$3,000	$4,538	$7,070	Over 40 Yrs	$1.249 M	$1.276 M	$1.269 M	$1.216 M	$895,215
$3,750	$5,672	$8,837	31 Y & 5 M	$1.197 M	$1.151 M	$1.046 M	$862,168	$146,102
$4,500	$6,807	$10,605	25 Y & 6 M	$1.144 M	$1.025 M	$822,822	$508,709	$0
$5,250	$7,941	$12,372	21 Y & 5 M	$1.091 M	$900,251	$599,773	$155,264	$0
$6,000	$9,076	$14,139	18 Y & 6 M	$1.039 M	$775,096	$376,709	$0	$0
$6,750	$10,210	$15,907	16 Y & 3 M	$985,920	$649,953	$153,657	$0	$0
$7,500	$11,344	$17,675	14 Y & 6 M	$933,247	$524,808	$0	$0	$0

4% COLA

Monthly Amount	15 Yr Inflated	30 Yr Inflated	Money Lasts	5 Years	10 Years	15 Years	20 Years	30 Years
$2,250	$3,896	$7,017	Over 40 Yrs	$1.299 M	$1.384 M	$1.446 M	$1.469 M	$1.315 M
$3,000	$5,195	$9,356	33 Y & 11 M	$1.245 M	$1.254 M	$1.207 M	$1.082 M	$456,418
$3,750	$6,494	$11,695	27 Y & 3 M	$1.192 M	$1.123 M	$968,861	$695,243	$0
$4,500	$7,792	$14,034	22 Y & 8 M	$1.138 M	$992,338	$730,437	$308,478	$0
$5,250	$9,091	$16,373	19 Y & 5 M	$1.084 M	$861,665	$491,952	$0	$0
$6,000	$10,390	$18,712	16 Y & 11 M	$1.030 M	$731,015	$253,524	$0	$0
$6,750	$11,689	$21,051	15 Y & 2 M	$976,714	$600,351	$15,058	$0	$0

$1,200,000 Balance	5% Return On Investment

No COLA

Monthly Amount	15 Yr Inflated	30 Yr Inflated	Money Lasts	5 Years	10 Years	15 Years	20 Years	30 Years
$3,750	$3,750	$3,750	Over 40 Yrs	$1.277 M	$1.375 M	$1.499 M	$1.659 M	$2.122 M
$4,500	$4,500	$4,500	Over 40 Yrs	$1.226 M	$1.258 M	$1.300 M	$1.354 M	$1.509 M
$5,250	$5,250	$5,250	Over 40 Yrs	$1.175 M	$1.142 M	$1.101 M	$1.049 M	$896,042
$6,000	$6,000	$6,000	34 Y & 5 M	$1.124 M	$1.026 M	$902,216	$743,690	$283,144
$6,750	$6,750	$6,750	26 Y & 4 M	$1.073 M	$910,396	$703,157	$438,662	$0
$7,500	$7,500	$7,500	21 Y & 7 M	$1.022 M	$794,364	$504,093	$133,626	$0
$8,250	$8,250	$8,250	18 Y & 5 M	$970,825	$678,334	$305,033	$0	$0

2% COLA

Monthly Amount	15 Yr Inflated	30 Yr Inflated	Money Lasts	5 Years	10 Years	15 Years	20 Years	30 Years
$3,000	$3,958	$5,327	Over 40 Yrs	$1.320 M	$1.451 M	$1.593 M	$1.748 M	$2.098 M
$3,750	$4,948	$6,659	Over 40 Yrs	$1.267 M	$1.324 M	$1.368 M	$1.389 M	$1.326 M
$4,500	$5,938	$7,991	36 Y & 4 M	$1.214 M	$1.198 M	$1.142 M	$1.030 M	$554,250
$5,250	$6,927	$9,323	28 Y & 2 M	$1.161 M	$1.072 M	$916,809	$671,242	$0
$6,000	$7,917	$10,655	23 Y & 1 M	$1.108 M	$946,316	$691,384	$312,275	$0
$6,750	$8,907	$11,987	19 Y & 8 M	$1.055 M	$820,279	$465,979	$0	$0
$7,500	$9,896	$13,319	17 Y & 1 M	$1.002 M	$694,234	$240,563	$0	$0

3% COLA

Monthly Amount	15 Yr Inflated	30 Yr Inflated	Money Lasts	5 Years	10 Years	15 Years	20 Years	30 Years
$3,000	$4,538	$7,070	Over 40 Yrs	$1.316 M	$1.429 M	$1.534 M	$1.621 M	$1.691 M
$3,750	$5,672	$8,837	38 Y & 3 M	$1.262 M	$1.297 M	$1.293 M	$1.230 M	$816,814
$4,500	$6,807	$10,605	29 Y & 7 M	$1.208 M	$1.166 M	$1.053 M	$839,376	$0
$5,250	$7,941	$12,372	24 Y & 2 M	$1.154 M	$1.035 M	$812,668	$448,609	$0
$6,000	$9,076	$14,139	20 Y & 6 M	$1.100 M	$903,101	$572,363	$57,833	$0
$6,750	$10,210	$15,907	17 Y & 9 M	$1.046 M	$771,657	$332,066	$0	$0
$7,500	$11,344	$17,675	15 Y & 8 M	$991,842	$640,216	$91,789	$0	$0

4% COLA

Monthly Amount	15 Yr Inflated	30 Yr Inflated	Money Lasts	5 Years	10 Years	15 Years	20 Years	30 Years
$2,250	$3,896	$7,017	Over 40 Yrs	$1.367 M	$1.543 M	$1.725 M	$1.905 M	$2.201 M
$3,000	$5,195	$9,356	Over 40 Yrs	$1.312 M	$1.406 M	$1.469 M	$1.478 M	$1.206 M
$3,750	$6,494	$11,695	31 Y & 6 M	$1.257 M	$1.269 M	$1.213 M	$1.052 M	$211,534
$4,500	$7,792	$14,034	25 Y & 7 M	$1.201 M	$1.132 M	$956,085	$625,859	$0
$5,250	$9,091	$16,373	21 Y & 6 M	$1.146 M	$994,754	$699,606	$199,429	$0
$6,000	$10,390	$18,712	18 Y & 7 M	$1.091 M	$857,636	$443,193	$0	$0
$6,750	$11,689	$21,051	16 Y & 4 M	$1.036 M	$720,502	$186,737	$0	$0

$1,200,000 Balance	6% Return On Investment

No COLA

Monthly Amount	15 Yr Inflated	30 Yr Inflated	Money Lasts	5 Years	10 Years	15 Years	20 Years	30 Years
$4,500	$4,500	$4,500	Over 40 Yrs	$1.292 M	$1.416 M	$1.581 M	$1.803 M	$2.495 M
$5,250	$5,250	$5,250	Over 40 Yrs	$1.240 M	$1.294 M	$1.365 M	$1.462 M	$1.762 M
$6,000	$6,000	$6,000	Over 40 Yrs	$1.188 M	$1.172 M	$1.150 M	$1.121 M	$1.029 M
$6,750	$6,750	$6,750	34 Y & 2 M	$1.136 M	$1.049 M	$933,955	$779,540	$296,365
$7,500	$7,500	$7,500	25 Y & 9 M	$1.083 M	$927,158	$718,187	$438,538	$0
$8,250	$8,250	$8,250	20 Y & 11 M	$1.031 M	$804,971	$502,418	$97,535	$0
$9,000	$9,000	$9,000	17 Y & 11 M	$978,801	$682,786	$286,651	$0	$0

2% COLA

Monthly Amount	15 Yr Inflated	30 Yr Inflated	Money Lasts	5 Years	10 Years	15 Years	20 Years	30 Years
$3,750	$4,948	$6,659	Over 40 Yrs	$1.335 M	$1.486 M	$1.658 M	$1.854 M	$2.336 M
$4,500	$5,938	$7,991	Over 40 Yrs	$1.280 M	$1.354 M	$1.415 M	$1.455 M	$1.424 M
$5,250	$6,927	$9,323	34 Y & 11 M	$1.226 M	$1.221 M	$1.171 M	$1.056 M	$513,284
$6,000	$7,917	$10,655	27 Y & 2 M	$1.172 M	$1.089 M	$927,888	$657,479	$0
$6,750	$8,907	$11,987	22 Y & 4 M	$1.118 M	$956,280	$684,404	$258,607	$0
$7,500	$9,896	$13,319	18 Y & 11 M	$1.063 M	$823,749	$440,903	$0	$0
$8,250	$10,886	$14,651	16 Y & 7 M	$1.009 M	$691,218	$197,397	$0	$0

3% COLA

Monthly Amount	15 Yr Inflated	30 Yr Inflated	Money Lasts	5 Years	10 Years	15 Years	20 Years	30 Years
$3,750	$5,672	$8,837	Over 40 Yrs	$1.329 M	$1.459 M	$1.580 M	$1.684 M	$1.769 M
$4,500	$6,807	$10,605	36 Y & 4 M	$1.274 M	$1.320 M	$1.321 M	$1.251 M	$743,911
$5,250	$7,941	$12,372	28 Y & 3 M	$1.219 M	$1.182 M	$1.062 M	$818,151	$0
$6,000	$9,076	$14,139	23 Y & 2 M	$1.164 M	$1.044 M	$802,868	$385,223	$0
$6,750	$10,210	$15,907	19 Y & 8 M	$1.108 M	$906,100	$543,739	$0	$0
$7,500	$11,344	$17,675	17 Y & 2 M	$1.053 M	$768,004	$284,632	$0	$0
$8,250	$12,479	$19,441	15 Y & 2 M	$997,615	$629,901	$25,512	$0	$0

4% COLA

Monthly Amount	15 Yr Inflated	30 Yr Inflated	Money Lasts	5 Years	10 Years	15 Years	20 Years	30 Years
$3,000	$5,195	$9,356	Over 40 Yrs	$1.380 M	$1.573 M	$1.772 M	$1.965 M	$2.257 M
$3,750	$6,494	$11,695	38 Y & 4 M	$1.324 M	$1.429 M	$1.496 M	$1.494 M	$1.098 M
$4,500	$7,792	$14,034	29 Y & 8 M	$1.268 M	$1.285 M	$1.219 M	$1.023 M	$0
$5,250	$9,091	$16,373	24 Y & 3 M	$1.211 M	$1.141 M	$943,378	$552,075	$0
$6,000	$10,390	$18,712	20 Y & 7 M	$1.155 M	$997,301	$667,335	$81,198	$0
$6,750	$11,689	$21,051	17 Y & 10 M	$1.099 M	$853,332	$391,252	$0	$0
$7,500	$12,988	$23,390	15 Y & 9 M	$1.042 M	$709,364	$115,181	$0	$0

$1,250,000 Balance　　　　3% Return On Investment

No COLA

Monthly Amount	15 Yr Inflated	30 Yr Inflated	Money Lasts	5 Years	10 Years	15 Years	20 Years	30 Years
$3,000	$3,000	$3,000	Over 40 Yrs	$1.255 M	$1.261 M	$1.268 M	$1.276 M	$1.296 M
$3,750	$3,750	$3,750	Over 40 Yrs	$1.207 M	$1.156 M	$1.098 M	$1.030 M	$861,074
$4,500	$4,500	$4,500	38 Y & 11 M	$1.158 M	$1.052 M	$928,053	$784,875	$426,469
$5,250	$5,250	$5,250	29 Y & 11 M	$1.110 M	$946,838	$758,153	$539,416	$0
$6,000	$6,000	$6,000	24 Y & 5 M	$1.061 M	$842,115	$588,250	$293,952	$0
$6,750	$6,750	$6,750	20 Y & 8 M	$1.013 M	$737,393	$418,351	$48,494	$0
$7,500	$7,500	$7,500	17 Y & 11 M	$964,104	$632,670	$248,448	$0	$0

2% COLA

Monthly Amount	15 Yr Inflated	30 Yr Inflated	Money Lasts	5 Years	10 Years	15 Years	20 Years	30 Years
$2,250	$2,969	$3,996	Over 40 Yrs	$1.298 M	$1.338 M	$1.366 M	$1.380 M	$1.346 M
$3,000	$3,958	$5,327	Over 40 Yrs	$1.247 M	$1.223 M	$1.172 M	$1.088 M	$783,633
$3,750	$4,948	$6,659	32 Y & 10 M	$1.197 M	$1.109 M	$978,690	$795,278	$220,935
$4,500	$5,938	$7,991	26 Y & 7 M	$1.147 M	$995,196	$784,937	$502,803	$0
$5,250	$6,927	$9,323	22 Y & 4 M	$1.096 M	$881,084	$591,197	$210,354	$0
$6,000	$7,917	$10,655	19 Y & 3 M	$1.046 M	$766,964	$397,438	$0	$0
$6,750	$8,907	$11,987	16 Y & 11 M	$995,323	$652,854	$203,694	$0	$0

3% COLA

Monthly Amount	15 Yr Inflated	30 Yr Inflated	Money Lasts	5 Years	10 Years	15 Years	20 Years	30 Years
$2,250	$3,403	$5,302	Over 40 Yrs	$1.295 M	$1.322 M	$1.326 M	$1.297 M	$1.097 M
$3,000	$4,538	$7,070	35 Y & 3 M	$1.243 M	$1.203 M	$1.118 M	$976,175	$450,796
$3,750	$5,672	$8,837	28 Y & 3 M	$1.192 M	$1.084 M	$911,157	$655,835	$0
$4,500	$6,807	$10,605	23 Y & 6 M	$1.141 M	$964,748	$703,887	$335,456	$0
$5,250	$7,941	$12,372	20 Y & 2 M	$1.089 M	$845,559	$496,626	$15,083	$0
$6,000	$9,076	$14,139	17 Y & 8 M	$1.038 M	$726,364	$289,353	$0	$0
$6,750	$10,210	$15,907	15 Y & 8 M	$986,424	$607,174	$82,085	$0	$0

4% COLA

Monthly Amount	15 Yr Inflated	30 Yr Inflated	Money Lasts	5 Years	10 Years	15 Years	20 Years	30 Years
$1,500	$2,598	$4,678	Over 40 Yrs	$1.344 M	$1.431 M	$1.504 M	$1.554 M	$1.543 M
$2,250	$3,896	$7,017	38 Y & 11 M	$1.292 M	$1.306 M	$1.282 M	$1.203 M	$797,484
$3,000	$5,195	$9,356	30 Y & 6 M	$1.239 M	$1.182 M	$1.060 M	$850,750	$51,787
$3,750	$6,494	$11,695	25 Y & 1 M	$1.187 M	$1.057 M	$837,654	$499,081	$0
$4,500	$7,792	$14,034	21 Y & 4 M	$1.135 M	$932,688	$615,724	$147,424	$0
$5,250	$9,091	$16,373	18 Y & 6 M	$1.082 M	$808,140	$393,734	$0	$0
$6,000	$10,390	$18,712	16 Y & 5 M	$1.030 M	$683,611	$171,792	$0	$0

$1,250,000 Balance					4% Return On Investment			

No COLA

Monthly Amount	15 Yr Inflated	30 Yr Inflated	Money Lasts	5 Years	10 Years	15 Years	20 Years	30 Years
$3,750	$3,750	$3,750	Over 40 Yrs	$1.272 M	$1.299 M	$1.332 M	$1.372 M	$1.480 M
$4,500	$4,500	$4,500	Over 40 Yrs	$1.222 M	$1.189 M	$1.148 M	$1.099 M	$965,088
$5,250	$5,250	$5,250	38 Y & 5 M	$1.173 M	$1.079 M	$964,464	$825,365	$450,230
$6,000	$6,000	$6,000	29 Y & 2 M	$1.123 M	$968,577	$780,648	$552,002	$0
$6,750	$6,750	$6,750	23 Y & 9 M	$1.073 M	$858,360	$596,829	$278,636	$0
$7,500	$7,500	$7,500	20 Y & 1 M	$1.024 M	$748,146	$413,016	$5,279	$0
$8,250	$8,250	$8,250	17 Y & 6 M	$973,876	$637,929	$229,198	$0	$0

2% COLA

Monthly Amount	15 Yr Inflated	30 Yr Inflated	Money Lasts	5 Years	10 Years	15 Years	20 Years	30 Years
$3,000	$3,958	$5,327	Over 40 Yrs	$1.314 M	$1.371 M	$1.416 M	$1.444 M	$1.425 M
$3,750	$4,948	$6,659	Over 40 Yrs	$1.262 M	$1.251 M	$1.207 M	$1.121 M	$767,710
$4,500	$5,938	$7,991	31 Y & 2 M	$1.211 M	$1.131 M	$997,892	$796,827	$110,361
$5,250	$6,927	$9,323	25 Y & 5 M	$1.159 M	$1.011 M	$789,029	$473,178	$0
$6,000	$7,917	$10,655	21 Y & 6 M	$1.107 M	$890,993	$580,141	$149,498	$0
$6,750	$8,907	$11,987	18 Y & 7 M	$1.056 M	$771,089	$371,274	$0	$0
$7,500	$9,896	$13,319	16 Y & 5 M	$1.004 M	$651,171	$162,393	$0	$0

3% COLA

Monthly Amount	15 Yr Inflated	30 Yr Inflated	Money Lasts	5 Years	10 Years	15 Years	20 Years	30 Years
$3,000	$4,538	$7,070	Over 40 Yrs	$1.310 M	$1.350 M	$1.359 M	$1.325 M	$1.057 M
$3,750	$5,672	$8,837	32 Y & 11 M	$1.257 M	$1.225 M	$1.136 M	$971,723	$308,269
$4,500	$6,807	$10,605	26 Y & 8 M	$1.205 M	$1.099 M	$912,871	$618,267	$0
$5,250	$7,941	$12,372	22 Y & 5 M	$1.152 M	$974,264	$689,821	$264,821	$0
$6,000	$9,076	$14,139	19 Y & 4 M	$1.099 M	$849,110	$466,758	$0	$0
$6,750	$10,210	$15,907	16 Y & 11 M	$1.047 M	$723,963	$243,701	$0	$0
$7,500	$11,344	$17,675	15 Y & 2 M	$994,080	$598,822	$20,669	$0	$0

4% COLA

Monthly Amount	15 Yr Inflated	30 Yr Inflated	Money Lasts	5 Years	10 Years	15 Years	20 Years	30 Years
$2,250	$3,896	$7,017	Over 40 Yrs	$1.360 M	$1.458 M	$1.536 M	$1.578 M	$1.478 M
$3,000	$5,195	$9,356	35 Y & 5 M	$1.306 M	$1.328 M	$1.297 M	$1.192 M	$618,586
$3,750	$6,494	$11,695	28 Y & 4 M	$1.252 M	$1.197 M	$1.059 M	$804,799	$0
$4,500	$7,792	$14,034	23 Y & 8 M	$1.199 M	$1.066 M	$820,481	$418,031	$0
$5,250	$9,091	$16,373	20 Y & 3 M	$1.145 M	$935,677	$582,000	$31,154	$0
$6,000	$10,390	$18,712	17 Y & 9 M	$1.091 M	$805,026	$343,570	$0	$0
$6,750	$11,689	$21,051	15 Y & 9 M	$1.038 M	$674,360	$105,100	$0	$0

$1,250,000 Balance   5% Return On Investment

No COLA

Monthly Amount	15 Yr Inflated	30 Yr Inflated	Money Lasts	5 Years	10 Years	15 Years	20 Years	30 Years
$3,750	$3,750	$3,750	Over 40 Yrs	$1.340 M	$1.456 M	$1.603 M	$1.791 M	$2.338 M
$4,500	$4,500	$4,500	Over 40 Yrs	$1.290 M	$1.340 M	$1.404 M	$1.486 M	$1.725 M
$5,250	$5,250	$5,250	Over 40 Yrs	$1.239 M	$1.224 M	$1.205 M	$1.181 M	$1.112 M
$6,000	$6,000	$6,000	38 Y & 6 M	$1.188 M	$1.108 M	$1.006 M	$876,357	$499,246
$6,750	$6,750	$6,750	28 Y & 8 M	$1.137 M	$991,839	$807,100	$571,321	$0
$7,500	$7,500	$7,500	23 Y & 3 M	$1.086 M	$875,810	$608,041	$266,292	$0
$8,250	$8,250	$8,250	19 Y & 8 M	$1.035 M	$759,777	$408,977	$0	$0

2% COLA

Monthly Amount	15 Yr Inflated	30 Yr Inflated	Money Lasts	5 Years	10 Years	15 Years	20 Years	30 Years
$3,000	$3,958	$5,327	Over 40 Yrs	$1.384 M	$1.532 M	$1.697 M	$1.881 M	$2.314 M
$3,750	$4,948	$6,659	Over 40 Yrs	$1.331 M	$1.406 M	$1.472 M	$1.522 M	$1.542 M
$4,500	$5,938	$7,991	39 Y & 1 M	$1.278 M	$1.280 M	$1.246 M	$1.163 M	$770,342
$5,250	$6,927	$9,323	29 Y & 11 M	$1.225 M	$1.154 M	$1.021 M	$803,905	$0
$6,000	$7,917	$10,655	24 Y & 6 M	$1.172 M	$1.028 M	$795,331	$444,941	$0
$6,750	$8,907	$11,987	20 Y & 9 M	$1.119 M	$901,725	$569,926	$85,989	$0
$7,500	$9,896	$13,319	17 Y & 11 M	$1.066 M	$775,680	$344,511	$0	$0

3% COLA

Monthly Amount	15 Yr Inflated	30 Yr Inflated	Money Lasts	5 Years	10 Years	15 Years	20 Years	30 Years
$3,000	$4,538	$7,070	Over 40 Yrs	$1.379 M	$1.510 M	$1.637 M	$1.754 M	$1.907 M
$3,750	$5,672	$8,837	Over 40 Yrs	$1.326 M	$1.379 M	$1.397 M	$1.363 M	$1.033 M
$4,500	$6,807	$10,605	31 Y & 3 M	$1.272 M	$1.247 M	$1.157 M	$972,042	$158,912
$5,250	$7,941	$12,372	25 Y & 6 M	$1.218 M	$1.116 M	$916,615	$581,275	$0
$6,000	$9,076	$14,139	21 Y & 6 M	$1.164 M	$984,546	$676,310	$190,498	$0
$6,750	$10,210	$15,907	18 Y & 8 M	$1.110 M	$853,101	$436,014	$0	$0
$7,500	$11,344	$17,675	16 Y & 6 M	$1.056 M	$721,661	$195,736	$0	$0

4% COLA

Monthly Amount	15 Yr Inflated	30 Yr Inflated	Money Lasts	5 Years	10 Years	15 Years	20 Years	30 Years
$2,250	$3,896	$7,017	Over 40 Yrs	$1.430 M	$1.625 M	$1.829 M	$2.038 M	$2.418 M
$3,000	$5,195	$9,356	Over 40 Yrs	$1.375 M	$1.488 M	$1.573 M	$1.611 M	$1.422 M
$3,750	$6,494	$11,695	33 Y & 1 M	$1.320 M	$1.350 M	$1.316 M	$1.185 M	$427,628
$4,500	$7,792	$14,034	26 Y & 9 M	$1.265 M	$1.213 M	$1.060 M	$758,520	$0
$5,250	$9,091	$16,373	22 Y & 6 M	$1.210 M	$1.076 M	$803,555	$332,097	$0
$6,000	$10,390	$18,712	19 Y & 5 M	$1.155 M	$939,079	$547,138	$0	$0
$6,750	$11,689	$21,051	17 Y & 1 M	$1.100 M	$801,947	$290,684	$0	$0

| $1,250,000 Balance | | | | | 6% Return On Investment | | | |

No COLA

Monthly Amount	15 Yr Inflated	30 Yr Inflated	Money Lasts	5 Years	10 Years	15 Years	20 Years	30 Years
$4,500	$4,500	$4,500	Over 40 Yrs	$1.359 M	$1.505 M	$1.701 M	$1.963 M	$2.782 M
$5,250	$5,250	$5,250	Over 40 Yrs	$1.307 M	$1.383 M	$1.485 M	$1.622 M	$2.049 M
$6,000	$6,000	$6,000	Over 40 Yrs	$1.255 M	$1.261 M	$1.270 M	$1.281 M	$1.316 M
$6,750	$6,750	$6,750	39 Y & 5 M	$1.202 M	$1.139 M	$1.054 M	$939,897	$583,542
$7,500	$7,500	$7,500	28 Y & 5 M	$1.150 M	$1.017 M	$838,014	$598,894	$0
$8,250	$8,250	$8,250	22 Y & 10 M	$1.098 M	$894,515	$622,249	$257,896	$0
$9,000	$9,000	$9,000	19 Y & 3 M	$1.046 M	$772,330	$406,482	$0	$0

2% COLA

Monthly Amount	15 Yr Inflated	30 Yr Inflated	Money Lasts	5 Years	10 Years	15 Years	20 Years	30 Years
$3,750	$4,948	$6,659	Over 40 Yrs	$1.401 M	$1.576 M	$1.778 M	$2.014 M	$2.623 M
$4,500	$5,938	$7,991	Over 40 Yrs	$1.347 M	$1.443 M	$1.535 M	$1.616 M	$1.712 M
$5,250	$6,927	$9,323	38 Y & 4 M	$1.293 M	$1.311 M	$1.291 M	$1.217 M	$800,455
$6,000	$7,917	$10,655	29 Y & 2 M	$1.239 M	$1.178 M	$1.048 M	$817,840	$0
$6,750	$8,907	$11,987	23 Y & 10 M	$1.184 M	$1.046 M	$804,232	$418,963	$0
$7,500	$9,896	$13,319	20 Y & 2 M	$1.130 M	$913,292	$560,731	$20,080	$0
$8,250	$10,886	$14,651	17 Y & 7 M	$1.076 M	$780,762	$317,226	$0	$0

3% COLA

Monthly Amount	15 Yr Inflated	30 Yr Inflated	Money Lasts	5 Years	10 Years	15 Years	20 Years	30 Years
$3,750	$5,672	$8,837	Over 40 Yrs	$1.396 M	$1.548 M	$1.700 M	$1.844 M	$2.056 M
$4,500	$6,807	$10,605	39 Y & 1 M	$1.341 M	$1.410 M	$1.441 M	$1.411 M	$1.031 M
$5,250	$7,941	$12,372	30 Y & 1 M	$1.286 M	$1.272 M	$1.182 M	$978,510	$6,358
$6,000	$9,076	$14,139	24 Y & 7 M	$1.230 M	$1.134 M	$922,697	$545,582	$0
$6,750	$10,210	$15,907	20 Y & 10 M	$1.175 M	$995,642	$663,567	$112,639	$0
$7,500	$11,344	$17,675	18 Y & 1 M	$1.120 M	$857,546	$404,459	$0	$0
$8,250	$12,479	$19,441	15 Y & 11 M	$1.065 M	$719,444	$145,341	$0	$0

4% COLA

Monthly Amount	15 Yr Inflated	30 Yr Inflated	Money Lasts	5 Years	10 Years	15 Years	20 Years	30 Years
$3,000	$5,195	$9,356	Over 40 Yrs	$1.447 M	$1.663 M	$1.891 M	$2.125 M	$2.544 M
$3,750	$6,494	$11,695	Over 40 Yrs	$1.391 M	$1.519 M	$1.615 M	$1.654 M	$1.385 M
$4,500	$7,792	$14,034	31 Y & 4 M	$1.335 M	$1.375 M	$1.339 M	$1.183 M	$226,709
$5,250	$9,091	$16,373	25 Y & 7 M	$1.278 M	$1.231 M	$1.063 M	$712,437	$0
$6,000	$10,390	$18,712	21 Y & 7 M	$1.222 M	$1.087 M	$787,163	$241,558	$0
$6,750	$11,689	$21,051	18 Y & 9 M	$1.166 M	$942,876	$511,083	$0	$0
$7,500	$12,988	$23,390	16 Y & 6 M	$1.109 M	$798,903	$235,002	$0	$0

$1,300,000 Balance   3% Return On Investment

No COLA

Monthly Amount	15 Yr Inflated	30 Yr Inflated	Money Lasts	5 Years	10 Years	15 Years	20 Years	30 Years
$3,000	$3,000	$3,000	Over 40 Yrs	$1.313 M	$1.328 M	$1.346 M	$1.366 M	$1.417 M
$3,750	$3,750	$3,750	Over 40 Yrs	$1.265 M	$1.223 M	$1.176 M	$1.121 M	$982,436
$4,500	$4,500	$4,500	Over 40 Yrs	$1.216 M	$1.119 M	$1.006 M	$875,183	$547,839
$5,250	$5,250	$5,250	31 Y & 11 M	$1.168 M	$1.014 M	$836,048	$629,717	$113,231
$6,000	$6,000	$6,000	25 Y & 10 M	$1.119 M	$909,313	$666,150	$384,260	$0
$6,750	$6,750	$6,750	21 Y & 9 M	$1.071 M	$804,589	$496,248	$138,796	$0
$7,500	$7,500	$7,500	18 Y & 10 M	$1.022 M	$699,867	$326,347	$0	$0

2% COLA

Monthly Amount	15 Yr Inflated	30 Yr Inflated	Money Lasts	5 Years	10 Years	15 Years	20 Years	30 Years
$2,250	$2,969	$3,996	Over 40 Yrs	$1.356 M	$1.405 M	$1.444 M	$1.471 M	$1.468 M
$3,000	$3,958	$5,327	Over 40 Yrs	$1.305 M	$1.291 M	$1.250 M	$1.178 M	$904,997
$3,750	$4,948	$6,659	34 Y & 4 M	$1.255 M	$1.177 M	$1.057 M	$885,589	$342,307
$4,500	$5,938	$7,991	27 Y & 9 M	$1.205 M	$1.062 M	$862,835	$593,109	$0
$5,250	$6,927	$9,323	23 Y & 4 M	$1.154 M	$948,279	$669,093	$300,658	$0
$6,000	$7,917	$10,655	20 Y & 1 M	$1.104 M	$834,161	$475,337	$8,190	$0
$6,750	$8,907	$11,987	17 Y & 8 M	$1.053 M	$720,050	$281,591	$0	$0

3% COLA

Monthly Amount	15 Yr Inflated	30 Yr Inflated	Money Lasts	5 Years	10 Years	15 Years	20 Years	30 Years
$2,250	$3,403	$5,302	Over 40 Yrs	$1.353 M	$1.390 M	$1.404 M	$1.387 M	$1.218 M
$3,000	$4,538	$7,070	36 Y & 8 M	$1.301 M	$1.270 M	$1.196 M	$1.066 M	$572,163
$3,750	$5,672	$8,837	29 Y & 4 M	$1.250 M	$1.151 M	$989,053	$746,138	$0
$4,500	$6,807	$10,605	24 Y & 6 M	$1.199 M	$1.032 M	$781,785	$425,760	$0
$5,250	$7,941	$12,372	20 Y & 11 M	$1.147 M	$912,755	$574,524	$105,388	$0
$6,000	$9,076	$14,139	18 Y & 4 M	$1.096 M	$793,560	$367,252	$0	$0
$6,750	$10,210	$15,907	16 Y & 4 M	$1.044 M	$674,372	$159,987	$0	$0

4% COLA

Monthly Amount	15 Yr Inflated	30 Yr Inflated	Money Lasts	5 Years	10 Years	15 Years	20 Years	30 Years
$1,500	$2,598	$4,678	Over 40 Yrs	$1.402 M	$1.498 M	$1.581 M	$1.645 M	$1.664 M
$2,250	$3,896	$7,017	Over 40 Yrs	$1.350 M	$1.373 M	$1.359 M	$1.293 M	$918,847
$3,000	$5,195	$9,356	31 Y & 6 M	$1.297 M	$1.249 M	$1.137 M	$941,053	$173,147
$3,750	$6,494	$11,695	25 Y & 11 M	$1.245 M	$1.124 M	$915,557	$589,392	$0
$4,500	$7,792	$14,034	22 Y & 1 M	$1.193 M	$999,882	$693,618	$237,725	$0
$5,250	$9,091	$16,373	19 Y & 2 M	$1.140 M	$875,334	$471,630	$0	$0
$6,000	$10,390	$18,712	16 Y & 11 M	$1.088 M	$750,809	$249,693	$0	$0

$1,300,000 Balance   3% Return On Investment

No COLA

Monthly Amount	15 Yr Inflated	30 Yr Inflated	Money Lasts	5 Years	10 Years	15 Years	20 Years	30 Years
$3,000	$3,000	$3,000	Over 40 Yrs	$1.313 M	$1.328 M	$1.346 M	$1.366 M	$1.417 M
$3,750	$3,750	$3,750	Over 40 Yrs	$1.265 M	$1.223 M	$1.176 M	$1.121 M	$982,436
$4,500	$4,500	$4,500	Over 40 Yrs	$1.216 M	$1.119 M	$1.006 M	$875,183	$547,839
$5,250	$5,250	$5,250	31 Y & 11 M	$1.168 M	$1.014 M	$836,048	$629,717	$113,231
$6,000	$6,000	$6,000	25 Y & 10 M	$1.119 M	$909,313	$666,150	$384,260	$0
$6,750	$6,750	$6,750	21 Y & 9 M	$1.071 M	$804,589	$496,248	$138,796	$0
$7,500	$7,500	$7,500	18 Y & 10 M	$1.022 M	$699,867	$326,347	$0	$0

2% COLA

Monthly Amount	15 Yr Inflated	30 Yr Inflated	Money Lasts	5 Years	10 Years	15 Years	20 Years	30 Years
$2,250	$2,969	$3,996	Over 40 Yrs	$1.356 M	$1.405 M	$1.444 M	$1.471 M	$1.468 M
$3,000	$3,958	$5,327	Over 40 Yrs	$1.305 M	$1.291 M	$1.250 M	$1.178 M	$904,997
$3,750	$4,948	$6,659	34 Y & 4 M	$1.255 M	$1.177 M	$1.057 M	$885,589	$342,307
$4,500	$5,938	$7,991	27 Y & 9 M	$1.205 M	$1.062 M	$862,835	$593,109	$0
$5,250	$6,927	$9,323	23 Y & 4 M	$1.154 M	$948,279	$669,093	$300,658	$0
$6,000	$7,917	$10,655	20 Y & 1 M	$1.104 M	$834,161	$475,337	$8,190	$0
$6,750	$8,907	$11,987	17 Y & 8 M	$1.053 M	$720,050	$281,591	$0	$0

3% COLA

Monthly Amount	15 Yr Inflated	30 Yr Inflated	Money Lasts	5 Years	10 Years	15 Years	20 Years	30 Years
$2,250	$3,403	$5,302	Over 40 Yrs	$1.353 M	$1.390 M	$1.404 M	$1.387 M	$1.218 M
$3,000	$4,538	$7,070	36 Y & 8 M	$1.301 M	$1.270 M	$1.196 M	$1.066 M	$572,163
$3,750	$5,672	$8,837	29 Y & 4 M	$1.250 M	$1.151 M	$989,053	$746,138	$0
$4,500	$6,807	$10,605	24 Y & 6 M	$1.199 M	$1.032 M	$781,785	$425,760	$0
$5,250	$7,941	$12,372	20 Y & 11 M	$1.147 M	$912,755	$574,524	$105,388	$0
$6,000	$9,076	$14,139	18 Y & 4 M	$1.096 M	$793,560	$367,252	$0	$0
$6,750	$10,210	$15,907	16 Y & 4 M	$1.044 M	$674,372	$159,987	$0	$0

4% COLA

Monthly Amount	15 Yr Inflated	30 Yr Inflated	Money Lasts	5 Years	10 Years	15 Years	20 Years	30 Years
$1,500	$2,598	$4,678	Over 40 Yrs	$1.402 M	$1.498 M	$1.581 M	$1.645 M	$1.664 M
$2,250	$3,896	$7,017	Over 40 Yrs	$1.350 M	$1.373 M	$1.359 M	$1.293 M	$918,847
$3,000	$5,195	$9,356	31 Y & 6 M	$1.297 M	$1.249 M	$1.137 M	$941,053	$173,147
$3,750	$6,494	$11,695	25 Y & 11 M	$1.245 M	$1.124 M	$915,557	$589,392	$0
$4,500	$7,792	$14,034	22 Y & 1 M	$1.193 M	$999,882	$693,618	$237,725	$0
$5,250	$9,091	$16,373	19 Y & 2 M	$1.140 M	$875,334	$471,630	$0	$0
$6,000	$10,390	$18,712	16 Y & 11 M	$1.088 M	$750,809	$249,693	$0	$0

$1,300,000 Balance　　　5% Return On Investment

No COLA

Monthly Amount	15 Yr Inflated	30 Yr Inflated	Money Lasts	5 Years	10 Years	15 Years	20 Years	30 Years
$3,750	$3,750	$3,750	Over 40 Yrs	$1.404 M	$1.537 M	$1.707 M	$1.924 M	$2.554 M
$4,500	$4,500	$4,500	Over 40 Yrs	$1.353 M	$1.421 M	$1.508 M	$1.619 M	$1.941 M
$5,250	$5,250	$5,250	Over 40 Yrs	$1.302 M	$1.305 M	$1.309 M	$1.314 M	$1.328 M
$6,000	$6,000	$6,000	Over 40 Yrs	$1.251 M	$1.189 M	$1.110 M	$1.009 M	$715,342
$6,750	$6,750	$6,750	31 Y & 4 M	$1.200 M	$1.073 M	$911,047	$703,987	$102,442
$7,500	$7,500	$7,500	24 Y & 11 M	$1.149 M	$957,253	$711,985	$398,955	$0
$8,250	$8,250	$8,250	20 Y & 11 M	$1.098 M	$841,221	$512,921	$93,920	$0

2% COLA

Monthly Amount	15 Yr Inflated	30 Yr Inflated	Money Lasts	5 Years	10 Years	15 Years	20 Years	30 Years
$3,000	$3,958	$5,327	Over 40 Yrs	$1.447 M	$1.613 M	$1.801 M	$2.013 M	$2.531 M
$3,750	$4,948	$6,659	Over 40 Yrs	$1.394 M	$1.487 M	$1.576 M	$1.654 M	$1.758 M
$4,500	$5,938	$7,991	Over 40 Yrs	$1.341 M	$1.361 M	$1.350 M	$1.296 M	$986,443
$5,250	$6,927	$9,323	31 Y & 11 M	$1.289 M	$1.235 M	$1.125 M	$936,566	$214,480
$6,000	$7,917	$10,655	25 Y & 11 M	$1.236 M	$1.109 M	$899,276	$577,603	$0
$6,750	$8,907	$11,987	21 Y & 11 M	$1.183 M	$983,169	$673,871	$218,652	$0
$7,500	$9,896	$13,319	18 Y & 11 M	$1.130 M	$857,122	$448,454	$0	$0

3% COLA

Monthly Amount	15 Yr Inflated	30 Yr Inflated	Money Lasts	5 Years	10 Years	15 Years	20 Years	30 Years
$3,000	$4,538	$7,070	Over 40 Yrs	$1.443 M	$1.592 M	$1.741 M	$1.886 M	$2.123 M
$3,750	$5,672	$8,837	Over 40 Yrs	$1.389 M	$1.460 M	$1.501 M	$1.495 M	$1.249 M
$4,500	$6,807	$10,605	32 Y & 11 M	$1.335 M	$1.329 M	$1.261 M	$1.105 M	$375,003
$5,250	$7,941	$12,372	26 Y & 10 M	$1.281 M	$1.197 M	$1.021 M	$713,937	$0
$6,000	$9,076	$14,139	22 Y & 7 M	$1.227 M	$1.066 M	$780,255	$323,161	$0
$6,750	$10,210	$15,907	19 Y & 7 M	$1.173 M	$934,546	$539,960	$0	$0
$7,500	$11,344	$17,675	17 Y & 3 M	$1.119 M	$803,105	$299,682	$0	$0

4% COLA

Monthly Amount	15 Yr Inflated	30 Yr Inflated	Money Lasts	5 Years	10 Years	15 Years	20 Years	30 Years
$2,250	$3,896	$7,017	Over 40 Yrs	$1.494 M	$1.706 M	$1.933 M	$2.170 M	$2.634 M
$3,000	$5,195	$9,356	Over 40 Yrs	$1.439 M	$1.569 M	$1.677 M	$1.744 M	$1.639 M
$3,750	$6,494	$11,695	34 Y & 7 M	$1.384 M	$1.432 M	$1.420 M	$1.317 M	$643,719
$4,500	$7,792	$14,034	27 Y & 11 M	$1.329 M	$1.295 M	$1.164 M	$891,191	$0
$5,250	$9,091	$16,373	23 Y & 6 M	$1.274 M	$1.158 M	$907,503	$464,765	$0
$6,000	$10,390	$18,712	20 Y & 3 M	$1.219 M	$1.021 M	$651,084	$38,450	$0
$6,750	$11,689	$21,051	17 Y & 10 M	$1.164 M	$883,389	$394,627	$0	$0

$1,300,000 Balance   6% Return On Investment

No COLA

Monthly Amount	15 Yr Inflated	30 Yr Inflated	Money Lasts	5 Years	10 Years	15 Years	20 Years	30 Years
$4,500	$4,500	$4,500	Over 40 Yrs	$1.426 M	$1.595 M	$1.821 M	$2.123 M	$3.069 M
$5,250	$5,250	$5,250	Over 40 Yrs	$1.374 M	$1.473 M	$1.605 M	$1.782 M	$2.336 M
$6,000	$6,000	$6,000	Over 40 Yrs	$1.322 M	$1.351 M	$1.389 M	$1.441 M	$1.604 M
$6,750	$6,750	$6,750	Over 40 Yrs	$1.269 M	$1.228 M	$1.174 M	$1.100 M	$870,712
$7,500	$7,500	$7,500	31 Y & 8 M	$1.217 M	$1.106 M	$957,845	$759,254	$137,849
$8,250	$8,250	$8,250	24 Y & 10 M	$1.165 M	$984,055	$742,074	$418,247	$0
$9,000	$9,000	$9,000	20 Y & 9 M	$1.113 M	$861,870	$526,307	$77,247	$0

2% COLA

Monthly Amount	15 Yr Inflated	30 Yr Inflated	Money Lasts	5 Years	10 Years	15 Years	20 Years	30 Years
$3,750	$4,948	$6,659	Over 40 Yrs	$1.468 M	$1.665 M	$1.898 M	$2.175 M	$2.910 M
$4,500	$5,938	$7,991	Over 40 Yrs	$1.414 M	$1.533 M	$1.655 M	$1.776 M	$1.999 M
$5,250	$6,927	$9,323	Over 40 Yrs	$1.360 M	$1.400 M	$1.411 M	$1.377 M	$1.088 M
$6,000	$7,917	$10,655	31 Y & 5 M	$1.306 M	$1.268 M	$1.168 M	$978,192	$176,366
$6,750	$8,907	$11,987	25 Y & 5 M	$1.251 M	$1.135 M	$924,062	$579,323	$0
$7,500	$9,896	$13,319	21 Y & 5 M	$1.197 M	$1.003 M	$680,558	$180,437	$0
$8,250	$10,886	$14,651	18 Y & 7 M	$1.143 M	$870,304	$437,055	$0	$0

3% COLA

Monthly Amount	15 Yr Inflated	30 Yr Inflated	Money Lasts	5 Years	10 Years	15 Years	20 Years	30 Years
$3,750	$5,672	$8,837	Over 40 Yrs	$1.463 M	$1.638 M	$1.820 M	$2.005 M	$2.343 M
$4,500	$6,807	$10,605	Over 40 Yrs	$1.408 M	$1.499 M	$1.561 M	$1.572 M	$1.318 M
$5,250	$7,941	$12,372	31 Y & 11 M	$1.353 M	$1.361 M	$1.302 M	$1.139 M	$293,528
$6,000	$9,076	$14,139	25 Y & 11 M	$1.297 M	$1.223 M	$1.043 M	$705,936	$0
$6,750	$10,210	$15,907	21 Y & 11 M	$1.242 M	$1.085 M	$783,397	$272,999	$0
$7,500	$11,344	$17,675	18 Y & 11 M	$1.187 M	$947,089	$524,289	$0	$0
$8,250	$12,479	$19,441	16 Y & 10 M	$1.131 M	$808,985	$265,168	$0	$0

4% COLA

Monthly Amount	15 Yr Inflated	30 Yr Inflated	Money Lasts	5 Years	10 Years	15 Years	20 Years	30 Years
$3,000	$5,195	$9,356	Over 40 Yrs	$1.514 M	$1.752 M	$2.011 M	$2.286 M	$2.831 M
$3,750	$6,494	$11,695	Over 40 Yrs	$1.458 M	$1.608 M	$1.735 M	$1.815 M	$1.673 M
$4,500	$7,792	$14,034	33 Y & 1 M	$1.402 M	$1.464 M	$1.459 M	$1.344 M	$513,883
$5,250	$9,091	$16,373	26 Y & 11 M	$1.345 M	$1.320 M	$1.183 M	$872,787	$0
$6,000	$10,390	$18,712	22 Y & 8 M	$1.289 M	$1.176 M	$906,990	$401,912	$0
$6,750	$11,689	$21,051	19 Y & 8 M	$1.233 M	$1.032 M	$630,907	$0	$0
$7,500	$12,988	$23,390	17 Y & 4 M	$1.176 M	$888,447	$354,833	$0	$0

$1,350,000 Balance   3% Return On Investment

No COLA

Monthly Amount	15 Yr Inflated	30 Yr Inflated	Money Lasts	5 Years	10 Years	15 Years	20 Years	30 Years
$3,000	$3,000	$3,000	Over 40 Yrs	$1.371 M	$1.395 M	$1.424 M	$1.456 M	$1.538 M
$3,750	$3,750	$3,750	Over 40 Yrs	$1.323 M	$1.291 M	$1.254 M	$1.211 M	$1.104 M
$4,500	$4,500	$4,500	Over 40 Yrs	$1.274 M	$1.186 M	$1.084 M	$965,488	$669,200
$5,250	$5,250	$5,250	33 Y & 11 M	$1.226 M	$1.081 M	$913,949	$720,024	$234,594
$6,000	$6,000	$6,000	27 Y & 4 M	$1.177 M	$976,509	$744,050	$474,567	$0
$6,750	$6,750	$6,750	22 Y & 11 M	$1.129 M	$871,785	$574,147	$229,103	$0
$7,500	$7,500	$7,500	19 Y & 10 M	$1.080 M	$767,062	$404,246	$0	$0

2% COLA

Monthly Amount	15 Yr Inflated	30 Yr Inflated	Money Lasts	5 Years	10 Years	15 Years	20 Years	30 Years
$2,250	$2,969	$3,996	Over 40 Yrs	$1.414 M	$1.472 M	$1.522 M	$1.561 M	$1.589 M
$3,000	$3,958	$5,327	Over 40 Yrs	$1.363 M	$1.358 M	$1.328 M	$1.268 M	$1.026 M
$3,750	$4,948	$6,659	35 Y & 11 M	$1.313 M	$1.244 M	$1.134 M	$975,893	$463,666
$4,500	$5,938	$7,991	28 Y & 11 M	$1.263 M	$1.130 M	$940,733	$683,415	$0
$5,250	$6,927	$9,323	24 Y & 4 M	$1.212 M	$1.015 M	$746,993	$390,965	$0
$6,000	$7,917	$10,655	20 Y & 11 M	$1.162 M	$901,356	$553,235	$98,495	$0
$6,750	$8,907	$11,987	18 Y & 5 M	$1.111 M	$787,245	$359,489	$0	$0

3% COLA

Monthly Amount	15 Yr Inflated	30 Yr Inflated	Money Lasts	5 Years	10 Years	15 Years	20 Years	30 Years
$2,250	$3,403	$5,302	Over 40 Yrs	$1.411 M	$1.457 M	$1.481 M	$1.477 M	$1.339 M
$3,000	$4,538	$7,070	38 Y & 1 M	$1.359 M	$1.338 M	$1.274 M	$1.157 M	$693,527
$3,750	$5,672	$8,837	30 Y & 6 M	$1.308 M	$1.218 M	$1.067 M	$836,447	$47,800
$4,500	$6,807	$10,605	25 Y & 5 M	$1.257 M	$1.099 M	$859,683	$516,065	$0
$5,250	$7,941	$12,372	21 Y & 9 M	$1.205 M	$979,949	$652,419	$195,690	$0
$6,000	$9,076	$14,139	19 Y & 1 M	$1.154 M	$860,757	$445,152	$0	$0
$6,750	$10,210	$15,907	16 Y & 11 M	$1.102 M	$741,568	$237,885	$0	$0

4% COLA

Monthly Amount	15 Yr Inflated	30 Yr Inflated	Money Lasts	5 Years	10 Years	15 Years	20 Years	30 Years
$1,500	$2,598	$4,678	Over 40 Yrs	$1.460 M	$1.565 M	$1.659 M	$1.735 M	$1.786 M
$2,250	$3,896	$7,017	Over 40 Yrs	$1.408 M	$1.441 M	$1.437 M	$1.383 M	$1.040 M
$3,000	$5,195	$9,356	32 Y & 7 M	$1.355 M	$1.316 M	$1.215 M	$1.031 M	$294,508
$3,750	$6,494	$11,695	26 Y & 10 M	$1.303 M	$1.192 M	$993,454	$679,697	$0
$4,500	$7,792	$14,034	22 Y & 10 M	$1.251 M	$1.067 M	$771,518	$328,032	$0
$5,250	$9,091	$16,373	19 Y & 10 M	$1.198 M	$942,530	$549,530	$0	$0
$6,000	$10,390	$18,712	17 Y & 7 M	$1.146 M	$818,003	$327,589	$0	$0

$1,350,000 Balance	4% Return On Investment

No COLA

Monthly Amount	15 Yr Inflated	30 Yr Inflated	Money Lasts	5 Years	10 Years	15 Years	20 Years	30 Years
$3,750	$3,750	$3,750	Over 40 Yrs	$1.394 M	$1.447 M	$1.512 M	$1.591 M	$1.804 M
$4,500	$4,500	$4,500	Over 40 Yrs	$1.344 M	$1.337 M	$1.328 M	$1.318 M	$1.289 M
$5,250	$5,250	$5,250	Over 40 Yrs	$1.294 M	$1.227 M	$1.145 M	$1.044 M	$774,572
$6,000	$6,000	$6,000	33 Y & 11 M	$1.245 M	$1.117 M	$960,741	$771,114	$259,708
$6,750	$6,750	$6,750	27 Y & 1 M	$1.195 M	$1.006 M	$776,925	$497,751	$0
$7,500	$7,500	$7,500	22 Y & 8 M	$1.145 M	$896,170	$593,110	$224,389	$0
$8,250	$8,250	$8,250	19 Y & 7 M	$1.096 M	$785,954	$409,293	$0	$0

2% COLA

Monthly Amount	15 Yr Inflated	30 Yr Inflated	Money Lasts	5 Years	10 Years	15 Years	20 Years	30 Years
$3,000	$3,958	$5,327	Over 40 Yrs	$1.436 M	$1.519 M	$1.596 M	$1.663 M	$1.749 M
$3,750	$4,948	$6,659	Over 40 Yrs	$1.384 M	$1.399 M	$1.387 M	$1.340 M	$1.092 M
$4,500	$5,938	$7,991	34 Y & 9 M	$1.332 M	$1.279 M	$1.178 M	$1.016 M	$434,704
$5,250	$6,927	$9,323	28 Y & 1 M	$1.281 M	$1.159 M	$969,119	$692,285	$0
$6,000	$7,917	$10,655	23 Y & 8 M	$1.229 M	$1.039 M	$760,237	$368,611	$0
$6,750	$8,907	$11,987	20 Y & 5 M	$1.177 M	$919,112	$551,366	$44,942	$0
$7,500	$9,896	$13,319	17 Y & 11 M	$1.126 M	$799,194	$342,484	$0	$0

3% COLA

Monthly Amount	15 Yr Inflated	30 Yr Inflated	Money Lasts	5 Years	10 Years	15 Years	20 Years	30 Years
$3,000	$4,538	$7,070	Over 40 Yrs	$1.432 M	$1.498 M	$1.539 M	$1.544 M	$1.382 M
$3,750	$5,672	$8,837	36 Y & 1 M	$1.379 M	$1.373 M	$1.316 M	$1.191 M	$632,608
$4,500	$6,807	$10,605	29 Y & 2 M	$1.326 M	$1.247 M	$1.093 M	$837,378	$0
$5,250	$7,941	$12,372	24 Y & 5 M	$1.274 M	$1.122 M	$869,915	$483,934	$0
$6,000	$9,076	$14,139	21 Y & 1 M	$1.221 M	$997,134	$646,852	$130,484	$0
$6,750	$10,210	$15,907	18 Y & 6 M	$1.168 M	$871,990	$423,798	$0	$0
$7,500	$11,344	$17,675	16 Y & 6 M	$1.116 M	$746,844	$200,759	$0	$0

4% COLA

Monthly Amount	15 Yr Inflated	30 Yr Inflated	Money Lasts	5 Years	10 Years	15 Years	20 Years	30 Years
$2,250	$3,896	$7,017	Over 40 Yrs	$1.481 M	$1.606 M	$1.716 M	$1.798 M	$1.802 M
$3,000	$5,195	$9,356	38 Y & 3 M	$1.428 M	$1.476 M	$1.477 M	$1.411 M	$942,926
$3,750	$6,494	$11,695	30 Y & 7 M	$1.374 M	$1.345 M	$1.239 M	$1.024 M	$84,189
$4,500	$7,792	$14,034	25 Y & 6 M	$1.320 M	$1.214 M	$1.001 M	$637,148	$0
$5,250	$9,091	$16,373	21 Y & 10 M	$1.267 M	$1.084 M	$762,092	$250,263	$0
$6,000	$10,390	$18,712	19 Y & 2 M	$1.213 M	$953,051	$523,665	$0	$0
$6,750	$11,689	$21,051	16 Y & 11 M	$1.159 M	$822,384	$285,193	$0	$0

$1,350,000 Balance	5% Return On Investment

No COLA

Monthly Amount	15 Yr Inflated	30 Yr Inflated	Money Lasts	5 Years	10 Years	15 Years	20 Years	30 Years
$3,750	$3,750	$3,750	Over 40 Yrs	$1.468 M	$1.619 M	$1.811 M	$2.057 M	$2.770 M
$4,500	$4,500	$4,500	Over 40 Yrs	$1.417 M	$1.503 M	$1.612 M	$1.752 M	$2.157 M
$5,250	$5,250	$5,250	Over 40 Yrs	$1.366 M	$1.387 M	$1.413 M	$1.447 M	$1.544 M
$6,000	$6,000	$6,000	Over 40 Yrs	$1.315 M	$1.271 M	$1.214 M	$1.142 M	$931,431
$6,750	$6,750	$6,750	34 Y & 5 M	$1.264 M	$1.155 M	$1.015 M	$836,654	$318,542
$7,500	$7,500	$7,500	26 Y & 11 M	$1.213 M	$1.039 M	$815,932	$531,620	$0
$8,250	$8,250	$8,250	22 Y & 6 M	$1.162 M	$922,666	$616,868	$226,584	$0

2% COLA

Monthly Amount	15 Yr Inflated	30 Yr Inflated	Money Lasts	5 Years	10 Years	15 Years	20 Years	30 Years
$3,000	$3,958	$5,327	Over 40 Yrs	$1.511 M	$1.695 M	$1.905 M	$2.146 M	$2.747 M
$3,750	$4,948	$6,659	Over 40 Yrs	$1.458 M	$1.569 M	$1.679 M	$1.787 M	$1.975 M
$4,500	$5,938	$7,991	Over 40 Yrs	$1.405 M	$1.443 M	$1.454 M	$1.428 M	$1.203 M
$5,250	$6,927	$9,323	34 Y & 1 M	$1.352 M	$1.317 M	$1.229 M	$1.069 M	$430,584
$6,000	$7,917	$10,655	27 Y & 6 M	$1.299 M	$1.191 M	$1.003 M	$710,271	$0
$6,750	$8,907	$11,987	23 Y & 1 M	$1.246 M	$1.065 M	$777,818	$351,320	$0
$7,500	$9,896	$13,319	19 Y & 11 M	$1.193 M	$938,568	$552,403	$0	$0

3% COLA

Monthly Amount	15 Yr Inflated	30 Yr Inflated	Money Lasts	5 Years	10 Years	15 Years	20 Years	30 Years
$3,000	$4,538	$7,070	Over 40 Yrs	$1.507 M	$1.673 M	$1.845 M	$2.019 M	$2.339 M
$3,750	$5,672	$8,837	Over 40 Yrs	$1.453 M	$1.542 M	$1.605 M	$1.628 M	$1.465 M
$4,500	$6,807	$10,605	34 Y & 10 M	$1.399 M	$1.410 M	$1.365 M	$1.237 M	$591,107
$5,250	$7,941	$12,372	28 Y & 2 M	$1.345 M	$1.279 M	$1.125 M	$846,606	$0
$6,000	$9,076	$14,139	23 Y & 9 M	$1.291 M	$1.147 M	$884,201	$455,826	$0
$6,750	$10,210	$15,907	20 Y & 6 M	$1.237 M	$1.016 M	$643,905	$65,038	$0
$7,500	$11,344	$17,675	17 Y & 11 M	$1.183 M	$884,551	$403,630	$0	$0

4% COLA

Monthly Amount	15 Yr Inflated	30 Yr Inflated	Money Lasts	5 Years	10 Years	15 Years	20 Years	30 Years
$2,250	$3,896	$7,017	Over 40 Yrs	$1.558 M	$1.788 M	$2.037 M	$2.303 M	$2.850 M
$3,000	$5,195	$9,356	Over 40 Yrs	$1.503 M	$1.650 M	$1.781 M	$1.876 M	$1.855 M
$3,750	$6,494	$11,695	36 Y & 3 M	$1.448 M	$1.513 M	$1.524 M	$1.450 M	$859,815
$4,500	$7,792	$14,034	29 Y & 3 M	$1.393 M	$1.376 M	$1.268 M	$1.024 M	$0
$5,250	$9,091	$16,373	24 Y & 6 M	$1.338 M	$1.239 M	$1.011 M	$597,427	$0
$6,000	$10,390	$18,712	21 Y & 2 M	$1.283 M	$1.102 M	$755,029	$171,112	$0
$6,750	$11,689	$21,051	18 Y & 7 M	$1.228 M	$964,833	$498,571	$0	$0

$1,350,000 Balance   6% Return On Investment

No COLA

Monthly Amount	15 Yr Inflated	30 Yr Inflated	Money Lasts	5 Years	10 Years	15 Years	20 Years	30 Years
$4,500	$4,500	$4,500	Over 40 Yrs	$1.493 M	$1.685 M	$1.941 M	$2.284 M	$3.357 M
$5,250	$5,250	$5,250	Over 40 Yrs	$1.441 M	$1.562 M	$1.725 M	$1.943 M	$2.624 M
$6,000	$6,000	$6,000	Over 40 Yrs	$1.389 M	$1.440 M	$1.509 M	$1.602 M	$1.891 M
$6,750	$6,750	$6,750	Over 40 Yrs	$1.336 M	$1.318 M	$1.293 M	$1.261 M	$1.158 M
$7,500	$7,500	$7,500	35 Y & 7 M	$1.284 M	$1.196 M	$1.078 M	$919,608	$425,017
$8,250	$8,250	$8,250	27 Y & 2 M	$1.232 M	$1.074 M	$861,904	$578,608	$0
$9,000	$9,000	$9,000	22 Y & 5 M	$1.180 M	$951,413	$646,134	$237,604	$0

2% COLA

Monthly Amount	15 Yr Inflated	30 Yr Inflated	Money Lasts	5 Years	10 Years	15 Years	20 Years	30 Years
$3,750	$4,948	$6,659	Over 40 Yrs	$1.535 M	$1.755 M	$2.018 M	$2.335 M	$3.197 M
$4,500	$5,938	$7,991	Over 40 Yrs	$1.481 M	$1.622 M	$1.774 M	$1.936 M	$2.286 M
$5,250	$6,927	$9,323	Over 40 Yrs	$1.427 M	$1.490 M	$1.531 M	$1.537 M	$1.375 M
$6,000	$7,917	$10,655	33 Y & 11 M	$1.372 M	$1.357 M	$1.287 M	$1.139 M	$463,545
$6,750	$8,907	$11,987	27 Y & 2 M	$1.318 M	$1.225 M	$1.044 M	$739,677	$0
$7,500	$9,896	$13,319	22 Y & 9 M	$1.264 M	$1.092 M	$800,387	$340,794	$0
$8,250	$10,886	$14,651	19 Y & 8 M	$1.210 M	$959,846	$556,882	$0	$0

3% COLA

Monthly Amount	15 Yr Inflated	30 Yr Inflated	Money Lasts	5 Years	10 Years	15 Years	20 Years	30 Years
$3,750	$5,672	$8,837	Over 40 Yrs	$1.530 M	$1.727 M	$1.940 M	$2.165 M	$2.630 M
$4,500	$6,807	$10,605	Over 40 Yrs	$1.475 M	$1.589 M	$1.681 M	$1.732 M	$1.605 M
$5,250	$7,941	$12,372	34 Y & 1 M	$1.420 M	$1.451 M	$1.421 M	$1.299 M	$580,711
$6,000	$9,076	$14,139	27 Y & 7 M	$1.364 M	$1.313 M	$1.162 M	$866,294	$0
$6,750	$10,210	$15,907	23 Y & 2 M	$1.309 M	$1.175 M	$903,219	$433,347	$0
$7,500	$11,344	$17,675	19 Y & 11 M	$1.254 M	$1.037 M	$644,117	$0	$0
$8,250	$12,479	$19,441	17 Y & 8 M	$1.198 M	$898,529	$384,997	$0	$0

4% COLA

Monthly Amount	15 Yr Inflated	30 Yr Inflated	Money Lasts	5 Years	10 Years	15 Years	20 Years	30 Years
$3,000	$5,195	$9,356	Over 40 Yrs	$1.581 M	$1.842 M	$2.131 M	$2.446 M	$3.118 M
$3,750	$6,494	$11,695	Over 40 Yrs	$1.525 M	$1.698 M	$1.855 M	$1.975 M	$1.960 M
$4,500	$7,792	$14,034	34 Y & 11 M	$1.469 M	$1.554 M	$1.579 M	$1.504 M	$801,059
$5,250	$9,091	$16,373	28 Y & 3 M	$1.412 M	$1.410 M	$1.303 M	$1.033 M	$0
$6,000	$10,390	$18,712	23 Y & 9 M	$1.356 M	$1.266 M	$1.027 M	$562,266	$0
$6,750	$11,689	$21,051	20 Y & 7 M	$1.299 M	$1.122 M	$750,734	$91,310	$0
$7,500	$12,988	$23,390	18 Y & 1 M	$1.243 M	$977,990	$474,663	$0	$0

$1,400,000 Balance   3% Return On Investment

No COLA

Monthly Amount	15 Yr Inflated	30 Yr Inflated	Money Lasts	5 Years	10 Years	15 Years	20 Years	30 Years
$3,000	$3,000	$3,000	Over 40 Yrs	$1.429 M	$1.463 M	$1.502 M	$1.547 M	$1.660 M
$3,750	$3,750	$3,750	Over 40 Yrs	$1.380 M	$1.358 M	$1.332 M	$1.301 M	$1.225 M
$4,500	$4,500	$4,500	Over 40 Yrs	$1.332 M	$1.253 M	$1.162 M	$1.056 M	$790,560
$5,250	$5,250	$5,250	36 Y & 3 M	$1.283 M	$1.148 M	$991,849	$810,331	$355,959
$6,000	$6,000	$6,000	28 Y & 11 M	$1.235 M	$1.044 M	$821,947	$564,870	$0
$6,750	$6,750	$6,750	24 Y & 3 M	$1.186 M	$938,982	$652,046	$319,410	$0
$7,500	$7,500	$7,500	20 Y & 10 M	$1.138 M	$834,260	$482,147	$73,951	$0

2% COLA

Monthly Amount	15 Yr Inflated	30 Yr Inflated	Money Lasts	5 Years	10 Years	15 Years	20 Years	30 Years
$2,250	$2,969	$3,996	Over 40 Yrs	$1.472 M	$1.539 M	$1.600 M	$1.651 M	$1.710 M
$3,000	$3,958	$5,327	Over 40 Yrs	$1.421 M	$1.425 M	$1.406 M	$1.359 M	$1.148 M
$3,750	$4,948	$6,659	37 Y & 7 M	$1.371 M	$1.311 M	$1.212 M	$1.066 M	$585,027
$4,500	$5,938	$7,991	30 Y & 3 M	$1.320 M	$1.197 M	$1.019 M	$773,719	$22,366
$5,250	$6,927	$9,323	25 Y & 4 M	$1.270 M	$1.083 M	$824,892	$481,271	$0
$6,000	$7,917	$10,655	21 Y & 10 M	$1.220 M	$968,551	$631,133	$188,800	$0
$6,750	$8,907	$11,987	19 Y & 2 M	$1.169 M	$854,440	$437,387	$0	$0

3% COLA

Monthly Amount	15 Yr Inflated	30 Yr Inflated	Money Lasts	5 Years	10 Years	15 Years	20 Years	30 Years
$2,250	$3,403	$5,302	Over 40 Yrs	$1.469 M	$1.524 M	$1.559 M	$1.567 M	$1.461 M
$3,000	$4,538	$7,070	39 Y & 6 M	$1.417 M	$1.405 M	$1.352 M	$1.247 M	$814,892
$3,750	$5,672	$8,837	31 Y & 7 M	$1.366 M	$1.286 M	$1.145 M	$926,750	$169,158
$4,500	$6,807	$10,605	26 Y & 4 M	$1.315 M	$1.166 M	$937,583	$606,373	$0
$5,250	$7,941	$12,372	22 Y & 7 M	$1.263 M	$1.047 M	$730,318	$285,996	$0
$6,000	$9,076	$14,139	19 Y & 9 M	$1.212 M	$927,953	$523,049	$0	$0
$6,750	$10,210	$15,907	17 Y & 7 M	$1.160 M	$808,763	$315,783	$0	$0

4% COLA

Monthly Amount	15 Yr Inflated	30 Yr Inflated	Money Lasts	5 Years	10 Years	15 Years	20 Years	30 Years
$1,500	$2,598	$4,678	Over 40 Yrs	$1.518 M	$1.632 M	$1.737 M	$1.825 M	$1.907 M
$2,250	$3,896	$7,017	Over 40 Yrs	$1.466 M	$1.508 M	$1.515 M	$1.473 M	$1.162 M
$3,000	$5,195	$9,356	33 Y & 7 M	$1.413 M	$1.383 M	$1.293 M	$1.122 M	$415,878
$3,750	$6,494	$11,695	27 Y & 8 M	$1.361 M	$1.259 M	$1.071 M	$770,000	$0
$4,500	$7,792	$14,034	23 Y & 7 M	$1.308 M	$1.134 M	$849,414	$418,335	$0
$5,250	$9,091	$16,373	20 Y & 6 M	$1.256 M	$1.010 M	$627,426	$66,570	$0
$6,000	$10,390	$18,712	18 Y & 2 M	$1.204 M	$885,199	$405,488	$0	$0

$1,400,000 Balance   4% Return On Investment

No COLA

Monthly Amount	15 Yr Inflated	30 Yr Inflated	Money Lasts	5 Years	10 Years	15 Years	20 Years	30 Years
$3,750	$3,750	$3,750	Over 40 Yrs	$1.455 M	$1.521 M	$1.602 M	$1.701 M	$1.966 M
$4,500	$4,500	$4,500	Over 40 Yrs	$1.405 M	$1.411 M	$1.418 M	$1.427 M	$1.452 M
$5,250	$5,250	$5,250	Over 40 Yrs	$1.355 M	$1.301 M	$1.235 M	$1.154 M	$936,732
$6,000	$6,000	$6,000	36 Y & 8 M	$1.306 M	$1.191 M	$1.051 M	$880,672	$421,881
$6,750	$6,750	$6,750	28 Y & 11 M	$1.256 M	$1.080 M	$866,973	$607,309	$0
$7,500	$7,500	$7,500	23 Y & 11 M	$1.206 M	$970,182	$683,156	$333,945	$0
$8,250	$8,250	$8,250	20 Y & 8 M	$1.156 M	$859,966	$499,340	$60,583	$0

2% COLA

Monthly Amount	15 Yr Inflated	30 Yr Inflated	Money Lasts	5 Years	10 Years	15 Years	20 Years	30 Years
$3,000	$3,958	$5,327	Over 40 Yrs	$1.497 M	$1.593 M	$1.686 M	$1.773 M	$1.912 M
$3,750	$4,948	$6,659	Over 40 Yrs	$1.445 M	$1.473 M	$1.477 M	$1.449 M	$1.254 M
$4,500	$5,938	$7,991	36 Y & 7 M	$1.393 M	$1.353 M	$1.268 M	$1.125 M	$596,874
$5,250	$6,927	$9,323	29 Y & 6 M	$1.342 M	$1.233 M	$1.059 M	$801,846	$0
$6,000	$7,917	$10,655	24 Y & 9 M	$1.290 M	$1.113 M	$850,284	$478,168	$0
$6,750	$8,907	$11,987	21 Y & 4 M	$1.238 M	$993,125	$641,414	$154,500	$0
$7,500	$9,896	$13,319	18 Y & 9 M	$1.187 M	$873,207	$432,532	$0	$0

3% COLA

Monthly Amount	15 Yr Inflated	30 Yr Inflated	Money Lasts	5 Years	10 Years	15 Years	20 Years	30 Years
$3,000	$4,538	$7,070	Over 40 Yrs	$1.493 M	$1.572 M	$1.629 M	$1.654 M	$1.544 M
$3,750	$5,672	$8,837	37 Y & 8 M	$1.440 M	$1.447 M	$1.406 M	$1.300 M	$794,773
$4,500	$6,807	$10,605	30 Y & 5 M	$1.387 M	$1.321 M	$1.183 M	$946,935	$45,494
$5,250	$7,941	$12,372	25 Y & 6 M	$1.335 M	$1.196 M	$959,961	$593,488	$0
$6,000	$9,076	$14,139	21 Y & 11 M	$1.282 M	$1.071 M	$736,901	$240,041	$0
$6,750	$10,210	$15,907	19 Y & 3 M	$1.229 M	$946,000	$513,843	$0	$0
$7,500	$11,344	$17,675	17 Y & 2 M	$1.177 M	$820,857	$290,808	$0	$0

4% COLA

Monthly Amount	15 Yr Inflated	30 Yr Inflated	Money Lasts	5 Years	10 Years	15 Years	20 Years	30 Years
$2,250	$3,896	$7,017	Over 40 Yrs	$1.542 M	$1.680 M	$1.806 M	$1.907 M	$1.964 M
$3,000	$5,195	$9,356	39 Y & 8 M	$1.489 M	$1.550 M	$1.567 M	$1.520 M	$1.105 M
$3,750	$6,494	$11,695	31 Y & 9 M	$1.435 M	$1.419 M	$1.329 M	$1.133 M	$246,360
$4,500	$7,792	$14,034	26 Y & 6 M	$1.381 M	$1.288 M	$1.091 M	$746,703	$0
$5,250	$9,091	$16,373	22 Y & 8 M	$1.327 M	$1.158 M	$852,140	$359,820	$0
$6,000	$10,390	$18,712	19 Y & 10 M	$1.274 M	$1.027 M	$613,712	$0	$0
$6,750	$11,689	$21,051	17 Y & 8 M	$1.220 M	$896,398	$375,243	$0	$0

$1,400,000 Balance	5% Return On Investment

No COLA

Monthly Amount	15 Yr Inflated	30 Yr Inflated	Money Lasts	5 Years	10 Years	15 Years	20 Years	30 Years
$3,750	$3,750	$3,750	Over 40 Yrs	$1.532 M	$1.700 M	$1.915 M	$2.189 M	$2.986 M
$4,500	$4,500	$4,500	Over 40 Yrs	$1.481 M	$1.584 M	$1.716 M	$1.884 M	$2.373 M
$5,250	$5,250	$5,250	Over 40 Yrs	$1.430 M	$1.468 M	$1.517 M	$1.579 M	$1.760 M
$6,000	$6,000	$6,000	Over 40 Yrs	$1.379 M	$1.352 M	$1.318 M	$1.274 M	$1.148 M
$6,750	$6,750	$6,750	37 Y & 11 M	$1.328 M	$1.236 M	$1.119 M	$969,315	$534,632
$7,500	$7,500	$7,500	29 Y & 2 M	$1.277 M	$1.120 M	$919,878	$664,284	$0
$8,250	$8,250	$8,250	23 Y & 11 M	$1.226 M	$1.004 M	$720,817	$359,252	$0

2% COLA

Monthly Amount	15 Yr Inflated	30 Yr Inflated	Money Lasts	5 Years	10 Years	15 Years	20 Years	30 Years
$3,000	$3,958	$5,327	Over 40 Yrs	$1.575 M	$1.776 M	$2.009 M	$2.279 M	$2.963 M
$3,750	$4,948	$6,659	Over 40 Yrs	$1.522 M	$1.650 M	$1.783 M	$1.920 M	$2.191 M
$4,500	$5,938	$7,991	Over 40 Yrs	$1.469 M	$1.524 M	$1.558 M	$1.561 M	$1.419 M
$5,250	$6,927	$9,323	36 Y & 4 M	$1.416 M	$1.398 M	$1.333 M	$1.202 M	$646,687
$6,000	$7,917	$10,655	29 Y & 1 M	$1.363 M	$1.272 M	$1.107 M	$842,936	$0
$6,750	$8,907	$11,987	24 Y & 4 M	$1.310 M	$1.146 M	$881,762	$483,980	$0
$7,500	$9,896	$13,319	20 Y & 11 M	$1.257 M	$1.020 M	$656,350	$125,033	$0

3% COLA

Monthly Amount	15 Yr Inflated	30 Yr Inflated	Money Lasts	5 Years	10 Years	15 Years	20 Years	30 Years
$3,000	$4,538	$7,070	Over 40 Yrs	$1.571 M	$1.755 M	$1.949 M	$2.152 M	$2.555 M
$3,750	$5,672	$8,837	Over 40 Yrs	$1.517 M	$1.623 M	$1.709 M	$1.761 M	$1.681 M
$4,500	$6,807	$10,605	36 Y & 8 M	$1.463 M	$1.492 M	$1.469 M	$1.370 M	$807,203
$5,250	$7,941	$12,372	29 Y & 7 M	$1.409 M	$1.360 M	$1.228 M	$979,267	$0
$6,000	$9,076	$14,139	24 Y & 10 M	$1.355 M	$1.229 M	$988,148	$588,490	$0
$6,750	$10,210	$15,907	21 Y & 5 M	$1.301 M	$1.097 M	$747,852	$197,704	$0
$7,500	$11,344	$17,675	18 Y & 10 M	$1.247 M	$965,996	$507,576	$0	$0

4% COLA

Monthly Amount	15 Yr Inflated	30 Yr Inflated	Money Lasts	5 Years	10 Years	15 Years	20 Years	30 Years
$2,250	$3,896	$7,017	Over 40 Yrs	$1.622 M	$1.869 M	$2.141 M	$2.436 M	$3.066 M
$3,000	$5,195	$9,356	Over 40 Yrs	$1.567 M	$1.732 M	$1.885 M	$2.009 M	$2.071 M
$3,750	$6,494	$11,695	37 Y & 10 M	$1.512 M	$1.595 M	$1.628 M	$1.583 M	$1.076 M
$4,500	$7,792	$14,034	30 Y & 6 M	$1.457 M	$1.458 M	$1.372 M	$1.157 M	$81,067
$5,250	$9,091	$16,373	25 Y & 7 M	$1.402 M	$1.321 M	$1.115 M	$730,092	$0
$6,000	$10,390	$18,712	21 Y & 11 M	$1.347 M	$1.183 M	$858,976	$303,777	$0
$6,750	$11,689	$21,051	19 Y & 4 M	$1.292 M	$1.046 M	$602,522	$0	$0

$1,400,000 Balance	6% Return On Investment

No COLA

Monthly Amount	15 Yr Inflated	30 Yr Inflated	Money Lasts	5 Years	10 Years	15 Years	20 Years	30 Years
$4,500	$4,500	$4,500	Over 40 Yrs	$1.560 M	$1.774 M	$2.061 M	$2.444 M	$3.644 M
$5,250	$5,250	$5,250	Over 40 Yrs	$1.508 M	$1.652 M	$1.845 M	$2.103 M	$2.911 M
$6,000	$6,000	$6,000	Over 40 Yrs	$1.455 M	$1.530 M	$1.629 M	$1.762 M	$2.178 M
$6,750	$6,750	$6,750	Over 40 Yrs	$1.403 M	$1.408 M	$1.413 M	$1.421 M	$1.445 M
$7,500	$7,500	$7,500	Over 40 Yrs	$1.351 M	$1.285 M	$1.197 M	$1.080 M	$712,190
$8,250	$8,250	$8,250	29 Y & 10 M	$1.299 M	$1.163 M	$981,731	$738,964	$0
$9,000	$9,000	$9,000	24 Y & 2 M	$1.246 M	$1.041 M	$765,964	$397,963	$0

2% COLA

Monthly Amount	15 Yr Inflated	30 Yr Inflated	Money Lasts	5 Years	10 Years	15 Years	20 Years	30 Years
$3,750	$4,948	$6,659	Over 40 Yrs	$1.602 M	$1.845 M	$2.138 M	$2.496 M	$3.485 M
$4,500	$5,938	$7,991	Over 40 Yrs	$1.548 M	$1.712 M	$1.894 M	$2.097 M	$2.573 M
$5,250	$6,927	$9,323	Over 40 Yrs	$1.494 M	$1.580 M	$1.651 M	$1.698 M	$1.662 M
$6,000	$7,917	$10,655	36 Y & 7 M	$1.439 M	$1.447 M	$1.407 M	$1.299 M	$750,712
$6,750	$8,907	$11,987	28 Y & 11 M	$1.385 M	$1.314 M	$1.164 M	$900,031	$0
$7,500	$9,896	$13,319	24 Y & 2 M	$1.331 M	$1.182 M	$920,212	$501,147	$0
$8,250	$10,886	$14,651	20 Y & 9 M	$1.277 M	$1.049 M	$676,708	$102,247	$0

3% COLA

Monthly Amount	15 Yr Inflated	30 Yr Inflated	Money Lasts	5 Years	10 Years	15 Years	20 Years	30 Years
$3,750	$5,672	$8,837	Over 40 Yrs	$1.597 M	$1.817 M	$2.060 M	$2.325 M	$2.917 M
$4,500	$6,807	$10,605	Over 40 Yrs	$1.542 M	$1.679 M	$1.800 M	$1.892 M	$1.893 M
$5,250	$7,941	$12,372	36 Y & 4 M	$1.486 M	$1.540 M	$1.541 M	$1.460 M	$867,881
$6,000	$9,076	$14,139	29 Y & 2 M	$1.431 M	$1.402 M	$1.282 M	$1.027 M	$0
$6,750	$10,210	$15,907	24 Y & 5 M	$1.376 M	$1.264 M	$1.023 M	$593,707	$0
$7,500	$11,344	$17,675	20 Y & 11 M	$1.321 M	$1.126 M	$763,943	$160,831	$0
$8,250	$12,479	$19,441	18 Y & 6 M	$1.265 M	$988,072	$504,826	$0	$0

4% COLA

Monthly Amount	15 Yr Inflated	30 Yr Inflated	Money Lasts	5 Years	10 Years	15 Years	20 Years	30 Years
$3,000	$5,195	$9,356	Over 40 Yrs	$1.648 M	$1.931 M	$2.251 M	$2.606 M	$3.406 M
$3,750	$6,494	$11,695	Over 40 Yrs	$1.592 M	$1.787 M	$1.975 M	$2.135 M	$2.247 M
$4,500	$7,792	$14,034	36 Y & 9 M	$1.535 M	$1.643 M	$1.699 M	$1.664 M	$1.088 M
$5,250	$9,091	$16,373	29 Y & 8 M	$1.479 M	$1.499 M	$1.423 M	$1.194 M	$0
$6,000	$10,390	$18,712	24 Y & 11 M	$1.423 M	$1.355 M	$1.147 M	$722,626	$0
$6,750	$11,689	$21,051	21 Y & 6 M	$1.366 M	$1.212 M	$870,562	$251,665	$0
$7,500	$12,988	$23,390	18 Y & 11 M	$1.310 M	$1.068 M	$594,490	$0	$0

$1,450,000 Balance   3% Return On Investment

No COLA

Monthly Amount	15 Yr Inflated	30 Yr Inflated	Money Lasts	5 Years	10 Years	15 Years	20 Years	30 Years
$3,000	$3,000	$3,000	Over 40 Yrs	$1.487 M	$1.530 M	$1.579 M	$1.637 M	$1.781 M
$3,750	$3,750	$3,750	Over 40 Yrs	$1.438 M	$1.425 M	$1.410 M	$1.392 M	$1.347 M
$4,500	$4,500	$4,500	Over 40 Yrs	$1.390 M	$1.320 M	$1.240 M	$1.146 M	$911,921
$5,250	$5,250	$5,250	38 Y & 7 M	$1.341 M	$1.216 M	$1.070 M	$900,637	$477,323
$6,000	$6,000	$6,000	30 Y & 8 M	$1.293 M	$1.111 M	$899,845	$655,175	$42,720
$6,750	$6,750	$6,750	25 Y & 6 M	$1.244 M	$1.006 M	$729,943	$409,713	$0
$7,500	$7,500	$7,500	21 Y & 11 M	$1.196 M	$901,455	$560,044	$164,255	$0

2% COLA

Monthly Amount	15 Yr Inflated	30 Yr Inflated	Money Lasts	5 Years	10 Years	15 Years	20 Years	30 Years
$2,250	$2,969	$3,996	Over 40 Yrs	$1.530 M	$1.606 M	$1.678 M	$1.741 M	$1.832 M
$3,000	$3,958	$5,327	Over 40 Yrs	$1.479 M	$1.492 M	$1.484 M	$1.449 M	$1.269 M
$3,750	$4,948	$6,659	39 Y & 2 M	$1.429 M	$1.378 M	$1.290 M	$1.157 M	$706,390
$4,500	$5,938	$7,991	31 Y & 6 M	$1.378 M	$1.264 M	$1.097 M	$864,024	$143,728
$5,250	$6,927	$9,323	26 Y & 5 M	$1.328 M	$1.150 M	$902,789	$571,575	$0
$6,000	$7,917	$10,655	22 Y & 8 M	$1.278 M	$1.036 M	$709,029	$279,103	$0
$6,750	$8,907	$11,987	19 Y & 11 M	$1.227 M	$921,637	$515,287	$0	$0

3% COLA

Monthly Amount	15 Yr Inflated	30 Yr Inflated	Money Lasts	5 Years	10 Years	15 Years	20 Years	30 Years
$2,250	$3,403	$5,302	Over 40 Yrs	$1.527 M	$1.591 M	$1.637 M	$1.658 M	$1.582 M
$3,000	$4,538	$7,070	Over 40 Yrs	$1.475 M	$1.472 M	$1.430 M	$1.337 M	$936,255
$3,750	$5,672	$8,837	32 Y & 9 M	$1.424 M	$1.353 M	$1.223 M	$1.017 M	$290,525
$4,500	$6,807	$10,605	27 Y & 3 M	$1.373 M	$1.234 M	$1.015 M	$696,677	$0
$5,250	$7,941	$12,372	23 Y & 5 M	$1.321 M	$1.114 M	$808,219	$376,304	$0
$6,000	$9,076	$14,139	20 Y & 6 M	$1.270 M	$995,147	$600,946	$55,930	$0
$6,750	$10,210	$15,907	18 Y & 2 M	$1.218 M	$875,960	$393,683	$0	$0

4% COLA

Monthly Amount	15 Yr Inflated	30 Yr Inflated	Money Lasts	5 Years	10 Years	15 Years	20 Years	30 Years
$1,500	$2,598	$4,678	Over 40 Yrs	$1.576 M	$1.700 M	$1.815 M	$1.915 M	$2.028 M
$2,250	$3,896	$7,017	Over 40 Yrs	$1.524 M	$1.575 M	$1.593 M	$1.564 M	$1.283 M
$3,000	$5,195	$9,356	34 Y & 7 M	$1.471 M	$1.451 M	$1.371 M	$1.212 M	$537,235
$3,750	$6,494	$11,695	28 Y & 7 M	$1.419 M	$1.326 M	$1.149 M	$860,307	$0
$4,500	$7,792	$14,034	24 Y & 4 M	$1.366 M	$1.201 M	$927,315	$508,644	$0
$5,250	$9,091	$16,373	21 Y & 2 M	$1.314 M	$1.077 M	$705,325	$156,875	$0
$6,000	$10,390	$18,712	18 Y & 9 M	$1.262 M	$952,395	$483,387	$0	$0

$1,450,000 Balance   4% Return On Investment

No COLA

Monthly Amount	15 Yr Inflated	30 Yr Inflated	Money Lasts	5 Years	10 Years	15 Years	20 Years	30 Years
$3,750	$3,750	$3,750	Over 40 Yrs	$1.516 M	$1.595 M	$1.692 M	$1.810 M	$2.129 M
$4,500	$4,500	$4,500	Over 40 Yrs	$1.466 M	$1.485 M	$1.508 M	$1.537 M	$1.614 M
$5,250	$5,250	$5,250	Over 40 Yrs	$1.416 M	$1.375 M	$1.325 M	$1.264 M	$1.099 M
$6,000	$6,000	$6,000	39 Y & 10 M	$1.366 M	$1.265 M	$1.141 M	$990,223	$584,044
$6,750	$6,750	$6,750	30 Y & 11 M	$1.317 M	$1.154 M	$957,020	$716,864	$69,192
$7,500	$7,500	$7,500	25 Y & 6 M	$1.267 M	$1.044 M	$773,203	$443,500	$0
$8,250	$8,250	$8,250	21 Y & 10 M	$1.217 M	$933,977	$589,386	$170,137	$0

2% COLA

Monthly Amount	15 Yr Inflated	30 Yr Inflated	Money Lasts	5 Years	10 Years	15 Years	20 Years	30 Years
$3,000	$3,958	$5,327	Over 40 Yrs	$1.557 M	$1.667 M	$1.776 M	$1.882 M	$2.074 M
$3,750	$4,948	$6,659	Over 40 Yrs	$1.506 M	$1.547 M	$1.567 M	$1.559 M	$1.416 M
$4,500	$5,938	$7,991	38 Y & 6 M	$1.454 M	$1.427 M	$1.358 M	$1.235 M	$759,044
$5,250	$6,927	$9,323	30 Y & 11 M	$1.402 M	$1.307 M	$1.149 M	$911,403	$101,780
$6,000	$7,917	$10,655	25 Y & 11 M	$1.351 M	$1.187 M	$940,329	$587,723	$0
$6,750	$8,907	$11,987	22 Y & 4 M	$1.299 M	$1.067 M	$731,460	$264,054	$0
$7,500	$9,896	$13,319	19 Y & 7 M	$1.247 M	$947,219	$522,580	$0	$0

3% COLA

Monthly Amount	15 Yr Inflated	30 Yr Inflated	Money Lasts	5 Years	10 Years	15 Years	20 Years	30 Years
$3,000	$4,538	$7,070	Over 40 Yrs	$1.553 M	$1.646 M	$1.719 M	$1.763 M	$1.706 M
$3,750	$5,672	$8,837	39 Y & 4 M	$1.501 M	$1.521 M	$1.496 M	$1.410 M	$956,949
$4,500	$6,807	$10,605	31 Y & 8 M	$1.448 M	$1.395 M	$1.273 M	$1.056 M	$207,657
$5,250	$7,941	$12,372	26 Y & 6 M	$1.395 M	$1.270 M	$1.050 M	$703,049	$0
$6,000	$9,076	$14,139	22 Y & 10 M	$1.343 M	$1.145 M	$826,946	$349,593	$0
$6,750	$10,210	$15,907	19 Y & 11 M	$1.290 M	$1.020 M	$603,891	$0	$0
$7,500	$11,344	$17,675	17 Y & 10 M	$1.237 M	$894,869	$380,855	$0	$0

4% COLA

Monthly Amount	15 Yr Inflated	30 Yr Inflated	Money Lasts	5 Years	10 Years	15 Years	20 Years	30 Years
$2,250	$3,896	$7,017	Over 40 Yrs	$1.603 M	$1.754 M	$1.896 M	$2.017 M	$2.126 M
$3,000	$5,195	$9,356	Over 40 Yrs	$1.549 M	$1.624 M	$1.658 M	$1.630 M	$1.267 M
$3,750	$6,494	$11,695	32 Y & 11 M	$1.496 M	$1.493 M	$1.419 M	$1.243 M	$408,532
$4,500	$7,792	$14,034	27 Y & 5 M	$1.442 M	$1.362 M	$1.181 M	$856,258	$0
$5,250	$9,091	$16,373	23 Y & 6 M	$1.388 M	$1.232 M	$942,187	$469,377	$0
$6,000	$10,390	$18,712	20 Y & 7 M	$1.335 M	$1.101 M	$703,757	$82,598	$0
$6,750	$11,689	$21,051	18 Y & 3 M	$1.281 M	$970,411	$465,290	$0	$0

$1,450,000 Balance	5% Return On Investment

No COLA

Monthly Amount	15 Yr Inflated	30 Yr Inflated	Money Lasts	5 Years	10 Years	15 Years	20 Years	30 Years
$3,750	$3,750	$3,750	Over 40 Yrs	$1.596 M	$1.782 M	$2.019 M	$2.322 M	$3.202 M
$4,500	$4,500	$4,500	Over 40 Yrs	$1.545 M	$1.666 M	$1.820 M	$2.017 M	$2.589 M
$5,250	$5,250	$5,250	Over 40 Yrs	$1.494 M	$1.550 M	$1.621 M	$1.712 M	$1.977 M
$6,000	$6,000	$6,000	Over 40 Yrs	$1.443 M	$1.434 M	$1.422 M	$1.407 M	$1.364 M
$6,750	$6,750	$6,750	Over 40 Yrs	$1.392 M	$1.318 M	$1.223 M	$1.102 M	$750,735
$7,500	$7,500	$7,500	31 Y & 7 M	$1.341 M	$1.202 M	$1.024 M	$796,949	$137,834
$8,250	$8,250	$8,250	25 Y & 9 M	$1.290 M	$1.086 M	$824,762	$491,915	$0

2% COLA

Monthly Amount	15 Yr Inflated	30 Yr Inflated	Money Lasts	5 Years	10 Years	15 Years	20 Years	30 Years
$3,000	$3,958	$5,327	Over 40 Yrs	$1.639 M	$1.858 M	$2.113 M	$2.411 M	$3.179 M
$3,750	$4,948	$6,659	Over 40 Yrs	$1.586 M	$1.732 M	$1.887 M	$2.052 M	$2.407 M
$4,500	$5,938	$7,991	Over 40 Yrs	$1.533 M	$1.606 M	$1.662 M	$1.694 M	$1.635 M
$5,250	$6,927	$9,323	38 Y & 8 M	$1.480 M	$1.480 M	$1.437 M	$1.335 M	$862,780
$6,000	$7,917	$10,655	30 Y & 9 M	$1.427 M	$1.354 M	$1.211 M	$975,600	$90,785
$6,750	$8,907	$11,987	25 Y & 8 M	$1.374 M	$1.228 M	$985,711	$616,649	$0
$7,500	$9,896	$13,319	21 Y & 11 M	$1.321 M	$1.101 M	$760,295	$257,696	$0

3% COLA

Monthly Amount	15 Yr Inflated	30 Yr Inflated	Money Lasts	5 Years	10 Years	15 Years	20 Years	30 Years
$3,000	$4,538	$7,070	Over 40 Yrs	$1.635 M	$1.836 M	$2.053 M	$2.284 M	$2.771 M
$3,750	$5,672	$8,837	Over 40 Yrs	$1.581 M	$1.705 M	$1.813 M	$1.893 M	$1.897 M
$4,500	$6,807	$10,605	38 Y & 7 M	$1.527 M	$1.573 M	$1.573 M	$1.503 M	$1.023 M
$5,250	$7,941	$12,372	30 Y & 11 M	$1.473 M	$1.442 M	$1.332 M	$1.112 M	$149,364
$6,000	$9,076	$14,139	25 Y & 11 M	$1.419 M	$1.310 M	$1.092 M	$721,157	$0
$6,750	$10,210	$15,907	22 Y & 5 M	$1.365 M	$1.179 M	$851,800	$330,371	$0
$7,500	$11,344	$17,675	19 Y & 8 M	$1.311 M	$1.047 M	$611,520	$0	$0

4% COLA

Monthly Amount	15 Yr Inflated	30 Yr Inflated	Money Lasts	5 Years	10 Years	15 Years	20 Years	30 Years
$2,250	$3,896	$7,017	Over 40 Yrs	$1.686 M	$1.951 M	$2.245 M	$2.568 M	$3.282 M
$3,000	$5,195	$9,356	Over 40 Yrs	$1.631 M	$1.813 M	$1.989 M	$2.142 M	$2.287 M
$3,750	$6,494	$11,695	39 Y & 6 M	$1.576 M	$1.676 M	$1.732 M	$1.715 M	$1.292 M
$4,500	$7,792	$14,034	31 Y & 9 M	$1.521 M	$1.539 M	$1.476 M	$1.289 M	$297,167
$5,250	$9,091	$16,373	26 Y & 7 M	$1.466 M	$1.402 M	$1.219 M	$862,754	$0
$6,000	$10,390	$18,712	22 Y & 11 M	$1.411 M	$1.265 M	$962,921	$436,442	$0
$6,750	$11,689	$21,051	20 Y & 1 M	$1.356 M	$1.128 M	$706,468	$10,053	$0

$1,450,000 Balance   6% Return On Investment

No COLA

Monthly Amount	15 Yr Inflated	30 Yr Inflated	Money Lasts	5 Years	10 Years	15 Years	20 Years	30 Years
$4,500	$4,500	$4,500	Over 40 Yrs	$1.627 M	$1.864 M	$2.180 M	$2.604 M	$3.931 M
$5,250	$5,250	$5,250	Over 40 Yrs	$1.575 M	$1.741 M	$1.965 M	$2.263 M	$3.198 M
$6,000	$6,000	$6,000	Over 40 Yrs	$1.522 M	$1.619 M	$1.749 M	$1.922 M	$2.465 M
$6,750	$6,750	$6,750	Over 40 Yrs	$1.470 M	$1.497 M	$1.533 M	$1.581 M	$1.732 M
$7,500	$7,500	$7,500	Over 40 Yrs	$1.418 M	$1.375 M	$1.317 M	$1.240 M	$999,363
$8,250	$8,250	$8,250	32 Y & 11 M	$1.366 M	$1.253 M	$1.102 M	$899,324	$266,506
$9,000	$9,000	$9,000	26 Y & 2 M	$1.313 M	$1.130 M	$885,791	$558,317	$0

2% COLA

Monthly Amount	15 Yr Inflated	30 Yr Inflated	Money Lasts	5 Years	10 Years	15 Years	20 Years	30 Years
$3,750	$4,948	$6,659	Over 40 Yrs	$1.669 M	$1.934 M	$2.258 M	$2.656 M	$3.772 M
$4,500	$5,938	$7,991	Over 40 Yrs	$1.615 M	$1.802 M	$2.014 M	$2.257 M	$2.860 M
$5,250	$6,927	$9,323	Over 40 Yrs	$1.561 M	$1.669 M	$1.771 M	$1.858 M	$1.949 M
$6,000	$7,917	$10,655	39 Y & 8 M	$1.506 M	$1.537 M	$1.527 M	$1.459 M	$1.038 M
$6,750	$8,907	$11,987	30 Y & 11 M	$1.452 M	$1.404 M	$1.284 M	$1.060 M	$126,647
$7,500	$9,896	$13,319	25 Y & 7 M	$1.398 M	$1.271 M	$1.040 M	$661,509	$0
$8,250	$10,886	$14,651	21 Y & 11 M	$1.344 M	$1.139 M	$796,537	$262,605	$0

3% COLA

Monthly Amount	15 Yr Inflated	30 Yr Inflated	Money Lasts	5 Years	10 Years	15 Years	20 Years	30 Years
$3,750	$5,672	$8,837	Over 40 Yrs	$1.664 M	$1.906 M	$2.179 M	$2.486 M	$3.205 M
$4,500	$6,807	$10,605	Over 40 Yrs	$1.609 M	$1.768 M	$1.920 M	$2.053 M	$2.180 M
$5,250	$7,941	$12,372	38 Y & 8 M	$1.553 M	$1.630 M	$1.661 M	$1.620 M	$1.155 M
$6,000	$9,076	$14,139	30 Y & 9 M	$1.498 M	$1.492 M	$1.402 M	$1.187 M	$130,330
$6,750	$10,210	$15,907	25 Y & 8 M	$1.443 M	$1.354 M	$1.143 M	$754,067	$0
$7,500	$11,344	$17,675	22 Y & 1 M	$1.387 M	$1.216 M	$883,771	$321,188	$0
$8,250	$12,479	$19,441	19 Y & 5 M	$1.332 M	$1.078 M	$624,650	$0	$0

4% COLA

Monthly Amount	15 Yr Inflated	30 Yr Inflated	Money Lasts	5 Years	10 Years	15 Years	20 Years	30 Years
$3,000	$5,195	$9,356	Over 40 Yrs	$1.715 M	$2.021 M	$2.371 M	$2.767 M	$3.693 M
$3,750	$6,494	$11,695	Over 40 Yrs	$1.659 M	$1.877 M	$2.095 M	$2.296 M	$2.534 M
$4,500	$7,792	$14,034	38 Y & 9 M	$1.602 M	$1.733 M	$1.819 M	$1.825 M	$1.375 M
$5,250	$9,091	$16,373	31 Y & 2 M	$1.546 M	$1.589 M	$1.543 M	$1.354 M	$216,411
$6,000	$10,390	$18,712	26 Y & 1 M	$1.490 M	$1.445 M	$1.266 M	$882,981	$0
$6,750	$11,689	$21,051	22 Y & 5 M	$1.433 M	$1.301 M	$990,393	$412,027	$0
$7,500	$12,988	$23,390	19 Y & 9 M	$1.377 M	$1.157 M	$714,319	$0	$0

| **$1,500,000 Balance** | | | | | **3% Return On Investment** | | | |

No COLA

Monthly Amount	15 Yr Inflated	30 Yr Inflated	Money Lasts	5 Years	10 Years	15 Years	20 Years	30 Years
$3,500	$3,500	$3,500	Over 40 Yrs	$1.513 M	$1.527 M	$1.544 M	$1.564 M	$1.613 M
$4,250	$4,250	$4,250	Over 40 Yrs	$1.464 M	$1.422 M	$1.374 M	$1.318 M	$1.178 M
$5,000	$5,000	$5,000	Over 40 Yrs	$1.416 M	$1.318 M	$1.204 M	$1.073 M	$743,552
$5,750	$5,750	$5,750	34 Y & 10 M	$1.367 M	$1.213 M	$1.034 M	$827,300	$308,949
$6,500	$6,500	$6,500	28 Y & 6 M	$1.319 M	$1.108 M	$864,475	$581,839	$0
$7,250	$7,250	$7,250	24 Y & 2 M	$1.270 M	$1.004 M	$694,575	$336,378	$0
$8,000	$8,000	$8,000	20 Y & 11 M	$1.222 M	$898,834	$524,673	$90,917	$0

2% COLA

Monthly Amount	15 Yr Inflated	30 Yr Inflated	Money Lasts	5 Years	10 Years	15 Years	20 Years	30 Years
$2,750	$3,629	$4,884	Over 40 Yrs	$1.554 M	$1.597 M	$1.627 M	$1.637 M	$1.578 M
$3,500	$4,618	$6,215	Over 40 Yrs	$1.504 M	$1.483 M	$1.433 M	$1.344 M	$1.015 M
$4,250	$5,608	$7,547	35 Y & 1 M	$1.453 M	$1.369 M	$1.239 M	$1.052 M	$452,727
$5,000	$6,597	$8,879	28 Y & 11 M	$1.403 M	$1.255 M	$1.045 M	$759,403	$0
$5,750	$7,587	$10,211	24 Y & 9 M	$1.352 M	$1.141 M	$851,509	$466,895	$0
$6,500	$8,577	$11,543	21 Y & 7 M	$1.302 M	$1.027 M	$657,767	$174,435	$0
$7,250	$9,566	$12,875	19 Y & 1 M	$1.252 M	$912,749	$464,007	$0	$0

3% COLA

Monthly Amount	15 Yr Inflated	30 Yr Inflated	Money Lasts	5 Years	10 Years	15 Years	20 Years	30 Years
$2,750	$4,160	$6,481	Over 40 Yrs	$1.550 M	$1.579 M	$1.577 M	$1.534 M	$1.273 M
$3,500	$5,294	$8,248	36 Y & 3 M	$1.499 M	$1.460 M	$1.370 M	$1.214 M	$627,054
$4,250	$6,429	$10,016	29 Y & 11 M	$1.448 M	$1.340 M	$1.162 M	$893,758	$0
$5,000	$7,563	$11,783	25 Y & 5 M	$1.396 M	$1.221 M	$955,190	$573,384	$0
$5,750	$8,697	$13,550	22 Y & 1 M	$1.345 M	$1.102 M	$747,931	$253,022	$0
$6,500	$9,832	$15,318	19 Y & 7 M	$1.293 M	$982,882	$540,669	$0	$0
$7,250	$10,966	$17,085	17 Y & 6 M	$1.242 M	$863,696	$333,417	$0	$0

4% COLA

Monthly Amount	15 Yr Inflated	30 Yr Inflated	Money Lasts	5 Years	10 Years	15 Years	20 Years	30 Years
$2,000	$3,463	$6,237	Over 40 Yrs	$1.599 M	$1.684 M	$1.745 M	$1.771 M	$1.653 M
$2,750	$4,762	$8,576	38 Y & 4 M	$1.547 M	$1.559 M	$1.523 M	$1.420 M	$907,235
$3,500	$6,061	$10,915	31 Y & 3 M	$1.494 M	$1.435 M	$1.301 M	$1.068 M	$161,737
$4,250	$7,360	$13,255	26 Y & 4 M	$1.442 M	$1.310 M	$1.079 M	$716,115	$0
$5,000	$8,659	$15,594	22 Y & 10 M	$1.389 M	$1.186 M	$857,208	$364,411	$0
$5,750	$9,957	$17,932	20 Y & 2 M	$1.337 M	$1.061 M	$635,277	$12,752	$0
$6,500	$11,256	$20,272	17 Y & 11 M	$1.285 M	$936,558	$413,292	$0	$0

| $1,500,000 Balance | | | | | 4% Return On Investment | | | |

No COLA

Monthly Amount	15 Yr Inflated	30 Yr Inflated	Money Lasts	5 Years	10 Years	15 Years	20 Years	30 Years
$4,250	$4,250	$4,250	Over 40 Yrs	$1.543 M	$1.596 M	$1.660 M	$1.738 M	$1.948 M
$5,000	$5,000	$5,000	Over 40 Yrs	$1.494 M	$1.486 M	$1.476 M	$1.464 M	$1.433 M
$5,750	$5,750	$5,750	Over 40 Yrs	$1.444 M	$1.375 M	$1.292 M	$1.191 M	$917,837
$6,500	$6,500	$6,500	35 Y & 10 M	$1.394 M	$1.265 M	$1.108 M	$917,540	$402,976
$7,250	$7,250	$7,250	28 Y & 9 M	$1.344 M	$1.155 M	$924,521	$644,176	$0
$8,000	$8,000	$8,000	24 Y & 3 M	$1.295 M	$1.045 M	$740,706	$370,816	$0
$8,750	$8,750	$8,750	20 Y & 11 M	$1.245 M	$934,514	$556,891	$97,456	$0

2% COLA

Monthly Amount	15 Yr Inflated	30 Yr Inflated	Money Lasts	5 Years	10 Years	15 Years	20 Years	30 Years
$3,500	$4,618	$6,215	Over 40 Yrs	$1.584 M	$1.661 M	$1.727 M	$1.776 M	$1.798 M
$4,250	$5,608	$7,547	Over 40 Yrs	$1.532 M	$1.541 M	$1.518 M	$1.453 M	$1.140 M
$5,000	$6,597	$8,879	34 Y & 9 M	$1.481 M	$1.421 M	$1.309 M	$1.129 M	$483,162
$5,750	$7,587	$10,211	28 Y & 8 M	$1.429 M	$1.301 M	$1.100 M	$805,166	$0
$6,500	$8,577	$11,543	24 Y & 5 M	$1.377 M	$1.181 M	$891,132	$481,505	$0
$7,250	$9,566	$12,875	21 Y & 3 M	$1.325 M	$1.061 M	$682,243	$157,812	$0
$8,000	$10,556	$14,207	18 Y & 10 M	$1.274 M	$941,287	$473,367	$0	$0

3% COLA

Monthly Amount	15 Yr Inflated	30 Yr Inflated	Money Lasts	5 Years	10 Years	15 Years	20 Years	30 Years
$3,500	$5,294	$8,248	Over 40 Yrs	$1.579 M	$1.636 M	$1.660 M	$1.637 M	$1.369 M
$4,250	$6,429	$10,016	35 Y & 3 M	$1.526 M	$1.511 M	$1.437 M	$1.284 M	$619,553
$5,000	$7,563	$11,783	29 Y & 2 M	$1.474 M	$1.386 M	$1.214 M	$930,398	$0
$5,750	$8,697	$13,550	24 Y & 10 M	$1.421 M	$1.261 M	$991,343	$576,962	$0
$6,500	$9,832	$15,318	21 Y & 8 M	$1.368 M	$1.136 M	$768,286	$223,515	$0
$7,250	$10,966	$17,085	19 Y & 2 M	$1.316 M	$1.011 M	$545,248	$0	$0
$8,000	$12,101	$18,852	17 Y & 3 M	$1.263 M	$885,453	$322,212	$0	$0

4% COLA

Monthly Amount	15 Yr Inflated	30 Yr Inflated	Money Lasts	5 Years	10 Years	15 Years	20 Years	30 Years
$2,750	$4,762	$8,576	Over 40 Yrs	$1.628 M	$1.741 M	$1.827 M	$1.868 M	$1.716 M
$3,500	$6,061	$10,915	36 Y & 5 M	$1.574 M	$1.611 M	$1.589 M	$1.482 M	$857,037
$4,250	$7,360	$13,255	29 Y & 11 M	$1.521 M	$1.480 M	$1.350 M	$1.095 M	$0
$5,000	$8,659	$15,594	25 Y & 6 M	$1.467 M	$1.349 M	$1.112 M	$707,861	$0
$5,750	$9,957	$17,932	22 Y & 2 M	$1.413 M	$1.219 M	$873,293	$321,100	$0
$6,500	$11,256	$20,272	19 Y & 8 M	$1.360 M	$1.088 M	$634,812	$0	$0
$7,250	$12,555	$22,610	17 Y & 7 M	$1.306 M	$957,322	$396,387	$0	$0

$1,500,000 Balance	5% Return On Investment

No COLA

Monthly Amount	15 Yr Inflated	30 Yr Inflated	Money Lasts	5 Years	10 Years	15 Years	20 Years	30 Years
$4,250	$4,250	$4,250	Over 40 Yrs	$1.626 M	$1.786 M	$1.990 M	$2.251 M	$3.010 M
$5,000	$5,000	$5,000	Over 40 Yrs	$1.575 M	$1.670 M	$1.791 M	$1.946 M	$2.397 M
$5,750	$5,750	$5,750	Over 40 Yrs	$1.524 M	$1.554 M	$1.592 M	$1.641 M	$1.784 M
$6,500	$6,500	$6,500	Over 40 Yrs	$1.473 M	$1.438 M	$1.393 M	$1.336 M	$1.171 M
$7,250	$7,250	$7,250	37 Y & 9 M	$1.422 M	$1.322 M	$1.194 M	$1.031 M	$558,226
$8,000	$8,000	$8,000	29 Y & 6 M	$1.371 M	$1.206 M	$995,064	$726,260	$0
$8,750	$8,750	$8,750	24 Y & 6 M	$1.320 M	$1.090 M	$795,999	$421,223	$0

2% COLA

Monthly Amount	15 Yr Inflated	30 Yr Inflated	Money Lasts	5 Years	10 Years	15 Years	20 Years	30 Years
$3,500	$4,618	$6,215	Over 40 Yrs	$1.667 M	$1.855 M	$2.066 M	$2.305 M	$2.880 M
$4,250	$5,608	$7,547	Over 40 Yrs	$1.614 M	$1.729 M	$1.841 M	$1.946 M	$2.108 M
$5,000	$6,597	$8,879	Over 40 Yrs	$1.561 M	$1.603 M	$1.616 M	$1.587 M	$1.336 M
$5,750	$7,587	$10,211	34 Y & 11 M	$1.508 M	$1.477 M	$1.390 M	$1.228 M	$564,222
$6,500	$8,577	$11,543	28 Y & 7 M	$1.456 M	$1.351 M	$1.165 M	$868,970	$0
$7,250	$9,566	$12,875	24 Y & 3 M	$1.403 M	$1.225 M	$939,368	$509,989	$0
$8,000	$10,556	$14,207	21 Y & 2 M	$1.350 M	$1.099 M	$713,956	$151,040	$0

3% COLA

Monthly Amount	15 Yr Inflated	30 Yr Inflated	Money Lasts	5 Years	10 Years	15 Years	20 Years	30 Years
$3,500	$5,294	$8,248	Over 40 Yrs	$1.663 M	$1.830 M	$1.997 M	$2.156 M	$2.405 M
$4,250	$6,429	$10,016	Over 40 Yrs	$1.609 M	$1.698 M	$1.757 M	$1.766 M	$1.531 M
$5,000	$7,563	$11,783	34 Y & 10 M	$1.555 M	$1.567 M	$1.516 M	$1.375 M	$656,752
$5,750	$8,697	$13,550	28 Y & 9 M	$1.501 M	$1.436 M	$1.276 M	$984,072	$0
$6,500	$9,832	$15,318	24 Y & 6 M	$1.447 M	$1.304 M	$1.036 M	$593,309	$0
$7,250	$10,966	$17,085	21 Y & 4 M	$1.393 M	$1.173 M	$795,561	$202,559	$0
$8,000	$12,101	$18,852	18 Y & 11 M	$1.339 M	$1.041 M	$555,283	$0	$0

4% COLA

Monthly Amount	15 Yr Inflated	30 Yr Inflated	Money Lasts	5 Years	10 Years	15 Years	20 Years	30 Years
$2,750	$4,762	$8,576	Over 40 Yrs	$1.713 M	$1.941 M	$2.178 M	$2.417 M	$2.835 M
$3,500	$6,061	$10,915	Over 40 Yrs	$1.658 M	$1.803 M	$1.922 M	$1.990 M	$1.840 M
$4,250	$7,360	$13,255	35 Y & 4 M	$1.603 M	$1.666 M	$1.665 M	$1.564 M	$844,697
$5,000	$8,659	$15,594	29 Y & 3 M	$1.548 M	$1.529 M	$1.409 M	$1.138 M	$0
$5,750	$9,957	$17,932	24 Y & 11 M	$1.493 M	$1.392 M	$1.152 M	$711,236	$0
$6,500	$11,256	$20,272	21 Y & 9 M	$1.438 M	$1.255 M	$895,886	$284,826	$0
$7,250	$12,555	$22,610	19 Y & 3 M	$1.383 M	$1.118 M	$639,468	$0	$0

$1,500,000 Balance   6% Return On Investment

No COLA

Monthly Amount	15 Yr Inflated	30 Yr Inflated	Money Lasts	5 Years	10 Years	15 Years	20 Years	30 Years
$5,000	$5,000	$5,000	Over 40 Yrs	$1.659 M	$1.872 M	$2.156 M	$2.537 M	$3.729 M
$5,750	$5,750	$5,750	Over 40 Yrs	$1.607 M	$1.750 M	$1.941 M	$2.196 M	$2.997 M
$6,500	$6,500	$6,500	Over 40 Yrs	$1.554 M	$1.627 M	$1.725 M	$1.855 M	$2.264 M
$7,250	$7,250	$7,250	Over 40 Yrs	$1.502 M	$1.505 M	$1.509 M	$1.514 M	$1.531 M
$8,000	$8,000	$8,000	Over 40 Yrs	$1.450 M	$1.383 M	$1.293 M	$1.173 M	$797,969
$8,750	$8,750	$8,750	30 Y & 8 M	$1.398 M	$1.261 M	$1.078 M	$832,343	$65,099
$9,500	$9,500	$9,500	24 Y & 11 M	$1.345 M	$1.139 M	$861,773	$491,339	$0

2% COLA

Monthly Amount	15 Yr Inflated	30 Yr Inflated	Money Lasts	5 Years	10 Years	15 Years	20 Years	30 Years
$4,250	$5,608	$7,547	Over 40 Yrs	$1.700 M	$1.935 M	$2.215 M	$2.550 M	$3.451 M
$5,000	$6,597	$8,879	Over 40 Yrs	$1.646 M	$1.803 M	$1.972 M	$2.152 M	$2.540 M
$5,750	$7,587	$10,211	Over 40 Yrs	$1.591 M	$1.670 M	$1.728 M	$1.753 M	$1.629 M
$6,500	$8,577	$11,543	35 Y & 9 M	$1.537 M	$1.538 M	$1.485 M	$1.354 M	$717,575
$7,250	$9,566	$12,875	28 Y & 10 M	$1.483 M	$1.405 M	$1.241 M	$954,804	$0
$8,000	$10,556	$14,207	24 Y & 4 M	$1.429 M	$1.273 M	$997,530	$555,928	$0
$8,750	$11,546	$15,539	21 Y & 1 M	$1.374 M	$1.140 M	$754,019	$157,011	$0

3% COLA

Monthly Amount	15 Yr Inflated	30 Yr Inflated	Money Lasts	5 Years	10 Years	15 Years	20 Years	30 Years
$4,250	$6,429	$10,016	Over 40 Yrs	$1.694 M	$1.904 M	$2.126 M	$2.358 M	$2.809 M
$5,000	$7,563	$11,783	Over 40 Yrs	$1.639 M	$1.766 M	$1.867 M	$1.925 M	$1.784 M
$5,750	$8,697	$13,550	34 Y & 11 M	$1.583 M	$1.627 M	$1.608 M	$1.492 M	$759,070
$6,500	$9,832	$15,318	28 Y & 8 M	$1.528 M	$1.489 M	$1.349 M	$1.059 M	$0
$7,250	$10,966	$17,085	24 Y & 4 M	$1.473 M	$1.351 M	$1.090 M	$625,852	$0
$8,000	$12,101	$18,852	21 Y & 2 M	$1.418 M	$1.213 M	$830,865	$192,969	$0
$8,750	$13,235	$20,620	18 Y & 9 M	$1.362 M	$1.075 M	$571,715	$0	$0

4% COLA

Monthly Amount	15 Yr Inflated	30 Yr Inflated	Money Lasts	5 Years	10 Years	15 Years	20 Years	30 Years
$3,500	$6,061	$10,915	Over 40 Yrs	$1.744 M	$2.014 M	$2.307 M	$2.613 M	$3.208 M
$4,250	$7,360	$13,255	Over 40 Yrs	$1.688 M	$1.870 M	$2.030 M	$2.142 M	$2.049 M
$5,000	$8,659	$15,594	34 Y & 11 M	$1.632 M	$1.727 M	$1.754 M	$1.671 M	$889,840
$5,750	$9,957	$17,932	28 Y & 10 M	$1.575 M	$1.583 M	$1.478 M	$1.200 M	$0
$6,500	$11,256	$20,272	24 Y & 7 M	$1.519 M	$1.439 M	$1.202 M	$729,336	$0
$7,250	$12,555	$22,610	21 Y & 5 M	$1.463 M	$1.295 M	$926,189	$258,471	$0
$8,000	$13,853	$24,949	18 Y & 11 M	$1.406 M	$1.151 M	$650,131	$0	$0

www.ingramcontent.com/pod-product-compliance
Lightning Source LLC
Chambersburg PA
CBHW071427170526
45165CB00001B/431